The Middling Sort of People

The Middling Sort of People

Culture, Society and Politics in England, 1550–1800

Edited by

JONATHAN BARRY *and* CHRISTOPHER BROOKS

St. Martin's Press   New York

First published in the United States of America in 1994

Printed in Hong Kong

ISBN 0-312-12356-6

Library of Congress Cataloging-in-Publication Data applied for

Contents

Introduction

JONATHAN BARRY

I

Few historical essays can have had a more enduring effect than Jack Hexter's article attacking 'the myth of the Tudor middle class'.[1] Though literary critics, politicians and students have continued to see early modern England in terms of the rise of the middle class, few professional historians have dared to do so; indeed, the issue has hardly seemed worthy of discussion. With a few exceptions, even Marxist historians have adopted alternative social classifications, playing down the importance of middle-class or bourgeois groups during this period.[2] Meanwhile, the attention of historians has focused elsewhere. The great storm over the gentry in the 1950s and 1960s was succeeded by an emphasis on 'history from below', concentrating on the lower classes and 'popular culture'. This has in turn given way to renewed concern with the gentry, even the aristocracy. The common feature of all this work has been an acceptance of Hexter's contention that the main changes in English society, not just in the Tudor period but for centuries afterwards (until 1832, he suggested), can be understood without detailed reference to the character and impact of a middle class. Hence social classifications have been adopted which divide society in a bipolar fashion – into gentry and non-gentry, elite and people, rich and poor, patrician and plebeian.[3] When necessary, historians have preferred less analytic terms such as 'the middling sort' rather than the contentious 'middle class', employing a contemporary terminology whose origins are identified in Keith Wrightson's essay.

This collection has itself followed this convention, but its purpose is to reopen the debate about the nature of the 'middling sort' and to reconsider how far Hexter's strictures should still be accepted in the light of recent research. It is based on the editors'

1

belief that such critical consideration is urgently required both by researchers and by students, who are regularly exasperated by the lack of a full-scale study of the theme based on recent scholarship. It will become clear from this introduction and from their individual contributions that the editors themselves consider that the middling sort form as meaningful and important a social category as, say, the poor or the gentry of early modern England. Not all our fellow-contributors, however, necessarily share our understanding of this category, as their essays make clear. This is understandable, indeed welcome, for, as Peter Earle observes, one of the virtues of studying the middling sectors of society is that such analysis reveals the imprecision and variability of all efforts to pin down social structure and relationships. What the contributors share is the belief that issues surrounding this group require direct analysis and that our understanding of early modern English society will be incomplete without a self-conscious consideration of where to place the middling sort and how to assess the significance of those groups occupying the social space between the landed elite, on the one hand, and the poor, on the other. What is at stake here is not simply the history of the middling sort, but the way in which we characterise and understand early modern society as a whole. Hexter's essay was, after all, a plea for precisely such reflection about the use of class terminology, although it has been honoured more for its own suggestions than for this methodological aim.

As the essays that follow demonstrate, there is no simple way to define 'the middling sort'.[4] However, a compact definition that conveys many important characteristics is given by Shani d'Cruze: independent trading households. The middling sort had to work for their income, trading with the products of their hands (for example, yeomen and husbandmen farmers and artisans) or with the skills in business or the professions for which they had trained (for example, merchants, attorneys and apothecaries). Moreover, they were rarely employed by others in this – even the emerging group of government officials mostly depended on fees or viewed their offices as a property investment, as did the professions. The middling sort defined themselves in relation to households, which often formed the heart of a trading unit – in farm, shop or craft workplace – but also acted as the key unit for the reproduction and security of the family, centred on the figure of the adult male householder. The work of this household ensured its independence from poverty and thus laid the foundation for social, cultural and political independence. As the nature of economic and social life changed, there were important changes in the incomes, occupations and nature of the groups that might compose this middling sort, and these chronological variations were matched by important geographical differences – between London and small towns, between different agricultural regions. As a consequence, no attempt is made here to quantify the overall size of the middling sort, though each new investigation into the social composition of early modern England seems to suggest an upward revision of the numbers involved, with recent suggestions ranging from 30–40 per cent up to nearly 50 per cent of families.[5] Ultimately, however, social analysis is about relationships not numbers; the necessary imprecision involved in linking the relationships outlined above to specific people may be a source of strength rather than weakness.

A starting point has to be an understanding of the contemporary language of social analysis, and there have been some outstanding recent attempts to tackle this issue, notably by Keith Wrightson and Penelope Corfield.[6] These have revealed the co-existence of a range of social vocabularies, each linked to different interests and prejudices on the part of social commentators. In his essay here, Wrightson takes this analysis further by uncovering the origins of the language of 'sorts', and how this term could serve both bipolar and tripartite analyses. Equally, Corfield's account of 'class' shows how this term was entering the language slowly in the seventeenth century and was quite regularly used by the 1750s (earlier than classic accounts, such as that of Asa Briggs, had assumed) but that a tripartite division was still far from universal. Interestingly, she cites several examples of four or five-fold social divisions which distinguish large-scale traders from smaller-scale ones, thus anticipating the suggestions of the Marxist historian, R. S. Neale, that we subdivide the middling sort into 'middle' and 'middling' classes.[7] Equally, greater sensitivity to issues of gender and family have alerted historians to the need for a social analysis in which gender, age and position in the life-cycle are integrated with notions of class derived from birth, occupation or wealth.

The conceptual tools are therefore emerging, with which to reconsider the identity of the middling sort in our period. At the same time, empirical research is slowly appearing, to fill out our picture of society at this level. Urban history, in particular, has flourished over the last few decades, initially in the Tudor and Stuart centuries and subsequently in the eighteenth century.[8] Urban historians can scarcely ignore the middling sort, though Barry argues, in his essay, that they have often adopted perspectives that prevent direct analysis of the identity of the middling. One honourable exception has been Peter Earle, whose work on the wealthier tradesmen in London c.1660–1730 has given rise to his ambitiously titled study, *The Making of the English Middle Class* (1989). Earle's essay in this volume draws out the implications of his research for our definitions of the middle class, but he rightly emphasises the problems of generalising from specific groups within London to the middling sort of the mass of smaller towns. Shani d'Cruze offers an alternative approach to Earle, concerned less with income and lifestyle than with household and political independence, and highlighting the intermediary role of the middling sort as 'community brokers', both within urban society and in the wider community. Chris Brooks's two contributions examine two other key elements within the formation of the urban middling sort: the institution of apprenticeship and the role of the professions. Apprenticeship, after long neglect while historians explored the 'educational revolution' of literacy, schools and universities, is again receiving the attention it deserves as a key element in the social, cultural and economic development of successive generations. Brooks's chapter is the first recent synthesis of this material.

The professions have been better served in recent decades, but their relationship with other middling occupations has generally been played down, not least because of the 'professional' label attached, sometimes unhelpfully, to what were, in early modern times, as much trades as professions, whatever they were to become later.[9] Brooks not only shows the numerical significance of this sector of the middling sort but also highlights the close relationship between the professions and their middling clients, socially and ideologically, and the ways in which the middling sort contributed to the articulation of major discourses, such as those connected to law and religion.

Research into the rural middling sort is much less well developed – with no synthesis yet replacing Mildred Campbell's classic *The English Yeoman*. Sadly, it has not proved possible to obtain an essay for this collection on this theme, in part because of the shortage of active research in this area. Agrarian historians have been primarily concerned with economic rather than social analysis, and have preferred to study regional or local communities as a whole, rather than analysing a particular social group across space or time.[10] The greatest attention to the rural middling sort has come from those interested in their political and cultural identity. The work of Wrightson and Levine, on Essex, and subsequently of David Underdown, on the West Country, has drawn attention to the attitudes of the so-called 'parish elites' before and during the Civil War, and their critique of the gentry-centred nature of early 'county community' studies has been extended by Clive Holmes. The electoral importance of the forty-shilling freeholder by the early seventeenth century has been demonstrated by Hirst and Cust, and Brooks shows how the language associated with the property rights of the freeholder provided a crucial metaphor in the constitutional criticism that was directed by early Stuart MPs towards unpopular royal policies. As yet, similar work on the eighteenth century is conspicuously lacking, though Nicholas Rogers offers evidence on the electoral independence of county freeholders that suggests strong continuities.[11]

Our growing understanding of local communities has provided a vital infusion of knowledge about the middling sort, but the community focus of such studies has rarely encouraged historians to speculate about national pattern or significance – indeed, as we shall see, many historians of localities are wedded to a perspective that denies the existence either of national trends or of a national identity for the middling sort. Some of the most important observations about the place of the middling sort have come, instead, from historians interested in national political developments, above all in the eighteenth century. John Brewer and Paul Langford have both highlighted middle-class influence on state formation well before the 1780s, after which it is customary to emphasise the role both of provincial manufacturing interests and of middle-class radicals, often dissenters.[12] Rogers's essay draws on this new work, as well as on his own research on urban politics. Less work has been done for the earlier centuries, but the centrality of the rule of law to earlier state formation created, as Brooks shows, a national discourse in which the specific property interests of the middling sort at local level could become articulated.

II

Despite developments since 1948, which have provided both conceptual and empirical guides to a reconsideration of the place of the middling sort in early modern England, no direct challenge has been offered to Hexter's formulation of and response to 'the myth of the middle class'. It is therefore useful to begin by exploring in more detail what Hexter argued and how his arguments have been developed in subsequent historiography. Hexter's objections centred on what he saw as the misapplication of nineteenth-century terminology to the analysis of early modern society. Like many other writers, he questioned the appropriateness of a language of class in studies of a society which did not use such terminology itself, and whose social features do not fit easily with notions of class that require a national horizontal division between self-consciously antagonistic social groupings. He drew attention first to the deceptive capaciousness of the notion of 'the middle class', and how hard it was to use properly a term which at one moment embraced the landed gentry – as agrarian capitalists opposed to feudal aristocrats – and at another referred to small artisans. He urged that the term be confined to groups such as merchants, traders and yeomen more akin to the nineteenth-century 'middle classes' whose origins were being sought.

But Hexter also denied that, even on this definition, one could find an early modern middle class that shared those features that were seen as crucial to the character of that class in the nineteenth century. Hexter correctly pilloried the effort to understand Tudor people as if they were Manchester manufacturers of the type familiar to Samuel Smiles, Karl Marx or Benjamin Disraeli. Far from upholding bourgeois liberal, individualist or entrepreneurial values, Hexter argued, those in the middle of Tudor society were characterised chiefly by their desire to emulate the culture and values of their landed superiors. Not until the Industrial Revolution and the rise of provincial cities did a middle class emerge with interests and values self-consciously opposed to those of the landed elite. It should be noted here that Hexter made no effort to identify an alternative 'middle-class' consciousness that might have existed prior to the nineteenth-century version; by implication he left intact the traditional type as the only conceivable model for a middle class.

Instead, Hexter's chief concern was to identify how and why the middling sort was subordinate to the landed elite. Traditionally, the 'rise of the middle class' had been exemplified by pointing to the individual mobility of figures such as Wolsey or Burghley, or of groups such as the gentry or merchants. Hexter therefore concentrated his attention on the issue of social mobility, introducing into the subject a much needed methodological and statistical rigour, but also turning on its head the normal conclusion drawn from the evidence. He pointed to the impossibility of generalising from stray cases, the need to distinguish between the mobility of individual members of a class and the rise of a whole class, and the need to see social mobility as a multi-generational affair. In particular he drew attention to the characteristic circulation of English families between countryside and town, whereby younger sons moved into urban trade or professions before, if they were successful, then purchasing or marrying back into land, or establishing their children in a position to do so. In this way, Hexter argued, both the intellectual and physical capital and the leadership of towns was constantly removed, so that the very success of individuals from the middling sort ensured that the rentier lifestyle of the landed gentleman retained its position as the dominant ideal of English society. At the same time, Hexter denied strenuously that the label 'middle class' could be applied to the gentry, emphasising their common identity with the peerage within a landed aristocracy.

Most of the subsequent empirical work done on the middle classes has come within the framework established by this analysis. A number of studies have been made of the 'social origins and aspirations' (to cite one example) of urban elites, on the assumption that the movement of individuals and their sources of income between countryside and town is the best guide to the values of those involved. While such work has certainly underlined the importance of the circulatory process Hexter described (though at varying tempo over the period, as Brooks's chapter on apprenticeship shows), it has promoted controversy rather than consensus. One of the problems is that economic transactions are being used as proxies for social values. The purchase of land, interpreted by Hexter as commitment to the values of a landed elite, could be seen, rather, as a rational investment for groups who valued either its profitability (at times of high food prices) or at least its security, negotiability and transferability: commodities hard to find in other

sectors of the economy before 1700. After 1700 the growth of alternative safe investments, in urban property, the stock market and
above all government debt, which made it possible to retire or pass
on to children a secure non-landed estate, was matched by a
decline in investment in large-scale landed purchase by merchants
and the like.[13] Alternative social explanations of this trend have
been offered, but are they necessary? In any case, how far did land
purchase imply withdrawal from entrepreneurial activity, and at
what level of estates should we set our standards to judge that the
middling have or have not returned to the ranks of the landed
elite? By definition, a circulatory process is hard to freeze in order
to apply a set of structural dichotomies.

Furthermore, if we stress circulation rather than the return to
land, we can begin to question the assumption that it is the landed
phase of the process that dominates. Would it not be as plausible
to talk about the renewed influence of the values of the middling
sort upon the landed as the other way around? This seems the
more likely, given the growing influence of urban life on the experience of the landed elite. London and the provincial towns played
an ever greater part, not just in generating the wealth of the
landed (via government service, commercial and financial investment), but also as the settings in which elite lifestyles had to be
lived. First the royal court, then London, as the centre of political
life and the social season, and finally spas and other urban centres,
attracted the landed elite for increasing periods of the year, bringing them in close contact with the urban middling sort, as did the
importance of urban constituencies in parliamentary politics.[14]

Yet, most historians have followed Hexter in portraying the
landed elite, not the urban middling sort, as the dominant and
leading partners in this relationship. It is now common to see the
landed elite as the first to become imbued with commercial, individualistic values, and most recent historians of the gentry and
aristocracy have emphasised their entrepreneurship. For Marxist
historians, in particular, the agrarian capitalism of the landlord
class has become the driving force of economic growth, rendering
otiose the search for a separate middle class of entrepreneurs.[15]
Culturally, however, the hegemony of the landed elite is believed
to have been maintained, even intensified. Crucial to this process,
it is argued, was the growth of a national culture centred on the
metropolis, but spread through religion, commercialisation and

emulation, which the landed elite dominated through their hold over the state and church, and through their place as the leaders of cultural fashion. By participating in this cultural world, even if it was increasingly urban in setting, the upper ranks of the middling sort were accepting, so it is argued, the leadership of the landed elite as surely as when they abandoned urban life for a landed estate.[16]

Most recent studies have therefore endorsed Hexter's contention that, if we focus on the social mobility of the upper reaches of the middling sort and their relationship with the landed elite, we lose sight of any identifiable middle-class identity. The leaders of the bourgeoisie wanted nothing more than to lose their identity, whilst the landed elite they sought to join or emulate was already sufficiently equipped with capitalist virtues to bring about political and economic change with no help from the middling sort. Whereas the nineteenth century was marked by struggles between the landed and manufacturing interests, in which class divisions were clear, the nature of a pre-industrial economy involved cooperation and mutual interests between the agrarian and commercial sectors. Though there were tensions over taxation and public policy, there was no ongoing class struggle, even during the clash between the so-called landed and moneyed interests in the decades after 1689. This was a dispute over the financial impact of the state and its control: one in which both sides appealed to commerce for support, and in which a part of the landed elite (the Whigs) stood on one side with certain London financial and mercantile groups, while the Tory landed were joined by other London middling groups, and many of the provincial middling sort, in opposition.[17] As this example suggests, divisions in this period were as much about ideology as about interest, and, above all, centred on religious and political divisions that cut vertically through society, starting with the elite.

Here we may return to Hexter, and to his further challenge to the conventional Marxist and Whig interpretations, that had associated the major political watersheds of the period (notably the Reformation and Civil War, but also the growth of the state and of political parties) with shifts in class power, whereby the middle classes had brought about political change to reflect their growing socio-economic importance. Hexter's critique of this, whether applied to Pollard on the Tudors or Christopher Hill on the Civil

War, has been reinforced both by so-called revisionism and by a rethinking of socialist historiography. It is now conventional to emphasise that the momentum for all these changes came from within the ruling elites or from splits within their ranks, rather than as a result of the pressure or participation of the middle classes. Thus, in explaining the Reformation and sixteenth-century growth of government, crown initiative is stressed; the upper ranks of the middling sort are seen as offering support to such changes, rather than leading the way. There is less of a consensus about interpreting the English Revolution (1640–60). Though a vigorous case has been made for seeing this, too, as a political and religious crisis within the landed elite, it is harder to ignore the obvious importance of the middling sort both during the war and in the nonconformist churches that it created. Many historians, however, are now playing down the long-term significance of the Civil War and of nonconformity, stressing, rather, an ongoing elite division culminating in 1688 and the establishment of Whig and Tory parties. Thus, events in which the role of the middling sort is accepted are seen as less significant than the struggle for national control between rival groups of the landed elite, in which the middling sort are once again relegated to the role of a supporting cast. Such a perspective on the eighteenth century has been characteristic both of the Namierites, who played down ideological divisions amongst the elite after 1689, and of those historians who have rediscovered the vitality of Tory or Jacobite opposition to the Whig supremacy.[18]

   This perspective has also recommended itself, not just to historians hostile to the notion of class analysis, but also to many sympathetic to it. Following the lead of E. P. Thompson, they have committed themselves to history from below, and thus to a focus on society in terms of a polarisation between the elite and the people. Preoccupied with the interplay between the ruling elite and the lower classes – above all in the supposed attack of capitalist national culture on traditional customs and moral economy – they have shown little interest in distinguishing amongst the people between the middling sort and the rest (with the honourable exceptions of Manning and Hill). Both by adopting the polarised vocabularies of elite and popular (or patrician and plebeian), and by the themes they have chosen for analysis, they have tended to obscure any distinctive role for a middling sort. The analysis has been chiefly rural (understandably, given the nature of the society), focusing on local disputes and, in particular, on issues such as crime, crowd activity and popular customs and beliefs.[19] As Barry's chapter argues, such an agenda ignores the largely urban world of association, where the particular values of the middling sort may be identified. Even within the topics studied, however, many historians are becoming increasingly unhappy with the 'popular' as a term of analysis. The crowd, for example, was not a simple entity. There can be different crowds, not just with different ideological allegiances but with different social compositions. The orderliness and relative success of many crowd actions is now seen as depending in large part on the support, open or tacit, of middling groups in the local community.[20] It has long been noted that 'popular radicalism', for example that of the Levellers or of nonconformist sects, was often sustained by artisan and other middling groups, and faced the hostility not just of the landed elites but of many in the lower orders (as well as others of the middling sort). Whether used by contemporaries or by historians, the notion of 'the people' is largely rhetorical, concealing its social connotations, though often encapsulating the genuine belief of those using it that they did indeed stand for the common interest.[21] As we shall see, this may have been a particularly important idea for members of the middling sort.

The paradigm established by Hexter has proved both fruitful and flexible, directing attention to urban–landed relationships affecting the upper middling sort and capable of surviving a shift of interest, from the flight of the urban to the countryside, to that of the landed into the town. Its effort to downgrade the political significance of the middling sort has appealed both to those eager to put politics and religion, rather than social relations, at the heart of the agenda about political change, and to those for whom the significant conflicts in society lay between the top and the bottom. Common to all these approaches has been a tendency to confine their working definition of the middling sort to its upper section – merchants, professionals, rich traders – and to ignore the rest of the middling sort, assuming either that they shared the deference to the landed elite of the upper middling, or that they fitted unproblematically into 'the people'. The rest of this introduction will consider what happens to our notion of the middling as a social category if we try instead to isolate the middling sort –

independent trading households – from those above and below
them and consider their common characteristics.

III

In seeking to define the middling sort as a meaningful social category, this essay is not committing itself to claiming that members
of the middling sort could only be defined as such or that the definition is ever unproblematic. But such an admission is not unique
to this enterprise, for, as historians have rejected simplistic socio-
economic categories and incorporated into their social classification such dimensions as culture and ideology, so they have come
to stress the problematic nature of *all* social categories in early
modern England. Those studying the gentry or the poor, for
example, have increasingly abandoned the effort to find a single
means of categorisation, even at one moment, let alone over time.
The key problems that arise are: the absence of legal and fiscal definitions of social position; the life-cycle changes in social position
associated with age and with both geographical and social mobility, not to mention their differential effects according to gender;
the overlapping yet sometimes contradictory implications of economic, social, political and cultural criteria; and the way in which
local and regional differences and community-based notions of
society cut across nationally based class definitions. Each of these
problems applies to the middling sort with particular force, but if
applied too strictly they would dissolve every social category, not
merely that of the middling.

(i) The Absence of Legal and Fiscal Definitions

Problems both of evidence and of definition are caused by the failure of the English State to classify its subjects with any consistency,
for either legal or fiscal purposes. With no equivalent to European
nobility, with its legal and fiscal privileges, the only precisely
defined poles of English society were the tiny group of peers at
one end of the scale and those on organised poor relief at the
other. Nobody would classify either of these groups amongst the
middling sort, but we are little advanced in our understanding of

the boundaries between the middling sort and either the gentry on the one hand, or on the other hand the lower orders, most of whom required poor relief only in exceptional circumstances (though this may be an important marker).[22] Other legal and political criteria, such as tenurial status (freeholders, copyholders and the like) or legal and electoral rights in towns (freemen, burgage-holders), were becoming increasingly unreliable as markers of socio-economic standing, though still important ideologically to the middling sort. Rural standing depended on access to land, however achieved, and many yeomen combined ownership, freehold and other tenancies and subtenancies of land in bewildering fashion. The specialisation of urban economies and the growth of new industries and service sectors made guild and freeman categories, whose legal and political importance required the preservation of traditional terminology, less and less accurate indicators of the occupations and income sources of the urban middling.[23] As Wrightson shows, the precise vocabulary of estates and degrees favoured in legal documents and in elite commentaries on society was rarely reproduced in more informal comments on social gradation.

English taxation combined the progressive assumption that the rich should pay their share with a preference for indirect taxation or self-assessed income taxes (especially on land). A major reason for this was that the sporadic efforts by the state to draw directly on middling wealth, usually when warfare threatened state finances, led directly to an upsurge in the political self-consciousness of the middling sort. The consequence has been a lack of national tax data that can easily be translated into good social statistics. The exceptional demands of the 1690s generated Gregory King's famous social tables, but his manipulation of the resulting figures renders them a most unsure guide; their status categories throw little light on the middling. For most of the period their chief tax burden (save for consumption taxes) probably came from local rates levied by parish and county. It would be tempting to use such rate-payer definitions, as nineteenth-century politicians did, to identify the middling sort, but at present we lack detailed studies of the incidence of rates. Since each parish had its own history, a great many such studies would be needed before generalisations would be possible; at present we can only be sure that early studies based on national taxation, which took those exempt to be poor, and hence portrayed English society as a pyramid with a base of massive poverty, are quite misleading.[24]

(ii) Life-cycle and Gender

Legally and fiscally, moreover, the state dealt not with the individual but with the household, or rather the head of the household. Recent interest both in demography and in gender has revealed the paramount importance of the life-cycle of the individual in relation to household formation, and its implications for understanding social position. It was amongst the middling sort that the division of social position according to life-cycle was most fully institutionalised and conceptualised, once again most sharply in the towns. The ideal passage for an urban male took him from apprentice to journeyman to small master or dealer in a given trade, followed by gradual advancement within a trade guild or other body, according to experience and seniority, which reinforced the divisions of wealth and power within a given occupation but also offered the prospect of controlled social mobility. The world of the yeoman farmer was less structured by age, but still affected sharply by changes in family fortunes: over his career a farmer might control a rapidly changing patchwork of freehold and rented land, of inherited and purchased acres, and its size might vary with family needs and labour capabilities, while downward social mobility for non-heirs would be countered by strategies involving education, marriage or the provision of capital to establish a business. If, as Brooks argues, apprenticeship declined as a formal means of training for the urban middling sort in the eighteenth century, then rural and urban experiences may have converged. It seems likely that less fragile family backgrounds (as fewer families were broken up by adult mortality) and greater use of schooling to provide initial cultural and vocational training were becoming middling characteristics during the eighteenth century: Earle's comments on the prerequisites for entry to genteel London trades suggests such a process at work.[25]

Other social groups shared much of this experience, but arguably the change in circumstance caused by the life-cycle was greater for the middling than for those above or below them. In so far as birth determined gentility, so all the children of a gentry family had some claim to a common social status throughout their lives, although lack of wealth or the appropriate life-style might jeopardise society's willingness to accept this claim. Brooks shows how gentry apprentices were reluctant to accept the temporary subordination to their social inferiors which their life-cycle position (and perhaps their economic prospects?) dictated, but that genteel codes of honour did not recognise. Youths of the middling sort were more likely to accept their lot, anticipating a future rise in status. Amongst the poor, on the other hand, their dependent status during childhood and youth was only a prologue to a lifetime of dependence on others. Without resources or support from their family, few could hope to rise above the status of labourers or servants. Some would never be able to establish their own households; for others, this phase of independence would be punctuated by reliance on poor relief or charity. In their old age, if they were spared, they could look forward only to further dependence. Like the gentry, their lives seemed determined at birth.

By contrast, among the middling it was assumed that, in charting their course through the cycle of life, the individual qualities of each person would play a key role in deciding his or her fortune. Whilst keenly aware of the differential start varied family backgrounds could bring, they tended to see success or failure in terms of the individual. Hence the emphasis on the classic virtues – industry, thrift, self-discipline, credit-worthiness – which brought success (measured as much by maintenance of social position and independence as upward mobility), and equally on the corresponding vices which spelt doom and downward mobility (the latter a good deal more sure than upward). These moral evaluations thus came to play a major part in the self-classification of the middling sort. Not only did they provide a vocabulary of differentiation within the middling sort, but they were often applied to distinguish the class as a whole from those above or below them.[26] Yet, as Barry's essay argues, although individual virtues and vices played a vital part in the vocabulary of the middling sort, this should not be mistaken for an ideology of individualism, since at every stage of the life-cycle the individual's progress was structured by a set of collective practices and associations. But, unlike the poor, the middling could view themselves as voluntary members of these collective groups, associating to ensure their successful passage through the hazards of life, and not dependent on others in the same way as, for example, those on charity or poor relief. Both Brooks and Earle note the importance of these bourgeois values in defining middling identity, and Earle argues that they form a direct ancestor for the self-consciousness of the Victorian middle class. However, he issues one important caveat: the Victorian middle class felt more confident and secure against misfortune; hence it was the lower middle class and respectable working class, still haunted by 'the poverty of disaster' who then adopted most strongly the defensive aspects of middling culture, including its mutual support mechanisms.

The most important of these mutual agencies was the household itself. The social position of males of the middling sort was measured against that of the head of the household. There seems little doubt that the household was just as vital for women, though their history is only just beginning to emerge. At present there is little to enable us to choose between a number of alternative accounts of the interplay between gender, the household and class identity. Davidoff and Hall's work on 1780–1850 has emphasised the role of women in producing a private domestic world, whose distance from work became a badge of middle-class identity for their menfolk, and Earle detects similar trends earlier, in London. Other historians see women's contribution as more basic, providing labour for the shop or business, or extra income to balance the household budget and so keep the family independent, and this argument is developed by d'Cruze in her essay. None the less she too stresses that the public figure of the male head of household relied on the private efforts of wife, children and servants – not least to give him the time for public activity.[27]

It is also unclear how far women's own labour or property could entitle them to middling status. Historians are divided, both over the property rights enjoyed by women during marriage (based on family trusts) and on the fate of widows. Arguably, the growth of retail and service sectors of the economy and of securer forms of rentier investment gave women an increasing chance of establishing their own middling status; set against this must be the growing exclusiveness of commercial and professional life and of established male trades. Unlike the male life-cycle, little public provision was made for the reproduction of female skills by training, nor was there any explicit recognition of female 'seniority' by occupation; domestic service, marriage and old age and/or widowhood were dangerous passages that women had to negotiate with much less formal support than men enjoyed. Earle suggests that this would have produced a 'deficit' of single or widowed women within the middling sort, reinforcing the centrality of marriage in ensuring women's entry into, and survival within, this group.[28]

(iii) The Consistency of Economic, Cultural and Political Criteria

Our third consideration is equally complex. As each specific measure of social differentiation has proved unreliable, historians have come to view social identity as an amalgam of factors – strongest when a number of different measures work together, but often less clearcut. The complete correlation of such indicators as occupation, wealth, birth, life-style and political power is only found at the very top and bottom of society. Like the lower gentry and some of the lower orders, the middling sort would rank differently according to different criteria. Thus, notoriously, merchants, professional men and even rich yeomen in some districts might earn more than many gentlemen, but were often adjudged non-gentle on grounds of occupation, birth, life-style and possibly lack of power. Equally, the poorest curate or humble artisan might not earn much more than an able-bodied labourer in his prime, yet still seem socially closer to those better off.

Economically, the middling sort appears much more fragmented than either the poor or the landed elite. What they all had in common – the need to work for their income using skill and engaging in a trade or profession, rather than relying on rentier income or labouring in another's employment, was also what separated them into a thousand different categories, depending on the character of the occupation and the balance it involved of head and hand, of labour and capital, of face-to-face trading or long-distance commerce, and so on. Although it would be misleading to portray the landed interest as monolithic, it was much easier to see what a minor squire had in common with a great aristocrat than to perceive the underlying similarities or shared interests of the middling. As traders they were in competition with others in their occupation and with rival occupations for the purses of consumers – and as consumers themselves they might question the practices of their fellow traders. Within one occupation there were often tensions between branches of the trade and between large or small-scale businesses, while masters had to deal with apprentices and journeymen, who might hope to be masters themselves, but for the moment might have contrary interests. Farmers equally were competing with each other much more directly than their rentier landlords, and also locked into uneasy dependence on urban commercial groups for the marketing of their products. All of this gave credibility to the claims of the gentry that they alone could stand above the babble of conflicting interest groups that formed the middling sort, and judge economic interests, and society more generally, objectively.[29] Such divisions certainly helped the landed to divide and rule, since few issues allied all the middling sort on one side against the landed on the other.

On the other hand, the very complexity of interests within the middling sort often generated a type of cohesion. The mixture of horizontal ties, say of merchants against artisans retailing their own goods, and vertical ones, for example of all those engaged in a certain trade locally, prevented long-term splits within the middling sort, even as they encouraged ever-changing alliances. As Shani D'Cruze observes, this gave a crucial role to the 'community brokers' who could link interests and mould common identities – often aided by ideological ties. Barry takes this point further by emphasising the degree to which urban association was devoted to bringing unity, or at least coherence, out of such diversity.

Such association, Barry argues, both reflected and strengthened common *cultural* assumptions among the middling sort, many of them based on the moral notions of virtues and vices discussed above. As Brooks notes, common experiences such as apprenticeship played an important role in creating this cultural identity, as did religious beliefs. The best guide to these ideas is still L. B. Wright's *Middle-Class Culture in Elizabethan England* (a study, in fact, of the reading and ideas of Londoners c.1550–1640), and many of the commonplaces recorded there retained their force, underlining the bourgeois notions of respectability we associate with the Victorian middle class. Paradoxically, however, these cultural stereotypes were seen not as progressive, pointing to modern urban civilisation, but more often as traditional values, closely bound in with reverence for custom and notions of honour. In this they overlapped heavily with concepts of gentility on the one hand, and the values of popular culture on the other. Historians have often concluded from this that middle-class culture was essentially imitative, subordinate to either elite or popular conceptions.[30] But, as Barry argues, such arguments depend largely on tacit assumptions that conservative cultural forms are inappropriate for this social grouping; in practice the appropriation of these cultural forms seems to have fitted well with middling experience of the world.

Many historians might agree with this characterisation of the middling sort before the Civil War, but argue that thereafter they were increasingly divided by the growth of a polite culture of gentility, to which the upper ranks of the middling aspired, leaving the lower groups excluded. There is no doubt that, in the towns at least, a more complex culture developed, in which those with more leisure and wealth could participate. However, middling cultures had never been unstratified, and other developments were occurring which worked in the opposite direction. By the late seventeenth century the middling sort were almost certainly all able to read and were increasingly provided with access, through print, to a world of knowledge denied to the poor. As yet, the mass market of the 'consumer society' was largely confined to the middling sort, and though the landed elite did provide its leaders of fashion, they soon found that they had to innovate constantly to maintain cultural distance from the middling. Furthermore, the meanings of cultural practices did not remain constant, but were assimilated into traditional middling values.[31] Alongside the commercial culture, moreover, survived and expanded a complex web of informal association depending little on any elite models, though often drawing on earlier civic or religious or guild practices.

Political concerns were often central to such groups, even if it was only the voracious interest in news which was common to the whole of the middling sort after the Civil War. Yet the middling sort's formal political position was highly variable. Whereas the exercise of power was the badge of the gentleman, and lack of formal power that of the poor, the middling's experience was diverse. The mercantile elite and the professions often exercised considerable power in their capacity as urban magistrates or members of the judicial or administrative systems. They considered themselves as entitled, because of this, to the status of gentleman or even esquire, though many gentry questioned this (partly because most landed gentry, not being JPs or above, had far less political power in practice than the elite of the middling sort). In one way, therefore, political power distinguished an elite of the middling from the rest and placed them in a status hierarchy alongside the gentry.

Running contrary to this oligarchic tendency, however, was the importance of participatory government and the common rights of the middling sort, summed up in the notion of freedom. Lacking paid bureaucracies, early modern government depended on the voluntary work, often in rotation or by election, of many of the middling sort, and on their cooperation with modes of government powered by legal processes and appeal to precedent. These sustained the ideological significance of notions such as freedom even when practices appeared oligarchic, while the growth of electoral and partisan politics in many urban constituencies, and even in non-parliamentary centres, gave new significance to local participation. Recent work, as Rogers shows, has indicated that the political support of the middling sort had to be earned rather than commanded (or bought), both by landed elites and by urban oligarchs, and this stimulated the intensification of vertical ties within the middling sort to rally and maintain allegiances. D'Cruze offers fascinating vignettes of this process at work in eighteenth-century Colchester.[32]

The possibilities for political action were different in rural areas. Holmes has shown the sophistication of the seventeenth-century yeomanry and their ability to organise and conceptualise their activity, once again drawing on the law and on concepts such as the freeholder. In jury service, in manorial courts and above all in the parish, the rural middling sort governed the poor and, in rotation, each other. As Wrightson observes, the vocabulary of the 'middling sort' was slow to develop precisely because locally the middling sort often *were* the elite, the rulers. In many parts of the country (such as pastoral areas where gentry were lightly scattered) they ran local affairs with little gentry interference, and when such interference by gentry or central government threatened their interests they were capable of vigorous responses. It is hard to believe that this was any less the case in the eighteenth century, though nobody really knows.[33]

(iv) Community versus Class?

For some historians, however, it is precisely the exercise of power parochially (in both senses) that prevents us from seeing the middling sort as a class. This brings us to our fourth and final consideration. Like the poor, whose riots and other actions in defence of local custom never, it is claimed, became part of a national class consciousness, so the middling were too rooted in local particularism, motivated by community rather than class. Hence Peter Laslett's contention that seventeenth-century England was a one-class society, because only the gentry operated on a national scale.[34] Certainly, as Wrightson suggests, it suited the middling sort to see themselves, in local affairs, as the representatives of government as a whole, while in defending their interests to a wider public they would tend to do so in the name of their community and its rights, rather than as 'the middling sort'. Brooks shows how, in the period before the Civil War, the interests of the middling sort were sometimes explicitly included in a political rhetoric which claimed to uphold the interests of 'the people' against the predatory landed elite on the one hand and the attacks on property rights by the crown on the other. Then, as Wrightson notes, the collapse of government, during the Civil War, forced some of the middling sort to claim a voice in national affairs in their own right, as soldiers or followers of a particular ideological cause, which led to the popularisation of the language of 'the middling sort'. Thereafter, community was restored as the most viable means of expressing middling interests (for all but a core of sectarian nonconformists who repudiated established community ties) until the late eighteenth and early nineteenth centuries, when oligarchic establishments in local government forced unrepresented groups to look elsewhere for an ideology (laissez-faire liberalism) that expressed their interests.[35]

Strategically, then, the language of community may have suited the middling sort better than that of class. The gentry, we should note, were hardly free of the same pressures, notably in their appeal to 'county community' and other local values. Historians of gentry politics have, however, increasingly questioned the reality of any dichotomy between the local and the national, and their arguments may also be extended to the middling sort. The early modern period saw an ever greater interdependence between local and national affairs. On the one hand, the actions of central government seemed of growing relevance to local interests, so that even the most parochially minded saw involvement in politics as necessary.[36] At the same time, the agenda of national politics was increasingly dominated by issues that arose from the everyday experiences of local communities. The two were linked ever more powerfully by party politics and the growth of the press and other media. Just as in the nineteenth (and indeed the twentieth) century, it makes no sense to see community as excluding class.

Indeed, reversing the argument, one might suggest that it was the intimate interrelationship of local and national in early modern England that gave the middling sort a central place in political and social developments. It hardly needs saying that the middling sort were divided – royalists and parliamentarians, Anglicans and dissenters, Whigs and Tories, all finding strong support at every level of the middling sort. It has been argued that, by this party identification, they became subordinate to the aristocratic groups that dominated these parties at a national level, and so lost their class identity. Leaving aside the question of how the aristocracy maintained *its* class identity whilst equally divided, this picture is far too simple in its emphasis on the downward direction of influence. It could equally be argued that elite division offered a much greater opportunity for the middling sort, especially through their domination of the electoral system, to exert upward pressure on crown and parliament. Equally, turning to relations within the middling sort, these divisions may have weakened the oligarchic tendencies within urban politics and strengthened those participatory aspects which helped to forge a common identity. Members of the elite and party politicians, whatever their private feelings, clearly found it expedient to appeal to civic identity and to a shared rhetoric of citizenship when they needed to gain the support of their fellow citizens – whilst denouncing their opponents' efforts to do so as rabble-rousing. When possible, all sides sought to appropriate traditional symbols of civic identity, such as public holidays, processions, public places, civic heroes, to their own cause. Culturally, therefore, partisanship did much to attract attention to the symbols and ideas of civic and bourgeois identity.

Clearly this process might involve, not genuine solidarity within the middling sort, but the exploitation of a rhetoric of community by cynical leaders. There was indeed a considerable distrust of elite manipulation among ordinary members of the middling sort. Hence the great resonance of successive anti-corruption, patriotic, independent campaigns in which the ideology of the independent citizen, resisting both central and local oligarchy, was exploited. The potency of this image – from the 1640s certainly until the Chartist movement – is often observed. The same rhetoric took on a particular resonance for the lesser middling sort, who felt threatened themselves by the danger of becoming dependent on those with greater access to capital, outside influence and so on.[37] In the countryside such fears could crystallise around issues such as common lands or enclosure, where the traditional rights of small property-holders were threatened. This tension was also a perennial feature of urban politics as far back as the medieval period, probably earlier. It found expression not just in corporate politics but also in disputes within and between guilds or interest groups. Its manifestations within London, or in other towns at times of political or social tension, such as during the mid-Tudor period, had characteristically triggered an alliance of interests between the urban elite and the crown in reshaping the boundaries of urban politics to strengthen the oligarchic aspects, for example by limiting electoral freedoms or shifting responsibility away from larger representative bodies towards self-perpetuating bodies of aldermen. Similar strategies were frequently attempted during the century or so after 1640, but rarely with any long-term success, not least because both urban and national elites were themselves too divided and too inconsistent in their own aims and allegiances to maintain a common front against those below them. Arguably, however, as noted before, these very divisions within the establishment, sustaining the struggle for power in the local community, may have prevented the lesser middling sort from turning to national political change to further their struggles. Whether we choose to set community against class, therefore, depends very much on whether we accept that class has to be both felt and acted upon at a national level, or whether we can conceive of class as primarily experienced within community.

IV

This essay began by adopting, from D'Cruze's work, the working definition of the middling sort as made up of 'independent trading households'. As the last section indicated, this combination of terms identifies a number of qualities that are both elusive to study and, in themselves, highly fragmentary over time and space. Rather than regarding this as a sign of failure, however, we might consider whether it is not a significant indication that we are grasping something of the reality of social identity. For, as historians of the modern middle classes have also stressed, elusiveness appears to be a characteristic feature of this class. A successful middling sort denied its own existence, because it regarded the continuation of its independent trading households as the natural state of affairs. Yet, for each such household, and for its individual members according to gender, age and so on, the continued independence, trading ability and household cohesion of that middling sort required constant activity, activity for which the household itself was responsible. In this respect, as Peter Earle has hinted, picking up E. P. Thompson's great insight into class formation, the middle classes are continuously making themselves. The remainder of this essay will be concerned with some of the key questions that remain to be asked about the maintenance and reproduction of independent trading households, and hence of the middling sort.

The first and most fundamental requirement is to try to recreate the way in which the early modern middling sort experienced and saw the world, rather than relying on Victorian stereotypes or elite perceptions. Major though the evidential problems facing such a 'history from the middle' may be, they are no greater, arguably less, than those involved in writing 'history from below'. We may indeed find that much of the study of 'popular' culture and experience will make more sense seen in this light, and the same may be said of local or community history. One intention of this volume is to indicate the possibilities for such work and to offer examples. But the urban bias of much of both this essay and this volume suggests that the task is much better developed for towns than for the rural middling sort, who must have comprised a numerical majority of the grouping throughout most if not all of our period. However, controversial new interpretations, both of agricultural innovation and of the importance of rural industry, may well spark off a debate about the transformative effects of the 'yeomen' or the 'landholding middle rank'.[38]

Barry's essay in this collection emphasises the specifically urban characteristic of a 'bourgeois culture' which he sees emerging both in response to the conditions of urban life and through the characteristically urban form of association. Implicit in his account is the suggestion that, in the town, middle-class formation may have grown more from the interrelationships within the middling sort, faced with urban conditions, than from relationships with those above or below them. It may be that the middling sort of the countryside, numerically weaker in any single community, were more likely to define themselves in terms of those above and below them – the landed and the poor. They were more directly affected by the power of the landed elite and, until the nineteenth century, also perhaps more vulnerable to the numerical weight and physical presence of the poor, than were town-dwellers. Recent work has emphasised the degree to which rural social relations were shaped by the growth of landless labour (whether in agriculture or rural industry) and the associated problem of poverty, and this is certainly the impression fostered by the poor-law documentation of the parish.[39] Such a generalisation obscures, of course, vital regional differences, between arable and pastoral agriculture, nucleated and scattered settlements, areas with and without resident gentry, manorial structures of which must have made each rural 'pays' almost as distinctive in its social and power structure as any town.[40]

We need, therefore, to begin the systematic study and comparison of rural middling sorts in different communities. But we also need to study the extent of circulation amongst the middling sort between urban and rural society, a topic much less considered than either pauper migration or the gentry/mercantile circulation discussed at the start of this essay. Studying this process may help us to understand both what common skills the middling sort required to establish independent trading households, regardless of location, and which skills were specifically urban or rural. Equally, how did families seek to diversify their assets, and hence perhaps secure themselves against risk, by basing themselves in both town and countryside? A fascinating insight into these issues, and much else about the rural middling sort, is offered by Richard Gough's contemporary account of life in that most aptly named Shropshire parish, Myddle.[41]

As these last points suggest, crucial to the reproduction and survival of independent trading households were decisions about the transmission of both property and skills to succeeding generations. Much studied among the landed classes, this issue has rarely been explored for the middling sort.[42] Fortunately, an indirect consequence of the flourishing study of both demography and gender has been a renewed concern for precisely these questions.

Studies of marriage decisions and their consequences, of life-cycle service, and of literacy and educational opportunities, are all potentially crucial to understanding the changing fortunes of the middle sort. Until recently, most of these topics tended to be examined by sources covering the whole social spectrum, thus obscuring the particular experiences of the middling sort, but here too there is now much greater concern to discover the varied social incidence and meaning of such practices, and this should make the middling sort more visible.[43]

While it is crucial that we should discover more about the workings of the households of the middling sort, as they took responsibility for their futures, we must be careful to avoid an unbalanced view of this process. Accustomed as we are to associating the middle classes with private life and individual responsibility, we may postulate a false dichotomy between such activity and the world of public, collective action. Just as such a rhetoric today ignores the dependence of middle-class security on the welfare state and the infrastructure of a modern society, so historians' emphasis on possessive individualism ignores vital aspects of both the experience and the values of the early modern middling sort. As various essays in this collection demonstrate, the collective framework provided by the law, by local and, to a lesser extent, national government, and by other forms of public and private association, were not only vital to the middling sort, but were recognised as such by contemporaries. As people of property, even if that property was limited to skill or a small business, they saw the law as a vital defence of their rights. Local government provided the framework for enforcement of this law, in which they often participated in positions of varying responsibility. National political involvement often arose out of this local role, but also from a broader sense of the connection between national institutions, such as parliament, and the interests of the middling sort. As Barry and others argue, all of these forms of activity spawned association, as did the countless other ways in which the middling sort sought to protect and advance their households. A new approach to public life in this period, which takes these efforts seriously, is just beginning to emerge, particularly for the later part of our period, but much further research will be required in this area.

The aim of this volume is to indicate the wealth of evidence already available for a reconsideration of the middling sort, but also, as these final remarks suggest, to suggest the new questions about early modern society that are raised once we begin to consider that society neither from above nor from below, but *from the middle*. Whatever we decide about the existence or otherwise of a middling sort (and perhaps too much is at stake historiographically for this to be universally accepted), this new perspective is surely too valuable to be ignored.

1. 'Sorts of People' in Tudor and Stuart England

KEITH WRIGHTSON

I

'A nobleman, a gentleman, a yeoman; the distinction of these: that is a good interest of the nation, and a great one!' Oliver Cromwell's famous words to the newly assembled members of the first Protectorate parliament provide an apt introduction to any discussion of the social structure of early modern England. Cromwell's purpose was to urge upon the members the necessity of 'Healing and Settling' the kingdom after more than a decade of civil war and revolution. In their 'endeavours after settlement', he argued, they should turn their attention first 'to the authority of the nation; to the magistracy; to the ranks and orders of men – whereby England hath been known for hundreds of years': the traditional pattern of social and political order which had been challenged by 'men of Levelling principles' who threatened 'the reducing all to an equality'.[1]

In alluding briefly but pointedly to the familiar status designations of the conventional hierarchy of 'ranks and orders', Cromwell doubtless knew that he was appealing to a conception of the social order that carried powerful ideological force for his listeners. Indeed, to make his point he needed to do no more than to rehearse the first three categories of the conventional list of 'estates and degrees of people' repeatedly described by the many writers who sought to anatomise the social order of Elizabethan and early Stuart England. This classical social hierarchy – noblemen; gentlemen; yeomen; citizens and burgesses; husbandmen; artisans; labourers – with its implications of oneness and order in a graduated ladder of subordination and reciprocal obligation, its reassuring sense of stability and continuity, must have been as familiar to his audience as the multiplication tables are to a twentieth-century schoolchild.

It is scarcely less familiar to modern students of the sixteenth and seventeenth centuries. Readily accessible in the works of such writers as Sir Thomas Smith, William Harrison and Sir Thomas Wilson, in the categories of sumptuary legislation, in the formal styles and 'additions' adopted in a host of legal documents, it dominates historical approaches to the social structure of early modern England. Widely accepted as an essentially accurate account of the principal social groupings distinguishable in Tudor and Stuart society, it provides the basic categories adopted in historical analyses of myriad aspects of contemporary life, ranging from the social distributions of wealth, status and power, to educational opportunity, religious affiliation, criminal behaviour, household structure, and patterns of domestic consumption. Moreover, it is commonly believed to have been so powerful a representation of the social order, so all-pervasive an influence on patterns of social relations, as virtually to have excluded any alternative definitions of social reality. This was the 'Old Society', the very essence of an *ancien régime sociologique* which was to be shattered only with industrialisation, the social and political conflicts of the early nineteenth century, the rise of political economy, and the 'birth of class'.

It is one of the underlying themes of this chapter that such comfortable assumptions need to be questioned and reappraised. Only by doing so can we gain a deeper appreciation of the social dynamism of the sixteenth and seventeenth centuries and the place of the early modern period in the long-term transition in perceptions of society and in social identities which took place between the fifteenth and the nineteenth centuries.

I have argued elsewhere that while the classical social hierarchy expounded by the writers of the Elizabethan and early Stuart period was indeed the dominant mode of formal social description of their age, it was not one which was of immemorial antiquity, 'known for hundreds of years'. On the contrary, its mature formulation was very much a product of the Elizabethan age; a reworking of traditional universalistic concepts of the social order in the light of the English experience of the sixteenth century; part and parcel of that heightening of national self-awareness which W. G. Hoskins dubbed 'the discovery of England'.[2] Nor was it necessarily so all-pervasive and exclusive a perception of the social order as is often assumed. For though there can be no doubt that it was widely accepted and routinely adopted as an appropriate model for the conceptualisation of the social order, one which exerted its influence throughout the seventeenth and deep into the eighteenth century, there is also reason to believe that it was, none the less, limited in both its currency and its significance.

There were certainly occasions enough when the people of the time appended to their names their 'estate, mystery or degree' – above all in the drawing up of formal legal documents, some of which required such identification. There were occasions also when they ordered themselves and their neighbours into the appropriate hierarchical pecking order, as for example in church seating plans, which were frequently structured in accordance with the 'conditions and estates', 'ranks qualities and conditions' or 'degrees and qualities' of the parishioners.[3] Yet it can also be argued that the language of 'estates and degrees', 'ranks and orders', remained to a very large extent a vocabulary of *formal* social description. As such, it undoubtedly enjoyed a long life. But there is far less evidence that it enjoyed great currency in the hurly burly of everyday affairs. Indeed, there is much evidence to suggest that for most purposes people employed much cruder, less precise and perhaps more effective terms to express the essential distinctions observable in their localised social worlds.

To take but one example, in his account of the parishioners of Myddle in Shropshire during the seventeenth century, Richard Gough showed himself to be highly sensitive to the social distinctions among his neighbours. He began his account of the families of the parish with the church seating plan of 1701, which presented them in rank order, the gentry at the front of the church, the cottagers at the rear. Yet though he wrote of 'the antient gentry' of the district, and of a family 'of Esquire's degree', and though he described himself as a 'yeoman', for the most part he eschewed such formal status 'additions'. Individual neighbours or inhabitants were most commonly identified by their specific occupations or by the tenements which they occupied. When he identified significant subgroups among the parishioners, he wrote not of gentlemen, yeomen, husbandmen and labourers, but simply of the 'cheife inhabitants', 'the best of the parish', 'good substantiall persons' and 'poore people'.[4]

Such informal terminology of social description and differentiation, which can be gleaned from a wide variety of sources, could be
very variegated. It included a host of terms unknown to the conventional hierarchy of estates and degrees.[5] But it too had its regu-
larities and its history, and, from the later sixteenth century, one
specific vocabulary of informal social description emerges into
prominence which deserves more consideration than it has
received hitherto. This involved a set of terms that I have called
'the language of "sorts"'. The remainder of this chapter will be
devoted to exploring its emergence alongside the conventional
conceptualisation of the social order, and its subsequent evolution
in the seventeenth century, in the belief that by examining this linguistic development, and considering its implications, a further
dimension can be added to our understanding of social change in
early modern England.[6]

II

All students of early modern England have encountered the language of 'sorts' of people – 'the better sort', 'the meaner sort', 'the
middle sort of people' – and many historians in recent years have
chosen to employ it extensively in their analyses of social and political change. Justifiably so, for it is, after all, an authentic contemporary terminology, and one that leaps out from the sources as
embodying the dynamism of social relations. As yet, however, the
chronological development and fuller implications of this useful
terminology have been very little investigated. As I hope to show,
these issues repay more careful study.

The word 'sort', meaning 'of a certain kind', and the verb 'to
sort', can be found in a variety of English vernacular works from at
least the fourteenth century.[7] Its widespread employment as a
term of social description, however, appears to have been a distinctively sixteenth-century development, and in particular an innovation of the mid-to-late sixteenth century.

As might be anticipated, occasional examples of its use in the
broad context of social description can be found from an early
date. Wycliffe wrote in 1380 of 'folk of this sort', and many more
examples can be provided from the literature of the earlier

sixteenth century. In such instances, however, the term was used in an essentially neutral and unspecific sense, implying no more than a broad category or type, or various kinds of people. Thus, in his *Dialogue between Pole and Lupset* (1529–32), Thomas Starkey wrote of 'al sortys and nature of pepul', and in *The Book Named the Governor* (1531) Sir Thomas Elyot referred to 'all sortes of men', though both greatly preferred to use the term 'state and degree' or 'estate and degree' for more specific discussion of particular social groups.[8]

Such essentially neutral usage was long to continue.[9] By the final quarter of the sixteenth century, however, the language of 'sorts' was also enjoying a much wider currency in social description in a distinctly different form – one which was maintained and elaborated in the seventeenth century. The key to its development appears to have been the addition to the neutral term 'sort' of a variety of resonant adjectives, frequently in the comparative form.

The gradual infiltration of language of this kind can be nicely illustrated by considering the two Books of Homilies, the officially promulgated sermons of the Church of England. The first book, published in 1549 and authored by the first generation of English Protestant divines, contains very little socially differentiating language at all, save for a prefatory aspiration that all people should serve God 'according to their degree, state and vocation', and the famous account of orders and degrees contained in the opening paragraphs of the homily on 'Good Order and Obedience'. It provides no examples of the language of 'sorts' whatsoever beyond an allusion to the disparagement of Protestants as being 'of the new sort'. The second book, however, written by the bishops of the Elizabethan church and published in 1563 and 1582, contains references not only to 'all states and sorts of people, high and low', but also specifically to 'the common sort', 'the meaner sort', 'the simpler sort', and 'the unlearned and simple sort', alongside a variety of other unflattering allusions to 'the rude people', 'the ignorant multitude', 'the weak, simple and blind common people' and the 'rascall commons'.[10]

Further illustration of the growing currency of the language of 'sorts' can be found in the varied renderings of certain passages of scripture in English translations of the Bible. In the 1537 Matthew Bible, for example, Nebuchadnezzar, after sacking Jerusalem, carried off into captivity all the inhabitants 'save ye poore people of ye lande' (2 Kings 24:14). In the 1539 Great Bible, he left 'the poore common people'. The Geneva Bible of 1583 reverted to 'the poore people of the lande', but the Authorized Version of 1611 broke new ground with '*the poorest sort* of people'. A more telling example, because it can be traced over more than two centuries, is provided by translations of Acts 17:5 – the raising of a riot against St Paul by the Jews of Thessalonica. In the Wycliffite version of 1378 they 'tooken of the comyn peple summe yuele men'. In 1526 Tyndale had them stir up 'evyll men which were vagabondes', a translation which was retained in the Matthew Bible, the Great Bible and (with slight modification) the Bishops' Bible. The Geneva Bible made the rioters 'certaine vagabondes and wicked fellowes'. To the translators of 1611, however, they were 'certain lewd fellowes of *the baser sort*'. One could scarcely ask for a better example of how shifting social prejudices could be incorporated into the Word of God. But there was no theological bias in this. The Catholic Rheims translation attributed the riot to 'certain naughtie men' drawn from '*the rascall sort*'.[11]

It was through the emergence of a particular set of favoured and widely adopted linguistic couplings of this kind (most of them with distinctive three-syllable rhythm, which may suggest the formulaic cadences of common speech) that the language of 'sorts' became conventionalised, stereotyped, and gained the prominence which it was to enjoy in the informal English terminology of social description for a century and a half. Closer consideration of the adjectives involved and their mode of employment can provide useful clues to its development over time.[12]

III

The elaboration of the language of 'sorts' of people appears to have begun in the second quarter of the sixteenth century with the adoption of the term 'the common sort' as a synonym for the older and still more frequently used terms 'the commonalty' or 'the common people' (i.e., all those of less than gentle status). One instance of this usage can be found in Starkey's *Dialogue*, though he generally preferred to write of the 'commynalty'.

Similarly, in 1548 John Hales distinguished 'the comen sorte of people' from those 'called to the degree of nobilitie', and thereafter the term was to enjoy a very long history alongside the increasingly archaic 'commonalty' and the perennial 'the common people'.[13]

Clearly such usage implied an essentially *dichotomous* perception of society, distinguishing the 'common sort' from people of gentility and authority, and it was a traditional enough dichotomy at that. Other linguistic coinages which were added to the vocabulary of 'sorts of people' under the later Tudors and early Stuarts also tended to imply an essentially dichotomous perception of the social world. Significantly, however, it was one which came to involve a rather broader range of criteria of differentiation, and to focus attention upon differentials of less traditional concern.

The crucial terms involved were 'the poorer sort' as against 'the richer sort'; the 'wiser' or 'learned' sorts as distinct from the 'simpler', 'ignorant', 'ruder' or 'vulgar' sorts; 'the better sort' in contrast to the 'poorer', 'ruder', 'ordinary'. 'vulgar', 'lower', 'inferior', 'meaner' or 'baser' sorts; and finally 'the meaner sort' as against anyone placed in a position of authority. As these commonly employed terms and juxtapositions indicate, the criteria of differentiation could be economic, cultural, related to authority and subordination, or combinations of all three. With the elaboration of the language of 'sorts', England acquired a vocabulary of social differentiation which was varied, resonant, flexible and wonderfully adaptable to particular contexts.

Thus, the 'poorer sort of people' of the Kentish parish of Strood, in 1598, were the members of the sixty-one families defined by the overseers as those 'which as yet are able to work and doth neither give nor take, but if the husband should die are likely to be a parish charge', as distinct from the eighty rate-paying households and the handful of paupers on relief. Those 'they do usually call the poorer sort' in Stanhope-in-Weardale, in 1609, were described as people who 'have little but live on[ly] by handlie labour or are in service to be cottagers', in contrast to 'such as are of better abilities and farm ground'. The 'Richer sort' of Malmesbury, c.1600, were members of the corporation; clothiers, drapers and glovers of substance: 'men that sway the whole towne'.[14]

Arthur Dent's best-selling *Plaine Man's Path-way to Heaven* (1601) was aimed at the edification of 'the ignorant and vulgar sort', as opposed to the 'learned', as were many of the scores of devotional works and catechisms published between the 1580s and the 1620s to instruct those 'of meanest capacity', namely the 'simpler', 'weaker', 'ruder' and 'vulgar' sorts.[15] In 1578 William Bourne attempted to present the principles of geometry not to the learned, but to 'the symplest sort of people' or 'common sort', while in 1623 Robert Record contrasted 'the learned sort' with the 'simple ignorant' or 'rude Readers'. The ecclesiastical lawyer, Henry Swinburne, advised in 1635 that great discretion should be used in interpreting testaments 'for as much as the ruder sort of people doe not know the difference of termes nor the naturall force of words'. It was the 'common and vulgar sorte of people' of Jacobstowe in Cornwall who formed the principal audience for a scandalous libel in 1616, while in Interregnum Wiltshire it was 'the ruder sort of the parish' of Everleigh who still hankered after Christmas ales.[16]

The 'better' or 'best' sorts of people were those considered in 1571 and 1584 to be fitter to serve on trial juries than 'men of weake Judgement and verie meane estate', alias 'the poor and simpler sort'. They were regarded by the bishop of St David's in 1583 as persons of sufficient local prominence to merit burial within parish churches. They provided references for would-be alehouse-keepers in Suffolk and Anglesey, while in Wellingborough, in 1612, the fact that one James Ball was 'held to be … a man of a troublesome disposition' by the 'better sorte of his neighboures' was damning evidence against him. In 1623, John Winthrop, incensed at the destruction of pheasants and partridges by 'many of very meane sort', proposed that hawking should be confined to 'the nobilitie, gentilitie and better sort of ample possessions'. The 'care and industry' of the 'better sort' kept the Blackfriars precinct of London 'in good order' in the 1590s. During the Norwich plague of 1603 it was 'the better sort of people' who were 'much grieved and offended that the ruder sort would not be stayed nor by the magistrates restrained', while in Warwick, in 1628, they were defined as 'men of estate and generally best affected to religion and of the discreetest sort of inhabitants', in contrast to the easily corruptible 'meaner sort'.[17]

As for the 'meaner sort of people' themselves, they were said to threaten disorders over high prices and against aliens in London in 1586. In Essex they were held to be extraordinarily ignorant of

religious doctrine. Throughout the kingdom they apparently bore
the brunt of suffering in times of dearth and plague. They were
regarded as inappropriate persons for enrolment in the trained
bands of the county militias in the 1620s, an unsuitability confirmed by their alleged prominence in riots against fenland drain-
age in the 1630s, and in London in 1663 they were supposedly
distinguished by their 'undutifulnesse and contempt of their supe-
riours, especially the Nobility and Gentry of the Kingdome'.[18]

The reports and orders which passed to and fro between
Westminster and the provinces in dearth crises such as those of
1596–8, 1622–3 and 1630–1 provide myriad examples of the
employment of the language of 'sorts' in its dichotomous forms, as
indeed do contemporary accounts of franchise disputes and electoral contests, and the documents relating to the fenland riots of
the 1630s and 1640s. In the crisis years of the 1590s the sufferings
of the 'poorer' and 'meaner' sorts were documented throughout
the kingdom. The 'richer' and 'better' sorts were enjoined to keep
hospitality, to relieve the hungry and to refrain from profiteering.
The disorders of the 'vulgar' or 'common' sorts were watched with
apprehension by anxious local and central governors.[19] Electoral
conflict in Sandwich revealed the 'wilfull and heddie' nature of
'the vulgar sort' and the 'mutinous opposition' of 'the meaner
sort'. In Warwick, Tewkesbury, Norfolk and Nottinghamshire, it
pitted the 'better sorte' against 'the meaner sort', 'the very scum
of the people', 'the factious and vulgar sort', or the 'plebs'.[20] The
riots in the fenlands of the east saw the 'better sort of inhabitants'
challenged by the 'common sort', 'ruder sort' and 'poorer sort' of
people.[21] But enough has been said to make the essential points
that in the later sixteenth century the English elaborated an alternative vocabulary of social description which reveals a world of
social meanings untapped by the formal social classifications of
literary convention, and that this language of 'sorts' of people was
ubiquitous in late Elizabethan and early Stuart England.

IV

How should this development be explained? We can begin to for-
mulate an answer by considering again some of the basic charac-

teristics of the language of 'sorts' and the manner in which it was employed.

First and most obviously, it was a terminology of social simplification, cutting across the fine-grained (and sometimes contested) distinctions of the formal hierarchy of estates and degrees and regrouping the English into two broad camps, which were evidently taken to encapsulate the basic realities of the social and economic structure. That this simplification involved the use of dichotomies and polarities may have owed something to the conventional logical methods of the day, and in particular to the common rhetorical device of dividing, or 'sortying', a complex problem for the purposes of exposition. 'Children of unbelief', according to the Book of Homilies, were 'of two sorts' – those who despair and those who are overconfident in their expectations of divine mercy. Good works were also 'of two sorts' – the outward and the inward. The homilists could, on occasion, rise to distinguishing 'three sorts', but they preferred a simple, logical dichotomy, and indeed, the rythmic rehearsal of lists of such polarities was a common feature of contemporary eloquence.[22]

The language of 'sorts', then, may have begun its development as a useful mode of classification embodying simple logical distinctions. And in certain forms it also retained a degree of descriptive neutrality. To distinguish the common from the gentle, the richer from the poorer, the wiser or learned from the simpler, implied a recognition of social, economic and cultural distance, but it did not necessarily carry any further implications. As it developed and acquired greater elaboration, however, the language of 'sorts' was to lose such classificatory disinterestedness and to acquire overtones of an altogether different nature.

To speak of the 'ruder', 'vulgar', 'baser', 'meaner' or 'inferior' sorts and to contrast them with 'the better sort' was to introduce a markedly pejorative element into the vocabulary of social description, with profound implications concerning the quality of social relations. It must be acknowledged immediately that the term 'better sort' was clearly derived from the medieval practice of characterising the leading inhabitants of parishes and manors or the governors of city companies as *meliores et antiquiores, seniores et meliores*, or *meillours et pluis sufficeants*, terms which already implied a superiority of experience, authority, capacity and wealth.[23] The novelty of the language of 'sorts' lay less in the identification of a 'better sort' of people than in the pointed and depreciating manner in which it was so often employed in specific social contexts to express the distinctions between this favoured group and those excluded from it: in its elaboration of what Professor Collinson has nicely termed the 'piebald mentality' of the age.[24] As it developed it became a terminology of *radical* differentiation, which could acquire economic, cultural or political overtones according to context, cleaving society into the haves and have nots, rulers and ruled, the respected and those who were dismissed with condescension or contempt. Moreover, it became not only a terminology of differentiation, but also one of *dissociation*, employed for the most part by those who identified themselves with the 'wiser', 'learned', 'richer', or 'better' sorts of people – magistrates, gentlemen, ministers, local rulers and worthies – and stigmatising those whom they excluded from that company with a barrage of denigratory adjectives. Finally, unlike the vocabulary of estates and degrees, which expressed distinctions within a unified social order, the language of 'sorts' was a terminology pregnant with actual or potential *conflict*. It aligned the learned against the simple, the richer against the poorer, the better against the meaner, vulgar, common, ruder or inferior sorts, and, as we have seen, it frequently did so in contexts which expressed the divergence and clash of their interests. All this gave to the language of 'sorts' a political significance which was largely absent from (or at least less pronounced in) other, earlier, modes of social classification.

Why, then, was such a language needed? It was needed, I would suggest, to express both the immediate social tensions and the longer-term reconstruction of social identities which arose from some of the well-known developments of the sixteenth and earlier seventeenth centuries. One of these was the polarisation of many local societies produced by demographic expansion and economic change, and the sense of greater social distancing which it entailed.[25] Another was the long-term impact of the English Reformation and of the cultural conflict and differentiation which attended the evangelical efforts of the Protestant clergy and their allies among the godly laity.[26] A third was the emergence of the cult of 'civility', an alternative conception of gentility which was open to all those who could acquire the ability 'to manipulate certain intellectual and cultural codes', but which bred also an exclusive contempt for uncultivated 'rudeness'.[27] And lastly there was the 'increase of governance' with which the Tudor and early Stuart State met the threats of economic, social, religious and political instability, and the consequent elaboration of the participatory role of local notables, which is so evident in the records of local administration.[28] These developments, separately and in conjunction, established the contexts within which the language of 'sorts' of people was coined, elaborated and disseminated. And if it took its original dichotomous forms in part as a consequence of the logical and rhetorical conventions of the age, it did so more by virtue of the fact that it expressed actual collisions of interests, authority and ideals.

In order to appreciate its full significance, it is important, finally, to reiterate that the language of 'sorts' was very much a terminology of those who identified themselves with authority, sound religion, civility – with the 'better sort of people'. Among the extensive records of the county of Essex, for example, it is to be found not so much in the recorded statements of witnesses and deponents, or in such personal records as wills, as in the reports of magistrates, the sermons and diaries of ministers and the petitions of groups of leading inhabitants of the townships and parishes. These were people whose position and responsibilities encouraged them to adopt a societal vision, whether it was one which encompassed a single community, a district, the county or indeed the nation. They were engaged also in functions which encouraged, even obliged, them to categorise others in terms which were meaningful beyond the confines of small-scale local communities.

In addition, it must be emphasised that the distinction between the 'better' and the 'meaner' sorts of people was not simply one between gentlemen and the common people. William Harrison, himself an Essex minister, recognised as much in 1577 when he exempted the yeomanry, who participated in the government of the commonwealth and enjoyed 'certain preheminance' among their neighbours, from inclusion among 'the vulgar and common sorts'. In this county, as in others, the 'better sort' included not only gentlemen but clergymen and the local notables of town and village; people of property, estimation and authority such as John Moreshead of Devon, described by his grandson Robert Furse in 1593:

he was xx yeres Cunstabell of the hundred of Stanbury he was retorned yn monye juryes he allwayes mentayned a good howse

a good plow good geldynges good tyllage good revynge and he
was a good hussebonde indede he wolde never be withowte iii
copell of good howndes he wolde surelye kepe companye with
the beste sorte.[29]

The 'better sort' were, in effect, a composite local ruling group,
distinct from both the greater gentry and the mass of the common
people. They could be, and often were, alternatively described by
themselves and others as the 'principal', 'substantial' or 'chief'
inhabitants of a parish, or as 'the best men'. They included such
men as the mayor, vicar, two gentlemen, six yeomen and a glover,
from Thaxted, who in 1610 petitioned the Essex justices for action
against a disorderly alehousekeeper who had challenged the
authority of 'the chiefe men of our Towne'; the similar group from
Orsett who, as the 'ancientest and better sort of the parish',
requested the establishment of a close vestry which would exclude
'the inferior and meaner sort'; the minister and leading men of
Manningtree, who complained in 1627 that the denizens of their
alehouses had grown 'so Rusticall that for the better sort it is
almost no living with them'.[30]

Examples of this kind can be duplicated from most areas of
the kingdom. They suggest that the language of 'sorts', in its
Elizabethan and early Stuart form, may have acquired its widespread currency because of its value in expressing the essential
identity of interest between England's ruling gentry, the clergy,
and the more prominent members of what the early Tudors
would have termed the 'commonalty'. To speak of gentlemen,
clergy and commonalty, in the old idiom of the three estates, or to
rehearse the status designations of the full hierarchy of 'estates
and degrees', would have missed an essential social fact which the
employment of the 'better sort' and 'meaner', 'ruder' or 'vulgar'
sorts captured admirably, and for some flatteringly. To this extent
the dichotomous social world encapsulated in the usages of the
language of 'sorts' reflected not only the processes of economic,
social, and cultural change in English local society, but also the
realities of *power* relations in the local community. It expressed
divergences of interests and values and shifts in collective identity,
and in its reciprocal influence on both perceptions and actions it
may also have furthered and consolidated the social realignments
of the age.

V

Dichotomous usages of the language of 'sorts' were long to persist wherever they served the function of differentiating England's dominant and valued social groups from their 'meaner' countrymen. Many such examples could be cited from the later seventeenth and eighteenth centuries.[31] But persistence does not necessarily imply stasis. The language of 'sorts' was possessed of a developmental dynamism quite foreign to the rigidities of the conventional hierarchy of estates and degrees, and in the course of the seventeenth century a further term was added to the vocabulary of 'sorts of people' which was in common use by the 1640s. This was the 'middle sort' or 'middling sort' of people, a descriptive innovation which recast the language of 'sorts' into a more complex, tripartite form.

As with the 'better' and 'meaner' sorts, 'the middle sort of people' is a term familiar to all students of Elizabethan and Stuart England and one much employed by historians of the period. Despite its manifest popularity and utility, however, the origins of this term have never been adequately explored. It has been suggested by Peter Laslett that it was very probably of urban, even of metropolitan, origin, coined perhaps to describe the independent craftsmen and tradesmen who stood between the civic elite and the urban poor. This was almost certainly the case. The records of London and of some other English cities in the thirteenth and early fourteenth centuries (like those of urban communities elsewhere in Europe) provide references to people of middle rank, variously described as *mediocres, de medio statu,* or *de statu communum et mediocrum.* Such usages, however, appear to have been rare in England as compared with, for example, Italian cities, and to have been employed primarily in the context of urban political conflicts in the thirteenth and early fourteenth centuries, subsiding thereafter.[32] Nevertheless, when the concept of a middle rank reemerged in vernacular form as part of the developing language of 'sorts' it did so in an urban context. The earliest example so far known to me comes from the pen of the London moralist Henry Brinklow, who in 1542 wrote of the need to ease 'the pore and myddel sort of peple' of the burden of subsidy taxes. Another early reference can be found in the work of Richard Mulcaster, headmaster of Merchant Taylors' School, who regarded formal education as particularly appropriate for the children of 'the middle sorte of parents which neither welter in to much wealth, nor wrastle with to much want'. Again, the anonymous author of an 'Apologie' for the city of London, apparently written in the 1580s, possessed a tripartite perception of metropolitan society. He divided Londoners into 'three parts' or 'three sorts' – merchants and 'chief retailers'; 'the most part of retailers and all artificers'; and 'hirelings'. In his view, 'they of the middle place', who were 'neither too rich nor too poor, but do live in the mediocrity', were the most numerous group (a situation which he followed Aristotle in regarding as a healthy one for the urban body politic).[33]

Be this as it may, my research suggests that 'the middle sort' was a term rarely used in a sociological context in the late sixteenth and early seventeenth centuries, even in London. Henry Brinklow used the term once only; for the most part he was preoccupied with the dichotomy between rich and poor. John Stow, who printed the 'Apologie' quoted above in the 1603 edition of his *Survey of London*, showed no evidence in his own writing of sharing its author's perception. He made frequent reference to 'the mayor, aldermen and commonality of London', juxtaposed 'the rich and mighty' and 'the common people', and alluded to 'persons of good worship', 'the poor', 'the graver sort' (i.e. liverymen of the city companies), 'the poorer sort', and 'people of meaner sort'; but he had nothing at all to say about the 'middle sort'. Indeed, the now extensive literature on Elizabethan and Jacobean London provides no contemporary examples of the concept of a 'middle sort of people' beyond the much-cited 'Apologie'. As for other towns, the detailed accounts of franchise and electoral disputes in English provincial towns provided by Professor Hirst yield examples of all sorts of 'sorts of people', and above all of conflict between the 'better' and 'meaner' sorts, but none whatever of the 'middle sort'.[34]

Nor did the term spring readily into the minds of the authors of the English Renaissance. Sidney was at one with Skelton and with Chaucer in his apparent unawareness of the sociological language of 'sorts'. It was different with Spenser, who wrote of the 'meaner', 'rusticke' and especially 'vulgar' sorts, and with Shakespeare, who refers to the 'noble', 'better', 'common', 'meaner', 'vulgar' and 'weaker' sorts. George Herbert contrasted 'the better sort and meaner'. Milton wrote of the 'better', 'ruder', 'meaner' and 'common' sorts. Among these writers the growing currency of the language of 'sorts' is evident enough. Yet none wrote of the 'middle sort'.[35]

It might be expected that scholars engaged in the study of the political writers of classical antiquity, and in particular of Aristotle's *Politics*, would be forced to confront the concept of a 'middle sort'. The revival of Aristotelianism played a major role in the quickening of English intellectual life in the final quarter of the sixteenth century, and issues drawn from Aristotle's political philosophy were frequently the subject of the *quaestiones* set for disputation by Arts students in Oxford. Yet the terms employed by the first English translator of the *Politics* suggest unfamiliarity with any *vernacular* concept of a 'middle sort of people'. In the course of rendering the French translation of Loys Le Roy into English he was happy to employ such clearly familiar terms as 'the vulgar sort', 'the baser sort', the 'popular sort', 'richer sort', 'common sort' and 'better sort of the people'. But in coming to the famous passages where 'middle sort' might have seemed a most appropriate translation, he wrote instead of 'men of meane substance', 'men whose estate is meane' or 'meane men' (using 'mean' in the less familiar sense of 'equidistant' rather than in its common sense of 'inferior'). Clearly the phrase which we might anticipate simply did not occur to him.[36]

Where the term 'middle sort' *was* used frequently in Tudor and Jacobean England was in a quite different and less predictable context: a *commercial* context. From at least the fifteenth century, goods of all kinds had been habitually categorised as of 'dyvers sortes'. Quern stones, for example, could be distinguished into 'the greatest sort' and 'the small sorte', or coal into 'the best sort' and 'the meaner sort'. And alongside the other sorts, we find the 'middle sort'. Fitzherbert, in offering advice on the selling of timber, recommends the reader to 'sorte the trees, the polles by themselfe, the myddel sorte by them selfe, and the greatest by them-selfe'. In a treatise on navigation published in 1577, John Dee identified 'Myddle-Sort Markatable' fish as being 'most commodiously ... servisable', as compared with those which 'scant are to be iudged Markatable' and 'over growen fish'. The 1582 Book of Rates similarly classified 'Fish called Newland' into 'great', 'middle', and 'small' sorts, while that of 1609 included not only 'Newland fish middle sort', but also 'middle sort Ivory Combes', 'Caskets of iron middle sort', and 'Mastes for Ships middle sort'.[37]

What we have here, it seems, is a familiar commercial term which was eventually adopted for the purpose of social differentiation, initially in a metropolitan context. If so, however, it was adopted very slowly, for I have found very few examples of its sociological usage prior to the 1640s. At present it seems probable that although the term was known and very occasionally employed – as when William Lambarde addressed the jurors of a Kent special sessions in 1594 as 'you that be of the middle sort', as distinct from 'the rich and wealthy' and 'the poor that have more need than you'[38] – the concept of a 'middle sort of people' held few attractions as a mode of social description in the late sixteenth and earlier seventeenth centuries. Perhaps it was usually not needed. Contemporaries were certainly aware enough of the existence of a middle range of people in the social distributions of wealth, status and authority – who else were the yeomanry of the countryside and the citizens and burgesses of the towns? But if such people had an economic and social identity, and in many places an institutional identity (by virtue of their prominent participation in the affairs of manors and parishes, guilds, wards and city companies), it may have been the case that they lacked the distinctive political identity which might have given them greater social structural salience and recognition in Elizabethan and early Stuart England. The very people who might have been regarded nationally or regionally as the 'middle sort', were perhaps better described in their own localities as either belonging to or else aligned with 'the better sort'. The focus of contemporary concern in the reigns of Elizabeth and James was on the more radical differentiation encapsulated in the dichotomous usages of the language of 'sorts'. Perhaps the harsh glare of the anxieties and hostilities attending social and cultural polarisation cast the 'middle sort' into conceptual shadow.

VI

If this is so, they began to emerge in the third decade of the seventeenth century, for from the 1620s references to the 'middle sort of people' in both town and country become, if not common, then at least more frequent. At a revel in Tockenham Wick, Wiltshire, in 1620, a gang of Wooton Bassett men challenged their rivals with the stirring cry 'Where were the middle sort of men in Tockenham?' In December 1623, John Winthrop, who anticipated being delayed in London until after Christmas, urged his wife at Groton in Suffolk to see 'all our poore feasted, though I be from home', but added 'such as are of the middle sort let alone till I come home'. Clearly the latter required personal attention. Francis Bacon twice alluded to the 'middle people' of England in his writings, further defining them as being 'in condition between the gentry and the peasantry'. Richard Rawlidge lamented the taste for strong beer of Londoners 'of the middle and meaner ranke', namely 'handicraftsmen, workemen of all sorts, Labourers, Porters, Carmen, Water-bearers, and Watermen, Journeymen and Apprentices'. The London draper Clement Cotton recommended his biblical concordance, published in 1631, to neither 'the most learned or the most unlearned', but to 'the middle sort', and William Prynne, in a tract of 1637, complained of the inequitable burden of Ship Money upon 'the middle and poor sort of people' of 'cities and corporations'.[39]

One might well speculate on the circumstances underlying the apparently more frequent employment of the term 'middle sort' as a category of social description in the third and fourth decades of the seventeenth century. Did it perhaps indicate the emergence of a fuller and subtler appreciation of the complexities of social differentiation, an awareness possibly stimulated by the enhanced activities of local government? The listing and assessment of local populations necessitated by taxation and poor-law administration, for example, might conceivably have focused attention, as in the Lambarde instance cited above, on the 'middle sort' as a broad category of people lying between the exempted poor and the wealthy 'better sort', who governed parishes and townships. But whatever the case, these were essentially antecedents. The term finally seems to have come into its own in the pamphlet literature and memoirs occasioned by the English Civil Wars, above all in those works which described the social basis of parliamentarian allegiance and in those which attempted to define an interest group in politics, religion, or taxation policy which was distinct from the gentry and 'meaner sort' alike.

The question of political allegiance produced the most familiar examples. Thus, London demonstrators against episcopacy, in 1641, were characterised as being 'men of mean or a middle quality', as distinct from both 'aldermen, merchants or common councilmen' on the one hand, and 'the vulgar' on the other. In Worcester 'the middle sort of people' supported the parliamentarian cause. 'The middle and inferior sort of people' of Birmingham resisted Prince Rupert's advance in 1643 despite the defeatist fears of the 'better sort'. At Bristol 'the King's cause and party were favoured by two extremes in that city; the one the wealthy and powerful men, the other of the basest and lowest sort, but disgusted by the middle rank, the true and best citizens'.[40]

Such activism and the terms in which it was described were not confined to urban centres. In Somerset the royalists were said to consist of most of the gentry and their tenants, while parliament had the support of 'yeomen, farmers, petty freeholders, and such as use manufactures that enrich the country', under the leadership of some gentlemen and others of lesser degree, who 'by good husbandry, clothing and other thriving arts, had gotten very great fortunes'. In Gloucestershire the king was supported by both the rich and 'the needy multitude' who depended upon them. Parliament allegedly had the hearts of 'the yeomen, farmers, clothiers, and the whole middle rank of the people'. According to Lucy Hutchinson, 'most of the gentry' of Nottinghamshire 'were disaffected to the parliament', but 'most of the middle sort, the able substantial freeholders, and the other commons, who had not their dependence upon the malignant nobility and gentry, adhered to the parliament'. Again, Richard Baxter saw the king as finding support among most of the lords, knights and gentlemen of England, together with their tenants and 'most of the poorest of the people', while parliament had a minority of the gentry 'and the greatest part of the tradesmen and freeholders and the middle sort of men, especially in those corporations and countries which depend on clothing and such manufactures'.[41]

Nor was the identification of the middle sort confined to the question of wartime allegiance, for it was also prominent in the radical literature of the Interregnum. John Lilburne denounced excise duties, in 1645, as laying the burden 'heavily upon the poore, and men of middle quality or condition, without all discretion', and four years later characterised both tithes and the excise

as 'those secret thieves, and Robbers, Drainers of the poor and
middle sort of people'. To John Wildman, writing in 1647, the
excise 'eateth the flesh and sucketh the blood of the poor and
middling sort', while an anonymous pamphleteer of the same year
also dwelt at some length on the tax burden of 'the middle rank of
men'. The *Declaration* of the Levellers of Buckinghamshire, published in 1649, spoke out for 'all the middle sort and poor people'
against landlords, base tenures, tithes, Westminster law and mar-
tial law. 'Abundance of the middle sort of people of London' were
also said to have celebrated John Lilburne's acquittal at his trial
for treason in 1649. Most striking of all as an example of the identification of the radicals with the interests and aspirations of the
'middle sort of people' was the vision of the millennarian George
Foster, published a year later. He saw a man on a white horse 'with
a sword in his hand ready drawn', riding across England 'cutting
down all men and women that he met that were higher than the
middle sort, and raised up those that were lower than the middle
sort and made them all equall'.[42]

In recounting these examples, many of them well known, I am
not attempting to enter the debate over the social basis of allegiance in the English Civil War, or to suggest, like Professor
Manning, that the English Revolution was above all a revolution
of the 'middle sort of people'. It is perfectly clear that the
'middle sort' were divided in their allegiances. The point is,
rather, that some people of such standing undoubtedly played a
vigorously independent part in the conflict in at least some areas,
and that where such activism involved repudiation of the established structure of authority it excited comment. As we have
seen, the *mediocres* of medieval English cities had first been identified in the political conflicts of the thirteenth century. In a similar way, the expanded use of 'the middle sort of people' as a
descriptive category, in seventeenth-century England, may have
been occasioned by the demands of describing novel forms of
participation in events of national significance by a hetero-
geneous body of people of intermediate status in town and country. The geographical context of their activity had expanded. Its
political significance had changed. In these circumstances a
modified language of social identification was required, and an
available, but previously little used, vocabulary was taken up and
employed.

This, however, can have been only part of the story, for the more frequent identification of the 'middle sort of people' was not merely the result of the convenience of the phrase as a descriptive term for particular groups of actors. It also involved a fuller recognition of their distinctiveness as an interest group. If, as I have argued, the elaboration of the distinction between the 'better' and 'meaner' sorts of people encapsulated one form of realignment in England's social fields of force, then the employment of the term 'the middle sort', and above all its use as a means of *self*-identification, involves awareness of a continuing process of realignment, a further modification of the principal dividing lines within the English social structure.

This further realignment may not have been observable in all places or at all times. When and where it *was* discernible, however, it grew first from a divergence of interests which had once run together, secondly from an awareness of a distinctive common interest among sectors of the population somewhat broader than the local ruling groups previously identified as the 'better sort' of people, and thirdly from the political expression of this nascent and perhaps fragile social identity in a variety of contexts. The grievances which underlay participation in the cataclysmic events of the 1640s, and the creative dynamic of those events themselves, may well have had the effect of both dramatising and advancing this further social realignment. If the 'middle sort of people' played a part in the making of the English Revolution, their involvement also helped to make *them*, in terms of both their identification by others and, in some instances at least, their own self-discovery in independent action.

This process may have been markedly partial in the context of English society as a whole, and its momentum may have slowed thereafter, as the traditional 'authority of the nation' was reasserted. Yet the crisis of the 1640s had been formative and educative, and it left a legacy in England's cities, and above all in London, in a popular political culture which continued to develop and in which the 'middle sort of people' played a prominent role. Divided by religion, by particular economic interests, by party preferences and by attitudes towards specific government policies, they none the less retained a presence in urban politics and, on occasion, influenced national events.[43]

The events of the mid-seventeenth century also left a legacy in the ways in which the English perceived their society and its constituent parts. For the term 'the middle sort of people', now rendered commonplace, stuck. In the later seventeenth and eighteenth centuries it was routinely adopted as an established mode of summing up the tradesmen, manufacturers, and farmers who occupied the middle ground in the hierarchies of wealth, status and power, and the outcome was the consolidation of a tripartite perception of the social order.

Such a perception might be implicit, as when Secretary Nicholas expressed his anxiety in 1661 about the affection of 'the middle sort of people in city and country' for the restored monarchy. It might be explicit, as when Richard Baxter wrote approvingly in 1673 of the presence 'in most places' of 'a sober sort of men of the middle rank, that ... are more equal to religion than the highest or lowest usually are', or when a visitor to Bath, in the mid-eighteenth century, distinguished 'the poor' and 'middling sort' from 'the rich and great'.[44] Even among those who attempted more complex social and economic analyses of English society, its influence was hard to escape. Gregory King's famous table distinguished twenty-six 'ranks' and 'degrees', but he wrote privately to Robert Harley in 1697 of 'the poorest sort', 'the middle sort' and 'the better sort'. Daniel Defoe differentiated seven consumption groups in 1709, but his use of 'the Middle sort' for those 'who live well' betrays his essentially tripartite perception of society. Guy Miège attempted a complex description of 'the several orders and degrees in England', an essentially conservative endeavour. Yet his account can be resolved into 'gentlemen', among whom he realistically included 'all that distinguish themselves from the common people by a genteel carriage, good education, learning, or an independent station'; 'a middle sort' (which explicitly included farmers); and the 'meaner' or 'inferior sort of people'. Joseph Massie, in 1756, produced calculations of the tax burdens of thirty income groupings and seven status and occupational categories, but in his text he referred to 'Gentlemen', and the 'middling and inferior classes'.[45]

In short, throughout the later seventeenth and early eighteenth centuries it was apparent to contemporary observers that a tripartite perception of society was both useful and appropriate. That perception of society was at once embodied in and furthered by the language of 'sorts' of people in its fully developed form. From the mid-eighteenth century, as the example of Massie indicates, it was perpetuated in a newer terminology, which had the capacity to express analytical precision as well as broad social identity: the language of 'class'.[46]

VII

Social identities and alignments, like medical conditions, may be defined by experts, but they are discovered by lay people in the immediacy of their own experience.[47] In the recovery of such processes of self-discovery the study of language has a special place. Examination of the language in which contemporaries formulated their paradigms provides deeper understanding of the manner in which they perceived the social world which structured their life experiences and provided the context for their actions as individuals. More, it can further an appreciation of the nature of social change. It can 'illuminate the problems that change caused everyday, unspoken assumptions – before these problems were explicitly recognized and long before they were resolved'. It can reveal 'the peculiar state of consciousness that emerges when a society has outgrown an old social ideology, but has not yet formulated a new one'.[48]

Early modern England provides an instructive example of such a situation. Older models of the social order persisted, albeit in modified form, together with their accompanying insistence upon order, subordination and mutual responsibility, and they could be appealed to, no less by the victims of change than by the Lord Protector. Yet they failed to provide an adequate account of contemporary reality, or to express the shifting alignments of a society undergoing profound, if gradual, social, economic and political change.

The language of 'sorts' filled that gap. In its dichotomous or its tripartite forms it could capture the mutability of social alignments and the plasticity of social identities. It could lump together the distinguishable estates and degrees of inherited social theory into broad groupings which anticipated the social classes of the nineteenth century. It could imply alternative conceptions of the fundamental nature of social differentiation, express conflicts of interests, and edge perceptive contemporaries along the path towards a thoroughgoing reappraisal of the structures of society, the basis of social inequality, and the dynamics of social process. In all these ways it has much to teach about the immediate antecedents of the concept of social class in its English form and about the deep roots of England's ambiguous class identities.

All that, however, was yet to come. To write back into the early modern period the class identities of the later eighteenth or nineteenth centuries would be as anachronistic as to insist upon the prolongation into the seventeenth century of the exclusive claims to social meaning of earlier conceptions of society. Early modern England encompassed both realities; the one fading slowly, the other stirring and quickening into life. It presented alternative definitions of social reality, one formulated, one only implied; both precariously poised. It invited choices between interests and ideals. What the language of 'sorts' of people reveals, above all, is the way in which such choices were made, confirmed, assimilated and perpetuated, generations before they could be intellectually justified.

2. Apprenticeship, Social Mobility and the Middling Sort, 1550–1800

CHRISTOPHER BROOKS

I

A particular concern for the education and future of their children may be the most distinctive single characteristic of the middle classes in modern British society, yet it is surprising how often we ignore the fact that in the sixteenth, seventeenth and eighteenth centuries this same worry about how to enable the next generation to establish itself was a problem common to all those social groups who had to work for their livings, the husbandmen and yeomen farmers, the merchants and the lawyers, the artisans and the doctors. Indeed, although social mobility in the early modern period is almost invariably discussed by historians in terms of the desire and ability of the middling sector of the population to buy into the landed elite, this way of formulating the question puts the cart before the horse. While it would be foolish to claim that owning broad acres was not an aspiration, the truly significant move for most people came not at the end of their lives, but at the beginning, when they set out in their teens on working careers. For the majority of parents, finding a niche for their children which would eventually enable them to set up and maintain a household, to provide for a wife and children and keep poverty at bay, was the overriding imperative.[1]

In the sixteenth and seventeenth centuries, the exact process through which this task of preparing for the next generation was carried out depended on the gender of the child as well as on the wealth and occupations of individual families. For the eldest sons of the gentry or yeomanry, there was of course an intergenera-

52

tional transferral of landed property. But for younger sons and daughters of such families, and for the children of the poor and urban social groups, some form of service in a household other than that of the biological family was likely to be involved.[2] For those with little wealth, service in husbandry for boys or domestic service for girls was a preparation for a career in agricultural labour or housewifery, and this was also the course most often chosen by parish officials when they made provision for orphans or pauper children of either sex by placing them in apprentice-ships.[3] Higher up the social scale, amongst the husbandmen, yeo-men, and lesser gentry in rural society, or the merchants, tradesmen, artisans and professionals in towns, the gender of the child probably had a much greater influence. Fathers in such families frequently made money available for their daughters' marriage portions, a practice which reflects the reality that matri-mony was considered the primary objective for most girls.[4] At the same time, however, throughout the period, a significant, but so far indeterminate, number of girls were formally apprenticed into trades, especially the various branches of sewing, weaving and needlecraft. Female occupations were largely, but by no means exclusively, distinct from those of males, and they are difficult to study because women are not well represented in the documents produced by largely male-dominated institutions such as guilds and urban corporations.[5] This was the world of their brothers, boys from similar backgrounds, who had been launched towards a potential livelihood by means of a formalised indenture of appren-ticeship. This legal agreement, which was accompanied by a pay-ment of money by the parents, set out the parameters of a process in which the young person, usually a male in his mid or late teens, was placed in a new family with a view to learning the details of an occupation and eventually setting up as a practitioner in his own right. In the well-known phrases of the indenture itself, the master was to instruct the apprentice in the 'craft, mastery, and occupa-tion which he useth' and provide him with meat, drink, linen, shoes, and anything else requisite for an apprentice in a particular trade. In return, the apprentice agreed to serve his master, keep his secrets, obey his commandments and to refrain from fornica-tion, gambling, or the haunting of alehouses.[6]

For those social groups within the middling sections of the population, therefore, apprenticeship was a characteristic family strategy for male children, a process which involved a considerable degree of geographical mobility, and, as we shall see, a powerful determinant in the careers and prospects of the boys who undertook it. At the same time, it was the primary means by which the urban social structure reproduced itself, and hence the focus of some of the most characteristic social and cultural values of the middling sort. As this chapter aims to demonstrate, however, during the course of the late seventeenth and, especially, the eighteenth centuries, apprenticeship both declined and changed character. Charting these transformations in one of the central institutions of the preindustrial world leads to two conclusions. First, some recent interpretations of eighteenth-century social history have overstressed prosperity and upward social mobility within the middling sort, especially in comparison with the seventeenth century.[7] There is also a story of diminishing prospects, the entrenchment of economic and social oligarchy, the decline of traditional institutions, and the growth of cultural differentiation. It follows from this that the late-eighteenth-century origins of modern English society lie as much in the transformation of the traditional culture of the middling sort as in 'the rise of the middle class'.

II

According to the law as laid down by the Statute of Artificers of 1563, a seven-year apprenticeship was an essential qualification for anyone who wanted to undertake a number of named trades, from that of blacksmith to merchant. In addition, apprenticeship was also the prime means by which boys trained to enter into practice in the most numerically significant ranks of the medical and legal professions, the attorneys and solicitors, and the surgeons and apothecaries.[8] Unfortunately, since the statutory regulations were never systematically enforced in smaller towns and villages, there are no records which permit a comprehensive study of apprenticeship in rural areas.[9] However, the evidence about the practice in larger towns is quite rich. Major towns kept records of the registrations of new apprentices, and so too did individual guilds or livery companies. Thanks to these sources it is possible to recover information about the social and geographical origins of the apprentice, as well as the name and occupation of the master. Consequently, for the period up until 1710, when government tax records provide more comprehensive information, the picture of apprenticeship which is presented in this paper is drawn largely from these urban sources.

Between 1550 and 1650, the number of boys who took up apprenticeships increased steadily (see Table 2.1). This point can be made most clearly by considering guild recruitment against the background of general demographic developments. The population of England nearly doubled during the late sixteenth and early seventeenth centuries. Although the rate varied from place to place, most towns were also growing. London experienced an astonishing increase in population from about 55,000 inhabitants in 1520 to 475,000 in 1640. No other town was nearly as large or as fast-growing as this, but a number of places, including the traditional provincial capitals, grew at about the same rate as the national population as a whole. If we add together the populations of London and all other towns with more than 5000 inhabitants, then the ratio of urban to national population increased from 5.25 per cent in 1520 to 13.5 per cent in 1670.[10] Since high death rates meant that the larger urban communities were incapable of sustaining, let alone increasing, their populations by natural means, there were high levels of migration into most early modern towns of any size, and the majority, if by no means all, of these immigrants came into them through a period of formal apprenticeship and participation in the guild system.[11] In London, for example, admissions to individual companies tripled over the period. By 1600, the four to five thousand apprentices enrolled each year in the metropolis accounted for a major proportion of the 6000 immigrants per year which were required to sustain its overall rate of population growth.[12] At Bristol, the numbers entered in the corporation registers increased from 193 in 1539–40 to 300 in 1629–30, and then remained at this level until the end of the seventeenth century.[13] Less systematic evidence from a number of other major towns, Exeter, Newcastle, Norwich and York, likewise suggests that in most places apprenticeship grew at about the same rate as local population.[14]

Before 1660, most new apprentices were young men who hailed from rural areas or from the smaller provincial towns and villages.

Table 2.1   *The social status of the fathers of entrants to some London and provincial guilds, 1551–1696*
(Percentages: total numbers given in round brackets; n/a = data not available)

	London[a] Freemen 1551–3	Newcastle[b] Merchant Adventurers 1580–5	London[c] Haberdashers 1583–4	London[d] Carpenters 1590–4	London[e] Carpenters 1600–3	London[d] Haberdashers 1603–4	Newcastle[b] Merchant Adventurers 1600–5
'Gent' and above							
From outside the town	n/a	24 (8)	10 (29)	n/a	2 (2)	n/a	27 (12)
From inside the town	n/a	–	0.6 (2)	n/a	–	n/a	2 (1)
Total	5 (46)	24 (8)	11 (31)	3 (6)	2 (2)	17 (37)	29 (13)
Yeoman	16 (136)	29 (10)	28 (80)	4 (7)	9 (10)	41 (87)	35 (16)
Husbandman	33 (289)	3 (1)	22 (63)	44 (85)	40 (43)	10 (20)	–
Professional*	2 (14)	–	3 (8)	n/a	3 (3)	n/a	9 (4)
Mercantile, Trade, or Craft							
From outside the town	n/a	9 (3)	27 (79)	n/a	40 (44)	n/a	9 (4)
From inside the town	n/a	32 (11)	1 (4)	n/a	4 (4)	n/a	11 (5)
Total	43 (378)	41 (14)	28 (83)	49 (93)	44 (48)	31 (65)	20 (9)
Citizens of London	n/a		4 (12)	n/a	2 (2)	n/a	
Not Given		3 (1)	4 (12)			1 (2)	7 (3)
Grand Total	100 (863)	100 (34)	100 (289)	100 (191)	100 (108)	100 (211)	100 (45)

SOURCES:

* The data in this table have been collected by different researchers, and this category in particular has not been defined in the same way by them all. It nearly always includes clergymen, but beyond that there is great variation. Also, the figures are almost certainly too low, because lawyers, especially attorneys, invariably called themselves 'gent' or esquire, and therefore usually end up with the 'gents' rather than the professionals.

a   Ramsay, 'The recruitment and fortunes of some London freemen', 531.
b   My counts from Dendy, *Merchant Adventurers of Newcastle*, vol. II, pp. 185–323.
c   GL MS 15,860/1.
d   Lang, 'Greater Merchants of London', pp. 75–8.
e   GL MS 4329/3. 25 Sept. 1600–25 Sept. 1603; GL MS 4337/3, 7 Jan. 1689 (o.s.)–Dec. 1693 (o.s.).
f   Bristol City Archive Office, Apprenticeship Books. April 1605–November 1606 (one and one-half years), April 1629–April 1631, April 1670–April 1671, March 1690 (o.s.)–March 1692 (o.s.).
g   Willis and Merson, *Southampton Apprenticeship Registers*, p. xxix.
h   GL MS 11, 593/1. Nov. 1629–Nov. 1632; GL MS 11,593/2. April 1690–April 1693.
i   GL MS 8200/1. April 1692–April 1632. GL MS 8200/3. May 1680–May 1681. April 1690–April 1692. In the figures for 1690–2, Citizens of London who were Apothecaries have been added to the 'Professional' category.
j   Smith, 'Social and Geographical Origins of London Apprentices', pp. 200–6.

Bristol[f] All trades 1605-6	Southampton[g] All trades 1610-20	London[d] Fishmongers 1614-16	Southampton[g] All trades 1620-31	Newcastle[b] Merchant Adventurers 1625-30	Bristol[f] All trades 1629-31	London[h] Grocers 1629-32	London[i] Apothecaries 1629-32	London[j] Grocers 1631-40
6 (17)	n/a	n/a	n/a	33 (25)	7 (41)	30 (132)	24 (25)	n/a
–	n/a	n/a	n/a	6 (5)	0.5 (3)	3 (14)	9 (9)	n/a
5 (17)	6 (6)	19 (24)	15 (15)	39 (30)	7.5 (44)	33 (146)	33 (34)	36 (590)
11 (35)	18 (18)	41 (53)	22 (22)	35 (27)	14 (84)	32 (142)	10 (11)	28 (461)
21 (64)	18 (18)	5 (7)	12 (12)	–	17 (105)	0.2 (1)	–	n/a
2 (5)	5 (5)	n/a	2 (2)	8 (6)	2 (15)	6 (26)	17 (17)	n/a
16 (51)	n/a	n/a	n/a	7 (5)	27 (165)	15 (67)	8 (8)	n/a
21 (65)	n/a	n/a	n/a	10 (8)	30 (178)	2 (10)	2 (2)	n/a
37 (116)	44 (44)	32 (41)	48 (48)	17 (13)	57 (343)	17 (77)	10 (10)	26 (426)
		n/a				12 (53)	16 (17)	n/a
23 (72)	9 (9)	3 (4)	1 (1)	1 (1)	2 (10)	–	14 (15)	n/a
100 (309)	100 (100)	100 (129)	100 (100)	100 (77)	100 (601)	100 (445)	100 (104)	90 (1477)

Table 2.1　*The social status of the fathers of entrants to some London and provincial guilds, 1551–1696 (contd)*
(Percentages: total numbers given in round brackets; n/a = data not available)

	London[j] Fishmongers 1631–40	London[k] Medical Entrants to Barber S. Co. 1658–60	Newcastle[b] Merchant Adventurers 1660–5	Bristol[l] All trades 1670–1	London[i] Apothecaries 1680–1	Newcastle[b] Merchant Adventurers 1680–5	Newcastle[l] Barber-Surgeons 1690–5
'Gent' and above							
From outside the town	n/a	n/a	37 (24)	12 (37)	22 (14)	49 (35)	–
From inside the town	n/a	n/a	3 (2)	0.2 (2)	3 (2)	3 (2)	12 (7)
Total	25 (168)	23 (42)	40 (26)	13 (39)	25 (16)	52 (37)	12 (7)
Yeoman	28 (190)	16 (28)	11 (7)	19 (59)	14 (9)	3 (2)	16 (9)
Husbandman	n/a	2 (3)	–	4 (12)	–	–	–
Professional*	n/a	9 (16)	11 (7)	3 (8)	25 (16)	1 (1)	5 (3)
Mercantile, Trade or Craft							
From outside the town	n/a	n/a	5 (3)	24 (72)	13 (8)	1 (1)	5 (3)
From inside the town	n/a	n/a	32 (21)	36 (109)	5 (3)	40 (29)	51 (29)
Total	37 (253)	46 (83)	37 (24)	60 (181)	18 (11)	41 (30)	56 (32)
Citizens of London	n/a	n/a			14 (9)		
Not given	n/a	4 (8)	1 (1)	1 (4)	3 (2)	3 (2)	11 (6)
Grand total	90 (611)	100 (180)	100 (65)	100 (303)	100 (63)	100 (72)	100 (57)

SOURCES:　
k　Shelton-Jones, 'Barber-Surgeons Company', p. 242.
l　TWAD MS 786/2.
m　GL MS 5576/2, July 1690–July 1693. Two men described as 'farmers' have been added to the 'Husbandman' category.
n　GL MS 5266/2, April 1690–April 1693. Those listed under Barbers include a number of miscellaneous trades.
o　*Records of the Company of Shipwrights of Newcastle upon Tyne, 1622–1967*, vol. II, ed. D. J Rowe (Surtees Soc., vol. CLXXXIV, 1966), pp. 240–5.
p　D. V. Glass, 'Socio-economic Status and Occupations in the City of London at the End of the Seventeenth Century', in *Studies in London History*, eds A. E. J. Hollaender and William Kellaway (London, 1969) pp. 387–8.

Bristol[f] All trades 1690–2	London[e] Carpenters 1690–3	London[h] Grocers 1690–3	London[m] Fishmongers 1690–3	London[i] Apothecaries 1690–3	London. Barber-Surgeons[n] Company 1690–3 Barbers	Surgeons	Newcastle[o] Shipwrights 1690–5	London[b] Freemen 1690
(35)	4 (10)	23 (48)	17 (40)	27 (51)	7 (13)	13 (11)	6 (6)	n/a
.5 (3)	1 (2)	5 (10)	4 (9)	7 (13)	4 (8)	8 (7)	–	n/a
7 (38)	5 (12)	28 (58)	21 (49)	34 (64)	11 (21)	21 (18)	6 (6)	10 (179)
1 (66)	11 (25)	9 (20)	16 (37)	5 (9)	20 (38)	1 (1)	76 (75)	13 (241)
7 (41)	8 (19)	–	3 (6)	–	–	–		9 (171)
2 (14)	2 (4)	9 (20)	6 (14)	15 (28)	6 (11)	19 (17)		2 (28)
26 (149)	36 (83)	18 (39)	18 (42)	14 (26)	27 (51)	15 (13)	2 (2)	n/a
45 (259)	21 (48)	14 (31)	11 (26)	22 (41)	31 (60)	34 (29)	13 (13)	n/a
71 (408)	57 (131)	32 (70)	29 (68)	35 (67)	58 (111)	49 (42)	15 (15)	n/a
	17 (39)	22 (47)	25 (59)	8 (15)	2 (3)	5 (4)		
2 (9)	–	–	–	3 (6)	3 (7)	5 (4)	3 (3)	n/a
100 (576)	100 (230)	100 (215)	100 (233)	100 (189)	100 (191)	100 (86)	100 (99)	34 (1850)

Predictably, the distance over which they were attracted depended primarily on the regional or national importance of the town to which they were migrating. For example, Newcastle, a fast-growing regional capital, drew most of its new blood from nearby Northumberland and County Durham. By comparison, London's long-distance magnetism was much more pronounced; migrants came from all over the country, including Wales, the north and south Midlands, and the upland regions north of the Trent.[15]

The social backgrounds of apprentices were diverse, but, since parents had to pay a sum of money (known as the apprenticeship premium), from a few to several hundred pounds to a potential master in order to get him to take on their son, few recruits came from the 30 per cent of the population which lived by wages alone. The vast majority were divided between the offspring of urban tradesmen, artisans and professional men on the one hand, and the sons of small to medium-sized landholders on the other (see Table 2.1).

The amount of the apprenticeship premium was determined primarily by the prestige and potential profitability of any given occupation, and early modern trades and crafts fell into a distinct status hierarchy which corresponded roughly to John Stow's division of the citizens of his native London into wholesalers, retailers and artisans, a division which also translated into a range of wealth and political influence. Wholesale traders in the City of London, whether engaged in inland or overseas trade, were the men who established legendary fortunes. They usually belonged to one of the twelve 'greater' City companies such as the Drapers, Fishmongers, or Haberdashers, whose members regularly dominated City government.[16] Similarly, in provincial towns, dealers in wholesale goods, such as the grocers of Norwich or the Hostmen and Merchant Adventurers of Newcastle, became leading political figures.[17] At the other end of the scale, a cordwainer of Newcastle, a weaver in Norwich, or a textile worker in Exeter might work as a journeyman rather than a master in his own right, and would have been one of the poorer members of the community.[18] Not surprisingly, therefore, the more elite business activities and the guilds which represented them generally attracted the richer and better-born recruits. For example, in London in the early 1600s, Haberdashers' apprentices included some 17 per cent of men whose fathers claimed the rank of gentleman or above, whereas the

Carpenters' Company found only 2 per cent of its recruits from among these groups.[19] In Newcastle, the elite Merchant Adventurers drew nearly 30 per cent of their members from the 'gent' category, whilst for the Housecarpenters, Millwrights, and Trunkmakers, a gentleman recruit was an exotic rarity.[20]

Between 1550 and 1650, the overall flow of boys from urban mercantile, trade, and artisan backgrounds remained fairly steady at between 35 and 45 per cent of all apprentices in both London and provincial towns, although they were always much more strongly represented in the handicrafts than in the commercial or trading occupations. However, there were some notable changes in apprenticeship recruitment from rural areas. In particular, the sons of men who described themselves as 'gentlemen' increased steadily as a percentage of all apprentices as the period progressed. About 5 per cent of the young men admitted to the freedom of London in the years 1551–3 claimed 'gent' backgrounds.[21] By comparison, composite figures for entrants to a group of London companies of different types (Haberdashers, Fishmongers, Carpenters, and Coopers) in the early seventeenth century record the sons of 'gents' at 9 per cent, and a similar list for 1630–60 indicates a further rise to 18 per cent.[22] Thus the relative presence of those who were the sons of 'gents' increased by a factor of three over the century from 1550 to 1650, although this was always much more pronounced in the more prestigious wholesale and retail trades than in the handicrafts, where there was hardly any increase at all.

There was, therefore, a significant, and increasing, degree of mobility between the gentry and trade during the sixteenth and seventeenth centuries, but it is important to be precise about its nature and extent. In this period, not all of those who used the status label 'gent' were landed gentlemen.[23] Status inflation was a characteristic of the period, and it is likely that as many as a fifth of 'gent' recruits were in fact the offspring of well-to-do townsmen, including professional men such as attorneys and surgeons, rather than landed gentlemen. Furthermore, most of the remainder of the 'gent' apprentices were the sons of what is known as the mere or parish gentry. While the word 'gent' frequently appears alongside the name of a father, the more elevated titles of 'esquire' and 'knight' are relatively rare. Even in an elite company such as the London Grocers, no more than 4 per cent of entrants in the period 1629–32 claimed to be the sons of men who were esquires and above.[24] Thus the majority of gentry apprentices came from families which occupied the borderline between the yeomanry on the one hand and the greater gentry on the other. Their fathers were solid members of the middle ranks of landed society but were more likely to measure their incomes in hundreds rather than thousands of pounds. In political terms, these were the families which supplied constables and grand jurymen rather than those who ruled their localities as justices of the peace.[25]

To a large extent, the increase in the number of the sons of 'gents' took place at the expense of two other rural groups which figure prominently in apprenticeship registers, the substantial small farmers who used the status designation 'yeomen', and the 'husbandmen', lesser landholders with incomes often not far above subsistence level. Before 1600, nearly half of the recruits to elite guilds such as the London Haberdashers and to craft companies such as the Carpenters came from such a background (see Table 2.1). However, after 1600, whilst recruitment from the lesser gentry continued to increase, first that from the ranks of the husbandmen and then that from the yeomanry began to decline, especially in the elite companies. For example, in 1583, 28 per cent of London Haberdashers' Company recruits were styled sons of yeomen, and 22 per cent the sons of husbandmen. By 1603, the percentage of yeoman backgrounds had risen to 41 per cent whilst that from the husbandmen had fallen to just under 10 per cent. But by the 1630s, the sons of yeomen, too, were no longer as numerous in the elite companies as they had been previously. Yeoman recruits to the London Fishmongers declined from 41 per cent in 1614–16 to 28 per cent in the years 1631–40, and developments in Southampton and Newcastle appear to have been similar.

III

Compared with the pattern of apprenticeship which we have been charting up to the middle of the seventeenth century, the most striking development of the period from 1660 to 1750 is that the steady increase in the number of apprentices, which had been characteristic of the late Elizabethan and early Stuart years, stopped and then entered into a relative decline. By 1640, recruitment through apprenticeship in most towns had reached a peak which was never exceeded thereafter. It is true that this needs to be placed against a general demographic picture in which the overall population of England stagnated at around 5 million in the years up to 1700 and then only gradually increased to 5.7 million by 1750. But the more telling point is that the levelling-off in the number of apprentices occurred despite the fact that many existing major towns continued to grow in size, and at a time when some unincorporated towns, such as Manchester and Birmingham, entered the urban league table for the first time.[26]

The pace of change varied from place to place. For example, at Bristol, late-seventeenth-century growth from 12,000 to 20,000 inhabitants was matched by a steady influx of about 300 new apprentices each year.[27] At Exeter, the expansion of the cloth industry, which contributed to rapid population growth, also marked a high point in new admissions to the Guild of Tuckers, Fullers and Weavers. Similarly, at Newcastle, guild membership reached a high point at the end of the seventeenth and early in the eighteenth centuries.[28] However, the very rapid growth of Norwich, from 20,000 people in 1670 to 30,000 in 1700, was accompanied by a decline in the number of apprentices registered,[29] and in London, too, guild membership was becoming less comprehensive. In 1700 it was still necessary to join a company in order to gain the freedom of the City, but throughout the seventeenth century there was an enormous growth in the suburbs beyond the city walls, where guild authority was not rigorously enforced. While London's late-seventeenth-century growth required a net inflow of approximately 8000 new migrants each year, the apprentices numbered about 4000 per year, a figure no greater than that for 1600.[30] In both London and Norwich, therefore, it would seem that significant numbers of people were migrating to the towns but not joining guilds, and very probably not entering into any very formal arrangements for apprenticeship either.

No less important, there were also significant changes in the geographical origins of those who took up apprenticeships. Whereas pre-1640 guild recruits to London and provincial towns came primarily from rural areas, or else the smaller towns and villages, by the 1690s London, Newcastle and Bristol guilds were refreshing their ranks increasingly from their own native popula-

tions. Twenty-seven per cent of those admitted to the freedom of
London in 1690 were from the City or adjoining suburbs.[31] At Bristol, the proportion of apprentices born and raised in the town
increased from about a quarter, under James I, to 45 per cent in
the reign of William III. In Newcastle, by the mid-1680s, some 41
per cent of apprentices to the Merchant Adventurers were from
Newcastle itself; 34 per cent were the sons of existing members of
the company.

This change in the geographical origins of guild recruits meant
that by the later seventeenth century the sons of resident merchants and craftsmen dominated the entry of new men into established positions in the urban hierarchies. By contrast, amongst
those with rural backgrounds, the sons of the lesser gentry continued to make up about the same percentage of apprentices as
they had in 1640, while the number of husbandman apprentices
continued the decline which had begun in the early seventeenth
century. At Bristol they dropped from 21 per cent of all new
recruits in 1606 to 7 per cent in 1690. In London they virtually disappeared from elite companies. Part of this apparent change in
the fortunes of husbandmen's sons may be attributable to status
inflation, which led more and more husbandmen to describe
themselves as yeomen, but this was clearly not the only factor at
work. Although 'husbandmen' largely disappeared from the
records of elite companies such as the Haberdashers or Grocers,
the style continued to be used right up until the end of the seventeenth century for recruits to the lesser companies such as the
Carpenters, which one would expect to have drawn more heavily
from smaller farmers of this type.

The yeomen, on the other hand, fared rather better. Their
presence in Bristol remained steady over the seventeenth century,
and much the same was true of the craft companies of London.
But the percentage of yeomen's children fell fairly sharply in the
more elite London companies such as the Fishmongers and
Grocers. At Newcastle, yeomen appear to have had difficulty gaining positions in the Merchant Adventurers, but at 16 per cent they
were well represented in the Barber–Surgeons Company, and the
majority of recruits to the company of Shipwrights came from the
yeomanry of nearby County Durham.[32]

Thus, the later seventeenth century saw a contraction in the
social and geographical range of apprenticeship recruitment.

After 1700, and especially from the 1720s and 1730s, apprenticeship itself, at least as it had previously been practised, began to decline. Contrary to a long-standing, but erroneous, historiographical tradition, English guilds continued to be vital institutions well into the eighteenth century, and in most places guild memberships remained high until the 1720s, from which point they began to drop off. However, it is also the case that most guildsmen, from at least the same date, were recruited not by apprenticeship, but either by redemption (the purchase of membership) or by patrimony, that is, as a result of a son following in his father's footsteps. In London, for example, the proportion of members of the Grocers, Fishmongers and Goldsmiths' Company who entered by apprenticeship declined steadily from the first decade of the eighteenth century, but particularly dramatically from 1720 to 1750. The fact that even many of those who did enter by apprenticeship were already descendants of freemen of London meant that the companies became 'increasingly inbred' during the first half of the eighteenth century.[33]

Further evidence about both the survival of apprenticeship as well as its gradual demise comes from the records produced by a tax which was first levied on premiums during the War of the Spanish Succession.[34] The material relates exclusively to formal, indentured arrangements, and is not without its shortcomings, but it does make it possible to chart the number of apprenticeships, both male and female, which were entered into from 1710 into the early nineteenth century. A statistical analysis of a sample of the tax records, which is displayed in Table 2.2, shows that, up until 1750, apprenticeship certainly remained important as a means of entering both manual trades and the more lucrative professions (especially those of attorney and surgeon) and mercantile occupations. Indeed, the absolute numbers of apprentices probably increased in growth towns such as Manchester, Birmingham and Liverpool, even though none of them had ever had strong guild traditions; for example, in the two years from 1752 to 1754, Liverpool averaged 189 new apprentices each year.[35] It is clear that apprenticeship continued to be used as a means of placing children in growth sectors of the eighteenth-century economy, such as cotton-dealing, merchandising, textile manufacturing, gardening, and the medical professions.[36]

Table 2.2   *Registered apprenticeship indentures, 1715–1801*

		Number	Average value of premiums
1715–18	(three years)	5283 (average)	£23
1730–1	(one year)	6139	£23
1752–4	(two years)	5491 (average)	£20
1770–1	(one year)	6144	£25
1790	(one year)	6275	£31
1801	(one year)	4771	£34

SOURCES: PRO IR1/4, 5, 6, 12, 19, 26–7, 34, 38, 44–5, 49, 51, 57, 65, 70, 71

A statute passed in 1709 (8 Anne, c. 9) laid a tax on candles as well as apprenticeship premiums. The rate was 6d. in the pound for premiums under £50, and 12d. in the pound for values over £50. The master was responsible for paying the duty to Stamp Officers either in London or in the provinces. The penalty for failure to comply was forfeiture by the master of double the value of the premium, half of which was to go to the Crown and half to any informer who reported him. Unstamped apprenticeship indentures were void and therefore deprived the apprentice of legal rights associated with formal apprenticeship. The statute explicitly excludes premiums paid for orphans or poor children at public expense, an important category of apprentices in the eighteenth century, but not one which figures significantly in the argument of this chapter. However, there is a much more serious question about how far tax evasion distorts the figures given in the table, and there can be no doubt that the figures are lower than they should be. The question is by how much. Statutes passed in 1745 and 1747 (18 George II, c. 22 and 20 George II, c. 45) granted an amnesty which was designed to encourage 'negligent' masters to pay the duty late without incurring the penalty. The second of the acts also enabled the apprentice to sue the master for double the amount of the premium if the master would not pay the duty after receiving a formal request in writing to do so. Especially during the early eighteenth century, proof of a legal indenture would have been valuable to the apprentice in enabling him to negotiate himself out of an unsuccessful apprenticeship, or, on completion of the term, gaining a settlement and entitlement to poor relief, practising a trade, or gaining the freedom from an urban corporation. Consequently, although there was undoubtedly under-reporting, it seems likely that the figures from the registers are a fairly accurate reflection of the numbers of formal agreements entered into in which significant sums of money were paid in the premium, and in this respect they may in fact be more accurate than other sources. For example, according to a local register kept by the city authorities, there was an increase in the number of 'apprentices' enrolled at Coventry, from 143 per annum in 1781–5 to 207 per annum in 1801–5 (J. Lane, *Coventry Apprentices and Their Masters 1781–1806* (Dugdale Society, vol. XXXIII, 1982) p. xii). But it is unlikely that the majority of these boys paid premiums or entered into formal agreements. This local register of apprentices was introduced in 1781 as a result of a statute (21 George III, c. 54) which was designed to prevent election fraud at Coventry, where the franchise was vested in freemen who had served a seven-year apprenticeship (see S. Lambert (ed.), *House of Commons Sessional Papers of the Eighteenth Century* (Wilmington, Del., 1975) vol. 33, p. 97ff). The majority of those enrolled in it were paupers and Coventry boys entering into the same trades as their fathers, or else taking up manual occupations such as weaving (Lane, pp. x, xi, xii). By comparison, between 1803 and 1805, an average of only 23 apprentices per annum were entered from Coventry in the Stamp Officers' registers (IR 1/71, pp. 4, 10, 205), but these were precisely those apprentices who originated from outside Coventry, who paid premiums, and who were indentured into the most prosperous occupations and trades.

Yet, it is also evident that apprenticeship, at least of the sort that we can measure and which enjoyed the benefits of legal recognition, did not keep pace with urban growth in the early eighteenth century. For instance, in the years around 1715, the number of London apprentices averaged only 3161 a year, a figure considerably lower than that for the 1690s. Furthermore, the vast majority of these apprentices were boys who came to masters in the City livery companies or the learned professions, and whose parents paid high apprenticeship premiums. Only 278 of this total were bound to masters in the fast-growing and highly industrialized suburbs of the metropolis, and, interestingly, half of these apprentices were girls, very often from clerical or minor gentry backgrounds, who paid premiums of as much as £30 for short terms of service in the sewing trades. At Bristol, the number of apprentices declined steadily throughout the first fifty years of the eighteenth century even though the town doubled in size during the same period.[37] More generally, as Table 2.2 shows, recorded apprenticeships grew only slightly in the years of modest overall population growth between 1715 and 1730. Thereafter, against the background of unprecedented increases in population during the later eighteenth century, the numbers remained constant until 1790, but had dropped off significantly in absolute terms by 1801.

Even in the early eighteenth century, it appears that some social groups were no longer willing or able to use apprenticeship of the traditional type to make the transition to working life, even though it is equally clear that it remained the best method of advancing into the most profitable occupations. At one level, pauper children and orphans continued to be put into service by their parishes.[38] Slightly higher up the social scale, many less wealthy families may well have been able to afford modest premiums, but many others evidently were not. Two-thirds of the forty new apprentices registered in Birmingham in 1715 paid premiums valued at less than the relatively modest sum of £10.[39] However, during the years 1700–26, between fifteen and forty migrants a year came to the town with settlement papers which absolved the Birmingham authorities of any financial responsibility if their bearers fell on hard times, and only 6 per cent of these were given an identifiable occupation.[40] Like many others born in towns or migrating to towns in the early eighteenth century, they were starting out in life by going directly into wage labour rather than going through the process of apprenticeship.

This is not to say that apprenticeship itself was not undergoing change. Long-distance migration and the formal placement of a child in the family of the master was increasingly replaced by arrangements in which the apprentice lived at home, and, perhaps, even earned a low wage. For example, evidence given during a lawsuit in 1725 tells of a boy who was not formally bound as an apprentice until two years after he first began to work for his master, and the agreement stipulated that the father would supply food, clothing, and lodgings. In return, the master agreed to pay the father two shillings a week.[41] By the later eighteenth century, it was evidently no longer uncommon for apprentices to marry during their terms, a state of affairs which had traditionally been forbidden by the formal apprenticeship indenture.[42]

Nevertheless, the fact remains that for many families, even amongst the moderately well-off, formal apprenticeship, and hence entry into the most profitable occupations, may have become prohibitively expensive. For instance, just over two-thirds of the premiums registered in the county of Surrey between 1711 and 1731 were valued at from £20 and upwards, sums which would have eaten quite heavily into the annual incomes of most members of the affluent middling sort, which Paul Langford has recently described as those worth between £40 and £100 a year.[43] In London, between 1715 and 1718, the average premium paid was £28; not surprisingly, the large number of apprenticeships in the City and to professional men such as attorneys and surgeons, which cost in excess of £100, were dominated by the sons of gentlemen and wealthy liverymen. Much the same was true of the potentially most lucrative occupations in both the older incorporated towns with guilds, such as Bristol and Norwich, and in new growth centres such as Liverpool, Manchester, Leeds or Birmingham. Recruits came primarily from amongst the relatives or associates of men already in the business, or else from the middling or lesser gentry.[44] In fact, according to the 1738 edition of Defoe's *Complete English Tradesman* one of the reasons for increased apprenticeship premiums was the willingness, particularly amongst the gentry, to pay more in order to ensure that their children received privileged treatment within the households of the masters with whom they were placed.[45] By the end of the century, although apprenticeship was by no means entirely irrelevant for tradesmen and artisans, it was perhaps more characteristic of the very poor and the moderately well-to-do. Before the passage of a statute, in 1802, which restricted the practice, large numbers of poor boys were apprenticed by parish authorities to work long hours for low wages in factories. The process frequently involved long-distance migration and offered little in the way of training.[46] By contrast, amongst the affluent middling sort, large premiums were found in order to enable children to get a foothold in profitable occupations such as that of attorney, architect or surgeon, or the more elite sectors of merchandising and manufacturing.

IV

The changes in the patterns of apprenticeship over the period from 1550 to 1800 were the product of significant transformations in both urban and rural society. In the first phase, that between 1550 and 1650, both the attractions of an urban occupation, in terms of its potential earning power, and 'push' factors arising from conditions in rural areas, were the most likely crucial features in the boom in the numbers of apprentices.[47] For example, the late Elizabethan influx of recruits into London from the lesser gentry, yeomanry, and husbandmen occurred at precisely the time when these social groups were riding a wave of unprecedented prosperity and the City was experiencing one of the fastest rates of growth in its history. For most of this period there was a shortage of labour in the capital, and wages, at least before the hard times of the 1590s, were high. While much less spectacular than the progress of London, many provincial towns, too, began slowly to recover from a period of early-sixteenth-century slump.[48] At the same time, demographic growth raised the value of agricultural produce, thereby creating excess wealth for those landholders who could grow enough food to feed themselves and have some left over for the market. This is the period in which yeomen and gentry farmers were able to build new houses, accumulate plate, buy joined furniture, and find the extra cash necessary to set up sons in business or trade.[49] Nevertheless, most apprentices presumably had little chance of inheriting significant amounts of land. Though they were hardly destitute, migration to a town was probably one of the few prospects open to them, hence apprenticeship levels remained high in the 1610s and 1620s even though urban economies were then at a relatively low ebb.

Furthermore, it is clear that the apprenticeship premium meant that changes in the financial position of a father had a direct influence on the point at which his son would be able to enter the urban hierarchy. This factor may explain why the sons of husbandmen, and to a lesser extent yeomen's sons, were gradually squeezed out of the more elite occupations during the later years of James I. Although our knowledge of the fortunes of these groups in this period is still incomplete, it is unlikely that the fall in recruitment was due to any substantial decline in the numbers of smallholders in favour of the gentry. But the former may well have been finding themselves in an increasingly uncompetitive position during these years as far as apprenticeship was concerned. There is evidence that the economic troubles of the 1590s and subsequent years caused increased stratification of village society, between greater yeoman farmers and smaller holders, which is perfectly consistent with the decline in the percentage of husbandmen apprentices in the first two decades of the century. Moreover, after 1618, and throughout the 1620s, the disruption of the cloth trade due to the Cockayne project, plague, and European wars, all contributed to a sustained period of economic hardship. Under these circumstances, only the richer yeomen and gentry would have been able to spare the extra cash necessary to establish a son in business or trade, especially when conditions in towns were not at the time particularly favourable to newcomers.[50]

It is hard to attach a very specific chronology to the cost of being apprenticed for any period before the eighteenth century, but there appears to have been a gradual rise, as more gentry recruits came forward and economic recession increased demands from within guilds that limits be put on the number of apprentices. The Jacobean period provides most of the earliest evidence of premiums, sometimes of as much as £100. After 1660, premiums of several hundred pounds became common, and by 1700 the amounts required to obtain an apprenticeship in elite wholesaling trades or with an overseas merchant could easily come to £400, a figure which does not include the capital required to set up a business once the term of apprenticeship had been completed.[51] Obviously, as values, particularly in the wholesaling and retailing trades, as well as the professions, increased only richer parents could afford to pay them.

This rise in premiums, like the other characteristics of apprenticeship in its next phase, that between the mid-seventeenth and the mid-eighteenth centuries, reflects a different, but no less complex, set of demographic, social, and economic circumstances. During the later seventeenth century in particular, overall population stagnation was accompanied by high mortality, low fertility, and a nadir in the ratio of children to adults. Furthermore, in a number of towns there were more female than male migrants.[52] All of this suggests that the high levels of late-seventeenth and early-eighteenth-century urban self-recruitment reflect to some degree a drop in the pressure pushing potential apprentices from the countryside to the towns. Nevertheless, apprenticeship remained vibrant enough to maintain the levels of premiums, and there is evidence of a growing differential between those willing or able to pay high premiums and those who were not. Population stagnation coupled with growing productivity led to lower agricultural prices (especially for the products of arable land), which damaged the fortunes of smallholders; significantly, the 1720s and 1730s were a period of agricultural depression.[53] Hence, small farmers feature less and less prominently in apprenticeship recruitment, especially in connection with the more profitable trades. On the other hand, by 1650, the squirearchy had consolidated a dominance of landed property which it was to maintain until the world war of 1914–18.[54] For lesser members of this group, the mere, or parish, gentry, the apprenticeship of sons had become a regular option in the life cycle of families, and they continued to buy into the elite occupations in London and established incorporated towns. At the same time, the undoubted late-seventeenth-century economic expansion benefited towns and their existing inhabitants. This, plus increased premiums, rendered it advantageous for the sons of merchants and tradesmen to follow in their fathers' footsteps.

The apprenticeship evidence points clearly to the formation, by 1730, of a very stable and more hereditary civic elite, and, very probably, to declining prospects for the sons of lesser landholders and rural artisans. Indeed, of all the possible explanations of the gradual atrophy of guild regulation over trades during the course of the first half of the eighteenth century, none seems more convincing than the view that increasing self-recruitment and a decline in the number of apprentices who migrated over long distances made the kinds of institutional control which guilds had traditionally exercised unnecessary. This trend towards economic oligarchy is perfectly consistent with the great prosperity of the urban middling sort in the early eighteenth century which has been so frequently commented on by recent historians. Nor is it likely to have been offset to any significant degree by developments either outside of the occupations traditionally associated with guilds or amongst the so-called professions. For example, the numbers of attorneys and solicitors increased hardly at all between 1730 and 1800 despite large increases in population during the later eighteenth century.[55]

Thanks to the apparent decline in guild regulation, and also to the emergence of new urban centres, mobility for the less well off from the countryside to towns was most probably easier after 1660 than it had been before. Also, apart from those who undertook domestic service, the material prospects of such migrants may not have differed greatly from that of those who entered the more lowly craft companies in the first half of the century. Population stability and economic expansion meant that real wage levels were higher throughout the period from 1660 to 1750 than they had been in the previous century. But this did not necessarily prevent a widening of the gap between the wealth of the richer and poorer urban inhabitants.[56] The disparity between the wealth of the centres of towns versus the poverty of their suburbs is a notorious fact. In London and elsewhere, from the 1690s, urban poverty caused by the growth in casual labour promoted demands for better measures for the relief of the poor and a reformation of their manners.[57] New industries and post-Restoration economic buoyancy did provide work for the children of the less well off, but they were not avenues towards the goal of self-employed mastership, which had been the traditional objective of apprenticeship. Except for the sons of the lesser gentry and men already established in urban occupations, the chances of breaking into the most lucrative sectors of urban life became more and more circumscribed.

From the mid-eighteenth century onwards, the further decline of apprenticeship was, of course, influenced by the dynamic changes introduced into English society by dramatic population increases and economic growth, which was eventually accompanied by technological innovation. In the period from the late 1740s through the 1760s, a shortage of labour, especially in London, may have induced adolescents either to abandon apprenticeships early or to forgo the process entirely in favour of immediate employment for wages. In 1747, for instance, the London common council cited a shortage of skilled labour as a justification for enabling the Lord Mayor to license employers to hire journeymen from the suburbs, even if they had not completed formal apprenticeships.[58] Similarly, a statute of 1766 indicates that masters were by then having difficulty in retaining the services of poorer apprentices beyond the first couple of years of their terms. Thereafter, as Keith Snell has observed, although the pace varied from place to place, it is likely that declining real wages led those who were apprenticed to manual trades to leave their terms early, and many others not to undertake apprenticeships at all.[59]

V

These changes in the social composition and frequency of apprenticeship were accompanied by alterations in the wide field of social and economic relationships with which it was traditionally connected. In the sixteenth and seventeenth centuries, apprenticeship was a central feature in the relationship between adults and children, and it generated a distinct set of educational and social values, values which were shared to a greater or lesser extent by all of the social groups which comprised the middling sort and which helped to establish a distinctive urban culture. By the middle of the eighteenth century, on the other hand, the institutional structures within which apprenticeship had formerly operated, most notably the guilds, had to a large degree atrophied and a relatively uniform social practice had given way to a much more differentiated set of experiences for those setting out in life. Even so, many of the values which characterised apprenticeship survived to become features of the identity of both the middle and the more elite, or respectable, sections of the working classes.

Some historians have found in apprenticeship, particularly as it was practised before 1700, evidence for a lack of affection in early modern family relations. They point to the fact that parents were evidently willing to send children aged between 14 and 17 off to serve in other families, often far from home, and some apprentices were undoubtedly badly treated by exploitative masters who ruled their households with the full force of absolute patriarchal authority.[60] But contemporary perceptions of the practice are probably best understood by starting instead with the proposition that, for most parents, finding a place for their child was a necessary responsibility. There is a great deal of evidence that care was taken to find a suitable occupation, a suitable master, and satisfactory living conditions. The ideal was sufficiently well-formulated for it to be expressed as a commonplace by Judge Henry Hobart in a court case of 1620. Parents made careful choices of masters because 'The putting of an apprentice is a matter of great trust for his dyet, for his health, [and] for his safety.'[61] Indeed, many parents must have made financial sacrifices in order to raise enough money to pay apprenticeship premiums. For example, the popular Puritan purveyors of moral advice, Dod and Cleaver, stressed the obligation of parents to bring up their children in a lawful and profitable calling which would enable them to live honestly and as Christians, but they also warned that parents should not turn themselves into slaves and drudges by sacrificing too much for the future of their offspring.[62] Finally, most families probably stayed in contact once the placement had been made. Parents were frequently involved in court cases which alleged the maltreatment of apprentices. In the more elite trading companies of London, where apprentices were often responsible for large sums of money, parents had to enter into bonds in which they agreed to indemnify masters against thefts by their sons.[63]

Nevertheless, the fact remains that a seven-year apprenticeship required a young man to live celibately within a strange household, often in a strange place, and to work for little or no pay. Not surprisingly, some such arrangements were notably more successful than others. Masters sometimes helped former apprentices to raise capital to enter into business for themselves; others actually passed on their businesses. On the other hand, as many as one-third to one-half of apprenticeships may have ended prematurely.[64] Some boys, especially amongst those who came up to London, undoubtedly intended to learn skills which they might take home with them to the country, and so never expected to become freemen. It was possible to set up in trade in the suburbs of London, or near towns like Bristol, Newcastle or Norwich without ever having obtained formal qualifications.[65] However, others must simply have run away, fallen into bad company, or been unable to live with their trade or their master and his family. Mobility from one occupation to another was by no means rare in the seventeenth century.[66] In addition, legal records reveal a steady stream of cases in which the master/apprenticeship relationship broke down. In London, the numbers of such cases were significant, but they in fact represent a tiny proportion of all the apprenticeships which were entered into. Some of them allege maltreatment of the apprentice or the failure of the master to teach his trade. Others claim intractability, lack of diligence, or dishonesty on the part of the apprentice. The formulaic quality of the accusations, on both sides, suggests that many of them were being employed in collusive actions in which the master and apprentice agreed to end the agreement by mutual consent, but others undoubtedly reflect real problems in the relationship.[67] In the 1720s, for example, there was a distinct increase in the number of cases in the county of Middlesex, largely because economic difficulties had driven many masters to abscond, thereby leaving their apprentice without either a trade or a home, and their parents out of pocket.[68]

Yet if apprenticeship as a social process was subject to human failings, it was also part of a broader set of urban values associated with the bringing up of the new generation. These were most clearly expressed within the culture of the guilds and livery companies which were the main channels through which apprentices came into incorporated towns. Ideally, guilds were fraternities of men (and sometimes women) who shared 'the secrets' of a 'mystery' or 'science', and who acknowledged a responsibility for maintaining it and passing it on. At York, the early-sixteenth-century city custumal declared that one purpose of guild meetings was 'the helping forward young men [in] time to come'.[69] In the early seventeenth century, trades as diverse as the Silkweavers of York and the Clockmakers of London still required those about to take up the freedom to produce a masterpiece, which might be displayed in the guildhall and inspected by the other members.[70] By the same date, a number of writers were producing books designed to contribute to vocational education.[71]

There was also a concern about general literacy and the relationship between practical trades and liberal sciences. Some apprenticeship indentures, particularly those of pauper children who were put out at young ages, specified that masters should instruct, or see that children were instructed, in basic literacy and numeracy.[72] From the mid-sixteenth century, members of London companies began to make a large number of bequests for general education. Skinners, Cutlers and Merchant Tailors endowed grammar schools, usually in the place of their birth. Even some of the more craft-oriented companies, such as the Carpenters, ran charities designed to provide university scholarships for members' children.[73] The merchant and adviser to monarchs, Sir Thomas Gresham, who founded his College in London with the avowed intention that it work to unite practical and liberal learning, is the most famous exemplar of this trend.[74] The playwright Thomas Dekker's pageant for the Lord Mayor's Show of 1612 provides a fulsome explanation of the kinds of thinking which lay behind such enterprises. One scene depicted 'Vertue', and

> Beneath her in distinct places, sit the seven liberal sciences; viz. arithmetic, geometry and astronomy ... as being mothers to all trades, professions, mysteries, and societies, and the readiest guide to vertue.

Next came a figure of Love being drawn by two horses, Desire and Industry. According to Dekker's script, 'all these (together) make men in love with arts, trades, sciences and knowledge, which are the only staires and ascensions to the throne of vertue, and the onely glory and upholdings of cities'.[75]

If precept was to any extent followed in practice, from the time a youth began his apprenticeship, through the completion of his service, and into his adult life, he became a part of a culture which subjected him to an indoctrination about standards of behaviour as energetic as that experienced by any other social group in the realm. The keys to this aspect of urban culture were two notions which had been central to the life of guilds during the Middle Ages and which survived the Reformation of the early sixteenth century to shape notions about correct behaviour well into the seventeenth. The first of these was Christian charity. As innumerable charters marking the foundation of guilds declared, their chief purposes included the promotion of love, unity and charity amongst the members.[76] The theological importance of these concepts rested primarily on the belief that being out of charity, or in conflict, with one's neighbour troubled the conscience and might ultimately place the soul in jeopardy.[77] But it is also clear that these doctrines, which stressed unity and so worked to defuse conflict, would have been essential features of urban environments, which had of necessity to accommodate a constant flow of newcomers, and where rivals in the same business or trade were forced to live in close proximity. In practice the maintenance of love and charity was facilitated by promoting a sense of community amongst members, providing a means of resolving conflicts, and establishing codes of acceptable behaviour.[78]

The second central ideal of pre-industrial urban life was 'honesty' and honest behaviour. On one level this included notions of fair dealing, probity, and uprightness of character. Thus, guilds punished dishonesty; for example, an apprentice to the London Carpenters was whipped for embezzling goods, and the elders of the Merchant Adventures of Newcastle made an elaborate public declaration against one of their fellows who had committed perjury.[79] But honesty was also associated with a certain mode of behaviour and speaking, a certain dignity of deportment, which conformed to generally accepted conventions. In the early sixteenth century, members of the Drapers' Company in London were supposed to go 'honestly' in processions. New members of the Cutlers' Company in London were to be of good fame and seemly behaviour and not addicted to quarrels or rioting. An early ordinance of the London Drapers pointed out that lapses in the 'fame' or 'behaviour' of individuals would bring slander and dishonour on the entire fraternity.[80] Perhaps the closest we get to a comprehensive statement of what constituted honest deportment comes from an ordinance issued by the Lord Mayor of London in 1560, which reminded all householders that they should behave themselves as citizens 'as well in outward gesture and sober behaviour as in decent and comely apparell'.[81]

Apprenticeship was, therefore, the locus of a set of family and educational values, and it served, at least in towns with guilds, as an introduction to a more general bourgeois culture. Yet, as the statistical evidence discussed earlier indicates, during the seventeenth and eighteenth centuries an increasingly large proportion of apprentices came from the gentry and lesser gentry. Thus, while apprenticeship was a distinctive institution of the middling sort, it was one in connection with which we can observe the interaction of bourgeois values and those characteristic of the gentry.

In many respects the two in fact had much in common. Guild moral injunctions against fornication or card playing were precisely the same as those laid down in the inns of court, the universities, or great magnate households, and suggest that such pastimes were popular in all four types of institution. London guildhalls frequently occupied buildings which had been converted from seats of the nobility, and in London as well as in the provinces their parlours, halls, libraries, bowling greens and formal gardens introduced members to many of the refinements of the great country house.[82] The Elizabethan writer, William Harrison, equated guild feasts with the large meals consumed by landed magnates, and, just as a young squire might learn table manners by serving in a great household, so too the apprentice could acquire them by waiting on tables at guild celebrations.[83] Throughout the period from 1500 to 1800, there was in fact a give and take between urban culture and that of the greater gentry and aristocracy. For example, by the late sixteenth century, the chivalric-hero tale, long a source of entertainment for the landed elite, had gained wider currency, and was adapted by dramatists and writers of popular stories into depictions of apprentices who won fame and glory through military feats in the service of the crown.[84] If the civic ritual of London sometimes praised industry and commerce, it also went to great lengths to celebrate the role of the livery companies and City in defending the realm in times of danger.[85] On the other side, sixteenth-century clerical writers and humanist authors from modest backgrounds did much to popularise the notion that the aristocracy should abandon its warlike ways and take up service to the State by acting as magistrates. By the end of the sixteenth century, the precept that every man, no matter how rich or how poor, had a duty to work, through his calling, for the good of the commonwealth was a commonplace shared (in theory at least) by the great nobleman and humble artisan alike.[86]

However, it is also true that gentlemanly attitudes towards apprenticeship were ambivalent. Leading sixteenth-century humanist writers, such as the enormously influential Erasmus and

Sir Thomas Elyot, devoted much of their work to promoting education as a social value amongst the aristocracy and gentry, but at the same time they also disparaged apprenticeship by associating it with dim wits and bondage. For them, and for other later sixteenth-century social theorists, there was a crucial distinction between the social and intellectual implications of what were described as the 'scientific' versus the 'mechanical' arts.[87] The liberal, scientific arts were those which involved book-learning and preparation for the role of magistrate or ruler, and they were explicitly associated with what went on at the inns of court in London or the universities at Oxford and Cambridge, institutions which contained a high proportion of gentlemen. The term 'mechanical' obviously applied to handicraftsmen, but it also came to be associated with any occupation, including that of attorney or surgeon, in which training was by apprenticeship.[88] Furthermore, unlike those who received a liberal education, mechanical men were not fit for government; indeed they were the subjects who needed to be governed. One logical implication of this distinction was that apprenticeship actually derogated or extinguished gentility in those who took it up, a point that was made by a number of late-sixteenth-century authors, most notably the lawyer, Sir John Ferne. Nevertheless, this extreme position was never upheld either at common law or by the arbiters of such matters, the College of Heralds.[89] Although echoes of it persisted in works describing the social structure of England until the end of the seventeenth century, they became increasingly faint.[90] By then, of course, some forms of apprenticeship had become significantly more exclusive, and, at the same time, the sons of gentlemen could increasingly help to shape urban institutions such as guilds and livery companies.

At the same time, while the values of the gentry had an impact on apprenticeship and guild culture, they did so in part by reacting against traditional urban values. Indeed, from the 1550s onwards, there are signs that increased numbers of gentry recruits were thought by townsmen to undermine guild discipline and ideals. At Newcastle, for example, the Merchant Adventurers noticed the haughtiness of wealthy young men who came to their apprenticeships with large sums of money ready to put into trade. In 1554, an act regulating the apparel of apprentices began with the preamble:

Whereas, in the education and bringing up of apprentices, no
little regard and study hath remained in our elders, that like as
the deuty of the apprentice was instructed him by God, so was
the same not forgotten, what reverence ought to be done to the
master and mistress, what obedience to their superiors, what
honest love unto there equals, what temperance in meat,
drinck, and apparell.

It then went on to detail how this older 'vertuous life' had been
replaced by a 'lewed liberty', which included carding, dicing,
tipling, dancing, familarity with harlots, fancy clothes and imper-
tinence towards masters.[91] In 1560, and in subsequent years over
the course of the sixteenth century, the Lord Mayor of London
reminded masters to discipline their apprentices, to stop them
from 'haunting evil women', and to keep them away from schools
of fencing, dancing, carding, and dicing.[92] By the early seventeenth century, it was a common lament that apprentices had
abandoned the traditional emblems of their calling, the flat
round cap, close-cut hair, narrow falling-bands, coarse side coat,
close hose, and cloth stockings, for the 'idol of fashion'.[93] In
1626, the London Butchers hired a barber to give haircuts to
all apprentices; in the 1630s, the Cutlers of London warned
members against appearing in the guildhall in boots, spurs, long
hair and other 'undecent habbet', which was in fact typical of the
gentry.[94]

To some extent, ordinances such as these may reflect nothing
more than the tendency for older generations to distrust innovation amongst the young. But new fashions which required,
amongst other things, gold and silver trimmings imply an
increased degree of affluence amongst apprentices, and some
observers were quick to associate the richer with the more undis-
ciplined servant. In warning apprentices that they should not
allow the vices of 'sawciness, impatiency, stoutness, distain and
arrogancy' to colour their relationships with their masters, the
long-serving parish priest of Blackfriars, London, William Gouge,
pointed out that,

Clerks, prentices, waiting-women and such like, being borne
Gentlemen, and men of good degree, are for the most part
guilty of this fault: the reason is because their birth and parent-

age maketh them forget their present place and condition; or else . . . maketh them wilfully presume above it.[95]

The conflict between traditional urban values and the disruptive influences of gentlemanly aspirations for riches and easy living appear as constant themes in late Elizabethan and early Stuart London literature. The satirical writer Robert Green created characters who contrasted the value of handicrafts and occupations which grew up to provide necessities for human life, and to profit the commonwealth, with the gentlemanly vice of pride, which brought deceit into every trade.[96] Ambitions above their station lead to the downfall of many of the characters of the playwright Thomas Middleton.[97]

Thus, by the early eighteenth century, when Daniel Defoe wrote his well-known attempts to reconcile gentility with the civic values of sound education and good manners, he was working within a long tradition. But it is no less significant that much had changed. His literary expression of the conflict came at a point when the opulence of some sectors of urban life, and the decline of guilds as institutions which managed apprenticeship and the regulation of trade, meant that the older urban values were under threat.[98] By then gentrification, self-recruitment and honorary admissions reduced many guilds to little more than gentlemen's clubs. It is revealing that by 1730, a nephew of the Lancashire tradesman, William Stout, could contrast what he saw as the desirable life-styles of mercers, drapers and gentlemen with that of the hard-working yeoman.[99] In this light, it is not surprising that the urban elite of the eighteenth century appears to have identified itself as much with the gentry, or at least ideals of gentility, as with a distinctive culture of the middling sort.[100]

Nevertheless, as we have also seen, apprenticeship, albeit in a diluted form, survived in the eighteenth century, and so, too, did the traditional values which were associated with it. For instance, in 1740, Sir John Barnard, a second-generation merchant, who served London as MP and Lord Mayor, published *A Present for an Apprentice or A Sure Guide to Gain both Esteem and an Estate*. A consistent opponent of the regime of Sir Robert Walpole, who was described by the elder Pitt as 'the great commoner', Barnard organised his work around a series of ideas long familiar in the world of apprenticeship – veracity, fidelity, temperance, moderation in dress ('fops in dress are the ridicule and scorn of all sober and intelligent persons'), frugality, industry, and honesty. The fact that this characteristic 'medley of Christianity and commerce' went through a number of subsequent editions suggests that such old-fashioned notions retained their relevance for some people.[101]

Furthermore, apprenticeship also helped to shape the artisanal world of work which emerged in the later eighteenth century. Early precursors of trade unions formed out of the traditions of association amongst apprentices and journeyman workers which had been characteristic of guilds.[102] As late as 1812, coachmakers, engineers, bricklayers, carpenters, and a number of other skilled workers who appeared before a parliamentary committee of investigation, defended apprenticeship on the grounds that the training it provided prevented the proliferation of faulty workmanship. They also expressed the traditional, but increasingly outdated, view that the paying of a premium and the completion of a term of apprenticeship entitled 'legal' or 'regular' men to a 'right' to their trade.[103]

However, it is also clear from this testimony, which was given on the eve of the repeal of the Statute of Artificers, that all trades by then had been affected by the willingness of masters to hire 'irregular' men, who had not undertaken apprenticeship, because they were willing to work for lower wages. In this respect, a more telling survival of the culture of apprenticeship and the traditional values of the middling sort comes from a work written in 1795 by Thomas Gisbourne, an Anglican political and social philosopher, who was an early expositor of what he claimed were the duties of men in the 'Higher and Middle Classes of Society'. Although Gisbourne accepted that fair and liberal competition was the principle on which trade of every kind ought to be conducted, he warned manufacturers in particular that this had to be balanced in practice by moral considerations. These included charity towards the poor, an awareness of the loss of employment which might result from technological innovation, and, above all, a concern that their 'servants' [employees] achieved at least a minimum of education and a maximum amount of moral and religious instruction. Neither the moral values Gisbourne espoused, nor the ideals they were supposed to achieve – 'robust, industrious, and honest' workmen – were new. But, whereas Sir John Barnard was writing at a time when apprenticeship could still be described as the means

through which people in a wide range of occupations were in-
doctrinated into a common set of religious and cultural values,
Gisbourne argued that members of the middle classes, who now
claimed such values as their own, should make sure that they
were imposed, through the household and the workplace, on
those who were distinctly their social inferiors.[104] The middling
sort had been replaced by the middle and working classes.

3. Bourgeois Collectivism? Urban Association and the Middling Sort

JONATHAN BARRY

I

Throughout the early modern period, townspeople participated in many types of association. Whereas countrydwellers had few places or occasions to meet save the parish church or the alehouse, the urban resident lived amongst a plethora of groups, formal and informal, voluntary and (in theory) compulsory that both reflected and reinforced the complexity of urban experience. The range of these associations naturally varied according to the size of the town and also over time, while opportunities for participation varied with social status, gender, wealth and pressures of work. But, for adult males above the labouring class, membership of some associations was axiomatic. For most of our period the great majority of such people were involved automatically in some level of local government, in the parish church, and often in an occupational guild. As householders, and especially if they were freemen of a corporate town, they might also play a part in military training and in both local and electoral politics. A substantial proportion of townspeople also joined nonconformist churches after 1640, building on an earlier tradition of informal religious groupings, which may have survived in some places and were revived by the various Methodist groups after 1737. Social and cultural associations mainly revolved around the countless inns, taverns and alehouses of the towns – home, for example, to clubs of journeymen (and perhaps small masters) in particular trades or to a friendly society. In the eighteenth century a range of more formal societies was established, including freemasons' lodges, charitable societies and countless other bodies based on a common interest or endeavour, such as gardening, music, literature, or for simple conviviality. The sheer diversity of such sociability precludes any comprehensive coverage in this chapter, and yet it was that very diversity that helped to set urban society apart. Thus the study of urban association can offer us an unrivalled insight into the nature and values of the urban middling sort, or, as they are called hereafter, the bourgeoisie.

Generally speaking, however, early modern historians have neglected this opportunity. Why? As well as describing urban association, this chapter also develops the historiographical critique offered in the Introduction to this collection.[1] It is argued there that historians have made unwarranted assumptions about the middling sort that have prevented proper study of the subject. This applies, I shall argue, with particular force to analysis of the relationship between urban identity and the middling sort, as indicated by urban association. Two features of this chapter are explained by this historiographical context and purpose. The first is the use of the term 'bourgeois' or 'bourgeoisie', which is done partly to avoid repetition of lengthy phrases such as 'the urban middling sort', and partly to force attention to the interrelationship between urban and class identity implied by 'bourgeois'. The second is the focus on *collective* identity, and in particular its establishment through association and collective action within a civic, and more merely an urban, context. This is not to deny the multiple nature of urban identities. The notion that urban identity was shaped by the pluralistic and fluid nature of urban life is fundamentally correct (indeed, it will be argued that this was a primary motivation for urban association). None the less, the emphasis here is on the identification of common urban values and collective responses to this condition, rather than consideration of the multiple forms and configurations that resulted from these when applied to individual urban dwellers of differing gender, age, family position, background, neighbourhood, occupation, status and religious or political standing. Both enterprises are equally important, but we need to establish the basic parameters of urban identity before we can begin to understand their individual impact. Indeed, as the chapter begins by stressing, we need to challenge the prevailing assumptions about the relationship between individual and collective identities before we can understand either properly.

Thus, the first historiographical assumption to be noted and challenged concerns the myth of bourgeois individualism, as applied particularly to English history. The nineteenth-century

conception (shared by liberals with their opponents, both aristocratic and socialist) that the middle-class ideal type was the individualistic entrepreneur, without whose presence the class could not
exist, still casts a heavy shadow over the early modern period.[2]
Although the classic early modern entrepreneur is assumed (correctly) to have been a merchant, not, as later, a manufacturer, it is
taken for granted that his (the male form of the adjective is
chosen deliberately) chief social concern was with individual
upward mobility (measured, above all, by his movement out of
urban society into landed ranks) and that such aspirations offer
the key to understanding the values of the entire bourgeoisie.[3]
Comparative historians searching for the roots of England's supposedly unique favourableness for industrialisation and modernisation have consistently identified its 'individualistic' society as a
key, although they have differed in their dating of this development. Without entering the debates about the 'peculiarities' of
English history, we should note the continued force of the model
when applied to urban association. For example, Anthony Black's
survey of *Guilds and Civil Society* in Europe takes it for granted that
England's experience was totally different from that of the
Continent, English individualism precluding the possibility of an
important 'corporatist' strand in English political culture.[4]

Yet historians of nineteenth-century England are now emphasising the inadequacy of the image of the bourgeoisie as one of
individualistic, male entrepreneurs. The classic self-made
manufacturer, it has been shown, formed only a tiny proportion of
the middle classes, although this minority was disproportionately
important to the self-image of the whole class. Historians recognise, as many contemporaries did, that the achievement of individual aims in urban society depended on collective action, both
official and voluntary, at the level of family, neighbourhood, parish, association, and the whole community.[5] Ironically, so little
have such topics been studied for the pre-industrial period that it
is not individualism, but rather, these collective forces, that such
writers are inclined to portray as new and distinctive in the nineteenth century. Yet, as we shall see, they are the neglected commonplaces of early modern bourgeois society as well.

To understand this neglect, we need to consider the recent
English historiography both of towns and of class in the early
modern period. The Reformation is generally seen as the start of an

identity crisis for urban communities, reaching its peak in the mid-seventeenth century, in which the collapse of traditional collective forces in town life was a central feature. The Reformation added religious weight to other tendencies that undermined the associational life of the guilds and the church, creating increasing social polarisation between a ruling oligarchy and the mass of townspeople, their numbers swelled by poor immigrants with no secure connection with urban collective life. Although London is often seen as the chief example of this tendency, the same process has been detected throughout the urban system. Peter Clark summarises the process as 'the fragmentation of the communal coherence, the diminution of the organized sociability, and the sundering of the powerful cultural identity of the older, medieval city'.[6]

In contrast to the picture of crisis and transition portrayed before and during the Civil War, a rosy picture is now emerging of 'urban renaissance' thereafter, especially in the eighteenth century. This involved not merely growing *urban* populations and prosperity, but the forging of a new sense of urban identity. However, this identity is seen as *urbane* rather than *civic*. A sense of civic identity, involving pride in and commitment to the particular traditions of a town and what are seen as the common values and attributes of its inhabitants, as members of a shared urban community, is not considered important in this period, but is associated with the later growth of the provincial cities of the Industrial Revolution. The urban renaissance is instead characterised as urbane – based on creating a common new identity for towns, emulating a single model, namely the metropolis (or rather, its fashionable West End). Furthermore, it was a process which, though occurring in towns, was to a large extent dominated by the landed elite and others (such as rentiers and professional people) not likely to identify with a specific civic tradition. To participate, townspeople had to cast off their old civic particularism and dissociate themselves from the culture of their fellow townsfolk. Although a whole new world of association for leisure and cultural purposes developed, the associations involved were restricted to those who could afford to aspire to the values and lifestyles of a refined elite.[7]

One feature of this urban historiography is its lack of interest in the culture and values of ordinary townspeople, because they are assumed not to be causally significant. Urban historiography is thus closely tied to the class historiography of the period, as discussed in the Introduction, notably Hexter's emphasis on England (before 1832) remaining under the control of a landed aristocracy, to which any middling groups were socially and culturally subordinate. In different ways, most subsequent writers on class have tended to follow this line, adopting various versions of the polarised, two-class visions of society – gentry and non-gentry, rich and poor, patricians and plebeians, elite and popular – which follow the excision of a middle ground from social classification. It should be noted, however, that most historians, following Hexter, have seen the landed elite whom the bourgeoisie emulated as themselves deeply imbued with the values of bourgeois individualism, pursuing commercial gain as agrarian capitalists and increasingly exercising their dominance as a class through their control of metropolitan government and culture.[8]

Through such arguments historians have found it possible to portray early modern England as an increasingly urban, commercial and individualistic society, whilst feeling little need to study the bourgeoisie. They confine their interest largely to London, and its growing role as both capital and cultural centre for the landed elite. Interest in the upper ranks of the urban middling is confined largely to their changing social relationships with the landed elite, rather than to their internal associations. Meanwhile the activities of other sectors of the bourgeoisie are normally discussed under the rubric of 'popular' politics or culture. Thus, despite the growing historical interest in popular culture, such work has focused on topics such as riots, crowd activity and traditional customs, where the middling and lower sort may have acted together, rather than on associations, where the bourgeoisie tended to operate exclusively of the poor.[9] Even though this work has exposed both the importance of the middling sort in the articulation of popular action and the strength of vertical ties within local communities, the framework of analysis has once again precluded systematic study of the links within the middling sort fostered by such movements.

II

In addition to these general features of urban and class historiography, a number of specific problems have been identified which seem to preclude the possibility of genuine association among the bourgeoisie. Before considering associations in more detail, therefore, three apparent obstacles require consideration: the economic and political diversity of middling groups in their local communities; the conditions of flux and mobility in urban life; and the supposed existence of a gulf within the bourgeoisie between an elite and the rest. Each of these factors appears inimical, not only to the formation and successful operation of associations, but also to any process whereby such associations might generate a sense of civic or bourgeois identity, rather than reinforce a sense of division within towns and the bourgeoisie. But each supposed obstacle emerges, on closer inspection, as a powerful factor impelling the bourgeoisie *towards* association and ensuring its centrality in their value-systems.[10]

There is no doubt that the bourgeoisie were fragmented in their sources of income. Economic and occupational specialisation was at the root of urban life – indeed it forms one of the most sensitive gauges of the size and development of an urban community. Furthermore, different groups within towns were in competition – the business rivalry of those who operated within a single trade, and the differing interests of producers, retailers and consumers of the different trades in the town dealing with each other. Tensions between, say, merchants trading to different areas, or within occupations, between masters and journeymen, or small and large-scale traders, are notorious. Equally well-known are the disputes between different towns as they vied for trade, most notably the rivalries between the capital and the out-ports or rival provincial centres. Surely such fragmentation prevented collective action by the bourgeoisie?

Though conflicts within the bourgeoisie clearly followed from such divisions, it can be argued that it was precisely this fragmentation that stimulated the bourgeoisie to seek to reconcile (or at least regulate) their differences by means of association. This was part of the traditional role of guilds within medieval towns (and continued to be so well into the eighteenth century), both as a means of managing rivalries within an occupational sector and, under the aegis of urban government and cultural life, ensuring that different groups could coexist in harmony, or at least without violence. Meanwhile other, non-economic forms of association, by neighbourhood, background, religious or political affiliation or cultural interests, could serve to soften these economic tensions. As for rivalry between towns, this was increasingly mediated through application to central authority, first the crown and later parliament and political parties. In some cases this generated informal associations of like-minded interest groups across the country, for example in petitioning and lobbying, but it was also a growing stimulus to association within each urban community. Those guilds which survived longest were those most active in such external lobbying, while the petitions to parliament of the eighteenth century reveal many associations that have left no formal record in their own towns.

As David Sacks's work on Bristol has shown, the manoeuvrings of rival commercial interests and associations for power, both locally and nationally, spilled over into cultural and ideological struggles as well. For a century or more after the Civil War, if not before, these politico-religious divides dominate the picture.[11] These split both the landed elite and the bourgeoisie – but they did so in a fashion which reflected the existing associational groupings within the bourgeoisie and stimulated further association. Above all, churches of every denomination retained enormous importance as places of middling association, while the partisanship bred of religious debates spilled over into a plethora of sociability, both party political and more generally related to public affairs. By rendering local government divisive, such partisanship in turn stimulated further forms of voluntary association, both to tackle urban problems that could no longer be settled consensually by local authorities, and in the search for non-contentious forms of sociability where social equals could get away from their potential disagreements. Thus political as well as economic pluralism stimulated association as a distinctive feature of bourgeois experience.

The second objection concerns issues of flux and mobility. Those who question whether towns had a civic identity often point to their fluid social quality. High levels of mortality, combined with heavy dependence on immigration from rural areas, ensured a steady turnover of urban personnel and a high level of first-generation towndwellers, many educated outside the town. Towns depended for much of their production and the bulk of their consumers on the countryside; a town was never more a town than when filled with country people for a fair or market. Historians have also been much exercised with a lack of dynastic continuity amongst the leadership of towns, partly due to heavy mortality, but also due to the return of wealthier townspeople to the countryside through marriage or the purchase of land. This very process is seen as itself an admission by townspeople that there was nothing *permanent* in towns – only the purchase of land offered a secure basis for continuity or upward mobility. Such problems were particularly severe in the pre-1660 period. Thereafter the most spectacular threats to urban populations receded (though infant and child mortality rates, in particular, remained high), immigration became less troublesome, and urban life grew more self-sustained. Yet, as mentioned before, Borsay and others see the new urban identity forged after the Restoration as based very heavily on rural demand and on visitors to the town rather than on permanent residents. Others question this, noting the emergence of a resident class of 'pseudo-gentry' in towns, in part because alternative sources of safe investment emerged in government finance, stocks and urban property. Everitt, for example, traces the emergence of urban dynasties back to this period, and even the most successful London businessmen now sought to combine urban and landed life, rather than desert the former for the latter permanently.[12]

We see here, again, the indivisibility of ideas about urban and class identity. The conditions of urban life undermined the stability of the bourgeoisie, whilst bourgeois instability weakened civic identity. Or did it? The connection rests on two questionable assumptions. The first is that *urban* flux and mobility during this period were particularly distinctive. It is doubtful whether our sense of a gentry class could stand up to rigorous testing of long-term stability, whether applied to the emerging parish gentry of the sixteenth and seventeenth centuries or to the demographically unstable gentry class as a whole after 1660. Many historians of nineteenth-century towns emphasise flux and mobility, but not only do they not find these a reason for denying civic or middle-class identity, but they actually see them as major causes and constituents of that identity.[13]

This leads to the second and crucial point: are conditions of flux and mobility in fact inimical to a sense of identity? This essay contends that it was precisely these conditions that encouraged the bourgeoisie to forge a civic identity based on association. It is now commonplace to see flux and mobility as creating the status anxiety amongst the sixteenth and early seventeenth-century gentry, for example, which led them to intensify their search for degree and order in society and to define their class by pedigree or life-style. As we shall see, the efforts of the bourgeoisie to achieve similar results depended on association. *Civic* identity had always been forged out of measures taken by townspeople to counter the effects of flux and mobility. The notion of a corporation and of corporate bodies, which lay at the heart of early modern definitions of a town, rested on the assumption that such institutions created the permanence and immortality which (mythically) landed property offered to the aristocracy, but which was otherwise unattainable in urban conditions. Equally, urban identities rested as much on the permanence of buildings (walls, gates, castles, churches, market halls, schools, almshouses) and economic privileges (fairs, markets, commercial courts) as on people: yet all these buildings and privileges required upkeep and management organised through urban association. The urban renaissance added to these traditional groupings a whole new set of institutions, such as infirmaries, theatres, walks, libraries and the like, all requiring supporting associations to handle their finance and management.[14]

At this point it is worth noting a major problem concerning the evidence for association in this period. The bodies just mentioned mostly dealt with property or legal affairs, and thus generated records which have some chance of survival. Other associations, especially those involving the lesser bourgeoisie, are much less likely either to have kept records or to have preserved them; this applies above all to the vast range of (often ephemeral) societies and clubs we know to have existed by the eighteenth century, but which met in public houses, held no property or public responsibility and are only known to us through stray references, above all in newspapers. Such groups rarely went more public than the public house; we believe they were far more common in the eighteenth century, but then the types of source likely to uncover them were far more common then. Unlike the nineteenth century, however, when the copious reports of the local press enable one to recreate in detail the activities of many such societies, even without their records, eighteenth-century (let alone earlier) information is usually extremely sketchy. Thus we have three inherent biases in our knowledge to contend with. First, our attention is directed towards forms of association where power and property were involved, which often brought to the fore the upper echelons of the bourgeoisie, sometimes in conjunction with visiting gentry. Secondly, new sources of information in the eighteenth century may lead us to regard as new, forms of association that were actually much older, but never recorded before. Thirdly, the inner life of many of these associations is very hard to uncover, and we rely heavily on examples from the best-recorded, but possibly unrepresentative, leading associations.

These evidential points lead directly to the third major obstacle to accepting the importance of civic and class identity, namely the notion of a large and growing gulf within urban society and the bourgeoisie between two social groups. In civic terms this is normally associated with the so-called rise of oligarchy in urban government. Post-Reformation towns supposedly lost their communitarian character, because small self-perpetuating elites of magistrates took control with State help. Any sense of civic identity that survived was based on the values and cultural hegemony of this elite, not on broader foundations. Socio-economically this elite consisted of the merchants and larger retailers, those whose livelihoods depended on access to large amounts of capital, together with the leading members of the professions and the pseudo-gentry (those on rentier incomes). There was, it is argued, increasingly little in common between *this* middle class and the small shopkeepers, artisans, minor professionals and others, who lacked access to political power, extensive capital or genteel culture. Instead, members of the elite group sought to be recognised by their superiors, the gentry, as part of the genteel in a polarised society. The implication is that they withdrew from urban association with their fellow townspeople.[15]

Once again we may note that very different conclusions tend to be drawn from evidence of similar stratification amongst both the early modern gentry and nineteenth-century urban society. Without denying conflicts of interest, between either upper and lower gentry or the upper and lower middle classes of Victorian towns, historians have been at pains to understand the relationship *between* these two groups within a single class. In particular they have studied under what circumstances they associated, politically and socially, and how such association served to forge a class identity. Ironically, towns are often seen as the places of association for the early modern gentry, whether it be the 'county community', meeting at the quarter sessions, or the gentry associating at a national level in London, the university towns or later the spas. Bob Morris has argued, for the nineteenth century, that it was through the effort to integrate the lower middle classes into the culture and ideology of the elite of the class that a distinctive middle-class culture was formed, and that the key to this integration was the forming of urban associations, to which both groups would belong, but which the elite could lead.[16] This appears an important suggestion to explore for the early modern period. Yet, as suggested above, the sources that survive are often fragmentary about the social significance of associations of the types that might bind the bourgeoisie together, and how this changed over time.

Some preliminary work of this kind has been undertaken for London, where one might expect differentiation within the bourgeoisie, together with integration of the upper bourgeoisie into the national elite, to be most advanced. In fact, studies, mostly on the political dimension of the process, have not confirmed either trend. There are certainly clear signs of an ongoing division between *an* elite – often identified with the aldermen – tied into international trade and government credit, and a large and potentially radical body of freemen, closely associated with the traditions of civic democracy and hostile to monopolies and large financial interests. However, social relationships changed rapidly according to circumstances and to religious and political divisions, which were vertical as well as horizontal. In a pattern which Mayer has encouraged us to look for more generally, the potential power of numbers of the lower middle classes in moments of crisis rendered them a perpetual subject of concern for the elite, and established the relationship as one of negotiation, not simply of hegemony. The aldermanic elite always excluded many very rich and socially important people, who often forged links with those of lesser standing, while frequent reversals in political fortunes after 1640 found different portions of the elite at different moments seeking such alliances. These alliances were generally forged through the capital's intensely rich world of association – city companies, parish and ward government, churches, neighbourhoods and informal clubs. Generally these brought the lower and upper bourgeoisie together, rather than segregating them. Thus, despite the unparalleled wealth of London's upper bourgeoisie, the general message for other urban historians appears to be the strength

of vertical ties and the difficulty of establishing a clear elite/
popular divide amongst the great mass of London's bourgeoisie.[17]

III

Thus, in short, the apparent obstacles to bourgeois association
were in fact stimuli to association. Civic and bourgeois identity was
forged out of efforts to establish dialogue within the bourgeoisie,
precisely because of the challenges posed by urban instability and
by economic and political fragmentation. As E. P. Thompson's
classic study of *The Making of the English Working Class* argued, class
formation is not an automatic process but results from struggle –
from a conscious and constantly renewed effort to establish identity.[18] Unlike the classic model of class formation, however, which
stresses the need for antagonistic relations with another class, in
the case of the bourgeoisie such struggles were related as much,
perhaps more, to urban conditions and the internal relationships
of the bourgeoisie, as to relationships with those above and below
in the social system. In every case, association was a critical factor
in the production of identity.

Take, for example, the family, or rather the household. The
notion of the city as a confederation of households, and of the
head of household as the citizen, lay at the heart of urban politics.
The household economy was fundamental, and the bourgeoisie at
all levels built their lives around the protection and development
of the family and household through a series of stages in the life-
cycle and in response to the challenges posed to it. Whereas the
poor had to depend on others for charity or poor relief, a fundamental characteristic of the bourgeoisie was the aspiration (not
always achieved) to use mutual support to secure their futures.
Unlike today, however, such insurance was based not on imper-
sonal commercial arrangements but on building up a network of
social and institutional relationships within the town, as well as
managing those that catered for the poor. Just as the town invested
in the household as the fundamental source of urban stability, so
the householder found urban association the necessary prerequisite for household maintenance, so strengthening the connection
between civic and bourgeois identity.

Apprenticeship (or other forms of domestic training and service) was fundamental both in introducing individuals to urban values and in their personal careers. Given high levels of immigration it was a key common experience, whose maintenance was high in civic priorities at least until the early eighteenth century. Thereafter, numbers may have fallen, but this resulted in part from the increasing internal recruitment of the bourgeoisie, lessening the need for such a formal introduction to town life. Even then, offering apprenticeship to the poor through charity and poor-law provisions remained a major bourgeois concern. The slow decline of guilds and civic apprenticeship does not signal a loss of interest, for increasingly these matters were handled not by guilds but by charitable societies and other agencies of government. The tradition of apprenticeship retained sufficient vitality, at least in the artisan sector, to be a major resource for these groups when, in the early nineteenth century, they sought to challenge the rise of deskilled factory labour. Meanwhile certain areas of middle-class life, such as the legal and medical professions, still depended on apprenticeship or its equivalent.[19]

Equally, at the other end of life, provision for retirement and death was originally regulated by guilds, not least through limitation of economic competition and privileges for seniority, as well as arrangements for pensions and help for widows and orphans. In the eighteenth century such provision was gradually assumed by voluntary groups, such as friendly societies and charities. These were an essential complement to private efforts to establish security for fragile family economies that relied on the skills of the male head. For all but a small elite of the middling they were surely more significant than landed purchase, although historians have been fixated with this particular solution to urban impermanence. In the nineteenth century a very significant alternative was investment in urban property (thus generating new associations such as building societies). Although this is a grossly neglected subject, such investment was probably less common before 1800, as a very high proportion of urban property was in the hands of corporate, religious and other collective bodies: control of this resource was dependent, once again, upon participation in urban associations.[20]

Thus both the ideal of the household, and the measures taken to support it against the frequent blows of fate, lay at the heart of both civic and bourgeois identity, even if their exact associational form changed. Generally, of course, women and children were the passive recipients of the fruits of such association by adult males, though sometimes their symbolic participation was encouraged, for example when children participated in parish perambulations, school processions or apprentice marches. Apprentices developed a social world with a degree of autonomy, and, at moments of crisis, might activate their latent status as bearers of the community's destiny by engaging in political action. The picture concerning female association is more problematic. Davidoff and Hall have argued that a growing separation between public and private was a middle-class characteristic after 1750 and that defining women's sphere as that of the individual within a private domestic space was crucial to class formation. Arguably this was less of a possibility in earlier periods, when family labour was more necessary for all of the middling groups, when suburban living, apart from work, was very rare and when, as emphasised, the uncertainties of life made provision for family security so dependent on public action. On the other hand, it could be argued that women were more excluded from public life and a civic identity in the earlier period, before polite society (geared to smoothing the path to marriage) and charitable work for women were better established. Once again, however, we may be misled by the survival of better documentation into positing a greater change than actually occurred. Courtship and marriage arrangements were no doubt always at the heart of many of the more informal types of association, and women's particular responsibilities for charity and hospitality had long been recognised. A largely urban movement like the Quakers, for example, saw supervision of marriage and relief as natural roles for their women acting collectively. As yet we lack the detailed work on women's social life that would enable us to unravel such contradictory indications.[21]

Protecting the household was, however, only one possible purpose for voluntary association, though unduly neglected. Whereas most historians would probably accept that there was a fundamental continuity in concern for the household, in other areas the emphasis has lain on discontinuity. The period 1550–1780 has been portrayed as one of crisis and rupture between two periods in which association created civic and bourgeois identity. The guilds and churches of the post-Reformation period are seen as the attenuated relics of a pre-Reformation civic order, which became increasingly incapable of expressing civic or bourgeois identity as time progressed. Economic irrelevance and oligarchic take-over weakened the guilds, while oligarchy, secularism and above all religious division undermined the churches. Thus the seventeenth century saw a crisis for urban association, as for civic identity. According to some historians, such as Morris, it was not until the 1780s that a real recovery took place; others, notably Peter Clark, see a new surge of sociability beginning after the Restoration and growing steadily through the eighteenth century. But Clark sees urban societies as a harbinger of new, secular, urban developments, forces for modernisation pointing to the nineteenth century. The emphasis is placed on their pluralistic diversity and lack of relationship either to traditional images of civic identity or to common class interests or values. Little attempt has yet been made to place these groups in the context of the continued activity of guilds and churches, now both Anglican and nonconformist, or to examine how far, collectively, they held the various sectors of the bourgeoisie together.[22]

Yet there are many points of obvious similarity and continuity between the new forms of association and the older civic forms. One overriding concern, already identified, was with the reinforcement of both the family and the wider community in the face of disorder of every kind. In addition to material provision, this included the promotion of a series of values seen as fundamental to the survival of urban society. Amongst the various virtues so promoted are all those qualities, such as thrift, respectability and industry, often labelled the Protestant work-ethic and seen as the foundation of individualism.[23] We may observe not only that their success was assumed to depend on *collective* rather than individual action, but also that they were matched by a set of overtly collective virtues, of sociability and good fellowship. The expression of these in communal gatherings, eating and drinking, and often in listening together to sermons and marching through the streets on holidays or anniversaries, was common to all these groups, old and new.

All these were practices drawn from the older organisations, in particular guilds and civic corporations, but adopted wholesale, along with many other characteristics, by new forms of association. These, I would argue, reflect the power of civic tradition and of an established vocabulary of associational form, though they also

grow out of what one might call the inner logic of urban organisation – prevailing patterns of urban space, wealth, leisure and the
like. Thus, to explain why a new philanthropic body such as an
infirmary instituted an annual procession, first to a sermon and
then to a dinner, one could stress the way in which this laid claim
to civic traditions, both of public display and of civic benevolence.
Equally, one could argue that the organisers of such events were
constrained by such factors as the availability of public meeting-
places, the preference for day-time over evening events and the
cheapness of this method of publicising and attracting participation, which ensured that new forms of association would imitate
older forms, without necessarily *intending* to evoke their traditions.
But even if the latter explanation is preferred (and the evidence
suggests a mixture of the two), the fact that new forms of association mirrored the older ones would have reinforced townspeople's
sense of continuity in values and aims.

Particularly crucial was the role of charity – both within the association and towards the wider community. To supply the needs of
others through charity and to provide for your own future needs
through mutual support was to establish one's place as an independent citizen. Though the prudential justification for such
charity, namely the maintenance of communal discipline, was
prominent, equally prominent was the insistence that such charity
cemented the mutual good fellowship of the bourgeoisie and displayed their capacity to overcome the temptations of possessive
individualism. This applied both to the individual and to the community as a whole – hence the centrality of charity, both in the way
towns presented themselves publicly and in the activities of their
key civic bodies, for example in those unincorporated towns where
a school or almshouse trust offered an unofficial centre of urban
government. This reminds us of the immensely close relationship
between such voluntary association and urban identity: towns
identified themselves through such actions, in part because such
associations were very rare in the countryside but ubiquitous in
urban conditions. Of particular significance here were the efforts
to bolster the fragile urban household, as discussed above. In supporting their women and children, bourgeoisie men were exercising a charity that was both self-interested and yet altruistic – a civic
duty, given contemporary assumptions about the household's
place as the foundation of civic order.[24]

As important as the aims of such groups was their organisation – if indeed the two can be distinguished. Whether we are talking about guilds, churches, clubs, freemasons' lodges, friendly societies or assemblies, we can trace throughout the early modern period a number of characteristic features, and in particular a characteristic tension between equality and inequality. Fundamental to all such bodies was the notion of a common bond of fellowship – a fraternity – between members. One aim of their rules or procedures was always to ensure the maintenance of good relations within the group and to prevent any divisions reaching the public domain. Yet, in a way that seems paradoxical to us, the rules and procedures usually also established hierarchies within such groups. How can we explain this, and does this undermine the vision of associations as places where urban identity, rather than division, was established?

One such form, typical of the guild and passed on to freemasons' lodges, for example, was the society of initiation, followed by rings of membership, with a strong principle of seniority. This built on the sense of civic life as a progressive process of incorporation, establishing a hierarchy, indeed an oligarchy, but offering a justification for this through the notion of seniority. A kindred but variant model was offered by the parish vestry, followed very often by nonconformist churches and other groups with property to administer, such as library societies or significant charities. This was to establish an inner group of trustees, answerable in some often ill-defined sense to a wider body of members or subscribers.[25] Finally, we find what was probably the most common but least visible type, namely the simple society of mutual members, joined for a specific purpose or just from good neighbourhood. Their chief characteristic was perhaps ephemerality, as they rarely lasted beyond the interest span of the groups that started them – a notorious problem, for example, of early friendly societies. They were therefore seen as ill-suited to any type of project that required permanence. This tended to require investment in property – usually urban property – rather than reliance on subscriptions alone, and entailed the establishment of rules of succession and decision-making, such as the trustee or seniority principle. Through such hierarchies and access to the patronage offered, such propertied associations attracted the support of the wealthier and more leisured of the bourgeoisie, with time and money to devote to the association's running.[26]

Urban associations thus reproduced the socio-economic in-equalities within the bourgeoisie, offering leadership to the mer-cantile and professional elite, at least in the cases of the most publicly visible societies. Thus they can legitimately be interpreted in terms of urban oligarchy and the dominance of an upper mid-dling class. Yet it is surely also important that the hierarchy within these organisations was justified organisationally (rather than on principle), that they brought different groups of the middling together, and that they often combined their hierarchical side with another emphasis, less often stressed by historians, on freedom and equality among and between members. The two dimensions, horizontal and vertical, were held together by the notion of 'trust', in a range of senses. The leading figures, often known as trustees, were responsible to the broader group for exercising authority in accordance with their agreed aims. Thus the relationships forged were not simple patron–client ones but ties strengthened by a sense of common, essentially voluntary, commitment to a shared cause, most notably in the case of churches. In this case consider-able power was given to the ministers of those churches to estab-lish and interpret the ideology of the group – an opportunity which other societies were often eager to offer to the clergy by get-ting them to preach to their annual meetings. The clergy thus formed perhaps the most powerful, or at least most visible, exam-ple of what Shani d'Cruze, in her essay, calls the community broker, those whose professions (especially clerical and legal), leisure or strategic location at common places of meeting, such as public houses or bookshops, placed them at the centre of large numbers of social networks.[27]

Too much emphasis can however, be placed on power relations, important though they were. Other sets of values were also embed-ded in associational life, once again in the form of dialectic ten-sions. These include those between self-control and obedience to others, between competition and cooperation, between restraint and liberality. We may see the practice of associational life as pro-viding the bourgeoisie with a constantly renewed experience and representation of how to manage their lives in accord with these values, and in particular how to balance their apparently contra-dictory requirements. The central notion here, one often evoked by contemporaries as they extolled the virtues of life in the 'middle station', was of the 'golden mean'. To be a member of the middling sort you had to learn how to practise moderation, but the middling sort were seen as uniquely placed to achieve this ideal state, if properly trained.

The role of associations in this process of training was twofold. On the one hand the *values* preached by the sermons, toasts, insignia, recitation of rules and the like at associational events provided a prudential code for bourgeois life. Its messages were, however, also embodied in the actual *practices* needed to carry off such occasions successfully. For example, the bourgeois learnt to balance the demands of sociability, expressed most commonly in expenditure on proper clothes, food and drink, with appropriate restraint, such as limits on expenditure and drunkenness, and insistence on correct clothing for one's position within the association. Plaudits for order and decency followed correct performance; criticism and penalties followed infractions. Both the group and the individual were thus under permanent scrutiny for the adequate expression of bourgeois self-management, itself the prerequisite for genuine independence. Association thus succeeded apprenticeship as the proving ground for the independent head of household.

Alongside the elaborate rituals involved in many of these associations, there was an elaborate social vocabulary to express these values – words such as fellowship, benevolence, decorum, respectability. Striking features include both the plurality of languages, besides that of 'gentility' (on which historians have lavished such attention), and the absence of direct appeals to the 'individualistic' creed of self-interest and self-advancement (such utility tends to be praised only if directed towards communal advantage, utilising such justificatory terms as 'helpful' or 'useful', or listing the civic benefits). Instead, two major clusters of terms can be discerned. The first concerns antiquity, honour and precedence. Here we can see the bourgeoisie vesting their associations with precisely those qualities, associated with continuity, that the gentry claimed, as individuals, from their relationship to land and family. Once established for the association to which he belonged, the individual bourgeois could then appropriate his share of this status.

The second, more complex, cluster of terms combine notions of freedom, citizenship and independence with the balancing requirements of loyalty, obedience, unity and impartiality. All of these terms, we may note, depend for much of their meaning on the legal and political arrangements of civic culture. They also embodied a tension, at the heart of the experience of the bourgeoisie, between independence and dependence. Unlike the poor, they saw themselves as fundamentally *free*, able to act voluntarily. Unlike Victorian liberals, however, they assumed that this freedom arose not just out of moral and economic autonomy, but also out of a set of legal rights and responsibilities, such as those of the freemen of incorporated towns. In this respect participation in established bodies like guilds, churches or local government was not so sharply differentiated from 'voluntary' participation in other associations as we might expect; both expressed involvement in civil society. Furthermore, as we have seen, freedom and independence were both recognised to be conditioned by duties and dependence. Individually, the bourgeoisie were unable to enforce their will either over the conditions of urban life or over each other; they depended on collective action to do so. Such collective action necessarily involved inequalities: it often expressed patriarchal and paternalistic sentiments towards women, children and the dependent poor and it often involved unequal responsibilities and power within the bourgeoisie themselves.

It may be possible to discern three distinct, if overlapping, groups within the bourgeoisie, marked by different relationships to association. For the mercantile elite of towns, urban association may have been a matter chiefly of power and responsibility, with their involvement limited to corporate and trade associations and to the most prestigious, property-owning associations, together with those that involved links with fashionable society, at least when this was useful for marriage purposes or when retired or semi-retired from business. For this group the collective strength of the association was perhaps of less importance, given their personal eminence, Hence, the most active organisers and attenders of most types of urban association appear to have been a middle rung of the bourgeoisie, including lesser merchants, professionals, shopkeepers, and skilled craftsmen. These people had the time and resources to devote to association, but needed to act collectively to make their mark in urban life. For some of them, such as lawyers, innkeepers or booksellers, these associations also brought business. Such people appear to dominate, first the world of guilds, wards and parish vestries, and then the clubs and societies of the later part of our period, such as freemasonry or charitable societies. Finally, there were those on the lower edge of independence, including many artisans and petty traders, for whom participation in such associations could be, as people like Defoe never tired of saying, a dangerous drain on resources. Their chief form of association was doubtless the more ephemeral clubs based in taverns. However, we should not underestimate the appeal of associations to this group. For them, too, association could be useful, not least in organising every aspect of employment, from displaying one's talents to striking for higher rewards. Furthermore, it was among the lesser bourgeoisie that dependence on the collective action of oneself and others was most intense. For example, without clubbing together such people could not even afford to read a newspaper. This arguably heightened their desire to assert the sense of freedom and independence that separated them from those below them.

Having suggested these three levels of bourgeois association, it is important to stress their schematic character. Some kinds of association allowed participation at all three levels, with nonconformist churches the most obvious example, with their trustees, members and 'hearers'. Individuals might become involved in different types of association at different stages of their career, according to the pressures of work and the availability of resources. Moreover, I wish to re-emphasise the common values involved in associational activity of every kind. Though the experience of the merchant and the humble artisan diverged dramatically, association provided a shared experience, in some respects at least, because it articulated values that seemed relevant to all the bourgeoisie.

IV

Yet English historians have generally been reluctant to take seriously either the practice or the ideology of association. We have already noted a number of historiographical assumptions and evidential problems that have prevented close analysis of associational practices, but it is worth considering further factors that have blocked serious study of the ideological aspect. Clearly there are problems in knowing how far to accept clerical interpretations of what association meant, and with the clash between rhetoric and reality in, say, the aims of freemasons' lodges. But resistance to taking this ideology seriously seems to rest on more fundamental historiographical objections. Both the continuity of themes across our supposedly divided period, and the associations' failure to articulate supposedly distinctive individualistic values have led historians to see the language and ideology within which civic and bourgeois identity were expressed as examples of *false consciousness*. If they are taken to indicate anything about the bourgeoisie, it is the hegemony of another culture, that of the aristocracy. Bourgeois, concern with order and hierarchy, great interest in notions of antiquity, precedence and honour, and the concern for gentility, have all been mocked since Tudor times by social commentators and writers from the landed classes, and historians have generally been content to echo the mockery. Before the Civil War, such values are taken to indicate the inability of urban groups to shake off their medieval past, itself subordinate to feudal ideology. Thereafter, such attitudes are regarded more indulgently, but no less condescendingly, as a sales-pitch to win genteel favour and to enable aspiring bourgeois to imitate the metropolitan values of the landed elite. Equally, historians have been dismissive of civic identities, as expressed, for example, in civic histories and public ceremonies, with their emphasis on antiquity, military and civic honour, legal and other precedents and values of freedom and honour.[28]

In part, such dismissive approaches arise naturally from the overall perspective on urban history outlined above. Yet they also reflect the latent power of the nineteenth-century model of bourgeois ideology. According to this, genuine middle-class values must relate to progress, liberalism and the self-made man, consciously rejecting the alternative value of landed conservatism or of working-class socialism. The upper bourgeoisie's failure to reflect such values must indicate their subordination to the landed, an advanced symptom of that 'gentlemanly capitalism' which it is now fashionable to see as the root of our current economic malaise. The appeal of traditionalist values to the lesser middling is either ignored or equated with the false consciousness of the modern petty bourgeoisie, often itself seen as pathological (leading, for example, to Fascism).[29] Yet, before dismissing these values as false consciousness, one might consider what experiences in urban life they reflected, no doubt imperfectly, and what they played in regulating relationships within bourgeois society.

As noted above, townspeople regarded themselves as living in a dangerous world where disorder and disaster constantly threatened. Continuity, as expressed by antiquity and ensured by corporate organisation and voluntary association, was thus a great value in itself. Amongst the dangers faced were those of war, civil strife and social discontent, not to mention the constant concern about crime. Although by European standards England was remarkably peaceful during this period, we should not forget that the impact of wars, civil and external, was borne disproportionately by the towns – in terms of sieges, disease, presence of soldiers or removal of sailors, effects of privateering and dislocation of trade. Just as urban defences proved remarkably stout during the Civil War, so notions of the urban community in arms proved very potent. Civic militias did not seem ridiculous to seventeenth-century townspeople, nor did the title of 'merchant adventurers' necessarily seem hyperbolic to those risking their fortunes in the dangerous seas of world trade. John Brewer has rightly emphasised that urban interest in news and political events (which supported countless clubs and societies by the eighteenth century) was perfectly rational (though scoffed at by snobs then and since) because war and government policy determined the conditions of trade and credit. In this respect the state was just adding to the already fragile conditions of credit in early modern towns, where bankruptcy was a constant threat and every trader, whether merchant, professional, shopkeeper or artisan, was part of a complex web of creditors and debtors. In this risky world, an obsession with one's own reputation and that of others, with honour and honesty and with demonstrating that one had friends and associations (which increased one's reliability) was a necessity of business, rather than the costly diversion from business which we might assume.[30] As we suggested above, the association performed multiple roles in this respect: training the bourgeoisie in self-management, displaying to others their mastery of this art and strengthening social ties with those on whom they relied.

We are dealing here with a world of complex interdependence, both on external factors and on other members of the town community. Although he applies the argument primarily to court

society, we may draw on Norbert Elias's observations on the so-
called civilising process (which arguably spread from cities and
bourgeois groups to the upper classes rather than the other way
round). Elias sees growing social interdependence as generating
that growing concern with manners and the feelings of others that
constitutes the civilising process.[31] Towns were obsessed with regulating their citizens' behaviour to ensure order and decency, two
of the highest terms of praise, though as we have seen they also
sought to provide conditions in which sociability and communal
solidarity could safely be expressed. Even the language of gentility
and genteelness, so often seen as a laughable attempt at social
climbing by the bourgeoisie, was in many cases adopted by them,
in changing fashions, as a convenient way of regularising relations
within civic society itself, especially as this grew racked with faction. In some respects it became easier for the bourgeoisie (especially the professional and mercantile elite) to share the same
language of respect as the gentry, because definitions of gentility
changed and the landed classes adopted a more urban lifestyle.
But it seems curious to regard this as marking a watershed or great
discontinuity within *urban* society, or to ignore the continued
power of other languages and cultural forms.

It would be wrong to imply, however, that it is only the false consciousness of historians that has prevented the proper study of
urban associations or concealed the continuities in bourgeois
values which this essay has highlighted. There remain genuine
problems, both evidential and methodological, in interpreting the
significance of urban association for its participants and in judging
between continuity and change, and the remainder of this chapter
will focus on these issues.

V

Any effort to construct a history of bourgeois association over the
early modern period is faced immediately with three phases of politics, each affecting both relations within the bourgeoisie and their
relationships with other social groupings and with the nation-state,
and, equally crucially, the types of evidence that survive concerning these. Our period begins with a new phase, linked with the

Reformation. Any forms of association not under public authority faced disapproval and discouragement from above. This undoubtedly strengthened the relative position within urban society of the upper bourgeoisie who led the town corporations, occupational guilds and parish vestries. Other forms of association were pushed off the public stage and into the alehouse or the home, and hence out of the records. How extensive and long-lasting this process of simplification was, however, is not clear: as in religion, responses to demands for wholesale change from above were often met by adjustments of existing practice rather than transformation. In itself, moreover, Protestantism soon became a motor of new forms of association, as the urban godly began to supplement parochial worship with other religious associations. Occupational guilds and other bodies, such as military trained bands, may have also taken over some of the associative functions of the now-banned religious fraternities. Compared with the pre-Reformation period, however, such urban association appears more self-contained, less likely to influence the wider society and perhaps more specific to each individual town.[32]

During this phase, our sources of evidence about urban life are restricted in certain key ways. We rely heavily on the legal and governmental contacts of urban elites with central government and on the legal records of their administration of civic affairs. Such records, by their very nature, draw our attention to the relationship between the bourgeoisie and the landed ruling class, on the one hand, and the poor, who threatened urban society, on the other. Few records survive that overtly record the values and practices of other middling groups. The one exception to this is the plethora of evidence, especially literary, for London, including the emergence of the printed advice books, stories and other printed material analysed by L. B. Wright in his *Middle-Class Culture in Elizabethan England*, a book which has been perhaps the most conspicuous and least worthy martyr to Hexter's polemic. Wright's book is, however, about London and it never surmounts the problem of identifying the authors and audience of the literature it discusses, and how far they wrote either as or for the urban bourgeoisie. As indicated earlier, subsequent historians have emphasised the cultural hegemony of the gentry over this material, although literary critics are increasingly exploring more sophisticated ways of understanding the ambivalent relationship between literature (notably the theatre) and civic life in the age of Shakespeare.[33]

According to the conventional wisdom, this period of civic particularism, with its deleterious effect on urban sociability, was overcome only by the opening up of towns after 1660 to broader patterns of sociability led by the gentry. But an alternative explanation can be given for the undoubted transformation in the place of association, both within the town and in defining the place of the bourgeoisie within society as a whole. The period from the Civil War to the mid-eighteenth century was marked by bitter divisions within the existing institutions of church and local government, and a proliferation, after a while, of alternative forms of association. Yet the intense partisanship of the period was matched by an equally intense devotion to the notion of impartiality and communal unity, a fervent desire to show that it was the other side, not one's own, who were threatening the civic community and that one's own side were only reinforcing traditional civic values. What better way to achieve this than to try to control the existing associations, or, if that was not possible (or they were somehow ideologically unacceptable) to establish new associations of one's own kind? On the other hand, if the achievement of commonly agreed values seemed threatened by partisan strife, then new voluntary bodies, such as philanthropic or cultural ones, might offer neutral ground on which rivals could meet. In many cases both motives probably mingled. The effect was a proliferation of new forms of association alongside the traditional world of guilds, parish and corporation, which had become so inextricably bound up with partisan politics. It is important to stress the 'alongside' here, because the traditional forms did not disappear, though their relative importance clearly lessened.[34]

As political historians begin to look beyond Westminster, they are increasingly aware of the richness of this urban world of ritual, association and public activity.[35] Furthermore, they have increasingly recognised the crucial role played in such urban politics by a language of citizenship and freedom, which, as we have seen, formed an integral part of the ideology of association, reflecting its concern with the conditions and expression of independence.[36] Once again, however, the issue of false consciousness arises. The increasingly political and factional character of many such associational activities requires the historian to be very cautious in interpreting their social significance. Not only could association be divisive, but its members might be appropriating values in which they no longer believed. How far were urban elites manipulating popular opinion, and how far were the rest of the bourgeoisie conscious of such manipulation? In terms of evidence, this problem is intensified by our continued dependence on sources generated by the mercantile and landed elite. Their recording of these processes is shaped both by their assumptions about the social order and by their own purposes, as well as by conventions of what was written and what was left unwritten. Just as our vision of the urban renaissance relies heavily on gentry correspondence, travellers' accounts and guides and advertisements for polite leisure, so our sense of the political process owes much to the electoral correspondence of the gentry and mercantile elites and their agents. As John Triffitt has shown, these can be fundamentally misleading. Instrumental in purpose, they portray townspeople in terms of 'interests' to be manipulated, and assume that power and ideological identities flow from above. They are thus highly flawed guides to the subjective significance of the urban identities involved in political campaigns, which the gentry, for example, often misunderstood.[37]

Yet these interest-based accounts seem vivid and realistic by contrast to the very formal descriptions of urban rituals and associations provided by the rhetorical literature that accompanied these, or by most other urban sources, such as the press. The latter tend to be brief and largely descriptive, while the former, because of the need to portray each cause as the natural product of urban community, claim always to be reflecting rather than constructing urban identity and deny the possibility of legitimate alternative forms of that urban identity. The continuing importance of making this claim – that there can only be one legitimate expression of civic identity (as of national identity) and that this associational activity was an authoritative expression of it – itself suggests the power of the appeal of civic identity and of the common images mustered to define that identity. But equally, the rhetoric prevents us from getting a firm purchase on how exactly that identity might be appropriated by the different groups within urban life. Only when denouncing their opponents' efforts to exploit the same civic and bourgeois values did contemporaries tend to reflect on the construction of identity, and then usually in purely negative terms, accusing their enemies of corruption and deceit.

For example, Tory partisans seeking to attract public support to their cause might establish a charitable society, complete with the usual public events and drawing on the civic image of charity to legitimate their activity, which might well be intended to challenge the patronage offered by a Whig-led corporation. Its own propaganda would make no mention of its partisan purpose, indeed would probably emphasise its impartial character and the social respectability of its members, and perhaps of outside patrons. Private letters about the society, say at election time, might emphasise its pragmatic aims as a means of organising and rewarding voters. In public its opponents would denounce it as a political device, using accusations, perhaps of Jacobitism or of appealing to mob prejudice, to deny the legitimacy of the society as an embodiment of civic and bourgeois values.

Thus, contemporary accounts of the ideological role of bourgeois associations tend either to see them as expressions of a self-evident series of values or systematically to deny them any meaning, save for emulation and self-interest. Significantly, it was this very polarity that helped to fuel one of the most important contemporary expressions of urban identity, namely the strain of political action (and association) that arose overtly from distrust by ordinary citizens of elite manipulation. Hence the great resonance of successive anti-corruption, patriotic, pro-'liberty' campaigns in which the ideology of the independent citizen, resisting both central and local oligarchy, was exploited. This movement, however, was itself deeply ambiguous. On the one hand, it thrived on unmasking the exploitation of power behind the rhetoric of urban politics and showing how rhetoric and action diverged, and it has thus provided much evidence for accounts of the subordination of ideology to interest. Yet, as an ideology, it rested, itself, on the continued potency of the image of the (adult male) freeman or citizen as a political agent.

By the later eighteenth century we enter a third political phase. Changes in urban society, combined with shifts in the politico-religious spectrum, were undermining the older notions of civic identity, just as new towns were growing with a different sense of themselves. A more pluralistic basis for sociability was established with, in the short term, less drive to relate this to civic identity or to ensure that such associations bound together the different sections of the bourgeoisie. A greater gulf probably did emerge between the associations of the lesser and upper bourgeoisie, though certain alienated elites, especially those linked to dissent, found a continued basis for alliance in the language of civic humanism. As a number of recent writers have observed, it was this section of the bourgeoisie which adopted most aggressively the language of 'middle class' to identify itself and the values it stood for, using them to mount a critique of the aristocratic establishment in church and state, but during the conservative backlash of 1776–1815 it failed, despite these appeals to a wider social spectrum, to attract extensive support.[38] Thus it was that when urban society faced its next crisis of identity, with the socio-economic upheavals and political tensions of the early nineteenth century, a rash of new voluntary associations had to rediscover the techniques and languages by which middle-class identity could be forged, as Morris has demonstrated. As ever, history never repeats itself exactly. Pressures from more aggressive working-class voices below, and a more intransigent aristocratic State above, led this new middle class to see itself in rather different terms from its predecessors, drawing heavily on that strain of the dissenting tradition which emphasised the individual conscience and voluntarism in religious and social life. Many of these new bourgeois associations adopted an ideology of liberal individualism, proclaiming the distinctive virtues of voluntary association and individual advancement, and setting these aggressively against establishment forms of collective action in church, State and civic life. Their success has established an image of bourgeois values which has obscured not only the older forms of bourgeois associations, but also the continued dependence of modern bourgeois life on collective action. Yet the enterprise of defining the bourgeoisie by association is as old as urban life itself.

4. Professions, Ideology and the Middling Sort in the Late Sixteenth and Early Seventeenth Centuries

CHRISTOPHER BROOKS

I

There is a long tradition in social theory and historical writing which makes a connection between 'the rise of the professions', the evolution of the middle classes, and the making of the modern industrial world. Consequently it is often taken for granted that before 1750 the professions were numerically insignificant and tied largely to the interests of the aristocracy and gentry.[1] Yet recent research on doctors, lawyers and clergymen is opening new perspectives which suggest that it is time to reconsider some of our preconceptions about the long-term history of the professions. Most notably, viewed from the sixteenth and seventeenth centuries, the social and numerical prominence of groups such as doctors and lawyers in the nineteenth and twentieth centuries appears much less singular than was previously imagined. For example, thanks to a ten-fold increase between 1485 and 1640 in the number of men qualified to practise as attorneys or barristers in England's two-tiered legal profession, the ratio of lawyers to population as a whole was roughly the same in the mid-seventeenth as it was in the early twentieth century.[2]

Nor were the professions mere adjuncts of the elite. Between 1500 and 1700, 70 per cent of the most numerous medical practitioners, the apothecaries and surgeons, came from social backgrounds outside the landed gentry, and a third of those who did claim gentry parentage were in fact the children of the 'lesser' or parish gentry rather than the greater gentry, those who sat on commissions of the peace.[3] In addition, well into the eighteenth century, apothecaries and surgeons were trained primarily by apprenticeship and were organised into guilds with institutional histories which closely resemble those of other occupations.[4] Although they were educated mainly in the universities, the social profile of the membership of the small and elitist Royal College of Physicians in London during the Tudor and Stuart period was much the same, and so too was that of the early-seventeenth-century parish clergy, between two-thirds and three-fourths of whom were of non-gentry origins.[5] Even the lawyers conform to this pattern. Before 1640, the practising bar was drawn just about equally from gentry and non-gentry backgrounds. Moreover, the much more numerous 'lower branch of the legal profession', the attorneys and solicitors, were recruited from the same social groups which supplied entrants to the more elite retail and mercantile trades, and clerkship, apprenticeship in everything but name, was the standard mode of training.[6]

Equally, although the rapacity and wealth of lawyers, in particular, were legendary, the prosperity of most professional men in the early modern period is best described as solid rather than spectacular. Some judges, barristers and crown law officers did achieve great riches, and married into the aristocracy or obtained titles on their own account. However, the law was a high-risk career. Many barristers failed to establish large practices although there is no doubt that some of them found their way into the gentry. Most attorneys lived in towns, and their social standing in the community was very likely to depend on the competition. In large, prosperous towns such as London, Bristol and Norwich, even a wealthy attorney would not have been as rich as the most successful merchant, and they would have wielded much less political power. By contrast, in smaller county towns, even shire towns which were administrative centres, such as Warwick or Stafford, attorneys had by 1640 emerged as part of the local elite, and much the same would have been true of the medical practitioners.[7]

These findings, which derive mainly from mass-biographical studies, locate professional occupations within the social world of the merchant, the artisan and the yeoman farmer, as much as within that of the aristocracy and gentry. In this chapter, they are the starting point for an attempt to explore further the relationship between the professions and the middling sort by looking at words rather than individuals. Concentrating mainly on lawyers and clergymen, it considers the professions as groups of men who produced and interpreted social and political ideology. It tries to probe the relationship between professional discourse and the urban and rural social groups between the gentry and the poor.

Religious, medical and legal rhetoric were important constituents of the early modern mental world. Clergymen, doctors and lawyers dealt with the state of men's souls, their bodies, and their relationship to the broader community. Their sermons, speeches, legal decisions and technical writings helped set the agenda and determine the content of public discourse in an age which was well aware of the importance of ideas in shaping consciousness and hence as a source of power. To give but one example, although medical rhetoric is explored much less thoroughly in this essay than it deserves to be, it was commonplace in the early modern period to diagnose problems in the body politic in terms of illnesses within the human body, and hence to draw on a language where harmony and balance were contrasted with distempers and corruption.[8]

Nevertheless, apart from notable exceptions in connection with theology and religion, there has been relatively little study of the making, propagation and reception of ideology in the sixteenth and seventeenth centuries.[9] Furthermore, much of the work of recent years has been influenced by an inclination of historians of many different outlooks to draw their conclusions in terms of a dichotomy between supposed realms of elite versus 'popular' culture. Some deny that learned or professional discourse had much impact on the actuality of political and economic relationships, which were dominated by the power and interests of the ruling elite.[10] Others have argued that law and religion were hegemonic ideologies which were controlled by the State and the elite, and which were imposed upon, and came into conflict with, traditional community values arising from family, neighbourhood, or civic relationships.[11] The middling sort rarely emerge from such studies as anything other than conduits for and absorbers of world views which they derived largely from other sources.[12] If they often seem to have been written out of the general political and social history of the period, that must be at least in part because they are assumed to have had little influence in determining the terms on which important issues were discussed. The failure to investigate the political and social idioms available to the social groups that composed the middling sort partly explains the confused and inconclusive state of recent writing about the relationship between social structure and politics in the Tudor and Stuart periods.[13]

The value of an examination of professional discourse in this connection is that its articulation in sermons, public speeches, private speculations and published tracts provides insight into the ways in which a broad range of social and economic interests were mediated and expressed. Lawyers and clerics operated within broader ideologies, which were to a degree manipulated and shaped by the Tudor and Stuart monarchs as well as by the aristocracy and gentry. But professional ideology was also influenced by the self-perceptions and interests of practitioners as well as by the fact that the middling sort was their largest single source of clients and composed the audience for many of their public pronouncements about society and the State.

The complexity of the social space occupied by the professions resulted in persistent tensions, which characterised legal and clerical thought throughout the period from the Reformation to the Civil War. There was a conflict between the professional desire to maintain a monopoly over specialised fields of knowledge, and a belief that these were too important to society at large for them to be withheld. Thus, the assertion of authority was counterbalanced by a tendency both to proselytise and to find a language of persuasion which would strike chords within the wider population. Despite the connections between the professions and the political and social elite, their dependence on a broader constituency meant that the ideologies they articulated, and hence the general political language of the day, was much less monolithic than is sometimes assumed. Although the term 'middling sort' does not appear all that often by name, the 'people' outside the ruling elite emerges as an important contemporary category of analysis, one that had a significant impact, for example, on the way in which legal and religious language was mobilised by propagandists for both the royalist and the parliamentarian causes during the Civil War. At the same time, by the later 1640s, one of the most powerful popular onslaughts in English history had been mounted on the professional monopolies and practices of clergymen, doctors and lawyers.

II

To say that the Tudor and Stuart monarchy and the learned professions were mutually supportive is hardly an exaggeration. The crown and its servants had considerable sources of patronage, not to mention the power to appoint bishops and judges. Equally, given the limited coercive powers available to the State, it was widely appreciated that rhetoric was an important weapon in securing the compliance of the subjects,[14] and in this respect the professions, like the middling ranks more generally, supplied loyal subjects of the crown. The famous Elizabethan *Homily on Obedience* was backed up by numerous sermons which put forward powerful arguments for the obedience that subjects owed to the monarchy, because kings had been appointed by God to rule and their subjects were obliged by this divine authority to obey.[15] Similarly, in the wake of the break from Rome in the 1530s, Henry VIII's government issued a set of general statements about the nature of political obligation, which were designed to be used by stewards in the charges which they addressed to juries of town courts, sheriff's tourns, and manorial courts. Apart from a defence of the new royal supremacy over the Church, the principal objective was to remind subjects all over the realm that the king had been appointed by God to rule over the commonwealth and that any disobedience was a violation of holy ordinances.[16] During the remainder of the period, speeches made primarily, though not exclusively, by lawyers on the nature of law and political authority became common features of the meetings of all local courts, from those of the manor to those presided over by the royal justices riding the assize circuits. Most of them undoubtedly promoted both royal authority and the existing social order. In 1588, for example, Sir Richard Crompton told the yeomen and lesser-gentry farmers who composed the grand jury in Shropshire that kings had been ordained by God to govern and that their subjects were commanded to obey. Even in the face of injustice or tyranny, subjects had no right to rebel against the prince. The laws of God, the

laws of nature, and the laws of the realm, all demanded obedience.[17] As Sir Edward Coke, the most famous lawyer of the age,
once put it, law and religion were twin pillars supporting the
king's throne.[18]

There were also many strong links between the aristocracy, the
gentry and at least the upper ranks of the professions. Clergymen
depended on gentry patronage.[19] Bishops and judges sat in the
House of Lords. Very few barristers made it this far in one lifetime,
but many established places for themselves in the gentry and
worked alongside other squires as justices of the peace, or sat as
MPs in the House of Commons.[20] Furthermore, learning of the
sort which was associated with the professions became an important element in a calculus of social differentiation which united the
professions and the gentry. Professional occupations successfully
claimed a special status because of their education and learning.
Physicians and barristers were regularly described as esquires.
Attorneys are difficult to identify as such in contemporary records
because they invariably have 'gent' written after their names, and
so are indistinguishable from minor country squires and the
upper reaches of the urban elite. On the other hand, the professions also had an important impact on the elite. During the late
sixteenth and early seventeenth centuries, it became fashionable
for the gentry to attend the universities of Oxford and Cambridge,
and the inns of court and inns of chancery in London, places
which were essentially academies for the professions.[21] While there
is good reason to question exactly how much the children of the
elite learned while they were attending these institutions, one of
the most striking features of the early Stuart era was the apparent
keenness of squires, and sometimes their wives, to sit down in the
wainscotted studies of their country houses to work out their views
on law, government and religion, or to add to the store of family
medical knowledge.[22]

Nevertheless, despite all this, professional practitioners also had
much in common with the middling sort, as well as an identity
which was to a large extent based on their own self image. As has
already been observed, many professional occupations recruited
from prosperous townsmen and yeomen who made up local
elites.[23] Based as it was on apprenticeship, the training of apothecaries, surgeons and attorneys was little different from that of
other moderately affluent urban and rural social groups. Indeed,

in an age when the culture of guilds was theoretically based on the possession of a specialised skill, which was mastered through a long period of training, contemporaries did not draw distinctions between 'professions' and other occupations as easily as we do today.[24] Instead, it was the type of learning which professionals possessed, rather than social status or institutional forms of organisation, which set them apart from other groups, and which also added an independent dynamic to their thought.

According to the influential Cambridge theologian, William Perkins, the callings of lawyer, schoolmaster, physician, and minister of the word occupied the first place amongst all occupations because they alone required academic learning and judgement.[25] Some clergymen and lawyers went so far as to define their own importance in terms of their disciplines. In 1632, for instance, the Leicestershire clergyman, Thomas Prestell, was accused of claiming that the calling of a minister was higher than that of a king, because, while the king had power only over the bodies of men, the minister had power over both the soul and the body.[26] If anything, lawyers were even more inclined than the clergy to promote their own self-esteem in terms of what they saw as the centrality of the institutions and ideas within which they worked. Thus, in a speech given at Grays Inn in 1589, Sir Christopher Yelverton began by saying that he could not 'sufficiently, nor amply enough magnifie the majestie and dignitie of the law'. He continued:

> The necessity of law is such that as in some nations, where all learning is forbidden, yet the houses of law be suffered, that thereby the people may the sooner be induced to civility and the better provoked to the performance of their duty ... to live without government is hellish and to govern without Lawe is brutish ... the Law (saith Tully) containeth all wisdom, and all the rules of philosophy.[27]

However, if learning and knowledge united the professions, they were also the most important sources of internal dissension within the various groups of doctors, lawyers and clergymen, and the cause of conflict with those whom they aimed to exclude from practice. The division which exists today within the English legal profession, between the bar, which specialises in pleading in court, and the solicitors, who traditionally have been associated with the practical side of legal work, has a history which stretches back into the Middle Ages, but it was strengthened during the early modern period largely because the inns of court, where barristers received their education, excluded the attorneys, who were trained by apprenticeship, from their membership.[28] Quarrels between the apothecaries and surgeons, who dealt in drugs or in the 'mechanical' or 'pragmatic' side of medical work, and the physicians, who were trained either at the universities or through the Royal College of Physicians, were a constant feature of medical history throughout the period from 1500 to 1730.[29] Furthermore, if plebeian tin-tub preachers and self-styled theologians were a thorn in the side of the clerics, there can be no doubt that any thorough consideration of the 'legal profession', and especially the medics, would have to include the numerous practitioners who were, in a formal sense, imperfectly qualified.[30]

Controversies between the qualified and outsiders were often about little more than the maintenance of social status and restrictive practices. But in the minds of contemporaries they were also associated with attempts to maintain standards of professional service. For example, in 1633, Alice Mays, 'a doctoress or Doctor Woman', was accused of murder by causing the death of patients she had treated in the vicinity of the town of King's Lynn. Although she claimed that she was qualified to dispense internal medicines by virtue of having studied 'learned physic' with eminent doctors in Cambridge and York, Alice's skills are perhaps best described as those of a 'cunning woman', an amateur herbalist who might also practise some magic. Despite several attempts by the authorities to try her, local juries refused to convict on the grounds that no one could convincingly establish that her prescriptions had killed. Thus it was left to the assize judge, Sir Robert Heath, to stop her from prescribing medicines to be taken internally. It was, he said, impossible that a 'silly woman' should have the skill to administer 'inward physic', but for 'outward applications' she might happily have some knowledge.[31]

In a period when the skill of 'empirics', especially in the medical field, was often likely to have been as effective for the patient as the Galenic learning of physicians, distinctions between theoretical, or 'scientific', knowledge, which could be obtained from books, and empirical knowledge, which was accumulated through practice and observation, very often amounted to little more than a weapon in the struggle to maintain professional (and gender) hegemony, especially when it is clear that many of the so-called empiric practitioners, such as apothecaries, surgeons and attorneys, were hardly ignorant.[32] But, although the evidence is ambiguous, those concerned with the case of Alice Mays were, after all, convinced that her cures were murderous. There was another side of professional attitudes towards knowledge which stimulated campaigns to improve standards of practice in the interest of the public, and to propagandise for the acceptance within society at large of the professionals' way of looking at the world.[33]

Inspired by the influence of humanist thought on education, and facilitated by the development of the printing trade, the first half of the sixteenth century in particular was notable for the production of a large number of books which aimed to propagate knowledge both within the professions and to the wider public. The phenomenon can be illustrated in a nutshell through the publishing career of the Oxford-educated physician and lawyer, Thomas Phaer (1510–60). He translated Vergil's *Aeneid*, put into English a French work on childhood health and diseases, *The Regiment of Life* (1545), and edited a compilation of legal instruments, *The New Book of Presidents* (1543). Like many other Protestant 'commonwealths men' of his time, Phaer's inspiration was the conviction that the information he possessed was potentially useful for all ranks of society, and a belief that it was wrong to keep 'the people in ignorance' by locking up the 'treasure' of knowledge in untranslated Latin works.[34] No less important, his example was followed frequently during the course of the sixteenth century as large numbers of works were written and published with the specific intention of making them available to the literate middling ranks of the population.[35] Amongst the more 'pragmatic' professions, especially, the power of the written word was perceived as a powerful tool for breaking through traditional ignorance.[36]

Yet, alongside this enthusiasm for publishing, there was also controversy about how far knowledge about religion or law should be opened to the wider public. Lawyers wanted to convince people of the benefits which would accrue to them by adhering to the rule of law. A powerful element in the vocational self-image of post-Reformation clergy was the idea that the objective of a Protestant preaching ministry was to guide their parishioners in the joint project of reading and interpreting the scriptures. But self-interest inevitably produced contrary arguments, which reinforced professional claims to an authoritative monopoly over their fields of expertise. No less important, many contemporaries, both lay and professional alike, were convinced that disseminating certain kinds of knowledge too widely might threaten the political and social *status quo*.

The paradigmatic issue in both respects was the ongoing debate which began in the reign of Henry VIII about whether the Bible should be translated into English, who should read it, and how far the Protestant notion of a 'priesthood of all believers' entitled any man or woman, armed with the scriptures, to make their own interpretation of their relationship to God and the Church.[37] This tension in religious life was mirrored in a parallel debate about whether the law, which was written primarily in barbarous forms of Latin and Norman French, should be translated entirely into English and perhaps even codified.[38] In the minds of many lawyers, the fact that the scriptures had already been put into English defeated arguments about the adverse social consequences of publication. In his *Advancement of Learning*, for example, the polymath lawyer, Sir Francis Bacon, argued that 'to say that a blind custom of obedience should be a surer obligation than duty taught and understood, ... is to affirm that a blind man may tread surer by a guide than a seeing man can by light'.[39] Nevertheless, Bacon was contesting the notion that widening the availability of knowledge would undermine reverence for laws and government, and, after the first decade of the seventeenth century, although the publication of English legal manuals continued, calls for reforms in the language and structure of the law largely disappeared, not to resurface again until the 1640s.[40] In short, an impulse which stressed the importance of understanding and conscience in human behaviour conflicted with social, political and professional imperatives which stressed unqualified obedience and the expediency for the elite of keeping those over whom they ruled in ignorance. To take an economic and social illustration, at the same time as a steward in Lancashire practised the archaic Aristotelian technique of using songs to help manorial tenants remember their rights at law, another lawyer, William Barlee, protested to Lord Treasurer Burghley that some members of his profession opposed making the law of copyholds openly available in print because this would enable 'the common sort of people' to vex lords of manors.[41]

III

These debates about access to learned discourse were of more than theoretical interest. They had a practical significance because, throughout the Elizabethan and early Stuart periods, professional success depended very largely on the cultivation of work for people from a surprisingly broad social range, not least those who composed the middling sort. The rate of civil litigation in 1600, for example, was probably higher than it has been in any other period of English history before or since, and no less than 70 per cent of those involved in pleas in the two main common law courts, King's Bench and Common Pleas, came from urban and rural social groups outside the landed gentry. Work for the lesser gentry, the yeomanry, urban merchants and artisans constituted the bread and butter of barristers and attorneys, as indeed it also did for the medical practitioners.[42]

Lawyers and clergymen, like apothecaries and surgeons, could not avoid, therefore, being aware of the interests of the population beyond the monarch, the aristocracy and the gentry. The important question is how far this fact can be said to have determined the character of social and political life during the period or to have influenced the content of professional ideology. For instance, whilst historians quite naturally accept that the rule of the gentry in the localities was based on both the deferential posture of their social inferiors and the control over legal processes which their positions as justices of the peace enabled them to exercise, the picture may not have seemed so clear-cut to contemporaries. Recent work on the criminal legal processes, on local officials such as constables, and the composition of juries at quarter sessions and assizes, has uncovered an important participatory role for members of the rural middling sort.[43] Equally, one of the most common criticisms of the increase in the number of lawyers during the period was that they encouraged ordinary people to go to law in the pursuit of their interests. Even in the relatively remote county of Lancashire, by the early seventeenth century, people of quite modest means employed local attorneys to present their cases at sessions, and it was one of the virtues of the notorious court of Star Chamber that it could be used to bring actions against JPs who arbitrarily exercised their powers.[44] As one clergyman put it in the 1630s, the problem with the lawyer was that he 'flatteringly sheweth every man a fairer face how illfavoured soever he be. Thus can he persuade the simple swaine that his matter will bear a strong action' no matter how weak it really was.[45]

No less important, a large amount of public professional rhetoric was addressed to middling urban and rural social groups, and for that reason alone could not afford to be too far out of tune with their perceptions. An unusually intriguing illustration of this was the admission of the long-serving minister of Blackfriars, William Gouge, that the women in his congregation disagreed with his interpretation of the Biblical duty of wives to subordinate themselves to their husbands.[46] But most clergymen had to preach to congregations composed of ordinary people of moderate status. Consequently many of the commonplaces of clerical thought were perfectly compatible with traditional urban and rural values. William Perkins's view of vocations, which stressed the importance of each man contentedly fulfilling his role in life, was little more than a theological gloss on a style of life which was familiar in urban guild culture.[47] Similarly, the puritan stress on sobriety and self-control had a counterpart in the more secular notion of 'honesty', which was to some extent summarised by the life-size statues on the entrance of the medieval guildhall in London, which depicted the civic virtues of Discipline, Justice, Fortitude, and Temperance.[48] Even the patriarchal turn of much clerical thought was tailored to the concerns of merchants and artisans, not to mention apothecaries and barristers, who managed large households of servants and apprentices, and who also found it necessary to define their position with regard to another potential claimant to authority, their wives.[49]

It is true that the lawyers' vision of social relations in certain respects contrasted with, even though it did not necessarily oppose, some traditional rural values based on neighbourliness, or urban ones which stressed the non-contentious settlement of disputes, in the search for 'charity' and 'love'.[50] But it is also notable that legal thought had little time for paternalism, deference, or a hierarchical society unified by great chains of being.[51] The rhetoric of the legal profession, moreover, consistently relied on persuasion as much as it did on authoritarian pronouncement. Speeches delivered to rural grand juries, whose ranks were filled by husbandmen, yeomen and the lesser gentry, or to urban corporations, frequently described the divine origins of monarchical authority, but the lawyers who made them were also quick to add that there was a practical inducement to obedience, one which was based on self-interest. Authority made possible the rule of law, and the rule of law prevented social and political chaos and protected the persons and property of the subjects from arbitrary power. In his address to the Shropshire grand jury in 1588 (which was later published), Richard Crompton stressed that in England loyalty was compensated for by traditional liberties such as the fact that the subjects were not liable to 'taxes or tallages' without their consent.[52] According to Sir Francis Ashley, who delivered a series of lectures on Magna Carta at the Middle Temple in 1616, the law enshrined not just franchises and special privileges, but 'liberties', and indeed 'freedoms', which were inheritable by all the freemen of England. These included the right to due process of law, trial by one's peers, and protection against the 'oppressions' of landlords, justices of the peace, or the ruling bodies of urban corporations. Like many other leading lawyers of the Jacobean period, he was clear that royal grants of monopolies, which lined the pockets of courtiers at the expense of ordinary tradesmen, were against the law of the land.[53]

There was also a well documented line in professional discourse which was openly hostile to abuses of power by the economically or socially overmighty. An often-repeated tenet of Christian humanism was that the powerful should not use their strength to oppress the weak.[54] In legal thought, this precept found a number of practical expressions in ideas about the foundation of political societies, the history of England, and in the notions of lawyers about the application of the rule of law itself. Thus, in his treatise on the *Origins of Cities*, the early-seventeenth-century town clerk of Winchester, Henry Trussell, developed a perfectly conventional theme in his explanation of the reasons why government according to law was first instituted.

When the distinction of property by *meum* and *tuum* had found out sufficient Combustible stuff to set Ambition on fire, and by the reflection thereof gave Avarice ... means ... to see how to increase its profit, as the other to extend its power, then the weakest went to the wall, And those that were simply modest were either enforced to serve others, or starve themselves, loosing either property, or liberty (nay often life) to the stronger.[55]

If one of the purposes of political society was to protect the weak, and indeed the moderately well off, from the overmighty, a natural corollary was that abuses of power by the great magnates were an evil. As Sir Henry Yelverton explained, in a charge to an Elizabethan meeting of quarter sessions in Northamptonshire, the disobedience and oppressions of the great were a major source of danger to the State. If there were no laws to bridle them, neither could the people live quietly nor the prince rule safely.[56] And in fact, apart from limited privileges accorded the titled nobility, the common law, as opposed to some parliamentary legislation, took little account of social status, as opposed to age or gender, as a criterion for decision-making.[57] In the words of an early-seventeenth-century recorder of London, Sir Anthony Benn, the value of the rule of law was that it allowed '*every man*' (my italics) to go his own way and accumulate wealth.[58]

Expressions such as these articulated a justification for political allegiance, and, indeed, the existing social order, in terms which took into account the interests of a 'people' outside the ruling elite.[59] Nor is there any doubt that, in this context, 'the people' included the middling sort. The Elizabethan legal writer, William Lambarde, made it plain that at least one of the many charges he delivered to Kentish grand juries was aimed specifically towards the 'middle sort' of small farmers.[60] A seventeenth-century treatise of knighthood refers to the 'yeomanry or common people', a group which was allegedly richer and more numerous in England than elsewhere.[61] Furthermore, since lawyers and clergymen, like other learned men of the period, drew their principal categories of political analysis from Aristotle, they would have been aware of the theoretical connection between the economic interests of various social groups and the ways in which these might find expression in the constitutional arrangements of particular states. The majority must, for example, have been familiar with the three fundamental types of government which Aristotle outlined in *The Politics:* monarchy, the rule of one person; aristocracy (or oligarchy), the rule of the best (or richest); and democracy, where political power was vested in 'the people'.[62] Apart from anything else, references to these alternatives not infrequently appeared in the speeches which were made at the opening of sessions of parliament by the lawyers appointed by the monarch to serve as speakers of the House of Commons.[63]

Given the potential significance of these simple equations about the relationship between social structure and the constitutions of states, it is hardly surprising that 'the people' was also a contested category. The legal notion that there was little technical difference between those below the rank of knight was important because it cut across other outlooks, which stressed social distinctions based on birth, status, education, or the holding of office, while at the same time enabling 'the people' to be an expansive term in political discourse, which could include the gentry as well as the middling sort.[64] But public descriptions of the forms of government inevitably came to the conclusion that monarchy was the most effective by far, and more hierarchical ideas about the social and political order had a wide currency. Judges and JPs, the holders of commissions from the king, certainly regarded themselves as the political superiors of the juries with whom they dealt at quarter sessions and assizes. In 1619, the judge, Sir John Dodderidge, was even the butt of a satire because he had apparently complained about the social quality of a Huntingdonshire jury.[65] In towns, the oligarchic progression from disenfranchised apprentice, to freeman, to common councillor, alderman, and mayor, tended to lead to a distinction between rulers and ruled. This boundary was in fact frequently challenged in the early seventeenth century, especially in connection with election disputes where freemen householders challenged oligarchic ruling bodies, but there were limits. It was entirely natural for the puritan lawyer, William Prynne, to argue in the Tewkesbury election case of 1640 that the granting of the parliamentary vote to every inhabitant, including servants, women and almsmen, would enable the 'very scum of the people' to overrule the 'better sort'.[66] Since professional men, like the middling sort more generally, included individuals who might at any given point be either rulers or ruled, professional opinion about the political significance of the people altered over time and according to individual dispositions and circumstances.[67]

Some lawyers, like James Morice or William Lambarde in the Elizabethan period, and John Selden in the early seventeenth century, envisaged the origins of political society emerging from a contract between ruler and people.[68] But, even if one concluded, as most probably did, that monarchical government was God-given rather than the product of human agency, it was a commonplace of humanist jurisprudence that laws worked best as a means of governing a society if the people had had a hand in formulating them through a representative institution.[69] On the other hand, especially during the early seventeenth century, lawyers who were themselves amongst the rulers frequently detected too much interest by the people in matters which were above their station. Sir Anthony Benn observed that 'as into the ark of the highest misteries every Tinker will in these days be peeping, and not satisfied will also be prating, so there are in government and state affaires certain Eavesdroppers and wise fellows that will not only let and hinder this chariot ... but others there are that will be ever reforming the reins.' Elsewhere, in an unpublished essay, he revealingly associated popular disquiet about James I's financial difficulties with the puritan emphasis on the personal interpretation of the Bible. The one might lead to chaos in the state, just as the other produced the religious confusion of anabaptism.[70]

Amongst the early seventeenth-century clergy, much of the surviving published material emphasises the importance of obedience to established authority, but it also reveals that the political role of the people was widely canvassed in controversial works which aimed to discredit the allegedly 'popular' political theories of the Papists. Sermons delivered at meetings of local courts such as quarter sessions and assizes in the first two decades of the seventeenth century relentlessly describe and then reject Catholic monarchomach theories which were based on the principle of popular sovereignty. Thus in 1614, Bartholomew Parsons, a chaplain to the Bishop of Salisbury, explained to the Wiltshire assize court the subversive doctrines of Cardinal Bellarmine, who allegedly held that all government depended on the 'consent of the multitude'.[71] But, intriguingly, such sermons also frequently suggest that other members of the profession might not have been following the same line, and that 'the people' themselves might have opinions of their own. For instance, at the Warwick assizes in 1619, Samuel Burton pointed out that since the beginning of Christianity, there had been foolish apostles who had mistakenly extended the idea of Christian liberty in order to argue that men were free from subjection and tribute. He claimed that the current age was addicted to speaking ill of rulers and criticised those 'zealous Preachers, which seem so dearly to tender the instruction of the people', who spent all their time attacking Maypoles rather than pressing 'the point of Obedience more closely to the Consciences of the People'.[72]

It is, of course, hardly surprising that sermons delivered before judges, lawyers and justices of the peace should emphasise the authority of the rulers, especially if, as seems the case, they evidently thought themselves under threat. But it is no less important to stress that in this period vigorous support for the divinely appointed nature of authority could also be cast in language which was designed to appeal to the merchants, tradesmen and professional men who composed the urban elites. At King's Lynn in 1634, the recorder, Francis Parlett, skilfully drew on the stock of traditional urban rhetoric about harmony and love in order to elaborate a patriarchal account of the authority of governors and government. He told the mayor on his installation that 'The government you are to enter into is over a town consisting of divers families, not by a natural necessity, but by a civil subordinate delegation from him that is the supreme natural parent.' The metaphors which appear most frequently in Parlett's numerous speeches to grand juries, and on occasions of civic ceremonial, were ones based on love, community and subordination. 'Love the town and it will love you. The oath of office is the vow of matrimony. The mayor is the civil husband of a civil wife.'[73] On a more practical level, moreover, this rhetorical support for the urban governors was backed up by legal decisions which reinforced their grip on power. In a famous opinion of 1598, the royal judges asserted that even in towns where charters prescribed that mayors, aldermen and other officials were elected by the commonalty [all the freemen], more recent ordinances limiting the franchise to selected members were agreeable to the law because they prevented popular disorder and confusion.[74]

Yet if judicial decisions in general favoured the interests of richer urban oligarchs, the law also formed the most effective means for townsmen outside the ruling circles to express their grievances and concerns. Attorneys were frequently to be found in the midst of the many challenges to local authorities which were based on differing interpretations of charters or customary practices.[75] A wide range of social relations arising out of apprenticeship and trade practices were tested in the courts, and in London and provincial towns it was common by the early seventeenth century for both individuals and guilds to employ legal advisors.[76] It is an error to say that the judiciary was completely hostile to guild control of economic activity, but prescriptive corporate powers did tend to be narrowly interpreted,[77] and in the famous case of the Merchant Tailors of Ipswich (1615), the judges decided that, within limits, the common-law right of every man to earn his own living outweighed the claims of corporate privilege.[78]

This last case, like a number of others initiated by individuals, revealed the tensions which existed in legal thought between the imperatives of order and the rights an Englishman might reasonably expect to enjoy. For instance, in 1616, James Bagg, a burgess of Plymouth, brought a suit in the court of King's Bench to have himself reinstated as a freeman, after he had been disenfranchised for criticising the mayor for carrying out his office 'foolishly', and calling for the support of the other burgesses to help throw him out of office and elect another.[79] The judges declared the disenfranchisement illegal because, in the words of Sir Edward Coke, such a course of action would force a man to close his shop and consequently ruin his trade, credit, and means of earning a living. The freedom belonged to Bagg as his freehold for life and could not arbitrarily be taken from him. Nevertheless, Lord Chancellor Ellesmere criticised Coke's claim, in this case, that the King's Bench had the authority to apply considerations of due process of law in order to prevent alleged misgovernment which tended to oppress or wrong the subject. Perhaps facetiously, Coke's own published report of the case reminds his readers to note that much was said at the trial 'to exort Citizens and Burgesses to yield obedience and Reverence to the Chief Magistrates in their Cities and Boroughs, because they derive their authority from the King'.[80]

IV

Neither the common law nor the Protestant religion were simply hegemonic ideologies which descended from London outwards and downwards to the rest of the population. Common access to the scriptures, and notions of spiritual equality, promised the literate middling sort some control over their religious lives, just as the ideal of the rule of law in theory guaranteed a certain degree of protection from arbitrary power in social and economic relationships, a protection which was enunciated in terms of equality before the law. At the very least, the public expressions of lawyers, like the sermons of the clergy, ensured that a generalised discourse about the nature of political life, and the place of the individual person in society, penetrated surprisingly deeply into the localities. Common-law ideology, for example, was largely consistent with the realities of a highly litigious society in which it was common for tenants to sue for their rights against landlords, or, indeed, to use the courts to challenge Puritan attempts to enforce moral regulation in the localities. Thomas Hobbes's premise, that one of the prime functions of civil society was to ensure that people kept their contracts, would have been easily appreciated by the thousands of artisans and yeomen who used courts to settle their business dealings.[81]

But it is at the same time clear that the more general political impact of professional ideologies was hardly straightforward. The common law and Puritan religious convictions have frequently been depicted as the enemies of early Stuart government, as part of the ideological armoury which was employed against the king on the 'high road' to the civil wars of the 1640s.[82] But this is to oversimplify highly complex cultural constructs. The participatory characteristics which meant that the common law represented the interests of those outside the political elite also meant that those same social groups could find much that was satisfactory in existing social and political arrangements. If the king was the fountain of justice, the protector of social order and the property of the subjects, then the logic of the case that obedience to the monarchy was a practical as well as a moral duty could well be compelling. Equally, as Patrick Collinson has argued, there was as much in Puritan thought which coincided with conventional values as there was to challenge them.[83]

Even so, it is no less misleading to reduce professional discourses to unifying or integrative ideologies which inevitably led to, or reflected, consensus within the wider population.[84] The Reformation and religious controversy during the sixteenth century meant that questions about political as well as moral authority were much more widely ventilated than they are, for example, today. Furthermore, as we have seen, the range of social interests and intellectual positions which influenced professional thought provided a potentially rich diversity of opinion. In times of political tension, like the 1620s and 1630s, when unpopular royal policies in connection with war, taxation and religion produced expressions of discontent, both arguments for the crown and its critics were articulated in legal and religious rhetoric which had multivalent resonances, but which, nevertheless, reveals distinctive views about the nature of politics and society.

Within the Church, conflict emerged between the so-called Arminian and Puritan factions of the clergy. The former advocated the suppression of debate about the contentious theological issues, increased episcopal control over the clergy, and a return to more ritualistic forms of worship. The latter, by contrast, maintained their adherence to a preaching ministry, Calvinist theological doctrine, and, according to their enemies, a greater say for ordinary laymen in the conduct of their spiritual lives.[85] As we have already seen, a range of political opinion also existed within the legal profession, and in both fields a general acceptance of the value of authority and an ambivalent attitude towards the people may well have provided common ground for the majority of practitioners. However, during the reigns of both James I and Charles I there were also a number of telling conflicts between some of the lawyers and some members of the Arminian faction of the clergy, which reflect the political impact of the 'people' outside the ruling elite on professional perceptions of politics.

In 1637, for example, just after the judges had delivered their decision in the famous case to determine the legality of Ship Money, a Northamptonshire clergyman called Thomas Harrison walked into the Court of Common Pleas at Westminster and accused Sir Richard Hutton, one of the judges who had dissented from the majority decision in favour of the king, of treason and moving 'the people' to sedition.[86] Justice Hutton eventually won an action of slander against Thomas Harrison, but the incident, along with others, appears to have stuck in the minds of members of the legal profession. In February 1640, the Northamptonshire lawyer, Edward Bagshaw, alluded to the case in the opening remarks of a lecture he gave at the Middle Temple on the relationship between the civil and ecclesiastical jurisdictions. In his view, both the ancient and honourable common law, as well as the lawyers, had recently been 'traduced in Pamphlets, jeered and derided in plays, and play books, and openly ridiculed and slandered at Bars at Law' by clergymen. In the event, Bagshaw's own lecture, which argued for limitations on the temporal authority of the churchmen, was suppressed by Charles I and Archbishop

Laud, a setback which did not, however, prevent the lawyer from riding out of London accompanied by fifty or sixty fellow members of the inns of court.[87]

To an extent, these and other similar incidents reflect a professional animosity between the lawyers and the clergy which dated back at least as far as the break from Rome in the 1530s.[88] But in the 1620s and 1630s broader issues were at stake. Thomas Harrison claimed that it was the opinion of all the 'Orthodox divines in this Kingdom' that it was unlawful to refuse to pay Ship Money, and in general, from the 1620s, if not before, clergymen of an Arminian persuasion were turning arguments about the divine ordination of government into reminders of the dangers of popular rule, the necessity for obedience to the monarchy, and the right of Charles I to make levies against the property of his subjects.[89]

By contrast, one of the most persuasive elements in traditional legal ideology was the proposition that the law protected the lands and goods of the subjects, hence legalistic arguments in defence of property rights formed the basis for much of the criticism which was directed against royal policies between 1625 and the autumn of 1641. Whether or not an individual happened to accept theories about the divine ordination of government, it was a commonplace of juristic thought that there was an important distinction to be drawn between what was described as a royal or lawful monarchy, where the king ruled according to the law of nature and protected the property of his subjects, and a seignorial or lordly monarchy, where the king was lord of the goods and persons of his subjects, and where he ruled as the father of a family ruled over his slaves.[90] This connection between seignorial monarchy and the absence of a clear right to property or freedom of the person lies behind much of the rhetoric of bondage, villeinage and slavery which was used by MPs critical of royal policies both in the later 1620s and during the early 1640s. In the parliament of 1628, for example, Francis Alford referred to the need to maintain a legal and royal monarchy. On the same occasion, Sir Dudley Digges said that a king that was not tied to laws was a king of slaves, and Sir Edward Coke pointed out that a lord might tax his villeins 'high and low, but this is against the franchise of the land for freemen'.[91]

These defences in parliament of rights to property obviously reflected the interests of the gentry as much as those of the middling sort. But, as the quotation from Coke suggests, what is particularly interesting is that they were couched in legal language associated with copyholders, that quintessential group of small farmers whose rights had undergone a significant transition during the Tudor period. Before the mid-sixteenth century, copyholders were largely denied access to the common law courts, and the judges held that copyhold was a form of base tenure, analogous to the bond-tenure or villeinage which was associated in the Middle Ages with serfdom.[92] The change came during the reign of Elizabeth, when the courts entertained the cases of copyholders and ruled against the claims of lords of manors to exact arbitrary or excessive entry fines from them. In 1600, Coke himself argued that 'if the lords might assess excessive fines at their pleasures', this would destroy copyholders and thereby ruin a 'great part of the realm'.[93] In his reading on Magna Carta in 1616, Sir Francis Ashley said that when a lord exacted excessive and unreasonable fines this amounted to oppression contrary to the liberties of Englishmen.[94] In short, copyholders had become freemen of England, not bondmen subservient to a feudal lord who could make arbitrary claims on their property.

Hence, by 1628, the rights of all landholders, large and small, with respect to the most powerful lord in the realm, the king, were being defended in a language which arose partly from professional jurisprudence and partly from the conflicts between small farmers and their landlords. There is no better single example of the influence of a group within the middling sort on professional discourse, and indeed, political ideology more generally. Furthermore, the message was certainly broadcast to a public outside parliament,[95] and, starting with King James I, there is a consistent line of hostile reaction which explicitly associated lawyers with a dangerous brand of populism. The king was irritated by the 'sharpe edge and vaine popular humour of Lawyers that think they are not eloquent and bold spirited enough except they meddle with the king's prerogative'.[96] In a bitter attack on Sir Edward Coke, Lord Chancellor Ellesmere warned Coke's successor as Chief Justice of England, Sir Henry Montague, that 'it is dangerous in a Monarchy for a man holding a high and eminent place, to be ambitiously popular'.[97] A correspondent writing in 1634, about the death of attorney general William Noy, noted that Noy had been held in high esteem amongst the people for his extraordinary ability in the law and his courage in pleading the 'subjects' cause though against the King, in the 1620s. But, since Noy had joined the King's service and been the architect of several notably unpopular fiscal policies, opinion had changed. 'Divers sorts of men now strike not to express a gladness that he is gone.'[98] Finally, one of Thomas Harrison's charges against Justice Hutton was that the judge had broadcast his dissenting opinion about Ship Money in speeches which he delivered on circuit. The alleged consequence was that all of Harrison's Northamptonshire parishioners were debating the validity of the levy, and it is worth noting that there are a number of known instances where grievances against royal policy in the 1630s were expressed through the medium of the grand jury.[99]

Yet, there was, as always amongst lawyers and the clergy, another line of thought which identified 'popularity' with a threat to the professions as well as to the king and the existing social order. Not surprisingly, given his background as a loyal servant to King Charles, the judge Sir Robert Health spied in the 1630s a dangerous time when witchcraft and popular sedition shared a common disregard for divine authority. Attempts to promote a popular belief that laws, liberties and the privileges of parliament were at stake were little different from the faith in charms which was characteristic of witchcraft.[100] In a sermon which he delivered at Lincoln assizes in March 1637, a royal chaplain, Thomas Hurste, hit with comprehensive clarity on the issues which united the professions with the divine authority of the monarchy.[101] Speaking a few months after the judgment in the Ship Money case, Hurste quipped that 'some' might think a discussion of 'the power of one man over another' either 'Apocryphall' or 'an Exchequer-chamber [the court where Ship Money was tried] case'. However, he justified his decision with a dark warning:

> Some (especially inferiors) think that one should be as good as another: that as we were at our births, and shall be at our deaths, so in our lives we should be equal. Being Christian brethren in Divinity, and partaking the same Sacraments, so (Anabaptistically) we should bee in Politics; and the perching of one man over another is but human invention and commanding policy.

Hurste went on to point out that insurrection and rebellion always began with 'noise' for the 'liberties' or privileges of the people, but only became particularly dangerous when the bonds of conscience which were upheld by religion came under attack. Predictably, his response to this dangerous state of affairs was to assert the view that the authority of 'emperors' stands 'not only upon the crutches or stilts of human power, but upon the firm basis of divine institution that some should ride on horse-back, while others walk on foot'. But he also warned his audience not to encourage the people by throwing 'dirt' at the king's government, and, aware that he was addressing a gathering of judges (including, incidentally, Sir Richard Hutton), lawyers and county magistrates, he also took particular care to point out how necessary it was for those who acted in the names of law and religion to maintain a solidarity with each other. 'The people' would neglect both callings if their practitioners did not substitute mutual support for mutual recrimination. '*Theologia [and] Ius* must *fraternizare*.'[102]

V

It is a commonplace of early modern historiography that contemporaries lacked the vocabulary to make a class analysis of society and politics. But the evidence presented in this essay suggests that the proposition is only half true. The intellectual tools available to the learned professions, as well as pressure from their congregations and clients, meant that social groups between the poor and the elite were a constant preoccupation. Sometimes referred to specifically as the middling sort, but more often described simply as the people, they had been appealed to ever since the break from Rome in campaigns to publicise professional ways of looking at the world. But, particularly during the 1620s and 1630s, a kind of populist politics was identified as a threat to authority, both monarchical and professional. In the hands of a writer like Thomas Hurste, moreover, the expression of this problem provides an extremely penetrating contemporary guide to the fate of both political authority and the learned professions themselves during the calamitous years of civil war in the 1640s and 1650s.

During the Short Parliament and the first year of the Long Parliament, lawyers and laymen alike attacked royal policies which threatened the property of the subjects, and criticised the clergy for telling people that they had no rights to their liberty or property.[103] But, as many historians have observed, the critical question about the outbreak of civil war is how did the king eventually gather a party which would fight in his defence, and in this connection the development of an attack on the established church and the traditional balance of the constitution played a major role.[104] As Thomas Hurste predicted in 1637, hostility to clerical politics and Arminian religious policies led to a profound questioning of both the episcopal structure of the English church and the control of the clergy over the profession of minister of God. In January 1641, the Root and Branch petition, which called for the abolition of bishops, was presented to parliament accompanied by 30,000 signatures. It ushered in more than two decades of deeply divisive controversy about the degree to which the English people were entitled to select their own path to salvation rather than accept the one which was purveyed to them by the authority of the bishops, the established clergy, and the Book of Common Prayer. Some of the sects which eventually emerged even went so far as to allow women into the pulpit.[105]

At the same time, a backlash of support for episcopacy was the principal cause around which a Royalist party began to coalesce in the autumn of 1641.[106] Although ostensibly religious matters, questions about the structure of the church were also professional problems, and seeing them as such can help us to understand that they involved the same fundamental questions about authority which had been at issue for more than a century. Royalist rhetoric was quick to draw the familiar analogy between a breakdown in the authority of the church and the collapse of civil authority more generally. For example, a petition from Cheshire criticised the use of pamphlets and pulpits to spread ideas 'dangerously exciting a disobedience to the established form of Government'. Stirring up the 'Common people' would lead to 'an Anarchy, which we have just cause to pray against, as fearing the consequence would prove the utter loss of learning and laws, which must necessarily produce an extermination of nobility, gentry, and order, if not religion'.[107]

Parliamentary propaganda, not surprisingly, exploited the more populist strand within professional thought. Writers like the sometime barrister of Lincoln's Inn, Henry Parker, aimed to show that since, as nearly everyone agreed, government was supposed to serve the people, it was logical to support parliament, the institution which claimed its authority in the name of the people. In addition, Parker, in particular, frequently buttressed his position by drawing on analogies from everyday legal practice. For instance, he explained that the right of the king to the property of his subjects was not the same as the property the king had in his horse. Instead, the king held his subjects' property in trust, and, as everyone knew, a trustee who held to the use of another was responsible for protecting the property of the beneficiary, not laying it to waste. Although the king might be said to rule his subjects in the same way as a husband ruled his wife, both relationships were in fact subject to the intervention of the law. Another author justified rebellion by arguing that since 'the People may be legally assembled to aprehend Robbers, nay to deliver a possession forceably detained against the sentence of some inferior court' it followed that they ought to 'bistirr themselves to keep in being and preserve that Government which maintains them in possession of their liberty and property'.[108]

As Conrad Russell has recently reminded us, the king, no less than parliament, had by 1642 adopted a stance which enabled him to claim that he was fighting for the rule of law and the maintenance of true religion. Yet to argue, as Russell does, from these facts to the conclusion that there were no significant expressions of ideological differences between the two sides, is to ignore the evidence which we have seen, from throughout the sixteenth and seventeenth centuries, for religious, legal and political discourse to polarise around notions which stressed absolute authority versus those which advocated openness and a greater or lesser degree of popular legitimisation.[109] For example, an understanding of the political allegiance of the rich Dorsetshire squire, Sir John Strangewayes, who had opposed royal policies in the 1620s, but who became a royalist in 1640–41, may be found less in his views on the rule of law than in the fact that he was the patron of the English translator of a Spanish work which explicitly warned that popular forms of government took no account of the wealthy or virtuous, and inclined towards the worst forms of tyranny. Indeed, Strangewayes was to gain first-hand experience of the threat. In November 1641, he complained to the House of Commons that he had been intimidated outside Parliament by armed citizens of London who were demanding that he vote against the bishops.[110]

At the same time, however, we have also seen that the language of authority, no less than that of popularity, had a wide currency and could strike chords within the many different constituencies within the middling sort. We should not dismiss the appeal of patriarchal arguments, which linked anarchy in the State with anarchy in the family, the disobedience of wives, and an attack on property, to householders who wanted to hang on to their land-holdings or maintain their position within the oligarchic, but fluid, course of life which was followed by urban merchants and artisans. Certainly, amongst the lawyers, as amongst the clergy, the choice of sides seems to have been a difficult one. As far as we can tell, a scant majority supported the parliamentary cause, but there were many waverers and defectors.[111]

Indeed, for many in the professions, the course of events bore out the worst prognostications of royalist propaganda. As Thomas Hurste had forecast in 1637, challenges to the authority of the king and the bishops led first to attacks in the form of impeach-ments of the Caroline judges deemed to have betrayed the liberty of the subject,[112] and, eventually, demands for root-and-branch reform of the law and the legal profession.[113] Just as the abolition of bishops and the clerical monopoly over the ministry of the word was advocated in the name of religion, so, too, change in the legal system was demanded in terms of ideas about justice, which had long been part of the populist vocabulary of legal discourse. For example, the Leveller John Warr based his case for radical reform on the principle that the primary function of the law was to pro-tect the poor against the rich and to keep the rulers within the bounds of just and righteous government. Although based on dif-ferent premises, many of his propositions could have come from the mouth of the likes of Sir Edward Coke three or four decades earlier.[114] On the other hand, a common denominator of most of the proposals was hostility to the professional monopoly of the law-yers, accompanied by a desire to open the secrets and benefits of the law to all the people. For many, the translation of legal pro-ceedings into English, which was accomplished, temporarily, in 1654, was the essential first step. To this, some added provisions for making justice available in local courts, where there would be few technicalities, professional advice would be unnecessary, and local freeholders would be the judges.[115] The radical ideal was that the resolution of disputes should be handed back to the community, and everyman should be able to act as his own lawyer. The values of the rule of law, which the lawyers themselves had done so much to promote, were accepted, but corrupt human agency, which depended on an unjust monopoly over a valuable field of knowledge, was attacked. In this respect, calls for law reform had much in common with similar proposals which advocated opening up all arts and sciences, from that of the medical men to that of ordinary trades, to wider public access.[116]

It is typical of the relationship between the professions and society in this period that many of these proposals failed because they evidently failed to generate sufficient support amongst the middling sort.[117] Furthermore, the Interregnum assault on the professions is final testimony to the influence of professional discourse in shaping the social and political values of the period. Despite the elements of self-interest which led professionals to maintain occupational closure or ally themselves with the ruling elite, many elements of professional thought also expressed the aspirations and values of 'the people' outside the elite, including the middling sort, and, although these were generally monarchical, they were not un-self-interested. At the same time, different aspects of professional thought also reflect the fear of 'the people' by the elite and by professionals themselves. What we now need are more studies of how this complex relationship between the professions, professional thought, and society at large changed and developed between 1650 and 1800.

5. The Middling Sort in London

PETER EARLE

This chapter will examine the expressions 'middling' and 'middle' as they were used of Londoners, with the emphasis being on the late seventeenth and early eighteenth centuries. An attempt will be made to define which of the many strata of metropolitan society should be considered as middling, and the chapter will also reflect on what these words meant to contemporaries and to what extent they anticipate the later use of the adjective 'middle-class'. However, before plunging into such considerations, it is worth noting that neither 'middling sort' nor 'middling' were very common as descriptions of Londoners during the period covered here.

Some writers certainly used such words, of whom Daniel Defoe was perhaps the most important, and the usage tends to catch the eyes of historians brought up on the class terminology of modern times. However, most writers used quite different words to distinguish between Londoners, such as the 'cits' and 'wits' of the playwrights and fashionable society, 'rich' and 'poor', 'people of quality' and 'common people', or if one is looking for a tripartite description, 'gentlemen', 'tradesmen' and 'mechanicks'. The upper part of this trinity is often divided into 'nobility and gentry', while the middling part is very often expanded to 'merchants and tradesmen', merchants always appearing first in such a description, while some writers go further by distinguishing 'merchants, wholesale-men and shop-keepers', all three being considered as 'tradesmen' and as socially and economically superior to 'mechanics, or handicrafts-men'.

Which of these status or functional strata are meant by writers who use the adjectives middling or middle? This is difficult to say since the meaning of such words is often ambiguous or, if it is

clear, varies with the context. This is certainly true of Defoe, who
used such words quite often in his many works. In *A Plan of the
English Commerce* (1728), for instance, he discusses the potential
market for imported groceries and refers to three groups below
the gentry, whom he describes as 'the mean, middling and trading people', a phrase which appears to place the 'middling'
below the 'trading people'.[1] However, they occupy a higher place
in society in *Robinson Crusoe*, where Crusoe reports his father as
saying

> that mine was the middle state, or what might be called the
> upper station of low life, which he had found by long experi-
> ence was the best state in the world, the most suited to human
> happiness, not exposed to the miseries and hardships, the
> labour and sufferings of the mechanick part of mankind, and
> not embarrassed with the pride, luxury, ambition, and envy of
> the upper part of mankind ... but in easy circumstances sliding
> gently through the world.

Crusoe's father was a merchant, who had retired to York, while
Crusoe himself was 'designed ... for the law' but, apart from these
hints, this nice description of 'the best state in the world' does not
allow us to know exactly who might belong to it.[2]

Ten years before he wrote *Robinson Crusoe*, Defoe had been
rather more precise on this matter. In a *Review* of June 1709, he
divided the people of England into seven categories based on a
very general description of their levels of consumption. In this
scheme, 'the middle sort, who live well' came third, below 'the
rich, who live plentifully' and above 'the working trades, who
labour hard but feel no want'. More clues come in another article
published in the same year. This time he divided the people into
four groups, by economic function rather than by consumption. If
we ignore 'the sailors, and all persons employed on the sea', we
find once again the tripartite division apparent in the quotation
from *Robinson Crusoe*, though this time with more precision as to
who belongs in each group. At the top, 'the upper part of mankind' are represented by 'the gentry, or such who live on estates,
and without the mechanism of employment, including the men of
letters, such as clergy, lawyers and physicians'. At the bottom, 'the
mechanick part of mankind' comprise 'the meer labouring people

who depend upon their hands, such as weavers, butchers, carpenters, shoemakers, labourers, with all kinds of manufacturers, and husbandmen etc. including apprentices, servants of all sorts, with vagabonds, loiterers, and unaccountable people'. In between, are those who belong to the middle station – 'the tradesmen, such as merchants, shop keepers of all sorts, and employers of others, either in trade or manufactures, farmers of land, public-houses, such as vintners, innkeepers, alehouse-keepers, coffee-houses, brewers'.[3]

This seems clear enough. Society can be divided into three sorts or stations: the gentry, who have a landed or investment income and live 'without the mechanism of employment'; the middling sort, who work but do not 'depend upon their hands', living as they do by the profits of capital and by the employment of others, 'either in trade or manufactures'; and those 'others' – 'the meer labouring people who depend upon their hands'. This is neat and functional but, nevertheless, immediately poses problems to the modern analyst. Where, for instance, do the professional people fit in? In the quotation above, 'the men of letters, such as clergy, lawyers and physicians' are lumped with the gentry, but Robinson Crusoe, 'designed for the law', was apparently going to end up in the 'middle state'. There are also problems in defining the cut-off point between the middling sort and the mechanicks. Where would one put a manufacturer who worked with his hands, but employed others, in other words an artisan? Were shopkeepers 'of all sorts' really middling? It is clear from inventories that many chandlers and haberdashers, to take just two 'sorts' of shopkeeper, were very poor, much poorer than most artisans, and the same is true of many coffee-house and alehouse-keepers. Such problems begin to make Defoe's categorisation look very blurred at the edges.

When one looks at the use of 'middling' by other writers on London, one gets the impression that the word is used for people fairly high up in London's social and economic hierarchy, far wealthier than small shopkeepers, alehouse-keepers and small manufacturers. Misson, for instance, links citizens and 'plain gentlemen' in a description of the marriage customs of people 'of a middling condition'. In another passage, he describes what 'the middling sort of people' in London ate for their dinner, and concludes that what he has described is 'the usual dinner of a substantial gentleman or wealthy citizen'. The middling sort thus overlap here into the 'plain' or even 'substantial' gentry and, in Defoe's seven-fold classification of 1709, they would seem to span the lower levels of 'the rich, who live plentifully' as well as 'the middle sort, who live well'.[4]

Such an impression of considerable wealth is reinforced by Jacob Vanderlint, who, in *Money Answers All Things* (1734), put a figure on the word 'middling' when he suggested that £250 a year was 'scanty to maintain a middling family in London'. The thrust of his argument required some exaggeration, but an expenditure of this order was by no means unusual amongst the better off 'merchants and tradesmen' of eighteenth-century London. Joseph Massie, in a paper written in 1761, subdivided merchants into three groups, spending £600, £400 and £200 a year. He also had six categories of tradesmen, three of Londoners, spending £300, £200 and £100 a year, and four categories of manufacturers, the two top ones spending £200 and £100 a year.[5]

Massie also provides a formula for converting expenditure into commercial wealth, suggesting as he does that a typical tradesman would make a profit of about 15 per cent a year on his capital and spend about two-thirds of this income, estimates which allow us to multiply expenditure by ten to get a rough idea of a tradesman's wealth.[6] Such a formula is of course arbitrary in the extreme, since it takes no account of age, competence or changing conditions of business. However, if we take it at face value and combine Vanderlint's and Massie's figures, we get a 'middling' mean expenditure of about £200 a year which multiplies up to a capital sum of £2000, while Massie's lower-bound expenditure of £100 a year produces a capital of £1000 at the lower end of the middling range.

What sort of people might be worth about £1000? Inventories show that virtually all merchants and wholesalers would come well above this figure, but that the shopkeepers were fairly evenly divided by the £1000 mark.[7] Wealthy shopkeepers, in the City or Westminster, would be likely to be worth more than £1000, sometimes very much more. Poorer shopkeepers, in the back streets and in the poor suburbs, would rarely be worth £1000 and might be worth very much less, just £100 or so, if that. The same division is apparent in the drink trade – most tavern-keepers and the better class of innkeeper would be worth at least £1000, while most coffee-house and alehouse-keepers would be worth much less, many being worth well under £100. We can see the same distinction amongst the manufacturers, with such people as shipbuilders, ropemakers, brewers, sugar refiners, soapmakers, coachmakers, printers and dyers, many of whom had considerable fixed capital as well as large working capital, all being likely to be worth well over £1000. Many masters in apparently artisan trades come into the same category – weavers, throwsters, hatters, 'shopkeeping tailors', many builders and metal-workers, people who might employ many journeymen in large workshops or have an extensive putting-out organisation or, like builders, work through and organise a network of subcontractors. Such people were all likely to be worth £1000 or more, but the typical artisan, employing a journeyman and an apprentice or two, would be much less substantial, with a likely fortune at death of between £50 and £500.

All this leaves the bottom end of the middling sort of people in a rather messy state. On the one hand, there is Defoe's functional description, which includes shopkeepers of all sorts and all 'employers of others'. On the other, there is Misson, who would include only the top range of such people and has a considerable overlap with gentlemen. In between, there is the quasi-quantitative definition provided by Vanderlint and Massie, which takes £200 a year or so to be the middling income of middling people. A common-sense compromise would suggest that the definition of the middling sort should include both function and money. They should be tradesmen in the broadest sense and employers of others, but they should not be so poor as to earn less or be worth less than the general run of 'mechanicks'. But where should the monetary cut-off point come? In the discussion above, a fortune of £1000 or perhaps £2000 has been suggested as some sort of boundary, but one could just as easily opt for another figure, as did the framers of taxation in the 1690s, who chose personal wealth of £600 and £300 as thresholds defining the payers of surtax.[8] The lower the figure one selects, the bigger becomes the middling sort of people, and possibly the less meaningful the concept. Misson, Vanderlint and Massie would hardly have thought of a man with a personal fortune of £300 and an income of well under £100 a year as middling, nor would Robinson Crusoe, though Defoe wearing some of his other hats might well have done.

II

Just to confuse the issue a little more, we might introduce here the concept of 'genteelness', a quality of fundamental importance to middling people but one which was not directly linked to wealth or income, in that one could be quite poor and still genteel or quite wealthy and not genteel at all. Such distinctions can be seen in Collyer's *Parents and Guardians Directory* and Campbell's *London Tradesmen,* two mid-eighteenth-century books which aimed to help parents make a choice of trade or profession for their children.[9] Both writers deplore the pride of parents which led them to push children into 'genteel' trades for which they had neither the necessary 'genius' nor sufficient funds to start up in business, but it is Collyer who provides a clearer guide as to which trades were genteel.

All people whom we would consider as professionals were genteel, as were those in the arts, such as portrait painters. Genteel tradesmen included merchants and such high-class wholesale and retail tradesmen as mercers, lacemen, silkmen, linen and woollen-drapers, threadmen and chinamen, most of these occupations being described not just as 'genteel' or 'very genteel and reputable' but also as 'in the first rank of tradesmen'. These occupations were genteel in themselves, in that they were respectable and could provide their practitioners with an income sufficient to support a certain style of life. They all required a very considerable start-up capital, thus ensuring that boys going into them should come from a wealthy background. These boys were also expected to be genteel before they started their apprenticeships, a quality made up of three different attributes – education, behaviour and person.

What is meant by a genteel education is shown in Collyer's description of youths who planned to be silkmen, who 'ought to have, besides a handsome fortune, the education of a gentleman, at least as far as relates to a polite behaviour'. The other two attributes are summed up in his description of the apothecary. 'He should have a genteel person and behaviour; for one who has naturally the clumsiness, the walk, the air, or the blunt rudeness of a plowman, can never be fit for this genteel profession.' The existence of a City (or middling) type of politeness, rather different from the manners of the West End, is suggested by Campbell's mercer, who 'must be a very polite man, and skilled in all the punctilios of City-good-breeding; he ought by no means to be an awkward clumsy fellow'.[10]

Lack of genteelness might take many forms, such as rudeness or unfashionable dress and manners, but it can also be discerned in decisions about consumption, as evidenced in inventories. Genteel tradesmen were quick to adopt new fashions in furniture. They also spent more on furnishing than the ungenteel, as can be seen by analysing the value of the furnishings of the best bedroom, in a sample of Londoners all worth more than £2000. The best bedroom was normally the primary focus of display in a London house and those who spent little on its furniture were almost invariably engaged in trades not considered genteel by Collyer and Campbell, men such as builders, coopers, coalmongers, soapmakers, distillers and cloth finishers. Those who spent a lot were either merchants or rich wholesalers or else were mercers, drapers and similarly genteel shopkeepers.[11] The analysis of this sort of social distinction could probably be done more subtly by examining such things as dress, handwriting and modes of expression in letters and other documents, but even at the fairly crude level of the contents of the best bedroom there is little doubt that a narrow definition of 'middling', in terms of wealth or income alone, may well miss the point.

III

We must now try to define the upper bound of the middling sort by considering the place of gentlemen and professionals in London's social structure. Do all people who could be so described belong to the 'upper part of mankind' or were some of them middling, as was suggested by Misson's use of the expression? There is no need to enter here into an extended discussion of just what the status 'gentleman' meant in early modern England, but it should be clear that by the late seventeenth century it was a very fluid and uncertain status in which anyone who looked and behaved like a gentleman might be accepted as one. This is perhaps best summed up by Guy Miège, who wrote that 'any one that, without a coat of arms, has either a liberal or genteel education, that looks gentleman-like (whether he be so or not) and has the wherewithal to live freely and handsomely, is by the courtesy of England usually called a gentleman'.[12]

Many of these attributes were clearly shared to some extent by the genteel tradesmen discussed above, all of whom had at least a genteel education and many of whom probably looked fairly 'gentleman-like'. Indeed, many of them were the sons and brothers of country gentlemen and esquires, as can be seen in their apprenticeship records, and would thus have the blood and upbringing as well as the appearance of gentlemen. But could working as a mercer or a linen-draper be described as living 'freely and handsomely'? Miège does not define these words, but, if 'handsomely' means having plenty of money and 'freely' means without working, then genteel tradesmen shared only one of these attributes, in that they had to work and so were not 'such as live on estates, and without the mechanism of employment' in Defoe's definition of the gentry.

Nevertheless, there was clearly much overlap between the gentle and the genteel. Merchants and financiers, for instance, worked for a living but they were not tied to shop hours and had no need to be servile to do business. They also tended to have had a liberal education, to be rich, very often styled themselves gentlemen and indeed were described as 'a species of gentry' in Steele's *Conscious Lovers* of 1722.[13] Some gentlemen of leisure derived their incomes from estates in the country, but an increasing number relied on investments in the city, on urban property, loans to other gentlemen or to tradesmen, stocks and shares and government debt. Since the inventories of merchants and other genteel tradesmen demonstrate that they often drew a substantial part of their income from the same investments, the distinction between those who lived on estates and those who did not becomes less compelling, especially as genteel tradesmen tended to withdraw progressively from active business as they got older and to rely increasingly on their investments.[14] When one remembers that both the gentleman of leisure and the genteel tradesman might well have come from the same country-gentry background, might indeed be brothers or at least cousins, were happy for their sons and daughters to intermarry and shared the same metropolitan culture of the well-to-do and well-educated, then it is no surprise that Misson might be somewhat confused in his distinction between the middling people and the urban gentry.

This does not of course mean that all gentlemen were middling. No one would have described the titular aristocracy as such, nor, indeed, the richer of those country gentlemen and esquires who had taken up residence in the West End. These were clearly representatives of 'the great, who live profusely' in Defoe's seven-fold categorisation of 1709. But there was a very considerable overlap in manners and life-style between the next two groups on the list, 'the rich who live plentifully' and 'the middle sort who live well'. One group was clearly richer than the other, but where the cut-off point should come is impossible to say, since many genteel tradesmen were far richer than many of the urban gentlemen of leisure.

Further problems occur in placing the professionals in London's social structure since their long hierarchies embraced people with such a wide range of wealth and income, from several thousands a year for the better off barristers and physicians to £30 or £40 a year for the poorer clergy and lesser members of the legal profession. Many professionals were as rich or richer than the wealthy or well-to-do gentlemen of leisure, merchants and genteel tradesmen who have already been considered. This group would include barristers, attorneys, senior government officials, most members of the medical profession, the better beneficed clergy and the higher-ranking army and navy officers. However, the lower ranks of the church and the law, not to mention such starveling professionals as the school-teachers, earned incomes far below the level enjoyed by genteel tradesmen; indeed, they often earned less than the better off artisans. And yet these poor curates and solicitors and grammar-school teachers shared many of the attitudes, and at least aspired to the life-style, of the middling sort if not the gentry. They were, after all, very often the sons of gentlemen or at least of those 'by the courtesy of England usually called a gentleman'. They had nearly all had not just a genteel but a liberal education and they were more than likely to 'have a genteel person and behaviour'. In short, they were almost invariably genteel and most would probably have thought of themselves as gentlemen even if they did not have 'the wherewithal to live freely and handsomely'.

Many other people in London's complex society considered themselves gentlemen but had little wherewithal. Virtually all military men down to the rank of sergeant (and often corporal) styled themselves gentlemen on documents, however miserable their half-pay or no pay.[15] The same was true of men in the lowest reaches of the law, such as solicitors, entering-clerks and bailiffs. Most writers (and indeed most other artists) thought themselves gentlemen and many certainly were, by birth and education at least. Even some servants styled themselves gentlemen – gentlemen's gentlemen, butlers, dancing and fencing-masters in high-class establishments.

The list becomes even longer when we consider those with only modest incomes who thought themselves to be at least genteel. Almost everyone in the growing numbers of the salaried would belong in this group, such people as excisemen, customs officers and other employees of the state and, in the commercial world, the book-keepers and clerks, a range of people with incomes from about £20 to £100 a year with a median of perhaps £50 a year, just enough to live a moderately genteel life and keep up some appearances. And indeed a well-dressed and reasonably well-educated book-keeper or exciseman, with a genteel person and behaviour, might well seem more middling to his contemporaries than a self-made builder or manufacturer, who, although worth ten or twenty times as much, might well be 'an awkward clumsy fellow' who could hardly write his own name.

IV

Up to now, there has been no discussion of life-cycle or social mobility, but these need to be considered in any approximation of the nature and size of the middling sort. Too many studies of social structure depend on an analysis at some particular frozen moment, either frozen for the community as a whole, in studies based on tax data, or frozen for the individual, usually at that moment when he has just died, in studies based on inventories. In reality, of course, people would be likely to move in and out of particular social strata in the course of their lives. Such mobility would be both upwards and downwards, but on balance the upwards movement was likely to be stronger, with the result that studies based on analysis of the dead will exaggerate the numbers in some social groups, while studies of the living under-estimate the numbers who would spend some part of their lives in that group.

Belief in the possibility of upwards mobility may well be an important harmonising factor in society, softening the potential conflicts between social groups as individuals discount their present lowly position in anticipation of a more elevated future. Steve Rappaport demonstrated the importance of such beliefs in his study of Elizabethan London, in which he was able to track the subsequent careers of a sample of apprentices.[16] He found that the chances of upward mobility were good, as apprentices became journeymen and as a surprisingly high proportion of journeymen became householders running their own shops or workshops. Further movement up the social ladder of livery companies to liveryman or assistant was less easy, but still sufficiently likely to minimise conflict between the higher and lower members of the hierarchy.

The sources probably do not exist for a similar study for the period here, since the records of the livery companies do not continue to include such detailed information on their members. However, it seems probable that, although such upward mobility was still possible, it was no longer such a powerful force for social improvement. Two factors were mainly responsible for the scale of social mobility in Rappaport's study, high adult mortality and the small scale of London business. Rates of adult mortality rose with age, so that more masters than journeymen died each year, thus providing opportunities in the form of dead masters and unoccupied workshops for the surviving journeymen, these opportunities being within the range of a high proportion of journeymen since entry costs were relatively low. By the early eighteenth century, the mortality of masters had probably fallen quite considerably, while entry costs had risen beyond the reach of all but a minority as the London economy became more highly capitalised.[17]

Nevertheless, there was still much upward mobility and this needs to be considered when examining the middling sort. At any point in time, there would be large numbers of apprentices and journeymen in London, people who, according to Defoe, would be members of the 'mechanick part of mankind'. Some of these would one day become members of the middling sort, whichever type of definition is employed. Indeed, some young men were probably considered as middling while they were still apprentices and therefore technically servants, since their genteel background and person and the wealth of their parents would make them the social equals and sometimes the social superiors of their masters. But, even if such rich young men were not considered to be middling during their apprenticeship, they and many others would soon become middling by function, as they finished their terms and set themselves up as merchants, shopkeepers or manufacturers.

It should also be noted that, if middling is defined by wealth, this means that there will be more middling people in each older age-group, as age and accumulation are fairly closely correlated, so that a man who might have been below some arbitrary middling wealth threshold at the age of 30 or 40 might well have accumulated enough to pass it by the time he was 50.[18] Beyond this age, it is possible that some middling people would sink below the threshold once again as they took large sums out of their capital to provide portions and dowries for their sons and daughters. On the other hand, some would rise above the middling sort altogether, on a functional definition, as they retired from business, invested their savings and became 'gentry, or such who live on estates, and without the mechanism of employment'. Indeed, such a move into the world of the leisured can well be seen as one of the main motivating factors in the lives of middling people whose gospel of work was interwoven with envy and admiration of those who could live comfortably without working.

Such success stories should not let us forget that social mobility was not always upwards, a point on which Defoe often lectured his middling readers. In a *Review* of 1707, he distinguished between two types of poverty, 'the poverty of inheritance' suffered by 'the people born to labour' and 'the poverty of disaster, and this falls chiefly on the middling sorts of people who have been trading-men, but by misfortune or mismanagement, or both, fall from flourishing into debt, bankruptcy, jails, distress, and all sorts of misery'.[19] Such disaster was quite common; indeed, I have estimated elsewhere that the career chances of bankruptcy for a London businessman were 10 or 15 per cent, and concluded that 'the commonest end to a business career was death, but bankruptcy must have run retirement very close in second place'.[20]

V

The discussion so far has been all about men, a group who made up rather less than half of the adult population of the metropolis. How do women fit into an analysis of the middling sort? The conventional approach of studies of social structure seems to be either to ignore women altogether or to treat them as appendages of men, in other words to consider women as belonging to the same sort, station or class as their fathers or husbands. Such an approach poses many problems in a study of late-seventeenth and early-eighteenth-century London.

How, for instance, does one define the social position of an adult spinster in a city where some two-thirds of all adult women and a rather lower proportion of men were immigrants?[21] It will be clear from other chapters in this book that the concept of middling was not necessarily the same in provincial England as it was in London, so it is quite likely that the daughter of provincial middling people would not make the grade in London. She might, for instance, not have enough money to qualify in a metropolitan milieu. Alternatively, she might be disbarred for lack of genteelness, her provincial background not providing her with the requisite genteel education, behaviour and person, attributes which would of course be rather different for young women as opposed to young men, but still easily discernible to her contemporaries. Such problems were likely to be compounded by the fact that the great majority of single immigrant women in London, even those who were the daughters of middling people in the provinces, earned their living as domestic servants and so were unlikely to be considered as middling in London. Such considerations suggest that the pool of middling spinsters in London would be quite small and would be drawn from those daughters of the London middling sort lucky enough to survive to adulthood in the urban graveyard, together with a small minority of immigrants whose social background, education and potential dowry raised them above the rest of their sisters. It is unlikely that any single woman who worked for her living would have been considered middling, since paid work was already normally seen as socially degrading for the female sex, a good example of the ambiguous middling attitude to idleness.

It seems probable that there would not have been enough middling spinsters to provide brides for all the middling men, so marriage would have provided an opportunity for upward mobility for many young women, a change of status often symbolised by their ceasing to work for their livings at marriage. Such upward mobility was no doubt a major factor in motivating the high level of female migration to London, but it was not necessarily a permanent state. Many married women, even those married to middling men, found it necessary to take paid employment later in marriage as the cost of children or the faltering business success of their husbands put a strain on the family finances. Some jobs, such as the better sorts of catering or shopkeeping, or high-class mantua-making, might have been compatible with middling status. However, most working wives were employed in occupations which would have put a serious strain on the world's ability to view them as being any longer members of the middling sort of people, while there would be serious doubts about a husband who could not maintain his wife.

The death of husbands was often the beginning of a decline in status. Fairly young middling widows might be seen as a good catch and so maintain their middling status with a new husband. Other middling widows were left wealthy enough to live a genteel life on an investment income, while some were able successfully to continue their husband's business. However, such fortunate women were a minority and the fate of most widows seems to have been a gradual slide into the 'poverty of disaster ... by misfortune or mismanagement, or both'. A widow only inherited a fraction, normally a third, of her husband's estate, and lack of business experience often meant that this third was much less than it might have been, as a result of failure to recover all the late husband's debts. Lack of experience and training also meant that few widows were able to get such a good return on this money as their husbands would have done, with the result that widowhood almost always meant a very big fall in household income. This necessarily implied a retreat from the genteel existence of marriage, as a house was exchanged for lodgings and servants were dismissed, or the house was given over to lodgers for whom meals and other services had to be provided. Many widows found that the attempt to maintain appearances ate into their capital and forced them to find some other means of livelihood, the fate of Elizabeth Green, who 'liveth upon what her husband left her and by needle work and lived entirely upon what her said husband left ... until about a year and a half since'.[22] Such poverty might continue to be genteel but it was certainly poverty, and increasingly so, and it seems unlikely that such widows still belonged to the middling sort of people.

In the present state of research, it is not easy to be certain of the gender aspects of the middling label. However, if the preceding discussion is accurate, it is clear that despite the female surplus in the metropolis there was a female deficit amongst the middling sort. Male advantages in education, occupational choice and money meant that there were likely to be more middling bachelors than spinsters. This disparity would have been much greater in widowhood, since widows were far more likely than widowers to descend into genteel or not so genteel poverty. Gregory King thought that widows in London were more than a quarter of the combined total of wives and widows, a figure which may well be an under-estimate, so that the female shortfall in the middling sort was probably quite large.[23]

VI

This discussion of the middling sort in London has posed more questions than it has answered, not surprisingly since middling meant different things at different times to the writers who employed it and was probably understood in a variety of ways by those contemporaries who read their books. In this chapter, three main types of definition have been considered – by economic function or source of income; by size of income and/or wealth; and by manners, the genteel/gentle spectrum of education, behaviour and person. The middling sort will vary in size depending on where one strikes a balance between these various attributes.

If we decide that no one worth less than £1000 or earning less than £100 a year fits the bill, we immediately remove most of the group of genteel salaried people considered earlier, as well as most small shopkeepers, though where we put them instead is another question, since few of them could be considered as 'mechanicks' or 'poor' or working-class. If we decide that only those whom contemporaries would have considered genteel belong to the middling sort, then we remove a lot more people. If all those whom contemporaries would have considered gentlemen are placed in another, higher sort, called 'gentry', then many professionals, merchants and other members of the 'mercantile bourgeoisie'[24]

will have to be removed and the middling sort will shrink to quite
a small number, composed mainly of the smarter shopkeepers and
the lesser merchants and wholesalers, perhaps too small to bear
the weight which the term is carrying in this book.

On the other hand, a big middling sort can be created by being
inclusive rather than exclusive, including everyone who could possibly be called genteel, whatever their income or wealth, together
with the lesser urban gentry, and also including everyone worth
more than some fairly low figure, perhaps the Poll Tax surtax sum of
£300, a figure which would bring in many of the lesser shopkeepers
and also the better off artisans. No doubt the 'real' middling sort, as
befits its name, lies somewhere between these extremes.

It has also been shown that, whatever definition or combination
of definitions is used, the size of the middling sort will depend on
a number of other factors – on the age-group or gender being
studied, on the age, sex and marital structure of the population,
the level of adult mortality, the structure and performance of the
economy and the level of entry costs into the London business
world. So many variables make it difficult and perhaps unwise to
come to any firm conclusions as to the size of the middling sort, a
group which will clearly expand or contract depending on who is
writing about it and what they wish to emphasise.

What then is the value of the concept of the middling sort to
the historian? First of all, it is perhaps valuable in that it makes
historians think about social structure, a worthwhile exercise even
if does not result in firm conclusions. But the adjectives 'middling' and 'middle' implied rather more to contemporaries than
just an expression descriptive of a certain position in the social
ladder. The meaning is never entirely clear, but it certainly seems
to be very similar to the meaning of 'middle-class' as this expression was used later in the eighteenth century[25] and as it is used in
popular speech today, as opposed to the meaning imposed on it
by sociologists.

This is to say that middling had a certain social structural meaning which was vague in the extreme, just as the popular use of middle-class is today. It also had a meaning as a description of a certain
sort of life-style which was different from that both of the aristocracy
and gentry and of the common people. The exact components of
this life-style are equally vague but, for all that, the word middling
probably elicited a fairly consistent response in the minds of con-

temporaries. Those who were middling would be well off and sometimes rich, would usually inhabit the whole of a fashionably
furnished house and would live a comfortable life and expect
(sometimes mistakenly) to do so until they died. They would be
moderately well educated, thirsty for further knowledge and self-
improvement and very interested in the education of their children.
They would be politely mannered, well spoken and fairly cultured.
In appearance, they would be quite fashionably dressed, clean by
the standards of the day, and would have a tendency to plumpness
as a result of being sufficiently well off to eat and drink well, if not
wisely, for the whole of their lives. In short, they would look and
behave or try to look and behave like genteel people.

They would also have a number of other qualities which there
has not been space to explore in this chapter. They would employ
servants, probably more than one since single-servant households
went well below the level of the middling sort of people. They
would take great care to maintain a respectable reputation in their
neighbourhood, would be fairly substantial payers of taxes and
poor-rates and would expect to take on the responsibilities of
office in their parish or ward. They would be interested in politics
and would normally have the franchise, either as householders in
Westminster or Middlesex or as liverymen of the City of London.
They would be regular attenders at their church or meeting
house, where they would sit in the front rows or pews and give the
impression of being pious and deeply religious people who wor-
ried seriously about the problem of salvation, sufficiently so to
earn an encomium from Bishop Burnet.

> As for the men of trade and business, they are, generally speak-
> ing, the best body in the nation, generous, sober and charitable
> ... more knowledge, more zeal, and more charity, with a great
> deal more of devotion. There may be too much of vanity, with
> too pompous an exterior, mixed with these in the capital city;
> but upon the whole, they are the best we have.[26]

It would not seem to be all that fanciful to describe these
middling qualities as middle-class, since they are very similar to the
qualities normally ascribed to the Victorian middle class. The
subjects emphasised in any general book on this subject, such as
Walter Houghton's book *The Victorian Frame of Mind*, induce a

feeling of *déjà-vu* in a student of the earlier period – respectability, conformity, an increasing interest in the home, a fairly puritanical religion and lots of it, hard work, accumulation and so on.[27] One passage in Houghton is called 'The Bourgeois Dream'. Here he emphasises the twin goals of Victorian middle-class life – respectability and salvation – and discusses the gospel of work and the middle-class view that idleness was a moral and a social sin, while both upper and lower class have high leisure preference; no surprises here for the student of early modern London. He goes on to describe what he sees as the two central paradoxes in Victorian middle-class ideas. This group who exalted work also valued idleness as a badge of status since it showed that one was a gentleman of independent means, all of which is nothing new to a student of Defoe and the early eighteenth century, where the same paradox is fundamental. The other paradox is equally apparent in both middling Augustan and middle-class Victorian society. This is the struggle between salvation and worldliness, between success in this world and the next, a clash which created a fundamental schism in the middling mind, since success was not always compatible with a moral code likely to lead to salvation.[28]

The middling sort of people thus carried within them many of the assumptions, values and beliefs, the mentalité in short, of the Victorian middle class. This is not to say that they were just the same – social history would be dull if this were true. Middling people were not quite so rich, confident or self-assured, not so well-imbued with upper-class ideas and culture through long residence in public schools. But they shared many of the Victorian ideals and ambitions just as they shared their worries and fears, worries about salvation, fears about reputation, fears above all about that 'poverty of disaster' which stalked the comfort of the middling sort of people. Nevertheless, it certainly was a comfortable state to be 'in easy circumstances sliding gently through the world' as Robinson Crusoe's father had suggested and as Crusoe himself was eventually to realise when he settled down after half a life-time of wandering. 'Now I thought indeed that I enjoyed the middle state of life that my father so earnestly recommended to me, and lived a kind of heavenly life.'[29]

6. The Middling Sort in Eighteenth-Century Politics

NICHOLAS ROGERS

I

The growing wealth, vigour and presence of the middling sort has recently been heralded as one of the distinguishing features of the eighteenth century,[1] yet controversy abounds concerning its impact upon national politics. The conventional, and still dominant, view is that its influence was negligible until the latter decades of the century, if not until the end of the French wars. Following Namier, historians have continued to insist that the eighteenth-century political system privileged birth, breeding, and, above all, landed wealth. This was reflected in the social composition of the House of Commons, in the aristocratic profile of eighteenth-century governments, in the pre-eminently landed character of the bench, the principal instrument of local administration, and in the perceptible increase in the political patronage of the great landowners, whose vast fortunes and influence determined the outcome of many elections. In these circumstances, it has been argued, the role of the middling sort was severely circumscribed. The network of patronage and the local, sometimes competing, interests of the middling classes ensured their subordinate position within the political structure. Clients to a culturally unified ruling class whose values they admired, they were marginal players in a grandee game.

Few, if any, historians would dispute the claim that the landed aristocracy and gentry dominated the political machinery of the state. But not all would agree that the problem of power can be reduced to the personnel of the state apparatus and to its myriad affiliations and dependences within society as a whole. Power did not reside exclusively with the official power-holders, even in the

159

heyday of Hanoverian oligarchy. Nor were the tentacles of clientage so pervasive or formidable as to encompass all men of property, let alone the labouring poor. In a politically literate nation, tetchily defensive of its liberties and lacking strong sanctions of force, power rested in large measure upon consent, upon the ability of the landed aristocracy to legitimate its rule. This necessarily involved complex reciprocities between patrons and their clients, or between aristocratic brokers and powerful regional or institutional interests, whose economic power was often considerable. As Eric Hobsbawm has rightly noted, 'the Whig grandees ... knew quite well that the power of the country, and their own, rested on a readiness to make money militantly and commercially'.[2] In other words, the power of the aristocracy rested less on its presumptive and prescriptive right to rule than on its capacity to shape national destinies in line with broader property interests, a predicament that necessarily forced it to come to terms with mercantile and financial interests with which it was not necessarily intimately associated.

Two further factors complicated the parameters of power in Hanoverian politics. The first was the independence of the larger counties and urban centres, particularly the freeman boroughs, whose cumulative presence as a counterpoint to executive authority and oligarchic politics could be considerable. The second was the changing dimensions of the political sphere itself, the ways in which the press and new forms of association transformed the terrain in which power was exercised. It is within these contexts, as well as in the interplay of interests in local and national politics, that the role of the middling sort can best be explored.

II

That said, there remains the vexed question of definitions. Who were the middling sort? Contemporaries tended to use the term impressionistically, as an interposition between persons of high rank and substantial landed wealth, and the servants, labourers and journeymen who lived off wages. In other words, the social boundaries of the middling sort were essentially indeterminate and could vary over time.[3] In the seventeenth century, when the language of sorts first appeared, the middling sort of people referred principally to the independent small producers in agriculture and industry.[4] With the development of agrarian capitalism and rural industry, many of these small producers became partially proletarianised, losing out to the large farmers and manufacturers who produced for the market and to the merchant-middlemen who controlled the distribution (and sometimes indirectly the production) of Britain's diverse products. These people, who turned over capital for profit, were the quintessential middling sort of the eighteenth century. They were joined by a diverse group of tradesmen and professional men whose presence illustrated the increasingly complex nature of Britain's market society and the dramatic development of the state after 1688. The term 'middling sort' still referred to those who could not be easily assimilated into a traditional perception of the social order based on birth, rank or gentility.[5] But its social connotations had changed. Generally speaking, the term now privileged urban occupations: merchants, tradesmen, substantial shopkeepers and master manufacturers, as well as the emergent professions of medicine, teaching, the law, the civil and armed services; most of whom expanded in wealth and numbers during the eighteenth century, although not perhaps as spectacularly as contemporaries assumed.[6] But the term 'middling sort' could still apply to the richer freeholders and tenant farmers, to the capitalists of the countryside, who numbered about 227,500 in 1688, rising to 320,000 by 1800. In some commentaries, the middling sort even included the smaller gentry, either because their families benefited from the rise of the professions, or within the conventional trinity of Crown, aristocracy and Commons, because they could be differentiated from the aristocratic elite. But such a definition was unusual.[7] Normally the 'middling sort' referred to persons who were not of gentle origin, however successfully they aspired to gentility; rather, to men of substance whose palpable economic and political contribution to society, as employers, consumers, office-holders and property owners, entitled them to recognition and respect.

In eighteenth-century parlance, then, the middling sort defied precise sociological definition, which explains why historians have had such a hard time delineating its boundaries.[8] At its uppermost level it could include the merchant princes and wealthy bankers of London and the major provincial towns, men who sometimes married into county society and rubbed shoulders with

the landed gentry.[9] At its lowest it could encompass the yeoman
farmer and master-craftsman, whose social horizons and tastes
were vastly different. What potentially united such men was their
independence from government and aristocratic domination,
however this might be negotiated, and the belief that their propertied stake in society should be suitably recognised. In the political
discourse of the century it was on these issues that the debate over
the participation of the middling sort often turned.

III

We might begin this analysis by considering the role of interests
in British politics. Interest politics, as such, were hardly new to
the eighteenth century. Generations of chartered companies had
sought privileges from the crown and had vigorously petitioned
the Privy Council to sustain their interests. But the dimensions of
interest politics changed dramatically during the eighteenth
century as the fiscal requirements of the State and its active
promotion of industrial protection touched a wider variety of
interests, and as parliament's status as a permanent and important policy-making body grew. As a result, lobbying parliament
became an increasingly sophisticated and necessary activity,
advanced through local representatives or professional lobbyists
and, where necessary, through large-scale petitioning campaigns.
Such campaigns were not simply the prerogative of the most
powerful mercantile and manufacturing groups in London and
the leading provincial towns. Quite modest men of property
could mobilise on a national scale against taxes or concessions
injurious to their trade. Over 100 different bodies petitioned for
the repeal of the leather duties between 1697 and 1699, some of
them tanners in small market towns across the country. Similarly,
shopkeepers from a wide range of towns deluged parliament
with petitions against measures that advantaged pedlars and
hawkers in the 1730s and again in the 1780s, in the latter case
forcing Pitt to amend and ultimately repeal his retail tax.[10] Their
success was testimony to the political acumen and vigour of the
middling sort in defending their livelihoods in an oligarchic
electoral system.

These tax revolts were largely intermittent and reactive. Small men of property could not hope to monitor the activities of parliament or the executive as closely as the Bristol Merchant Venturers, the West India planters and merchants, or the East India Company, all of whom regularly had representatives in the Commons and were intimately aware of its business. Nor could they afford to maintain active committees to promote legislative agendas, like some of the London livery companies. Such well-established interest groups inevitably had the edge in cornering the attention of parliament. Sometimes they were powerful enough to influence policies that disadvantaged landed property, despite its numerical preponderance in the legislature and the key institutions of the State. Textile manufacturers, for example, were able to influence the regulation of Anglo-Irish trade to their advantage, unlike English graziers. Regionally organised around committees of trade, they were also able to prohibit the export of wool despite repeated complaints from English growers. 'Merchants are artful as well as powerful,' commented one Lincolnshire grower in 1782, 'and have always seen when theirs and the landed interest have stood in competition, they have got the better.'[11]

In fact the situation was rather more complex. Despite the generalising tone of these remarks, broadly-based economic interests seldom stood in dramatic opposition to one another in the eighteenth century. The one exception to this rule was the battle between the monied and landed interests during the early eighteenth century, when the exigencies of war demanded a high land tax to pay off the interest on the funded debt. During the wool controversy of the 1780s, for example, textile manufacturers argued that an end to the prohibition of wool would inhibit output, increase unemployment and impose higher poor-rates upon landowners. Similarly, on the question of the export bounty upon corn, an issue which potentially raised wage costs for manufacturers and pitched industry against agriculture, commentators were quick to emphasise their intrinsic interdependence.[12] In practice, the economic questions brought before parliament were usually local and particular, disclosing tensions within sectors as much as between them. Grand sectoral alliances did occasionally crystallise in response to government policies. In the 1730s, for instance, Walpole faced considerable opposition from mercantile groups over his proposed excise tax on wine and tobacco, a measure that was widely regarded as a prelude to further imposts upon trade. Yet, by and large, eighteenth-century governments eschewed coherent economic policies beyond managing the funded debt and its taxable base, a base that heavily exploited consumers rather than specific fractions of capital. The result was that MPs were remarkably free to pursue whatever economic legislation appealed to themselves, to their constituents, or to the organised groups with which they were connected. In other words, political convention and the structural peculiarities of the British economy, which was imperfectly integrated before 1770, encouraged a contrariety of interests to engage in the business of lobbying government and parliament. Even in 1784, when Samuel Garbett ventured to create a national lobby for industry with the General Chamber of Manufacturers, such an experiment proved short-lived. Manufacturers could not agree over the 1786 commercial treaty with France. Many, in any case, felt that the best way to deal with economic grievances was by discreet lobbying and personal influence rather than by means of a national forum.[13]

The large-scale clash of interests, then, was not as salient a feature of eighteenth-century politics as it was to become in the early nineteenth century, when the battles over cash and corn generated discourses that pitched an entrepreneurial middle class against a predominantly landed oligarchy. Those that did occur grew out of the government's wartime activities and, in the mid-century decades at least, out of its pursuit of Eurocentric policies to the detriment of the rapidly expanding Atlantic trades. What was evident was the pragmatic pursuit of local interests, particularly vigorous once the party strife between Whig and Tory had subsided. Applications for turnpikes multiplied dramatically in the 1750s and 1760s, for example, to be followed by a veritable canal mania. Enclosure also grew apace, while improvements acts in provincial towns grew from 16 in the years 1689–1759 to 56 in the years 1760–89, transforming the urban landscape.[14]

Many of these local initiatives were promoted by large landowners. Yet turnpikes and canals did draw upon business support, as indeed did the varied schemes for urban improvement, whether for paving, lighting, sewage or the laying out of neat terraces and squares. Paul Langford has recently shown that the statutory bodies set up to deal with these local concerns frequently allowed for middling representation, although its extent could vary according to the project and the locale.[15] Turnpike trusts tended to be fairly exclusive, although prominent merchants and manufacturers were often involved. Street-lighting and paving commissions had a broader membership, save in the affluent parishes of Westminster, while small-debt courts tended to be presided over by men of commerce. The middling presence was also quite visible in the various voluntary associations that were rapidly becoming part of the new urban order such as hospitals and educational trusts. In Liverpool, for example, merchants and retailers made up nearly three-quarters of the trustees of the newly founded Infirmary in 1749, with the physicians and lawyers mustering a further 7.6 per cent.[16]

What the larger political ramifications of this local activism were is difficult to answer. Paul Langford has made a compelling case for a pluralistic, propertied, conservative order, in which substantial sections of the middling sort were co-sponsors of improvement. Local associations, whether statutory or voluntary, allowed many merchants, tradesmen and aspiring professionals to carve a niche in the social order, to raise their social standing and to combine 'patriotic' endeavour with self-advancement. Drawn into the process of government, they were well placed to press for local concessions from parliament and to capture the ear of MPs whose diverse interests made them attentive to issues where their own property interests were involved. Despite the electoral anomalies and corruption of the unreformed system, Langford has claimed, it was accessible enough to forge alliances among the propertied; a fact that explains why many unrepresented towns did not campaign for parliamentary reform at the end of the American war.

On the other hand, lobbying and local activism could breed its discontents. Merchants and local industrialists were often frustrated by the politics of persuasion, and frequently resented the time and expense of lobbying MPs unfamiliar with and sometimes indifferent to the technicalities of their case. The Midlands iron master, Samuel Garbett, complained to William Burke in 1766 that the 'old country families look upon themselves as patrons of the trade in the neighbourhood, and really have great inclination to serve it when they distinctly understand the subject. But we have troubled them very seldom, and indeed we sorely want somebody who is not only intelligent but hath enlarged views to take the lead in considering our commerce as a subject of politicks.'[17] Even where trades had direct representation, MPs could be tetchily indignant at the demands made of them, particularly if it cramped their gentlemanly style. 'The Duty of a Representative of Bristol', bemoaned Edward Southwell, MP for the city from 1739 to 1754, 'requires every hour of the day a constant attendance in Parlt., an extensive and regular correspondence, an attention to every Branch of Trade, an universal solicitation in all Offices and with all persons in power.'[18] To a man who prided himself upon his independence and held high offices of state in Ireland, this was all rather demeaning, and the leading businessmen in Bristol frequently had to flatter and sometimes cajole him into action.

Merchants and manufacturers did not always find the structures of landed power to their taste, and their experience of local associations sometimes reinforced their unease. Local improvement schemes occasionally raised middling shackles, as they did in Southampton in 1770, when some ratepayers and councillors opposed an increase in the rates to transform the town into an aristocratic spa.[19] Conversely, middling participation in similar schemes could generate a criticism of corporate privilege and 'aristocratic' habits of rule. Commissioners were sometimes elected by the ratepayers. Officials were customarily elected by ballot, whether by governors, subscribers or the commissioners. They were paid by salary, not by fees and perquisites, and they could not hold their position for life, nor delegate it to anyone else.[20] These principles of public accountability and scrutiny were sometimes honoured in the breach, but they did stand in stark contrast to the operations of many corporations, whose management of local charities, estates and markets too frequently smacked of proprietary interest, civic favouritism and graft. The lesson was not lost on city radicals, who frequently pressed for a more open, participatory style of politics consonant with the statutory commissions and voluntary associations. The Beckfords took this tack over the Bristol Watch bill in 1755, deploring the decision to confer statutory power to the aldermen of the closed corporation rather than to a more accountable body.[21] In Newcastle, the local radicals drew on their brethren's experience as surgeons and apothecaries of the local Infirmary to berate the corporation for its indulgent and self-serving paternalism.[22] Middling participation on statutory commissions and voluntary associations did not necessarily wed its local politicians to the status quo; it could serve as a tocsin for reform and greater political accountability.

IV

Most middling men lacked the resources and connections to be big players in the politics of interest. They were neither industrial giants, mercantile magnates, nor members of powerful corporations. Some of them could, however, make their presence felt as voters. The eighteenth-century franchise, derived from a hotchpotch of freedoms and customary privileges, was paradoxically socially diverse and restrictive. In a handful of boroughs it could include 80 per cent of all adult males; in others singularly few. On average, the electorate comprised 20 per cent of all adult males; at the Hanoverian accession rather more, about 24 per cent; at the end of the century rather less, about 17 per cent.[23]

The representation of the middling sort on this electorate is difficult to gauge with any precision, largely because of the ambiguous status of the craftsman, who could be a petty journeyman or his employer. Historians have guessed that probably 25–30 per cent of the borough electorate would normally be classified as middling, the proportion rising to at least 50 per cent in the shires.[24] Neither of these figures give any indication of the influence such a group might bring to bear on their constituencies, nor of the degree to which it might exercise an independent choice. On these matters, controversy abounds.

The conventional view has cast the middling sort – the merchants, tradesmen and shopkeepers of the towns, and the yeoman farmers of the countryside – in a distinctly subaltern role. Sir Lewis Namier, for example, argued that few cities outside the metropolis evinced any degree of political independence. Most deferred to the well-born and adhered to standards of political morality that were not intrinsically different from those of the smaller, aristocratic-dominated boroughs. Even the counties, conventionally portrayed as the classic, open, independent constituencies, remained dominated by the greater landlords. Namier himself doubted that 'one voter in twenty at county elections could freely exercise his statutory right'[25], rendering any discussion of public opinion, ideology, or party superfluous and anachronistic. This view was elaborated upon in the first volumes of the *History of Parliament* and became the dominant view of the 1960s.[26] Patronage, landlordism and deference became the key words.

These views have not gone unchallenged. Many years ago Sir John Plumb complained that the Namierite perspective remained too riveted to Whitehall and Westminster and to the detailed negotiations of patronage disclosed in the private papers of aristocrats such as the Duke of Newcastle. Drawing attention to the vitality of the extra-parliamentary political culture, he emphasised the uneasy relationship that existed between the political elite and the nation at large, one that periodically precipitated vigorous, if unsuccessful, movements for change.[27] Subsequent generations of scholars have developed these insights, pointing, among other things, to the growth in formal political participation. Although the political control of the greater landlords over the small boroughs intensified over time, especially in the south-west, the medium and large-sized boroughs continued to be contested, increasingly so after 1760. Since these boroughs represented the vast majority of the 110,000 urban electors, popular political participation remained a constituent feature of the 'unreformed' system.[28] Within the oligarchical structure of eighteenth-century politics there were opportunities for the middling sort to be heard.

Those historians who have sought to re-emphasise the role of the middling sort in English politics have tended to focus upon the urban context; that is, upon the merchants, manufacturers, professionals and tradesmen, who numbered over 300,000 by about 1760 and made up an influential minority of the borough electorate. They have been less attentive to the 248,000 farmers and freeholders, over half of whom were entitled to vote in county elections. These voters, of whom there were roughly 130,000 in the mid-century, constituted the majority of middling voters in the eighteenth century, although the rising size of farms and stricter electoral registration may have reduced their numbers.[29] This omission is a significant one, for it is here that the case for a marginal middling presence has been consistently advanced.

One plausible index for this marginality is the ratio of uncontested elections. It is an imperfect measure, for an uncontested election may well be the product of hard-fought compromises and does not necessarily imply a politically somnolent electorate. Yet it does register the ability of electors to exercise their statutory right to vote in environments where the political disposition of leading families was often extremely important. As Table 6.1 reveals, the number of English counties that went to the polls in

Table 6.1 *Proportion of contested elections, 1701–1802*

		1701–15	1722–61	1768–1801
English counties	(n = 40)	45.7	20.7	16.4
Industrial counties	(n = 10)	51.4	24.3	17.1
Big cities and towns	(n = 28)	53.6	56.6	59.7

the seven general elections between 1701 and 1715 was just under half (45.7 per cent). In the next seven, the proportion had fallen to just over a fifth, and by the end of the century, to only 16.4 per cent. This decline is equally noticeable in the more industrial and commercial counties, where landlord influence might have been mitigated by a substantial influx of urban voters and the density of voter affiliations. By contrast, over half of the 28 towns and cities with electorates of 1000 or more were regularly contested throughout the century, and the proportion grew as time progressed. Clearly the freeholders of the shires had less opportunity to exercise their vote than did their urban counterparts. The disposition of the landed elite to electoral compromise, encouraged by the tremendous costs of contesting a county seat, severely circumscribed their role in the formal political process.

Some historians, echoing Namier, have argued that this role was in any case a deferential one. G. E. Mingay has contended that 'both the servility of the lesser gentry and the complaisance of the farmers paid tribute to the greater landlords' and that most electors 'belonged to a particular family's interest and voted as directed'.[30] D. C. Moore has elaborated upon this by pointing to the marked incidence of bloc voting in county elections, a symptom of the extent to which electors saw themselves as cohorts of big houses or landed estates.[31] In his opinion, freeholders, especially those who had a tenurial relationship with local landlords, saw themselves as part of 'deferential communities', to a point that county elections simply reaffirmed the political dispositions of the leading landowners.

Yet the evidence for such homogeneity of sentiment is by no means conclusive. It is not difficult to find examples of 'village voting', that is, the tendency of villages to vote in a uniform manner.

Indeed, there was a higher unanimity among village voters than there was among urban voters who belonged to the same trading companies. But voter unanimity was not the typical experience of rural freeholders. Frank O'Gorman's analysis of eleven county elections in the eighteenth century reveals that more voters dissented from the dominant pattern of electoral allegiance within their villages than voted in uniform battalions. Certainly the number of uniform villages as a proportion of all villages could be high, reaching 40 per cent or over in a few county elections. Yet, generally speaking, uniform villages were small and untypical.[32] Even where freeholders from the same village or hamlet voted *en bloc*, one should not presume that they did so at the behest of their landlords. In the Oxfordshire election of 1754, which Hogarth immortalised for posterity, some 41.3 per cent of villages voted in a uniform fashion. Yet there was a low correlation between the choice of resident squires and that of their villagers. Of the sixteen villages where a squire was in residence, only two showed any disposition to follow his choice. At Kingham, where the squire and parson voted Tory, for example, only three of eleven freeholders followed suit.

The quantitative evidence derived from poll books, then, gives little support for the widespread prevalence of deferential communities. It is not entirely watertight. The networks of dependence that were operative in rural areas were not necessarily coterminous with village boundaries and doubtless some are difficult to detect. None the less, the poll-book evidence is compelling enough to suggest that landlords could not automatically command the allegiance of their tenants and that patronal control of the substantial county electorate was far from complete. Landlords might wish to pressure their tenants, but they had to consider carefully both the private and public ramifications of high-handed tactics. Good tenants were often hard to find. Evictions for defying a landlord's recommendation, even where this was possible under the terms of a tenancy, could be economically and politically counterproductive, sullying a local reputation. Consequently, politically ambitious landlords went out of their way to cultivate their interest through the recognised conventions of county politics. These included electoral hospitality and the courtesy of acknowledging a freeholder's formal independence, often his right to dispose of one vote. In the Leicestershire election of 1741, for example,

Wrightson Mundy was rebuked by the freeholders for not paying 'obeisance to 'em earlier'. When he 'entreated their vote', he reported, 'they have sagely reply'd ... that it was Long till the Elections: & that time must be taken to consider of it'.[33] Patrons had to court their clients; bullying them represented a loss of authority. When Sir John Trevor promised his tenants' vote to Lord Myddleton in the Denbighshire election of 1741, he expressly refused 'to give authority for any violence towards them'.[34]

Landlords not only had to observe the accepted proprieties of electoral behaviour; they also had to be attentive to the broader issues of an electoral campaign. Normally, county elections were fought on local issues and reputations, but there were occasions when national controversies rippled through the shires. In the Northumberland by-election of 1748, when Lord Tankerville attempted to wrestle control of the county from the shires by capitalising on the '45 rebellion, Lord Somerset found his control of the formidable Percy interest faltering. Of the 110 freeholders in Alnwick, 67 declined to follow his support of the Jacobite candidate, Lawrence Allgood. In 1763 Lord Coleraine found his standing whittled away in Gloucestershire, where his support of the cyder tax counted against him. In 'all the vale and forest, great cyder countries', he reported, not more than 7 per cent of the freeholders offered him their votes.[35]

Perhaps the most striking examples of national issues influencing county elections occurred in 1734 and 1784. In the former, anti-Walpolean coalitions registered substantial gains, with the lesser gentry and yeoman farmers voting solidly against pro-excise candidates. Even in Walpole's home county of Norfolk, where all the stops were pulled out to return ministerial men, freeholders defied landlord pressure. Although many villages complied with the wishes of their resident squires, at least a third did not, with the ministerial Whigs suffering the greatest casualties.[36]

Similar signs of voter truculence occurred in 1784, when the issues surrounding the dismissal of the Fox–North coalition and the early dissolution of parliament reverberated through the shires. In Yorkshire, the tide of opinion ran so strongly against Fox that his foremost supporter in the county, Earl Fitzwilliam, abandoned a contest. In Norfolk, the Foxite candidate, Thomas Coke, was shunned by the freeholders even though the county elite had been prepared to support his candidature. In Suffolk, too, Sir

Charles Bunbury was turned out despite his thirty years' experience as the knight of the shire and his reputation among the gentry. 'We the Yeomanry and common freeholder are only considered as a pack of hounds', complained one freeholder during the electioneering, 'and as such are to be obedient to the whistle of some neighbouring squire.' Too often the county elite had packed the nomination meetings with their own cronies, he continued, but if such meetings had been organised by division, the shire would soon see 'who can bring in most votes, the Aristocratic Few or the Democratical Many, the Arbitrary Squires or the oppressed Freeholders'.[37] Such attitudes doubtless contributed to Bunbury's defeat.

It would be wrong, therefore, to exaggerate the passivity and localism of eighteenth-century freeholders. While they had relatively little opportunity to exercise their collective rights after 1715, at critical junctures their collective voice could be considerable. This applied *a fortiori* to city electors. Not only did they have a greater chance to participate in the political process, they often did so in a manner that expressed their independence from magnate control.

Of course, it is possible to find large towns and cities that were dominated by powerful patrons. At least seven of the twenty-eight towns with electorates over one thousand returned members or nominees of prestigious landed families on a regular basis. A further four constituencies were dominated by closed corporations, whose ability to flush the electorate with new freemen perverted the course of demotic politics. But it would be misleading to infer from this evidence that large towns were as politically compliant as the smaller boroughs, where the grip of patrons made them almost electorally unassailable. With the urban renaissance of the eighteenth century and the thickening of urban economies, landed patronage became a more fragile form of control and more contingent upon the delivery of favours and services. It also had to contend with the persistence of party strife. As many as 75, even 90 per cent of the voters in large urban constituencies voted along party lines in the first half-century; and such partisanship was accompanied by high turnouts and a high level of voter consistency. In Bristol, for example, 78 per cent of the freemen who polled both in 1734 and again in 1739 voted along party lines. In Norwich, where four in five of the 1734 voters returned to the polls the following year, the corresponding figure was 92 per cent. Even with the abatement of party strife after 1754, voter turnout and regular participation in large urban elections remained high, although partisanship was more erratic, reassuming a more distinct party coloration towards the end of the century.[38]

But what was the role of the middling sort within these politically vibrant constituencies? In terms of participation this is difficult to determine, for historians have not ventured any figures. My own researches suggest that, in mid-century Bristol, 60–66 per cent of the master craftsmen, tradesmen and merchants who registered their apprentices voted in the elections of the 1730s and 1750s. So, too, did the leading importers and exporters. These were very respectable participation rates, comparable to those of the new voters who had been deliberately recruited for the poll, and in excess of some religious congregations.[39] Among those tradesmen who acted as churchwardens, vestrymen and trustees of the Quaker meeting, the participation rate was even higher, ranging from 68 per cent to 91 per cent. Such figures suggest that electoral commitment grew with civic or religious responsibilities.[40]

The importance of the middling sort in urban elections is enhanced if we look at two other aspects of their political behaviour, their partisanship and their networks. In Bristol, in the 1730s, roughly the same proportion of masters voted in consecutive elections as did the total electorate (62 per cent), but their political consistency was significantly higher, 97 per cent as opposed to 78 per cent. Comparable figures are lacking for other constituencies, but, leaving aside voter consistency, it is clear that middling participation was often more partisan than amongst those lower in the social scale, where the temptations of venality and personal dependence enhance split voting and deference to social superiors.[41] To be sure, client relationships were far from absent among the middling ranks. One correspondent of the Society for Constitutional Information reported in 1783 that in Hull the solicitations of the higher ranks were such that 'several tradesmen are totally at a loss how to conduct themselves with safety. ... Others, ... having more than one voter in their families, split their votes for the sake of peace and the preservation of their friends in Trade.'[42] Within Westminster's luxury economy, well-to-do tradesmen often felt the thraldom of aristocratic clientage, being called upon to muster votes for the Court and the great houses.[43] Yet, by and large, men of the middling sort had greater opportunities to assert their independence than poor journeymen and labourers, especially in towns with diverse and ramified socio-economic structures.

This did not mean that the middling sort voted *en bloc* in big city elections. As vestrymen, churchwardens and elders, as members of important societies, commercial fraternities and clubs, they were deeply implicated in the infrapolitics of urban life. In cities like Bristol and Norwich, middling businessmen were crucial players in the mobilisation of political support, gathering votes, organising parades, supervising scrutinies. In the first half-century they were deeply divided by religion and party affiliation, a schism that was often institutionalised in corporation and caucus politics. Such passions did not necessarily abate with the decline of party. The onset of the American war revived sectarian differences, giving rise to an anti-ministerial Dissent and an Anglican party of order. Such polarities have induced some historians to suggest that the fundamental social foundations of urban politics were religious rather than class-based.[44]

Such an interpretation is compelling but by no means conclusive, based as it is on a relatively small, and sometimes unrepresentative, sample of visible nonconformists. We need to know a good deal more about Anglican affiliations and their penetration and purchase before we can confirm its veracity. Politico-religious differences resonated in Bristol, Norwich and Great Yarmouth, but they were less apparent in the electoral politics of other towns, among them Liverpool, Newcastle, Hull and Colchester, where the charismatic leadership of Dissenting ministers and merchants carried less weight. Indeed, as Paul Langford has suggested, it is possible that 'it was political strife which exacerbated sectarian conflict rather than vice versa'.[45]

Although the middling sort did not speak with one voice in city politics, there were occasions when its influence was decisive. Urban merchants and tradesmen revolted against Walpole's fiscal policies in 1733 and campaigned dramatically against his Eurocentric foreign policy, which privileged continental interests over trans-Atlantic. By the late 1730s, country coalitions against the Whig 'Colossus' had been forged in a number of towns, fuelling demands for a purification of political life and a more open, accountable politics.[46] The coalition did not last. It was soon compromised by high political manoeuvre and inner contradictions. But it set important precedents for the future. In 1756, during the crisis over Minorca, whose loss was accredited to a corrupt Whig oligarchy, urban spokesmen again advocated a reform of Britain's electoral and parliamentary structure and a redefinition of political power to accommodate mobile sources of wealth. Pitt's entry into the war cabinet for a time satiated such demands, but they resurfaced once more in the wake of Wilkes's flamboyant entry upon the political scene, making headway among the small-to-middling voters of the large towns that had championed anti-ministerial politics three decades earlier. By this time, urban politics addressed a broader range of issues that were pertinent to the middling sort: reform of the debt laws, freedom of the press, accountability in law, due judicial process, a reformed magistracy. These themes broached conflicts in more immediate contexts as much as national ones, generating demands for a purification of local government as well as greater middling representation.

Electorally, Wilkite radicalism was arguably negligible; discursively it was not. As John Brewer has shown, the Wilkite movement proved an important catalyst in the development of a more open, commercialised style of politics that stood in stark contrast to the custodial politics of the aristocratic elite and afforded the middling sort greater space for the pursuit of public and private grievances.[47] Wilkes's supporters enhanced the power of the press by safeguarding printers from arbitrary arrest and opening parliamentary debates to public scrutiny. They revivified the politics of commemoration into a counter-calendar celebrating Wilkes's own victories against constituted authority. They also pioneered new forms of political association, such as mass petitioning; pressured MPs to adhere to their constituents' demands through electoral pledges and instructions; and encouraged men of movable property, even the propertyless, to play a more active, formal role within the political nation. By making Wilkite politics convivial, commercial and accessible, radicals enhanced what Habermas termed the public sphere, that 'realm of ... social life in which something approaching public opinion can be formed'.[48]

The expansion of this terrain owed much to the efforts of the middling sort. As the consumers of political news and more accurate business information, the merchants and urban tradesmen had fostered the growth of the press and a faster, denser network of communications between the metropolis and the provinces, eroding the forces of localism in the process. As men who had clubbed together to insulate themselves from the hazards of debt and social misfortune, whether in masonic lodges or pseudo-masonic fraternities, they provided much of the infrastructure of Wilkite politics, raising subscriptions and sponsoring celebrations.[49] So, too, did the conventions of civic and extra-parliamentary politics in which many middling tradesmen had participated. It was the shopkeepers and artisans of the local London wards who first developed the practice of electoral pledges and delegatory representation, and it was the tradesmen of the large towns who were most active in sending instructions to their members and addressing king and parliament in a collective capacity. A survey of the instructions, addresses and petitions on major political issues between 1733 and 1784 reveals a hard core of support from the larger towns, especially from Bristol, Coventry, Exeter, Gloucester, London, Nottingham, Southwark, Westminster, Worcester and York. These large constituencies, with electorates ranging from 1200 to 12,000, were the most consistent participants in the extra-parliamentary politics of the mid-century, framing instructions and addresses on three or more occasions in the reign of George II, and again in the reign of his successor.[50] In the petitioning movements of 1769, 1775 and 1784, in each of which approximately 60,000 signatures were successfully solicited, the middling sort in the towns and shires were conspicuously represented.[51]

This did not mean that the middling sort spoke in unison. Despite the salience of Wilkes's middling backers and the gravitation of the Dissenters to the opposition by the mid-1770s, some wealthy merchants, professionals and tradesmen rallied to the crown in 1769 and 1775 and rejected radical, even opposition, Whig candidates at the hustings. In the 1781 Bristol by-election, for example, the 'Tory' candidate, George Daubeny, drew proportionately more support from the gentlemen, professions, merchants and genteel trades than did his opponent, the radical Whig and American, Henry Cruger. Even so, the differences were not substantial, and, indeed, the larger manufacturers of the city divided their votes quite evenly between the two contestants. On these grounds it would be misleading to link opposition politics to any notion of a rising middle class.

But it would be possible to show how middling notions of respectability and virtue helped set the political agenda. The point can be made by looking at the changing manner in which politicians were subjected to public scrutiny. During the first half of the century the private lives of politicians were seldom censured. The main source of criticism centred on manifestly public behaviour and the structures of dependence spawned by the growth of the State and the money market, which had compromised political independence. This quintessentially country vision of corruption continued after 1760, but it was increasingly enjoined by a moral critique of high politics which denied any distinction between the public and private spheres. Middling spokesmen such as Vicesimus Knox, the headmaster of Tonbridge School, helped sway the public in this regard. His enormously popular essays, first published in 1778 and running into nine editions in as many years, emphasised the inextricable connection between private and public virtue and the need to promote 'decency and regularity', 'temperance and industry', and 'religion and fortitude' to uphold liberty.[52] The same line of argument was taken up by Richard Price, who in 1779 linked Britain's political troubles to her profligacy and impiety.[53] Such appeals inevitably attracted those of an Evangelical stamp who were alarmed by upper-class dissipation and its abrogation of true Christian stewardship. But amid the trauma of the Gordon riots and the loss of America, the call for moral virtue acquired the status of a patriotic venture as much as the more extensively studied campaigns for economic and parliamentary reform.[54]

The changing temper of late-eighteenth-century politics may be illustrated by looking at two of the most flamboyant politicians of the era, John Wilkes and Charles James Fox. During the 1760s and 1770s, Wilkes's libertinism proved no major impediment to his political career. Certainly there were some who never forgave him for the *Essay on Woman,* and deplored his open visits to brothels. Wilkes's own mother remonstrated with her son for visiting 'the *Infamous* Mrs Gardener' in the sheriff's coach. She saw 'fatal consequences' from such outlandish actions and warned him that 'Many of the Middling People (thank Heaven) revere Virtue and see Vice countenanced by a Magistrate with *double* Abhorrence.'[55] Yet, on balance, the exploits of the waggish, squinting, leering hero of liberty drew as many plaudits as recriminations. 'I knows that Wilkes is a rascal', proclaimed one correspondent of the *Middlesex Journal,* 'but dam me I likes him the better for it.'[56] He was, as one drayman put it in 1768, 'free from cock to wig'.[57]

By the mid-eighties, however, gentlemanly libertinism proved less marketable, at least among the middling sort. In the 1784 election Fox was taken to task for his rakish habits and compared unfavourably with the Younger Pitt. 'The years which most of his Opponents have consumed in shaking a Dice Box, in the Haunts of Debauchery, in the Follies of Fashion, have been faithfully devoted by Mr Pitt to the Improvement of his Mind', declared one commentator.[58] 'No honest Man can behold a profligate Gambler passing from the Gaming Table to the Counsels of his Sovereign, and the important Concerns of a Nation', wrote Thomas North-cote, 'without feeling a strong Disgust in his Mind and a sympathetic Nausea in the Stomach. It is an Example repugnant to all Principle and subversive of all Moral Character.'[59] Along with his boon companions and the libertine Prince of Wales, Fox was cast as a degenerate politician unfit to govern the country. By the same token, the moral respectability of the king had begun to restore his popularity among the middling sort, after the loss of America and his meddlesome favouritism towards Lord Bute. As a signifier of 'domestic probity and obstinate patriotism', he came to represent 'a reassuring stability in the midst of national flux and humiliation', a welcome, homely, and honest contrast to meretricious and immoral politicians.[60]

V

By the mid-eighties the foundations of what was to become a middle-class social and political sensibility had been laid. Political and social virtue no longer rested on a country-house ideal, with its acknowledged reciprocities between rich and poor and its conventions of landed stewardship, but on men of character, whose domestic felicity, moral integrity and forthright dealing made them, in Richard Price's words, 'the health and vigour of a state'.[61] Such a vision privileged men of mobile wealth and sought to reconcile the older traditions of civic humanism with the realities of a more dynamic commercial society. While it did not necessarily exclude landed proprietors, it challenged narrow definitions of landed hegemony, and denied virtue to both aristocratic voluptuaries and to those who lacked the cultural and economic means to

respectability and responsibility. Such a definition ultimately set
limits to the call for a more open, accessible politics, denying the
labouring poor their rights to full citizenship. Shocked by the
Gordon riots and the subsequent excesses of the French Revolution, the middling sort by the large rallied in defence of a propertied order in which they had staked out a claim.

The political means by which the middling sort asserted that
claim, I have suggested, were essentially three-fold. Although
under-represented in parliament, the more influential members
of the middling sort, particularly those that belonged to well-
organised pressure groups, proved adept at advancing their
interests through lobbying their local MPs and petitioning parliament and the departments of state. Sometimes these activities
were reinforced through electoral pressure, by building up a
commanding interest in town and even county politics. Such was
the case with the Birmingham manufacturers, whose dramatic
entry in the Warwickshire election of 1774 signalled that they
were a force to be reckoned with.[62] But electoral politics was normally a site of contention among middling groups, who, divided
by religion and party, struggled for local supremacy in an oligarchical, but by no means closed, political system. Large towns, in
particular, proved crucial sources of vitality in what was an
increasingly sclerotic electoral system. Predictably, they became
important sites for the expansion of the public sphere, drawing
upon the cultural and economic resources of middling associations and fraternities and fracturing the sinews of clientage and
localism which had hitherto made the landed aristocracy and
gentry the indispensable brokers of national politics. Such
brokerage continued to be important, but the associational
strength of the middling sort, its economic power and its moral
authority in the broader political sphere, meant that aristocratic
leadership could not be exercised in an unconditional or
unqualified manner. 'I used to make no scruple of maintaining',
reflected Joseph Priestley in the 1790s,

> that there is not only most virtue and most happiness, but even
> most true politeness in the middle class of life. For the propor-
> tion as men pass most of their time in the society of their equals
> they get a better established habit of governing their tempers;
> they attend more to the feelings of others, and are more

disposed to accommodate themselves to them. On the other hand, the passions of persons in higher life, having been less controlled, are more apt to be inflamed; the idea of their rank and superiority to others seldom quits them and though they are in a habit of concealing their feelings, and disguising their passions, it is not always well done.[63]

Priestley was a controversial figure, a Dissenting intellectual who had spent much of his life amid the bourgeoisie of the manufacturing North and Midlands. Like Adam Smith, he made a virtue of commercial self-interest, seeing it as the foundation of a sociability that would rationalise and harmonise the diverse interests of a more open, accessible market society. In his view such intercourse was vastly superior to the status-bound attitudes of the aristocracy, whose hauteur and brittle code of honour undermined its self-control and compromised its statecraft. Real civility, and by extension citizenship, rested fundamentally on middling, even middle-class manners and morals. Certainly Priestley's anti-aristocratic ethos was more assertive than many of his contemporaries, but it was not idiosyncratic. It was indicative of the distance the more progressive sections of the middling sort had travelled in the so-called aristocratic century.

7. The Middling Sort in Eighteenth-Century Colchester: Independence, Social Relations and the Community Broker

SHANI D'CRUZE

I

The urban middling sort are increasingly being identified by historians as a group with an identity and interests of their own in eighteenth-century English society. They proliferated and benefited from economic and social change and were a vocal component of out-of-doors political processes. This chapter will outline an hypothesis that links the business and household patterns of the middling sort, in an eighteenth-century provincial town, with a model of social relations and ideas reflecting their participation in the public and political sphere.[1]

An essential defining attribute of the Colchester middling sort throughout most at least of the eighteenth century, common between traders, manufacturers and professionals, was the business household, where the divide between working and domestic arrangements was minimal and the skills and labour of all household members contributed to both the economic and the domestic enterprise. The occupational title of the head of the household often described the enterprise of the whole family, though sometimes different occupations were carried out by household members and contributed to the overall family economy. Where the household head was 'pater familias', his occupational title served to accord him status in the public community. Male middling

household heads were also involved in public life through office-
holding in vestry or corporation and variously as trustees, will
executors, bond holders, churchwardens or chapel deacons. This
public activity, necessary to operate the unsalaried and amateur
institutions of local government and society, formed a second
component of the middling male's social persona. Such institutions provided a forum for political contest, divided by party.
Despite periods of formal political compromise, local party
remained important. The middling public presence also incorporated political participation, heightened by the comparatively wide
borough franchise. The rounded middling citizen could claim full
citizenship in the public sphere through this multiple social role.

Citizenship was predicated on independence, based on the avoid-
ance of waged labour and the rights and privileges of local institutions. Nevertheless, the independent middling citizen achieved his
position through hidden dependences, not only on the labour and
support of household members but also through interdependence
with his fellow citizens, especially those most publicly active. Within
what remained very much a face-to-face community, local social
relations were important in associating middling individuals
through networks of family, neighbourhood, religion, trade and
politics. Local sources show social networks tended to centre on a
significant minority of active middling individuals who had a
heightened public role and were in contact with multiple groups of
people. These 'community brokers' can be supposed to have held
power within the networks they linked. Their very activity made
them sought out as office-holders, creditors, executors or trustees.
In eighteenth-century terminology, these were one's 'friends'.

However, if independence for the bulk of the male middling
sort was limited, in that social connection centred on the brokers
who monopolised channels for credit, political status and office, it
was equally constrained for the brokers themselves. Despite the
apparent independence of an active public role and influence
within social networks, their position was ultimately only realised
though their connections with each other within the constraints of
local society as a whole. This hypothesis concerning social interaction must remain as such since the personalised character of much
brokering activity cannot be documented in detail, given the public nature of the available sources. Nevertheless, it offers a plausible interpretation of those incidences of crisis or scandal where

such informal activity tends to reach the written record. The recurrent conflict and crisis of local politics provides an excellent testing ground. At election times, when the distribution of local power was formally contested, the canvassers and managers of voting interests were exactly those middling individuals who maintained an active public role and a wide social connection, which they could then mobilise for political ends.

Colchester provides a good location for studying these issues. It was a medium-sized town within sixty miles of London, which, during the eighteenth century, was overtaken in the urban ranking by newly industrialising towns, and also lost its staple woollen cloth manufacture through progressive disruption of overseas markets during wartime and through mounting competition from the Yorkshire woollen industry. Nevertheless, it developed its role as a marketing centre for the region's grain trade and as an east coast port, its retail and craft manufacture servicing the agricultural sector as well as the town. Colchester survived its economic setbacks and participated in the growth then occurring in English towns. Economic change altered, diversified and multiplied the middling sort, to whom it proved far less disruptive than to the poor. Change, growth and 'improvements' throughout the urban network showed patterns which Peter Borsay has identified as an 'urban renaissance'. He discusses the improvement in town fabric and the increases in commerce and marketing. Above all, he analyses a distinctively urban culture which could be described, in the terminology of the times, as 'genteel'.[2]

In Colchester many new high-street shops sprang up after the 1730s, their bow-fronted windows illuminated at night. Better road links, especially to the capital, increased trade and mobility. Many older, jetted, timber-framed houses were rebuilt or re-fronted in Palladian style. Lime trees were planted beside new and elegant gravel walks. Colchester had two bowling greens and a commercial public gardens. Auricula and tulip growers mounted festivals and displays. A permanent theatre was built by subscription in 1763, where the Norwich Company of Comedians played. They had hitherto performed in the Moot Hall. Colchester had musical concerts, monthly assemblies and a coffee room as well as a book club and a subscription library.[3]

Genteel culture was far from being the province of the visiting and town gentry alone. Merchants, professionals, traders and superior artisans participated in genteel activities and acquisitions, as both producers and consumers. We cannot from this make the unqualified assertion that the middling sort were deeply implicated in the development of genteel culture without further considering how the middling sort is to be defined. Are we simply to use the term as a 'catch-all', to include all occupational groups between the gentry and the labouring poor? If so, should distinctions be made for struggling artisans, or for those affluent professionals who to all intents and purposes lived as gentry? Do we further wish to understand that there was some sort of shared social identity amongst these occupational groups, one aspect of which may be their active participation in the 'urban renaissance'?

What help do local sources offer us in identifying a middling sort? If we focus on the period 1735–50, we find the records mentioning many individuals from a range of artisan, manufacturing, and trading occupations, with comparatively few gentry or labourers. Admittedly, such local sources do not name only the middling sort, and even those with ostensibly middling occupations may be journeymen or impoverished artisans. However, the greater proportion named can be accommodated within wider definitions of the middling sort. The bay trade and the food and drink trades are well represented, as well as numbers of gardeners, yeomen and husbandmen reflecting the amount of agriculture and horticulture that took place within the borough and its liberties (see Table 7.1).

Definitions which rely on occupation seem at first sight to have the best methodological precision, but on closer examination the evidence becomes more opaque. Correlations between occupational criteria and social status are fraught with difficultly. Trades and occupations included men and sometimes women of widely diverging income – compare, for instance, the small market trader in meat with the very substantial and gentlemanly grazier, both of whom could be described at butchers. Neither those given titles of gentility, nor labourers and servants, were middling sort if we wish to narrow the definition to the families who operated independent trading households. A gentleman and his family lived on unearned income, servants were dependants within households, and labourers received a cash wage. However, Colchester was a popular parliamentary borough where a few gentlemen and labourers exercised a vote amongst the predominantly middling electorate. Furthermore, occupational mobility over a life-cycle could include moves from servant to tradesman to 'gent', since

Table 7.1 *Occupations in Colchester and district, 1735–50*

	Occupational Group	All Locations	Colchester Only
1	Baytrade (woollen trade)	99 (22.5)	96 (26.6)
2	Building	27 (6.1)	26 (7.2)
3	Dress	41 (9.3)	38 (10.5)
4	Drink	33 (7.5)	30 (8.3)
5	Food	27 (6.1)	25 (6.9)
6	Hythe*	15 (3.6)	11 (3.0)
7	Gents	18 (4.1)	10 (2.9)
8	Land	71 (16.1)	30 (8.3)
9	Medical	4 (.9)	4 (1.1)
10	Merchant	13 (2.9)	12 (3.3)
11	Metal	6 (1.4)	4 (1.1)
12	Misc	5 (.9)	5 (1.4)
13	Officers	9 (2.0)	7 (1.9)
14	Professions	33 (7.5)	30 (8.3)
15	Transport/Leather	12 (2.7)	11 (3.0)
16	Wood	5 (1.1)	5 (1.4)
17	Working	21 (4.8)	17 (4.8)
	TOTAL	440	361

Figures in brackets are occupation groups as a percentage of known occupations

*All occupations connected with Colchester's port at the Hythe, excluding substantial merchants, e.g. boatbuilder, mariner, porter.

Notes: This data is drawn from the database of Colchester sources between 1735 and 1750 presented in S. D'Cruze, 'The Middling Sort in Provincial England, Politics and Social Relations in Colchester, 1730–1800'. The database comprised 12,724 items of data on 5,421 individuals, some three-quarters of whom were resident in the urban parishes of the borough, the rest in the surrounding area of north-east Essex and south Suffolk.

The sources used to compile the database were: newspapers, *Ipswich Journal*, 1739–50, *Colchester Journal*, 1736, 1739; quarter sessions; Sessions Books and Rolls for Colchester Borough Sessions, Epiphany 1734/5 to Epiphany 1740/1 inclusive (Borough Sessions ceased at that point following the suspension of the Borough Charter); Petty Sessions for Colchester Borough, P/COR/1 and P/COR/1a, Lexden and Winstree Petty Sessions, Colchester Sittings P/LWR/1, P/LWR/4; administrations of estates: Archdeaconry of Colchester and the Commissary of London (Essex and Herts), 1735–1750, D/ACWb, D/ABWb, D/ABAc, D/ACAc; wills proved in the same jurisdiction for Colchester, 1735–50, D/ACR, D/ABR, D/ACW, D/ABW; Colchester Borough Assembly Book, 1735–1742; Colchester Borough Poll Books for 1735 and 1741.

This table uses an alpha-cluster sample of individuals in the database, whose surnames begin with A, G, I, J, M, R, and T. Individuals from all locations are compared with individuals in Colchester town only (i.e., excluding borough liberties). The 'All Locations' sample includes 1120 individuals in all, i.e. 20.7 per cent of the 5421 individuals in the database. The 'Colchester' sample includes 895 individuals in all, i.e. 16.5 per cent of total individuals in the database. Hence, Colchester individuals comprise 79.9 per cent of this alpha cluster sample.

Named occupations and 'gents' are classified here, hence no account is taken of widows and spinsters without an occupation named in the relevant sources.

retirement from trade or profession was often accompanied by the purchase of a genteel town house. Those calling themselves 'Esq.' were commonly gentry, but the title was also assumed by those of the middling sort elected Mayor or Alderman. Clergy and affluent professionals have elsewhere been described as 'pseudo-gentry', but in Colchester such individuals also retained considerable social connections amongst the middling sort.[4]

Rateable values can also give some indication of the size of the Colchester middling sort, since they should certainly be prosperous enough to pay more than the minimum rate. The very poor were excused rates and the minimum was calculated on a yearly rateable value of £1. In the later eighteenth century in Colchester around 14 per cent of the adult population were ratepayers on property valued at more than £2 rental per year (rateable values remained stable over decades and underestimated market values). An upper level for rateable values of the middling sort is more difficult to determine. In the large parish of St James, for example, 6 per cent of all ratepayers could be accounted as town gentry. Their rates, however, could well be lower than those of commercial enterprises. Wilshire Wilson Esq., who was sufficiently well off to bequeath his wife an annuity of £2000 per annum, was assessed on £10 rateable value, whereas Sarah Thornton, victualler at the Rose and Crown, had a rateable value of £30.[5] Ratepayers were heads of households and so wives and adult children were not included in the 14 per cent figure. We can therefore estimate, making allowance for widow or widower household heads, that the adult middling sort as a whole comprised something like 20 per cent of the town's adult population.[6]

It may, perhaps, be that the project of attempting to isolate a bounded occupational and status group labelled 'the middling sort' is so problematic because such a discrete group had little social identity. Nevertheless, the social and administrative aspects as well as the political life of eighteenth-century Colchester can, it will be argued, best be interpreted in terms of a recognizable middling sort. As a concept to understand what was going on in eighteenth-century towns, the term should best be understood more broadly. A middling sort cohered out of lived experience and social relations, through occupation, but also through other aspects of life. One attribute in particular was shared by traders, artisans and professionals. All organised their working and family lives around the small-producer household in which living and working space existed in close proximity and household members, including wives, older children, servants and apprentices, participated in both the household and business tasks.

Despite individual mobility through business failure or betterment migration, the Colchester middling sort had a substantial core of comparatively stable business and minor professional families. The Barnet Readings, father and son, ran the charity school in All Saints' for decades. The Agnis dynasty of gardeners can be traced over most of the century. Families could change trade as economic circumstances dictated. The Shillito family of All Saints' moved out of the declining bay trade into the drink trade and office-holding. Families could export members, often during young adulthood and especially to London. Meanwhile the core of the family business and property remained as a resource to be husbanded over time.[7]

Such families were not necessarily parochial, for they had an extended commitment to family and to small business. The Whiting family of cardmakers illustrate the point. At around the beginning of 1750, one John Stokes was apprenticed to Samuel Whiting, cardmaker of Braintree. Three years later he was transferred to Anthony Whiting, Samuel's father, who traded in St Nicholas, Colchester. When Anthony senior died, the business in Colchester was taken over by another son, Anthony junior. Despite the geographical separation, Samuel Whiting was trading as part of the family business and receiving financial support from his father.[8]

The Taylor family moved from Lavenham to Colchester in 1798, when father, Isaac Taylor, became minister at Stockwell Independent Chapel. Isaac was also an engraver, the work providing a much-needed supplement to the small stipend from his ministry. The Taylors, Isaac and Ann, produced eleven children, six of whom survived. Their large family strained limited finances and the health and energies of Ann Martin Taylor. Despite her heavy burden, Ann took measures to keep up her intellectual partnership with her husband and the couple were equally dedicated to providing a close, affective, educational and religious upbringing for their children. In this, they were part of the distinctive practices of middling domesticity, which were becoming widespread by the end of the century. All their children were educated at home, with additional teaching at the day school for the boys. From their mid-teens each child was also trained in engraving work and assisted their father in his workshop. The Taylor daughters, Jane and Ann, who also became the authors of popular children's books, poetry and adult moral tales, alternated between engraving and housework. The Taylor household was the workplace of family members engaged in engraving, intellectual, educational, religious and domestic work. It was operated by the parents and older children with one or two servants, as well as apprentices and often a few pupils.[9]

Although no comparably detailed descriptions survive of other Colchester middling households, similar structure and practice is apparent. The Wilders were saddlers living in a house perhaps a little smaller than the Taylors', but which also included workshops as well as living quarters. Father, Francis Wilder, died in 1743, leaving his wife and children to continue the business. His son seems to have died soon after. By 1755 a daughter, Ann, was operating a clear-starcher's trade from the family premises. This evidence of apparently successful business continuity betokens not only the work and skills of other family members after the father's death, but also indicates the degree of their involvement beforehand. Ann's move into a more genteel trade seems to have been associated with an attempt to make the most cost-effective use of her available skills, not with a distaste for, or inability to participate in the saddlery, as her later career shows. In 1757 she married James Bream, also a saddler, and they ran the business together. After his death in 1780 she continued alone.

The pattern of pooled labour supporting the middling and artisan family enterprise is repeated elsewhere. Thomas Hardy and his wife were weavers and worked together at their looms late into the night. Elizabeth Shillito was the daughter of cardmakers Ephraim and Elizabeth. She trained in millinery and traded from the family premises before marriage, to James Dunthorne, in December 1779. Dunthorne was by trade a limner, with artistic and musical talent, who, despite some showing at the Royal Academy, was unsuccessful in furthering his career in London and ran a print shop in Colchester High Street. The shop never made much money and Elizabeth continued her milliner's and perfumer's business as well as servicing the demands of a fast growing family. She continued in trade as a widow until her own death in 1807. We do not know whether the Dunthornes had similar ideas on child-rearing to the Taylors, but can surmise that their household similarly combined domestic and business duties (for two separate businesses) and involved the hard and continued work of both partners, as well, no doubt, as that of older children and one or two servants.[10]

In 1773, when Elizabeth Shillito wished to publicise her wares, she advertised in the local paper and begged 'leave to thank her *friends* for their past favours and ... (acquainted) ... them and the *public*, that she is just returned from London with a fresh assortment of Millinery Haberdashery and Linnen Drapery goods' (my emphasis). The distinction between one's friends and the public is common in the sources. When, in 1749, attorney William Mayhew wanted the assistance of the borough MP to regain the town's charter, he wrote on behalf of the 'poor Burgesses of Colchester', who had applied to him 'as one of ... (the MP's) ... Friends'. Harold Perkin has identified the concept of 'friendship' to describe ties of patronage and deference in an aristocratically dominated society, yet Leonore Davidoff and Catherine Hall have shown how, by the early nineteenth century, amongst England's emerging middle class: 'The stark world of political economy had been conceived within real lives deeply embedded in ties of kinship and traditional, if modified bonds of patronage.'[11]

So, who were your friends? Milliner Elizabeth Shillito's were no doubt her chief and most affluent customers, who could claim first choice of her delightful wares. Your friends were those who supported your status in the public world. It was to your friends you would apply for a pension, a pardon, or a loan. Friends would act as executor, trustee or witness to a will. They would put up a recognizance for your court appearance. They would witness your marriage. They were your landlord, your employer, the most affluent member of your parish vestry, the neighbourhood victualler, perhaps the local cleric. Across this wide spectrum of relationships both patronage and something nearer approaching reciprocity can be included.

When Hannah Hopkins, the widow of a prosperous mariner and ship-owner made her will, she appointed as executors her brother and John Bartholomew, a merchant at the port, a friend and neighbour, clearly a trade associate of her husband and the executor of his will. Bartholomew first appeared in Colchester as master of the sloop Ceres. He lived near the Hythe (Colchester's port) in the 1730s and married Hannah Pamplin, whose family owned the Fleece, a large inn in the town centre. Bartholomew was an active trader and used the local courts to enforce payment from his debtors. At about the time of his wife's death, in 1739, the Ceres was sold and Bartholomew seems to have developed his merchant activities. By the later 1740s he was selling marble and portland stone and employed a skilled mason from London. He was active in St Leonard's vestry. When, in 1740, a ring of timber thieves was discovered in the neighbourhood they were taken to his house by the constable to be examined, apparently before the JP was informed. Again in 1760, he took a leading role in examining and apprehending small-time crooks, sailors embezzling sugar from the Colchester to London pacquet. He maintained strong connections with the town's sea-going interest as well as the wider urban middling sort through executorships, administrations of estates and other business. If one needed a 'friend' in St Leonard's, John Bartholomew clearly had influence at his disposal and can be seen to have deployed it.[12]

One can use local records not just to build up data on the careers of named individuals but also to demonstrate connections between people. Individuals are rarely mentioned alone. A juror, a constable or an alderman is listed with his fellow office-holders. A will associates the will-maker with legatees, witnesses and executors. By plotting the connections between individuals mentioned in the sources, networks of social linkage can be built up. The networks discussed here are drawn from links in Colchester sources made over the period 1739 to 1741, a time of local political upheaval, as the Whigs sought to break the Tories' ten-year monopoly on the corporation. The local contest was further complicated by a highly contentious general election, in which the Walpole administration was struggling to prevent defeat.[13]

Two networks will be discussed here, those of Peter Alvis and William Mayhew. Networks were plotted to the second order (a first-order link is my friend; a second-order link is the friend of a friend). The techniques used borrow from the methodologies of social network analysis. Clearly the size of a network is important. Those who emerge as busier, from the sources, had a greater amount of social connection, and thus perhaps more social influence. A network's density measures how closely individuals are connected with each other. The members of the corporation, for example, formed a very dense network since all were connected to each. By contrast, the legatees named in a will may not all be known to each other, and form a less dense network. Someone having direct connections to many people in the network is said to have a high degree of centrality. Many lines of communication pass through that person, who therefore has the important ability to make connections between other people or, conversely, keep them apart.[14]

The network belonging to Peter Alvis (Figure 7.1) has 90 links between friends-of-friends and 39 individuals as well as Alvis. Links are made across a wide range of sources. Alvis was a shoemaker and sometime minor exciseman, living near the Castle. He was churchwarden at All Saints' and left money in his will of 1743 for a Wednesday lecture, as well as many small legacies to friends, neighbours and relatives. He seems to have been a bachelor. Alvis could muster ten first-order links between 1739 and 1741, spread over three wills, those of Joseph Tanner, Jonathan May and Peter Thorn. Though his role in All Saints' vestry would place him amongst middling office-holders, he was not on the corporation but sat once as a juror in quarter sessions and voted in the election of 1741. His position in the excise barred him from elected office, though he retained close contacts with the corporation through office-holders Tanner and May. His link with Tanner is reinforced by a kinship connection.[15]

Alvis's network shows separate clusters around the various wills, the corporation, and quarter sessions. Thirteen individuals, including Alvis, are mentioned in more than one source and have some degree of centrality between clusters. Characteristics of these thirteen are tabulated in Table 7.2. They appear in a good range of local sources – overall they were busy people. In terms of occupation they include a spread of the trades plus one member of the lesser clergy. They were all resident in Colchester town. Several lived in the small central parishes close to the Castle, but others (mostly in the second order) form a distinct subgroup, resident outside the town walls in the South Ward. As regards religion, the twelve tabulated are all Anglicans. Politically, they are virtually all Tory.

Alvis's network shows the effective links within the middling governing group. It locates Alvis as part of the group in a way that his biographical detail alone cannot do. It illustrates how neighbourhood, religion and politics can unify a network across the range of middling occupations, but also shows how more than one 'centre of

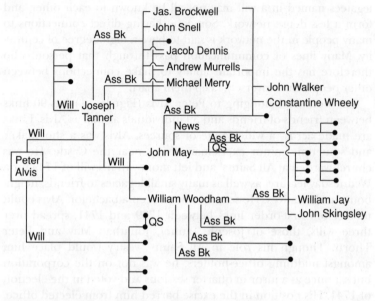

Figure 7.1 *Peter Alvis's network*
Total individuals, 39. Total links, 90. Density, 12.1%

The network maps in Figures 7.1 and 7.2 illustrate the social networks generated by the links between individuals shown in Colchester sources for the years 1739–41. For the composition of the original database, see notes to Table 7.1.

The original individual, ego, is shown to the left of the map and lines link him/her to other individuals. Networks are mapped to the second order, so the links of first-order contacts are then also portrayed. My friend is a first-order contact. My friend's friend is a second-order contact. Contacts who generate further links are shown by name. Those who have no further links within the second order of ego's network are shown as black dots. The sources that generate links are indicated alongside the connecting lines. Source names are abbreviated as follows:

Quarter Sessions	QS
Will	Will
Administration	Ad
Assembly Book	Ass Bk
Petty Sessions	PS
Newspapers	News

(Poll Books generate no links in this database).

For each map, the **density** (a measure of how much ego's contacts are linked with each other) as well as the number of individuals and links in the network are indicated.

A network's **density**, D, is obtained by the formula $D = 100Na/\frac{1}{2}N(N-1)\%$, where Na = total actual links excluding links with ego, and N = total individuals excluding ego.

gravity' can appear in a network, not only offering choice in the contacts that can be mobilised but also illustrating how one network can shade into the contacts of another individual. Andrew Murrells's network would include many people shown here.

The people who were central to Alvis's network were active in the borough sources. Murrells, for example, a gardener, held fourteen minor offices on the corporation between 1734 and 1740. He was called to the Borough Sessions petty jury in 1736 and 1739 and was juror in a criminal trial at Easter 1740. That same sessions he took over an apprentice from his recently-deceased father and stood £20 recognizance for his relative, Francis Murrells, accused of assault and robbery. It was not only in court or on the corporation that Murrells took a public role. In 1739 he was a steward at the town's annual Auricula Feast.[16] Such people had a not dissimilar social role to the merchant, John Bartholomew, described above. Their social role gave them social influence and connected them to a number of other people, in particular to each other.

Table 7.2 *Members of Peter Alvis's Network*

Name	Occupation	Place	Sources	Hits	Vote
Peter Alvis	Shoemaker/Excise	C	3	6	T
Joseph Tanner	Baker	C	5	13	T
John May	Weaver	C	6	36	T
William Woodham	?	C	4	28	T
Jacob Dennis	Weaver	H	3	10	T/W
Andrew Murrells	Cooper	H	4	24	T
Michael Merry	Papper	H	5	36	T
James Brockwell	Curate	H	4	10	T/W
John Walker	Shoemaker/Baker	H	5	44	T
Constantine Wheely	Barber	C	5	26	W
William Jay	?	T	3	14	T
John Skingsley	Baymaker	T	3	30	T

In this table, 'Place' indicates whether the individual lives in a parish near the Castle (C), in another town parish inside the walls (T), or in the parishes near the Hythe, outside the walls (H).

'Source' gives the number of sources in which the individual appears over the whole 15-year database. For sources, see Notes to Table 7.1.

'Hits' gives the number of times the individual is recorded in all sources over the full 15-year period.

'Vote' shows whether the individual voted Tory or Whig in the Colchester elections of 1735 and 1741. A vote in one election or a vote for the same party in both elections is indicated T or W. A voter who votes for a different party in each election is shown T/W, the vote for 1735 being given first.

Like Bartholomew, these individuals can be described as 'community brokers'. They are of the middling sort and hold local office. They are central to the local connection between other middling individuals in Colchester society.

William Mayhew was a very active community broker. He was a Tory attorney and participated fully in borough politics. His activities were augmented by large holdings of property (including two substantial Colchester inns), which he controlled either as administrator of two family estates, or as agent for the lessees of the corporation's extensive estates on Severalls Heath. As well as stewardships and agencies on land in Essex and Suffolk, he maintained an attorney's practice in Colchester. These property interests gave Mayhew leverage within the town and the borough to further his private and political interests.[17]

His network (Figure 7.2) has 316 links and 114 other people. Its density (4.9 per cent) is less than half that of Alvis's network (12.1 per cent). In other words, not only is Mayhew linked with far more individuals, but also his contacts are far less well known to each other. He has a much greater role in making social connection than does Peter Alvis. Mayhew's network includes a wide range of sources. Mayhew was on the committee which raised the corporation's legal expenses when, as part of the political crisis in 1739–41, several innkeepers took leading corporation members to court for extorting illegal fines from non-burgesses for alehouse licences. This connects him to the main protagonists of the case, including the elite group on the aldermen's bench. Thence there are contacts in the second order to many middling office-holders. Of these, William Seaber (tailor and high constable), John Skingsley (baymaker, distiller and multiple office-holder), and Ephraim Shillito (cardmaker and keeper of the house of correction), are central to wider networks among the lower officials.[18] Mayhew is clearly very busy in the town and the corporation – a thoroughgoing eighteenth-century man of business. His occupation itself facilitated his brokering activity and he balanced his activities in local politics with an extensive attorney's practice and fingers in very many lucrative propertied pies in the town and surrounding area.

The broker's centrality to the network is vital. It was in his interests to keep clients and patrons apart and thus render his services necessary. Time was also a prerequisite for successful broker activity. It took directed and sustained effort to manage a network of

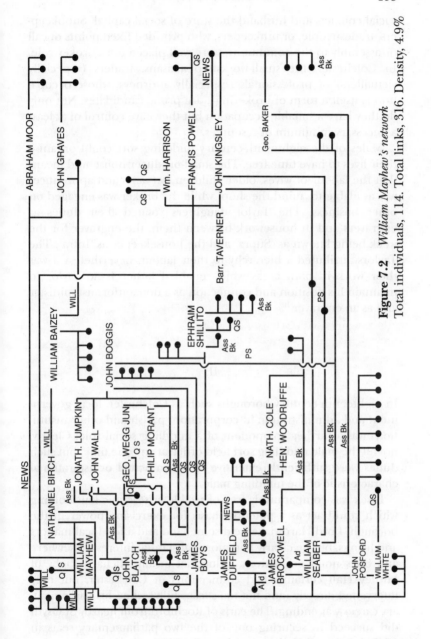

Figure 7.2 *William Mayhew's network*
Total individuals, 114. Total links, 316. Density, 4.9%

social contacts and husband the store of social capital. Shopkeepers, tradespeople, or innkeepers, who provided fixed points of call
or assembly to the community, were well placed for a broker role.
In Colchester, the small-workshop artisans, traders (especially
victuallers) or professionals (especially attorneys, whose occupation is itself a form of brokering), are prime candidates. Not only
do they have a suitable occupation but they have control of at least
a necessary minimum of resources.

Males of the eighteenth-century middling sort could organise
their lives to have time free. The small-producer household meant
that the labour of wives, older children, servants and apprentices
was available to 'mind the shop' while the broker was engaged on
other business. The Taylor daughters rotated their duties as
engravers and in housework between them, the engraver for the
week being known as 'Supra' and the housekeeper as 'Infra'. The
Taylors attributed a hierarchy to their labour, nevertheless it was
their work in both areas which enabled father Isaac Taylor to
maintain his position and connection as a nonconformist minister
and as an engraver.[19]

II

In eighteenth-century boroughs such as Colchester, local government and administration in corporation, parish and other institutions was a further component of a middling social role. Clearly,
not all the male middling sort held office at any one time, but such
duties were sufficiently extensive to be an actual or aspirational
characteristic of the middling male.

Essex was comparatively free of sizable aristocratic landholding
which could act as a potential basis for exercising power in the
borough. Lord Hardwicke held some land and a few local manors
and livings, but he clearly had more substantial interests elsewhere
and does not seem actively influential locally. Richard Rigby of
Mistley Hall certainly had connections in Colchester, but only
intervened directly (and not too successfully) when his parliamentary career was ending. The earls of Rochford from nearby St Osyth
did succeed in securing one of the two parliamentary seats in
1747, but lost their interest thereafter. Indeed the Essex landed

gentry seem to have concentrated their political and social influence in county rather than Colchester politics. Within the borough, the middling sort were able to participate fully in the competing nexus of interests and to use borough institutions as vehicles for social and political assertiveness.[20]

John Triffitt has argued that the extent of gentry and aristocratic patronage in eighteenth-century society has, in general, been over-stated, in terms both of economy and of institutions. His research on south-western towns reveals lively, independent, urban communities with an active middling sort as well as a degree of independence amongst craftsmen engendered by complex and diffuse organisation of trade. He finds community solidarity based around trade and neighbourhood, an important social role for parish churches, and active nonconformity. Local government was 'extensive, active, efficient and popular'. Institutions of government available in eighteenth-century boroughs had been designed to suit a far less complex society. Office-holders were unpaid amateurs, and, without the active participation of a local middling sort utilising the frame-work of these outmoded institutions, local administration would have failed and local autonomy would have been jeopardised.[21] The trading and professional middling sort could leave their businesses in the charge of wives, servants and apprentices whilst spending time on public business. Even superior artisans, paid by the piece, could make time to undertake the more humble offices. Hence, also, the tendency to mix public and private funds, to make money from office in ways that would later be condemned as corrupt.

There was automatic tension between competition for status between parties and individuals and the need to keep town government running in order to preserve the institutions and structures which were desired status vehicles. Conflict between varied interests was, Triffitt argues, endemic to town life. This contentiousness and high level of political awareness and activity balked attempts at incursion by either upper-class or central-government patronage and influence, which had to compete within the generalised local conflict. Much other recent historiography has emphasised the importance of the local dimension to eighteenth-century politics. The politics of interests, as well as the politics of party, was import-ant in linking the local to the national context.[22]

Similar conclusions emerge from studying Colchester, which was a 'popular' borough with some 1500 burgesses, about half of these

resident. Political participation in borough affairs and parliamentary elections could therefore extend over a wide range of traders,
artisans and professionals. Very few labourers were voters, and,
apart from retired tradesmen and the locally active town gentry,
very few 'gents' exercised a borough vote. This is not to argue that
local politics was entirely a middling concern. Both town gentry and
the labouring poor had differing interests to defend and promote
in the local political arena, without exercising a vote. Nevertheless,
for Colchester's trading, minor professional and superior artisan
groups, who had sufficient material and social stake in the town to
flesh out the exercise of a voting right with the demands and status
of office-holding, but who had not the scope and the capital to
acquire a political identity at county level, borough politics held a
particular importance. At the same time, their man-power was
necessary to operate the institutions of local government.

The borough institutions provided an official role for some 280
or so individuals in any year, counting Grand and Petty Sessions
jurors and constables: that is, about a third of the resident burgesses. However, allowing for duplications of office, this number can
be reduced to an estimate of 180–200 people – around a quarter
of resident burgesses and over 6 per cent of the adult male population. This office-holding group seems also to have been comparatively stable over time, changing only with shifts in power between
the town's political parties, Whig and Tory. Given this, the potential
office-holders in the 'out' party should reasonably be included in a
more generalised office-holding population. Amongst the 'in' party,
repeat office-holding, in more than one capacity, was common and
this group often additionally acted as recognizance or prosecutor in
the borough courts or as witness, executor or legatee in a local will.
Such a public role outside office was also available to the 'outs',
many of whom also held office in vestries, chapels, or sometimes as
charity trustees. Especially after the 1770s, for example, the Har-
bour Commission, which then also dealt with paving and lighting,
was an important forum for affluent merchants and traders,
including some scrupulous nonconformists, who did not sit on
the corporation. Despite the civil disabilities they suffered in
eighteenth-century England, nonconformists were represented on
Colchester corporation roughly in proportion to their presence in
the population. This was not necessarily the case in all towns. The
Colchester corporation of the late 1730s contained 23 per cent

dissenters, and the new corporation named in the charter of 1763 had 27 per cent nonconformists.[23]

III

Occupation, rateable value, participation in genteel culture, household structure, and office-holding, each define somewhat different but overlapping middling groups which comprised up to around 20 per cent of Colchester's adult population. Economically speaking, the middling sort were of sufficient economic standing to maintain a household and pay their rates and taxes. Socially, they were characterised by the merchant, manufacturing or professional household form, not markedly dissimilar for superior artisans than that for prosperous attorneys, and by at least some degree of participation in genteel pursuits or consumerism. Politically, their males had some sort of public role.

A definition of the middling sort which was too restrictive would not be able to capture the historical realities. Although any definition must be securely based in occupation and social structure, occupation alone is too unclear and limited a label. By taking account of the elements of economic standing, household formation, genteel culture and political participation, a middling sort can be seen as an organising concept for local social and political life rather than only as an occupational grouping. The concept could thus become available to mobilise local political interests composed substantially but not entirely of the middling sort. The rhetoric employed helped create this at least superficial community of interests between burgesses of the middling sort and other voters at its periphery. Furthermore, the mechanics of organising political interests seem also to have mobilised established social connections within the middling sort. If brokers were active in middling social life in eighteenth-century Colchester, can any connection be made between their activity and the operation of local politics? Clearly such questions are better posed than answered in an essay of this length; nevertheless, illustrations from the events of Colchester politics can prove helpful.

In 1739–42, the period for which the network maps were drawn, the town was sharply politically divided by party. Local Whigs strongly contested the Tory hold on the borough corporation, which had been reinforced by the success of an alliance of Tory and 'country' groupings in a by-election of 1735, fought on the issue of Walpole's excise proposals, which were perceived as threatening by middling traders. The struggle took place against a back-drop of a bad winter and food riots in 1741, wartime garrisoning in the town, and the national political difficulties of the Walpole administration, which intervened in the hopes of getting a favourable candidate (John Olmius) elected for Colchester. Finally, the Whigs were able to prove at law that most of the existing aldermen's bench had been invalidly elected because of improper election procedures, leaving no quorum of properly elected officials, so that the borough charter lapsed from 1742 until 1763.[24]

The political contest seems to have been all-consuming in Colchester in these years. This discussion will focus on one particular aspect, closely related to the party struggle, namely the prosecution of Whig alderman George Gray for sodomy. George Gray, gentleman, plumber and glazier, had been an alderman since 1719. His son, Charles Gray, became Tory MP in 1741 and the scandal of the sodomy prosecution may be associated with a rift between them. Charles did not benefit under his father's will, in 1747, and followed his political career with the support of the Tory Creffield family, into which he had married in 1726.[25]

If surviving records of the Gray affair are read at surface value, what emerges is a meticulously documented tale of a middle-aged, affluent, businessman being led astray by his sexual preference. A more careful reading indicates that his tastes were known, at least in some quarters, and long tolerated. The full-blown scandal developed only when John Wright, who had been in dispute with Gray over a lease, saw an opportunity to work off the grudge by laying information, coincident with a political crisis where the Tories sought any means to disgrace the opposition. The political dimension was crucial. Gray submitted 'That the Prosecutors were encouraged by a Party Interest to Distress ... [him] ... and that they carried on their Prosecutions to make Gain of him'.[26]

The three weeks before the prosecution commenced saw a whispering campaign and attempts to secure other witnesses to similar acts by Gray. Wright was heard to gloat that he could make £500 out of the matter as well as gaining his revenge on Gray, the 'Rich Old Rogue'. Wright's lawyer, Jeremiah Howlett, bragged around the town 'We Catcht Them and declared that he and Wright were concerned in the Prosecutions and that if they did not come down Handsomely they would blow them, but if they would come down Handsomely they should hear no more of it.' His remarks were reported by leading Whig tradesmen James Thorn, Benjamin Dikes and Edward Jones. Howlett offered 10 guineas reward for evidence against Gray and gained sufficient to begin two similar prosecutions, as well as a prosecution of Thomas Francis, the consenting party to the act overheard by Wright. Gray and Francis both provided recognizances of £200 apiece, and two sureties for each put up £100 apiece. At Chelmsford Assizes, in August 1739, Gray and Francis were found guilty. On 13 February 1740 the corporation expelled Gray from the aldermen's bench. Although Gray and Francis later obtained a pardon, Gray was unable to regain his place as alderman. The Tory corporation stalled when presented with a writ of mandamus to reinstate him. By the time Gray had obtained a fresh writ from King's Bench the corporation had collapsed following proof at law of the improper elections.

There is a clear party bias in those individuals named in the relevant sources as they line up, Whigs for Gray and Tories against. When nineteen Colchester individuals who were specifically identified with the case are traced in the 1735 and 1741 borough polls, eleven vote consistently with a party bias. All bar one of these are Whigs who appear in the record in support of George Gray (including Thomas Francis). James Weatherly (surety for Thomas Francis) voted Tory in 1735 but Whig in 1741. Francis and Weatherly later stood bond together and Francis witnessed Weatherly's will. Jeremiah Howlett and his father both voted Tory in 1735. Of the five non-voters, four were pro-Gray and one was against him. John Wright, the prosecutor, was a Whig voter and thus something of an anomaly. The original lease between Gray and Wright was an agreement made between two Whigs, and it seems that in Wright's case personal considerations took precedence over party ones. Political networks were important but they were not the sole determinants of behaviour.[27]

Unsurprisingly, the sources name more pro-Gray individuals, since the prosecutor's evidence does not survive in detail. However, the support for Gray from like-voting individuals is strong. This in itself demonstrates the importance of party in the matter. Not only this, however, but party ties can lead individuals to act in other matters. There was traditionally a strong public taboo against homosexuality in English society. Whatever the private opinions (and practices) of the eighteenth-century male middling sort, it can have been no light matter to give evidence or stand a very expensive surety in support of an accused sodomite. No doubt, conventional public politics did not alone determine the conduct of Gray's supporters, and politics certainly failed to stay John Wright's hand. My argument is that there undoubtedly *were* social bonds operating which influenced individuals' preference in the Gray case *and* their political choice.[28]

Moreover, in the hotbed of Colchester in 1739 and 1740 any such public actions were political in a more general sense. Gray's petition is quite specific that the issue was one of party, and the refusal of the mandamus to restore him to office put the matter beyond question. If the Tories were cheering Gray on to his downfall, Whig tradesmen would find an interest in preserving him to maintain their numbers on the aldermen's bench, to say nothing of damage limitation to their party's reputation in general. Gray's supporters in particular followed predicted patterns of social connection. This was echoed in 1793 when baptist clothier, Richard Patmore, was prosecuted for seditious publications. The most active prosecutor was the leader of the local corporation party, Tory Francis Smythies. Patmore allegedly distributed Paine's second part of the *Rights of Man* and other pamphlets. Of the men who stumped up sizable recognizances on his behalf, all but one were local, middling, pro-Reform, nonconformists of the opposition party.[29]

Such networks were mobilised in particular at election times. A surviving campaign account book demonstrates the importance of middling broker figures in working up and maintaining a political 'interest' around Isaac Martin Rebow, a successful Whig candidate in 1754. The accounts list many disbursements made by Rebow's main political manager (also his attorney and steward), Samuel Ennew. The total expenditure was £1251. The account opens on 31 May 1753, almost a year before the poll, and closes in December 1758, with settlement of the final balance outstanding to Ennew of £628.7s.3d, indicating the extent to which his own finances were implicated. The accounts consist largely of payments to named freemen (mostly resident in Colchester). Each promised vote seems to have attracted 5/- reward, generally paid in two stages of 2/6d.[30]

The first recorded half crown is paid to John Dobbs on 16 June 1753 and payments are maintained steadily thereafter. Even where a voter received only one named payment, he was often paid considerably before the poll. If voters were entirely venal and uncomprehending, a half crown paid nine months before the election would surely have diminished in effect by polling time. It would be bad business for candidates and managers to spend so much so early, especially if no other interest was campaigning at the time. These widely spaced payments do make sense, however, in the context of several consistently maintained and longer-term political groupings supported by the spade work of the local brokers.

Several figures stand out in the Rebow accounts. Their names appear frequently and they receive payments well in excess of remuneration for their own vote. They seem to be paying out to the freemen, organising treats, canvassing and campaigning. They are comfortable middling tradesmen, such as James Thorn, the clockmaker (a supporter of George Gray), Samuel Todd and Thomas Kendall, both distillers. They invested considerable time, effort and money in the campaign. Thorn, for example, was repaid a total of £201.11s.4d. Todd expended £122.14s.10d on matters including the cost of an indictment and travelling to secure the freemen at Woodbridge. Although Rebow's gentry relations gave financial support, and more affluent local merchants also incurred some expenses, the sums involved are not larger (and often far smaller) than the disbursements of these active middling brokers. All this group are long-term Whig voters. They are also, including the more prosperous merchants named, all nonconformists.[31]

IV

Much of the discourse in which the eighteenth century conducted its political affairs was 'rights-based and libertarian'. This language could be derived from elite, enlightenment, civic humanism, but also from far more popular conceptions of the 'rights of the freeborn Englishman'.[32] Both those whose politics entertained republicanism, and the popular Tory, country, 'Church and King' viewpoint, could invoke particularist rights of a publicly active citizenry. The possession of such rights was predicated on an assumption of independent action in the public political sphere, itself supported by some notion of economic 'independence'. In effect, this qualification excluded the dependent – wage labourers, women and children. It envisaged the independent citizen as the pater familias, the head of the small-producer or more affluent household. In terms of a borough such as Colchester, the citizenry, possessed of political rights, often implicated in the machinery of local government, could also identify their independence as the heads of small-producer households. Even those who were not voters were ratepayers and could exercise a public role in the vestry. Much of the discourse of Colchester politics was centred around the rights of just such independent citizens, very many of them middling sort.

The borough charter, enshrining burgesses' rights, had been lost as a result of the débacle of 1741–2. Tory Charles Gray and Whig Richard Savage Nassau (the latter in the interest of the earl of Rochford) were chosen in the 1747 general election. As a Tory implicated in the preparations for the 1745 rebellion, Gray could have little influence in obtaining a new borough charter. Nassau had made no progress two years after the election, despite campaign promises. William Mayhew, the attorney, actively campaigned on this issue. In declaring it was not a 'Party Cause', Mayhew could maintain the Tory interest in the town around the issue of the burgesses' lost rights and privileges. Mayhew approached Nassau with an interest evidenced by a petition of 200 signatures (claiming to be able to raise 500 more), asking that he obtain the charter. Nassau replied crossly that he was surprised to hear from Mayhew, whom he did not number amongst his 'friends', and felt the approach presumptuous as the attorney was not amongst the town's 'principal Burgesses'. Mayhew was nettled. He replied;

> Who the Princ[l] Burgesses were of y[r] Friends, I couldn't distinguish, besides principal persons are not the persons immediately aggrieved, for that reason not so ready to apply for a proper remedy.[33]

The correspondence ended and Nassau took the matter no further. He did not stand for election in Colchester again. Mayhew and the local Tories (and behind them the proscribed Gray) were not about to let the issue drop.

In 1750, a few months after Mayhew's last letter to Nassau, the Charter Club was founded. This association of burgesses in support of a new charter met at the King's Head Inn. Its rhetoric, of ancient rights and privileges in the popular Tory tradition, was a constitutionalist call to middling and artisan burgesses to defend their position against a section of property-holders. According to a Charter Club bulletin, 'to Acquaint the *Publick* as to why the *Burgesses* desire a Charter' (my emphasis), a charter would preserve:

> their estates, their Rights of Common, their Markets, their Tolls, their Quit-rents, their Charities, their Freedoms, their Exemptions, their Fines on Delinquents; and all their other prescriptive and customary Rights.[34]

Without a charter, cash and land-value benefits on corporation property 'to the Amount of £1000 a Year' fell into pockets not entitled to them. Tenants of borough lands (shopkeepers and Hythe merchants) were excused their rents and were accused of making huge profits pulling down buildings and selling materials. Loans made to baymakers under a local charity were not repaid. The owners of land on which burgesses held grazing rights were enclosing their holdings and vastly increasing their worth.

> Those who dread the Day of Accounting cry out for Peace and Quiet, and no Charter.[35]

There was no distinct socio-economic divide between pro- and anti-charter factions. Many affluent middling traders and leading baymakers were Tories, and pro-charter burgesses are also described as having estates. However, rights over property were bunched together with rights to a local court and to elect magistrates and with political rights to produce a package with which the whole socio-economic range of voters could identify, down to the most indifferent artisan. Add to this the clear decay of the town fabric that the Rev. Phillip Morant (Rector of St Mary-at-the-Walls and correspondent of tory MP, Charles Gray) laments in his history of the town, published in 1748, the additional expense incurred and revenue lost to the town through losing its market tolls and subjecting itself to county administration based 20 miles distant, not to mention the loss of many offices and perquisites that borough organisation could distribute amongst middling burgesses, and a constitutionalist campaigning platform of strength emerges.[36]

A Charter Club advertisement also laments the loss of benefit to the burgesses through 'a valuable fishery incroached upon and made common', the loss of grazing rights, 'our cattle are impounded, and no redress to be had', the loss of borough freedom to sons and apprentices, and employs the eternal cry of 'Our Markets spoiled by Forestallers, Regrattors and Ingrossers'. The identity constructed of the outraged burgess is defined by his rights as a small producer, practising a mixed domestic economy where grazing and fishing rights are important, planning to hand on the business and lifestyle to the next generation and beset by landowners and market entrepreneurs. With the licence of propaganda this rhetoric disguises the reality for many burgesses in a town where the declining wool trade was polarising the socio-economic profile, where the half-year grazing was a racket run by a clique of carriers, butchers and victuallers, and where demographic shifts were already beginning to show up in the declining proportion of Colchester burgesses compared with those from London and the country. Nevertheless, lived experience for many middling and artisan burgesses was close enough to this idealised image, especially outside the elite, for it to be an effective rallying call.[37]

Mayhew was also quite right in insisting to Nassau that the more affluent citizens of the town had the economic clout to operate outside the borough within county circles and institutions, though they would, of course, corner leading borough positions if they were there for the taking. The loss of the charter, above all, circumscribed the public role of the smaller man, and it was to him that Mayhew's rhetoric appealed. The charter campaign developed the constitutionalist stance of the proscribed Tory grouping, which lost political impetus and local leadership in the early 1740s. By appealing to the burgesses as a whole – in 1752 the Charter Club was keen to insist that it was not a 'Party Cause' – it moved local politics away from the pre-1742 parameters and into a more ambiguous mid-century configuration. The Whig, Rebow, also attracted a faction including numbers of active nonconformists, thus generating a three-cornered struggle with the Tories and the rump of town Whigs, until Rebow and Gray established a long-standing compromise from 1761.[38]

V

This chapter has attempted to approach an understanding of the identity and the place of the middling sort in eighteenth-century urban society. Definitions of the middling sort couched solely in terms of occupational criteria run into problems when considering a society and economy where occupation was a far less clear-cut category than it was later to become. A broader approach has been suggested which, while grounded in occupation and social structure, can perhaps better capture the lived experience of the middling sort. As well as participation in genteel culture and an 'urban renaissance', the small-producer household, which closely connected domestic and business concerns, and the public role of the middling male in office-holding and politics are seen not only to be shared across the range of middling occupations, but also to be relational factors, as the labour of wives and older children supported the private dependences of the pater familias and enabled him to take up the public role of citizen.

An investigation of social connection amongst the middling sort has indicated that social and political networks were related, though the complex and changing nature of local politics made the match far less than absolute. At this stage of research we can only speculate how far pre-existing social connection affected political choice or, conversely, how far shared political party extended linkages into other areas. This study has also shown socially active middling community brokers who seem equally busy in political life. Only further research can reveal exactly how important such brokers were in making connections that gave social cohesion to the middling sort. Nevertheless, if we can relate social connection and politics in this way, the contingencies of social interdependence through the networks and the conventional political rhetoric of the independent citizen and his rights can be contrasted, as can the pooled labour of middling families in the domestic sphere supporting the public role of the 'independent' middling citizen.

Bibliography

In a thematic collection such as this there would be a great deal of overlap between the suggested reading for each chapter. For this reason, we have decided to provide a single bibliographical guide. The notes for each chapter should be consulted for detailed references regarding their specific subject.

The place of publication for books is London, unless otherwise stated.

Students wishing to place the middling sort should begin with broader analyses of the social structure. There are a number of excellent textbooks dealing with English society. The most incisive of these is K. Wrightson, *English Society 1580–1680* (1982), while the most extended discussions of the middling sort occur in J. G. Rule, *Albion's People: English Society 1714–1815* (Harlow, 1992) pp. 55–104, and P. Langford, *A Polite and Commercial People: England 1727–83* (Oxford, 1989) ch. 3. Other useful works are J. Youings, *Sixteenth-Century England* (Harmondsworth, 1984); C. G. A. Clay, *Economic Expansion and Social Change: England 1500–1700*, 2 vols (Cambridge, 1984); J. A. Sharpe, *Early Modern England: A Social History 1550–1750* (1987); B. Coward, *Social Change and Continuity 1550–1750* (Harlow, 1988); R. Porter, *English Society in the Eighteenth Century* (2nd edn, Harmondsworth, 1990); D. M. Palliser, *The Age of Elizabeth* (2nd edn, Harlow, 1992).

There are also several fundamental articles on social classification, led again by Keith Wrightson, 'The Social Order of Early Modern England: Three Approaches', in L. Bonfield *et al.* (eds), *The World We Have Gained* (Oxford, 1986) pp. 177–202; Wrightson, 'Estates, Degrees and Sorts', in P. J. Corfield (ed.), *Language, History and Class* (Oxford, 1991) pp. 29–51; P. J. Corfield, 'Class by Name and Number in Eighteenth-Century Britain', *History*, 72 (1987) pp. 38–61, revised in Corfield (ed.), *Language, History and Class*, pp. 101–30. See also: R. Williams, *Keywords: A Vocabulary of Culture and Society* (1976) pp. 37–40, 51–9; R. S. Neale, *Class in English History 1680–1850* (Oxford, 1981); G. Stedman Jones, *Languages of Class* (Cambridge, 1983); D. Cressy, 'Describing the Social Order of Elizabethan and Stuart England', *Literature and History*, 3 (1986) pp. 29–44; S. Wallech, 'Class versus Rank: the Transformation of Eighteenth-Century English Social Terms and Theories of Production', *Journal of the History of Ideas*, 47 (1986) pp. 409–31; M. Shiach, *Discourse on Popular Culture: Class, Gender and History in Cultural Analysis, 1730 to the Present* (Cambridge, 1989); M. L. Bush (ed.), *Social Orders and Social Classes in Europe since 1500* (Harlow, 1992).

Alongside these should be considered the empirical studies that seek to quantify the social order: G. Holmes, 'Gregory King and the Social Structure of Pre-Industrial England', *Transactions Royal Historical Society*, 5th ser. 27 (1977) pp. 41–68; P. Mathias, 'The Social Structure in the Eighteenth Century', in his *Transformation of England* (1979) pp. 171–89; P. Lindert, 'English Occupations 1670–1811', *Journal of Economic History*, 40 (1980) pp. 685–712; P. Lindert and J. Williamson, 'Revising England's Social Tables 1688–1812', *Explorations in Economic History*, 19 (1982) pp. 385–408 and 20 (1983) pp. 94–109; J. Cornwall, *Wealth and Society in Early Sixteenth-Century England* (1988); J. James, 'Personal Wealth Distribution in the Late Eighteenth Century', *Economic History Review*, 41 (1988) pp. 543–65; K. Schurer and T. Arkell (eds), *Surveying the People* (Oxford, 1992).

In contrast to studies which seek to classify and number social classes can be set studies which focus on social relationships. The most influential exponents of this approach have been historians influenced by Marx, of whom the two greatest modern figures have been Christopher Hill and E. P. Thompson. Hill's work belongs, broadly speaking, to the Marxist school that has sought to identify a strong bourgeois presence during the early modern period; his prolific output can be sampled in his *Collected Essays*, 3 vols (Hassocks, 1985–6) and *A Nation of Change and Novelty* (1990). The other leading examples of this approach are: B. Manning, *The English People and the English Revolution* (revised edn, 1991); C. H. George, 'Making of the English Bourgeoisie 1600–1710', *Science and Society*, 35 (1971) pp. 385–414; M. Rosen, 'Dictatorship of the Bourgeoisie: England 1688–1721', *Science and Society*, 45 (1981) pp. 24–51; C. Mooers, *The Making of Bourgeois Europe* (1991); D. Rollison, *The Local Origins of Modern Society: Gloucestershire 1500–1800* (1992). Thompson's work belongs to an alternative school, which has played down any middling presence, though emphasising that the gentry acted as an 'agrarian bourgeoisie'. See Thompson, 'Patrician Society, Plebeian Culture', *Journal of Social History*, VII (1974) pp. 382–405; Thompson. 'Eighteenth-Century Society: Class Struggle without Class?' *Social History*, 3 (1978) pp. 133–65; Thompson, 'The Patricians and the Plebs', in his *Customs in Common* (Harmondsworth, 1993) pp. 16–96. See also R. W. Malcolmson, *Life and Labour in England, 1700–1780* (1981); P. Corrigan and D. Sayer, *The Great Arch: English State Formation as Cultural Revolution* (Oxford, 1985); K. D. M. Snell, *Annals of the Labouring Poor: 1660–1900* (Cambridge, 1985); T. Koditschek, *Class Formation and Urban Industrial Society: Bradford, 1750–1850* (Cambridge, 1990) pp. 1–78. This relates closely to the so-called 'Brenner debate' over the transition to capitalism, for which see E. Kamenka and R. S. Neale (eds), *Feudalism, Capitalism and Beyond* (1975); J. E. Martin, *Feudalism to Capitalism* (1983); T. H. Aston and E. Philpin (eds), *The Brenner Debate* (Cambridge, 1987); R. Brenner, 'Bourgeois Revolution and Transition to Capitalism', in A. L. Beier *et al.* (eds), *The First Modern Society* (Cambridge, 1989) pp. 271–304.

Other historians have questioned whether classes can be identified in terms of social relationships in early modern England. See, for example, P. Laslett, *The World We Have Lost* (1965), revised as *The World We Have Lost – Further Explored* (1983); L. Stone, 'Social Mobility in England

1500–1700', *Past and Present*, 33 (1966) pp. 16–55; A. Everitt, 'Social Mobility in Early Modern England', ibid., pp. 56–73; H. Perkin, *The Origins of Modern English Society 1780–1880* (1969); M. James, *Family, Lineage and Civil Society* (Oxford, 1974); M. James, *Society, Politics and Culture* (Cambridge, 1986); A. MacFarlane, *The Origins of English Individualism* (Oxford, 1978); J. C. D. Clark, *English Society, 1688–1832* (Cambridge, 1985). Helpful discussions of the alternative concepts of class involved in these debates can be found in R. J. Morris, *Class and Class Consciousness in the Industrial Revolution 1780–1850* (1979) and P. Calvert, *The Concept of Class: An Historical Introduction* (1982). Two helpful guides to defining a middle class are P. Stearns, 'The Middle Class: Towards a Precise Definition', *Comparative Studies in Society and History*, 21 (1979) pp. 377–96, and S. M. Blumin, 'The Hypothesis of Middle-Class Formation in Nineteenth-Century America: A Critique and Some Proposals', *American Historical Review*, 90 (1985) pp. 299–338, which is developed in Blumin, *The Emergence of the Middle Class: Social Experience in the American City, 1760–1900* (Cambridge, 1990). Also very stimulating is A. Mayer, 'The Lower Middle Class as a Historical Problem', *Journal of Modern History*, 47 (1975) pp. 409–36.

As discussed in the introduction, the starting point for the study of the middling sort as a class in early modern England is still J. H. Hexter, 'The Myth of the Middle Class in Tudor England', *Explorations in Entrepreneurial History*, 2 (1950), revised in his *Re-appraisals in History* (1961) pp. 71–116, which should be read in conjunction with L. B. Wright, *Middle-Class Culture in Elizabethan England* (new edn, Cornell, 1958), the best example of the approach which Hexter attacked. P. Earle, *The Making of the English Middle Class: London 1660–1730* (1989) is the only extended study of the middling sort as such, or at least those in London, but it eschews theoretical discussion of the nature of a middle class, despite its title. The October 1993 issue of the *Journal of British Studies* is devoted to the middle class of the late eighteenth and early nineteenth centuries.

The middling sort must therefore be approached largely through studies of sub-groups or themes in which their presence is significant. Earle's study of London can be supplemented by R. G. Lang, 'Social Origins and Social Aspirations of Jacobean London Merchants', *Economic History Review*, 27 (1974) pp. 28–47; L. D. Schwarz, 'Income Distribution and Social Structure in London in Late Eighteenth Century', *Economic History Review*, 32 (1979) pp. 250–9; L. D. Schwarz, 'Social Class and Social Geography: The Middle Classes in London at the End of the Eighteenth Century', *Social History*, 7 (1982) pp. 167–85; L. D. Schwarz, *London in the Age of Industrialization* (Cambridge, 1992); N. Rogers, 'Money, Land and Lineage: the Big Bourgeoisie of Hanoverian London', *Social History*, 4 (1979) pp. 437–54 and 6 (1981) pp. 365–9; D. T. Andrew, 'Aldermen and Big Bourgeoisie of London Reconsidered' *Social History*, 6 (1981) pp. 359–64; G. S. De Krey, *A Fractured Society: The Politics of London in the First Age of Party 1688–1715* (Oxford, 1985); A. L. Beier and R. Finlay (eds), *The Making of the Metropolis: London 1500–1700* (1986); H. Horwitz, 'The Mess of the Middle Class Revisited', *Continuity and Change,* 2 (1987) pp. 263–96; J. Boulton, *Neighbourhood and Society: A London Suburb in the Seventeenth Century* (Cambridge, 1987); S. Rappaport, *Worlds within Worlds: Structures of Life in Sixteenth-Century London* (Cambridge, 1989); I. Archer, *The Pursuit of Stability: Social Relations in Elizabethan London* (Cambridge, 1991); R. Brenner, *Merchants and Revolution: Commercial Change, Political Conflict and London's Overseas Traders 1550–1653* (Cambridge, 1993). Other urban studies are discussed in J. Barry (ed.), *The Tudor and Stuart Town* (Harlow, 1990) and P. Borsay (ed.), *The Eighteenth-Century Town* (Harlow, 1990), but of particular importance are Borsay, *The English Urban Renaissance* (Oxford, 1989) and A. Everitt, *Landscape and Community in England* (1985).

Studies of specific urban occupations contain much of value, though see J. Patten, 'Urban Occupations in Pre-Industrial England', *Transactions Institute of British Geographers,* 3 (1977) pp. 296–313 and P. J. Corfield and D. Keene (eds), *Work in Towns 850–1850* (Leicester, 1990) for the problems of identifying such occupational groups. Surprisingly little direct work has been done on the leading mercantile and retailing groups, except in London (see above), though see R. Grassby, 'The Personal Wealth of the Business Community in Seventeenth-Century England' *Economic History Review,* 23 (1970) pp. 220–34; R. Grassby, 'English Merchant Capitalism in the Late Seventeenth Century: The Composition of Business Fortunes', *Past and Present,* 46 (1970) pp. 87–107; R. Grassby, 'Social Mobility and Business Enterprise in Seventeenth-Century England', in D. Pennington and K. Thomas (eds), *Puritans and Revolutionaries* (Oxford, 1978) pp. 355–81; R. G. Wilson, *Gentlemen Merchants: The Merchant Community in Leeds 1700–1830* (Manchester, 1971); R. G. Wilson, 'Merchants and Land', *Northern History,* 24 (1988) pp. 75–100; D. H. Sacks, *The Widening Gate* (Berkeley, 1991); K. Morgan, *Bristol and the Atlantic Trade in the Eighteenth Century* (Cambridge, 1993). For the financial aspects see B. L. Anderson, 'Provincial Aspects of the Financial Revolution of the Eighteenth Century', *Business History,* 11 (1969) pp. 11–22; E. Kerridge, *Trade and Banking in Early Modern England* (Manchester, 1988); H. Roseveare, *The Financial Revolution* (Harlow, 1991). There are numerous studies of particular trades and industries; for general guides to these see D. C. Coleman, *Industry in Tudor and Stuart England* (1975); S. M. Jack, *Trade and Industry in Tudor and Stuart England* (1977); M. Berg, *The Age of Manufacturers 1700–1820* (1985). For entrepreneurs see R. B. Westerfield, *Middlemen in English Business, Particularly between 1660 and 1760* (New Haven, 1915); J. W. Gough, *The Rise of the Entrepreneur* (1969); F. Crouzet, *The First Industrialists* (Cambridge, 1985). The fundamental issue of business instability is tackled thoroughly only in J. Hoppit, *Risk and Failure in English Business 1700–1800* (Cambridge, 1987).

The last decade has seen a shift of interest to issues of consumption and retailing. On this see J. Thirsk, *Economic Policy and Projects: The Development of a Consumer Society in Early Modern England* (Oxford, 1978); N. McKendrick *et al.,* *The Birth of a Consumer Society: The Commercialization of Eighteenth-Century England* (1982); L. Weatherill, *Consumer Behaviour and Material Culture in*

Britain 1660–1760 (1988); B. Fine and E. Leopold, 'Consumerism and the Industrial Revolution', *Social History*, 15 (1990) pp. 151–79; C. Shammas, *The Pre-Industrial Consumer in England and America* (Oxford, 1990); J. Brewer and R. Porter (eds), *Consumption and the World of Goods* (1993), all of which throw much light on the middling sort as consumers. For the retailers themselves see T. S. Willan, *An Eighteenth-Century Shopkeeper* (Manchester, 1970); A. M. Everitt, 'The English Urban Inn, 1560–1760' in Everitt (ed.), *Perspectives in English Urban History* (1973) pp. 104–18; P. Clark, *The English Alehouse* (1983); M. Spufford, *The Great Reclothing of Rural England: Petty Chapmen and their Wares in the Seventeenth Century* (1984); H-C. and L. H. Mui, *Shops and Shopkeeping in Eighteenth-Century England* (1989) pp. 106–47; R. M. Berger, *The Most Necessary Luxuries: The Mercers' Company of Coventry 1550–1680* (Philadelphia, 1993).

Much more work has been done on the professions. The best general study of this, with excellent essays on all the main groups, is W. R. Prest (ed.), *The Professions in Early Modern England* (1987), and this provides many important qualifications to G. Holmes, 'The Professions and Social Change', *Proceedings of the British Academy*, 65 (1979) pp. 313–54, and G. Holmes, *Augustan England: Professions, State and Society, 1680–1730* (1982). Important recent studies include: G. E. Aylmer, 'From Office-Holding to Civil Service: The Genesis of Modern Bureaucracy', *Transactions of the Royal Historical Society*, 5th Ser. 30 (1980) pp. 91–108; W. R. Prest (ed.), *Lawyers in Early Modern Europe and America* (1981); C. W. Brooks, *Pettyfoggers and Vipers of the Commonwealth: The 'Lower Branch' of the Legal Profession in Early Modern England* (Cambridge, 1986); I. Loudon, *Medical Care and the General Practitioner 1750–1850* (Oxford, 1986); W. R. Prest, *The Rise of the Barristers: A Social History of the English Bar 1590–1640* (Oxford, 1986); R. Porter, *Health for Sale: Quackery in England 1660–1850* (Manchester, 1989); M. Hawkins, 'Ambiguity and Contradiction in the Rise of Professionalism: The English Clergy 1570–1730', in Beier *et al.* (eds), *The First Modern Society*, pp. 241–69; J. Brewer, *The Sinews of Power* (1989); D. and R. Porter, *Patient's Progress: Doctors and Doctoring in Eighteenth-Century England* (Cambridge and Oxford, 1989); D. Lemmings, *Gentlemen and Barristers: The Inns of Court and the English Bar 1680–1730* (Oxford, 1990); D. R. Hainsworth, *Stewards, Lords and People: The Estate Steward and his World in Later Stuart England* (Cambridge, 1992).

Much less work has been done specifically on craftsmen and artisans, especially before the eighteenth century, when they are often viewed from the perspective of industrial labour and unionism. For this approach see: C. R. Dobson, *Masters and Journeymen* (1980); J. G. Rule, *The Experience of Labour in Eighteenth-Century Industry* (1981); J. G. Rule, *The Labouring Classes in Early Industrial England* (1986); J. G. Rule, 'The Property of Skill in the Period of Manufacture', in P. Joyce (ed.), *Historical Meanings of Work* (Cambridge, 1987) pp. 99–118; J. Smail, 'Manufacturer or Artisan? The Relationship between Economic and Cultural Change in the Early Stages of Eighteenth-Century Industrialization', *Journal of Social History*, 25 (1991–2) pp. 791–814. For the earlier period see the general works on industry mentioned above, plus C. Hill 'Pottage for Freeborn Englishmen:

Attitudes to Wage-Labour', in his *Change and Continuity in Seventeenth-Century England* (1974) pp. 219–38; B. Sharp, *In Contempt of All Authority* (Berkeley, 1980) and P. Seaver, *Wallington's World: A Puritan Artisan in Seventeenth-Century London* (1985) for insights into aspects of the artisan's world.

The middling sort in rural society have not been the focus of any study since M. Campbell, *The English Yeoman under Elizabeth and the Early Stuarts* (1960) and sections of G. E. Mingay, *English Landed Society in the Eighteenth Century* (1963). R. C. Allen, *Enclosure and the Yeoman* (Oxford, 1992) is not a social history. The best guides are therefore the community and regional studies of the 'Leicester school' pioneered by W. G. Hoskins and pursued by Alan Everitt, Joan Thirsk, Margaret Spufford and others. For a synthesis of this work see C. Clay (ed.), *Rural Society: Landowners, Peasants and Labourers 1500–1750* (Cambridge, 1990) and for the current research in this area see J. Chartres and D. Hey (eds), *English Rural Society 1500–1800* (Cambridge, 1991). The most influential community studies from outside this perspective have been those of Keith Wrightson and David Levine, *Poverty and Piety in an English Village* (1979) and *The Making of an Industrial Society* (Oxford, 1991), together with D. Underdown, *Revel, Riot and Rebellion: Popular Politics and Culture in England 1603–1660* (Oxford, 1985).

As discussed in the introduction, one of the most complex issues concerning the middling sort is the extent to which any 'class' consciousness was overridden by their community focus and local status. A helpful introduction to these issues can be found in D. Underdown, 'Community and Class: Theories of Local Politics in the English Revolution', in B. Malament (ed.), *After the Reformation* (Manchester, 1980) pp. 147–66, and D. Wahrman, 'National Society, Communal Culture: An Argument about the Recent Historiography of Eighteenth-Century Britain', *Social History*, 17 (1992) pp. 43–72. Three crucial areas of interaction between the local and the national were criminal law, poor relief and taxation, on which see J. A. Sharpe, *Crime in Early Modern England 1550–1750* (Harlow, 1984); J. Beattie, *Crime and the Courts in England 1660–1800* (Oxford, 1986); C. Herrup, *The Common Peace: Participation and the Criminal Law in Seventeenth-Century England* (Cambridge, 1987); P. Slack, *Poverty and Policy in Tudor and Stuart England* (Harlow, 1988); P. O'Brien and P. Hunt, 'The Rise of a Fiscal State in England 1485–1815', *Historical Research*, 46 (1993) pp. 129–76. An excellent collection exploring these issues for the period 1688–1750 is L. Davison *et al.*, *Stilling the Grumbling Hive: The Response to Social and Economic Problems in England 1689–1750* (Stroud, 1992).

The role of the middling sort in national government and politics is still poorly explored before 1700, save in the debate over the Civil War. For the Tudor period P. Williams, *The Tudor Regime* (Oxford, 1979) remains the best guide. For the Civil War issues see D. Hirst, *The Representative of the People? Voters and Voting in England under the Early Stuarts* (Cambridge, 1976); C. Hill, 'A Bourgeois Revolution?', in J. G. A. Pocock (ed.), *Three British Revolutions* (Princeton, 1980) pp. 109–39, revised in his *Collected Essays*, vol. 3, pp. 94–124; C. Hill, 'The Poor and the People', in ibid., pp. 247–73; G. Eley and W. Hunt (eds), *Reviving the English Revolution* (1988);

R. Cust and A. Hughes (eds), *Conflict in Early Stuart England* (Harlow, 1989) as well as the writings of Hill and Manning noted above, against which should be set the sceptical views of C. Russell, *Unrevolutionary England* (1988) and J. Morrill, *The Nature of the English Revolution* (Harlow, 1993). The nearest approach to a social history of late seventeenth-century politics is T. Harris, *London Crowds in the Reign of Charles II* (Cambridge, 1987). A pioneering study of how the middling sort might use national political institutions is provided by C. Holmes, 'Drainers and Fenmen: The Problem of Popular Political Consciousness in the Seventeenth Century', in A. Fletcher and J. Stevenson (eds), *Order and Disorder in Early Modern England* (Cambridge, 1985) pp. 166–95.

The tide of recent work on the middling sort in eighteenth-century politics is reviewed by Nicholas Rogers in his chapter, especially those studies which focus on electoral politics. For the broader ties between the middling sort and the state see J. Torrance, 'Social Class and Bureaucratic Innovation, 1780–87', *Past and Present*, 78 (1978) pp. 56–81; J. Brewer, 'The Commercialization of Politics', in McKendrick *et al.*, *Birth of a Consumer Society*, pp. 197–262; Brewer, *Sinews of Power;* P. Langford, *Public Life and the Propertied Englishman 1689–1798* (Oxford, 1991); Davison *et al.*, *Stilling the Grumbling Hive*. The place of the middling sort in political debate can be approached through J. Brewer, 'English Radicalism in the Age of George III', in Pocock (ed.), *Three British Revolutions*, pp. 323–67; J. G. A. Pocock, *Virtue, Commerce and History* (Cambridge, 1985); I. Kramnick, *Republicanism and Bourgeois Radicalism: Political Identity in Late Eighteenth-Century England* (Cornell, 1990); D. Wahrman, 'Virtual Representation: Parliamentary Reporting and the Language of Class in the 1790s', *Past and Present*, 136 (1992) pp. 83–113. The best local study remains J. Money, *Experience and Identity: Birmingham and the West Midlands 1760–1800* (Manchester, 1977).

The religious history of the middling sort has long been seen through the lens of nonconformity, first puritan and then dissenting. The classic statement of the first is C. Hill, *Society and Puritanism in Pre-Revolutionary England* (1964). Recent studies of puritanism have questioned its specific link to the middling sort and its 'nonconformist' nature: the best work on this is P. Collinson, *The Religion of Protestants: The Church in English Society 1559–1625* (Oxford, 1982) and Collinson, *Godly People* (1983). However, historians such as Wrightson and Underdown (see above) have endorsed the broader view that Protestantism, especially in its puritan form, embodied an ethos of social discipline that suited the middling sort. Critiques of this include M. Spufford, 'Puritanism and Social Control?', in Fletcher and Stevenson (eds), *Order and Disorder,* pp. 41–57; E. Duffy, 'The Godly and the Multitude in Seventeenth-Century England', *The Seventeenth Century*, 1 (1986) pp. 31–55. The fundamental guide to later dissent is M. Watts, *The Dissenters: From the Reformation to the French Revolution* (Oxford, 1978), but see also J. F. MacGregor and B. Reay, *Radical Religion in the English Revolution* (Oxford, 1984); J. E. Bradley, *Religion, Revolution and English Radicalism: Non-conformity in Eighteenth-Century Politics and Society* (Cambridge, 1990); J. Innes, 'Politics and Morals', in E. Hellmuth (ed.), *The Transformation of Political Culture in Britain and Germany in the Late Eighteenth Century* (Oxford, 1990) pp. 165–84. The importance of the established church to the middling sort, and vice versa, is suggested in S. Wright (ed.), *Parish, Church and People: Local Studies in Lay Religion 1350–1750* (1988).

Cultural attitudes *about* the middling sort are considered in L. S. O'Connell, 'The Elizabethan Bourgeois Hero-Tale', in Malament (ed.), *After the Reformation*, pp. 267–90, expanded in L. Stevenson, *Praise and Paradox: Merchants and Craftsmen in Elizabethan Popular Literature* (Cambridge, 1984); J. McVeagh, *Tradefull Merchants: The Portrayal of the Capitalist in Literature* (1981); and, best of all, J. Raven, *Judging New Wealth: Popular Publishing and Responses to Commerce in England 1750–1800* (Cambridge, 1992). Whether these tell us much about the cultural attitudes *of* the middling sort is more questionable. The starting point for any such study remains Wright, *Middle-Class Culture in Elizabethan England*, which should now be read in conjunction with T. Watt, *Cheap Print and Popular Piety 1550–1640* (Cambridge, 1991). For useful guides to later work see M. Foss, *The Age of Patronage 1660–1750* (1971; reissued Bristol, 1988, as *Man of Wit to Man of Business*); B. Reay (ed.), *Popular Culture in Seventeenth-Century England* (1985); G. Newman, *The Rise of English Nationalism: A Cultural History 1740–1830* (1987); Borsay, *English Urban Renaissance*.

One of the most important and fruitful new areas concerns the interaction between class and gender. This is particularly important for the middling sort since various accounts of gender history have seen the erosion of the independence and public role of middle-class women as occurring during our period. For a critical review of this historiography see A. Vickery, 'Golden Age to Separate Spheres? A Review of the Categories and Chronology of English Women's History', *Historical Journal*, 36 (1993) pp. 383–414. The key texts examined by Vickery are A. Clark, *The Working Life of Women in the Seventeenth Century* (1919, new edn. 1982) and L. Davidoff and C. Hall. *Family Fortunes: Men and Women of the English Middle Class 1780–1850* (1987). Other valuable recent studies are: L. Charles and L. Duffin (eds), *Women and Work in Pre-Industrial England* (1985); M. Prior (ed.), *Women in English Society 1500–1800* (1985); S. Amussen, *An Ordered Society: Gender and Class in Early Modern England* (Oxford, 1988); B. Hill, *Women, Work and Sexual Politics in Eighteenth-Century England* (Oxford, 1989); P. Mack, *Visionary Women: Ecstatic Prophecy in Seventeenth-Century England* (Berkeley, 1992).

Finally, students of the early modern middling sort can learn much from recent work on the 'middle classes' in other periods and places. For medieval England see C. Dyer, *Standards of Living in the Later Middle Ages* (Cambridge, 1989); H. Swanson, *Medieval Artisans* (Oxford, 1989). For the rest of the British state in the early modern period see G. B. Nash, *The Urban Crucible* (Cambridge, Mass., 1979); J. P. Greene and J. R. Pole (eds), *Colonial British America* (Baltimore, 1984), especially pp. 233–89; S. Nenadic, 'The Rise of the Urban Middle Class', in T. M. Devine and R. Mitchson (eds), *People and Society in Scotland*, vol. I: *1760–1830* (Edinburgh, 1988) pp. 109–26; Blumin, *Emergence of the Middle Class*; R. A.

Houston and I. D. Whyte (eds), *Scottish Society 1500–1800* (Cambridge, 1989). For early modern Europe see M. Walker, *German Home Towns: Community, State and General Estate 1648–1871* (Ithaca, 1971); S. Schama, *The Embarrassment of Riches: An Interpretation of Dutch Culture in the Golden Age* (1987); M. Sonenscher, *Work and Wages: Natural Law, Politics and the Eighteenth-Century French Trades* (Cambridge, 1989); C. Jones, 'Bourgeois Revolution Revivified: 1789 and Social Change', in C. Lucas (ed.), *Rewriting the French Revolution* (Oxford, 1991) pp. 69–118; Bush (ed.), *Social Order and Social Classes*. For industrial Britain see R. J. Morris (ed.), *Class, Power and Social Structure in British Nineteenth-Century Towns* (Leicester, 1986); P. Jones, S. Nenadic and P. Hills, 'Studying the Middle Class in Nineteenth-Century Britain', *Urban History Yearbook*, 14 (1987) pp. 22–50; J. Wolff and J. Seed (eds), *The Culture of Capital: Art, Power and the Nineteenth-Century Middle Class* (Manchester, 1988); R. J. Morris, *Class, Sect and Party: The Making of the British Middle Class, Leeds 1820–1850* (Manchester, 1990); S. Nenadic, 'Businessmen, the Urban Middle Class and the "Dominance" of Manufacturers in Nineteenth-Century Britain', *Economic History Review*, 44 (1991) pp. 66–85; J. Seed, 'From "Middling Sort" to Middle Class in Late Eighteenth-Century and Early Nineteenth-Century England', in Bush (ed.), *Social Orders and Social Classes*, pp. 114–35.

Notes and References

The place of publication for books is London, unless otherwise stated.

INTRODUCTION *Jonathan Barry*

1. J. H. Hexter, 'The Myth of the Middle Class in Tudor England', *Explorations in Entrepreneurial History*, 2 (1950), revised in his *Reappraisals in History* (1961) pp. 71–116 (originally delivered as a paper to the American Historical Association in December 1948).

2. Notable exceptions include B. Manning, *The English People and the English Revolution* (1st edn 1976, revised with a new introduction 1991) and C. Hill, 'A Bourgeois Revolution?', in J. G. A. Pocock (ed.), *Three British Revolutions* (Princeton, 1980) pp. 109–39, revised in his *Collected Essays*, vol. 3 (Hassocks, 1986) pp. 94–124. See also C. H. George, 'Making of the English Bourgeoisie 1600–1710', *Science and Society*, 35 (1971) pp. 385–414; M. Rosen, 'Dictatorship of the Bourgeoisie: England 1688–1721', *Science and Society*, 45 (1981) pp. 24–51; C. Mooers, *The Making of Bourgeois Europe* (1991).

3. The most important examples of this are H. Perkin, *The Origins of Modern English Society 1780–1880* (1969); E. P. Thompson, 'Patrician Society, Plebeian Culture', *Journal of Social History*, VII (1974) pp. 382–405; E. P. Thompson, 'Eighteenth-Century Society: Class Struggle without Class?', *Social History*, 3 (1978) pp. 133–65; E. P. Thompson 'The Patricians and the Plebs', in his *Customs in Common* (Harmondsworth, 1993) pp. 16–96; K. Wrightson, *English Society 1580–1680* (1982); J. C. D. Clark, *English Society, 1688–1832* (Cambridge, 1985). The only social history textbook with an extended analysis of the middling sort as a defined category is J. G. Rule, *Albion's People: English Society 1714–1815* (1992) pp. 55–104.

4. Two helpful guides to defining a middle class are P. Stearns, 'The Middle Class: Towards a Precise Definition', *Comparative Studies in Society and History*, 21 (1979) pp. 377–96, and S. M. Blumin, 'The Hypothesis of Middle-Class Formation in Nineteenth-Century America: A Critique and Some Proposals', *American Historical Review*, 90 (1985) pp. 299–338, which is developed in S. M. Blumin, *The Emergence of the Middle Class: Social Experience in the American City, 1760–1900* (Cambridge, 1990). These and other recent studies of the nineteenth-century middle class are considered from an early modern perspective in J. Barry, 'The Making of the Middle Classes?', *Past and Present* (forthcoming).

217

5. For the estimates see B. Reay (ed.), *Popular Culture in Seventeenth-Century England* (Beckenham, 1985) p. 1, and L. Weatherill, *Consumer Behaviour and Material Culture in Britain 1660–1760* (1988) p. 235, n. 8. See also G. Holmes, 'Gregory King and the Social Structure of Pre-Industrial England', *Transactions of the Royal Historical Society*, 5th series, 27 (1977) pp. 41–68; P. Mathias, 'The Social Structure in the Eighteenth Century', in his *Transformation of England* (1979) pp. 171–89; P. Lindert, 'English Occupations 1670–1811', *Journal of Economic History*, 40 (1980) pp. 685–712; Lindert and J. Williamson, 'Revising England's Social Tables 1688–1812', *Explorations in Economic History*, 19 (1982) pp. 385–408 and 20 (1983) pp. 94–109; C. Husband, 'Regional Change in a Pre-Industrial Economy: Wealth and Population in England in the Sixteenth and Seventeenth Centuries', *Journal of Historical Geography*, 13 (1987) pp. 345–59; J. James, 'Personal Wealth Distribution in the Late Eighteenth Century', *Economic History Review*, 41 (1988) pp. 543–65. This builds on a growing awareness of how many English people were not employed primarily in agriculture; the already high estimates found in E. A. Wrigley, 'Urban Growth and Agricultural Change', *Journal of Interdisciplinary History*, 15 (1985) pp. 683–728, reprinted in his *People, Cities and Wealth* (Oxford, 1987), are seen as too low by G. Clarke, 'Labour Productivity in English Agriculture 1380–1800', in *Land, Labour and Livestock*, ed. B. Campbell and M. Overton (Manchester, 1991) pp. 211–36, especially p. 228.

6. K. Wrightson, 'The Social Order of Early Modern England: Three Approaches', in L. Bonfield et al. (eds), *The World We Have Gained* (Oxford, 1986) pp. 177–202; K. Wrightson, 'Estates, Degrees and Sorts', in P. J. Corfield (ed.), *Language, History and Class* (Oxford, 1991) pp. 29–51; P. J. Corfield, 'Class by Name and Number in Eighteenth-Century Britain', *History*, 72 (1987) pp. 38–61, revised in Corfield (ed.), *Language, History and Class*, pp. 101–30. See also: R. Williams, *Keywords: A Vocabulary of Culture and Society* (1976) pp. 37–40, 51–9; Holmes, 'Gregory King'; D. Cressy, 'Describing the Social Order of Elizabethan and Stuart England', *Literature and History*, 3 (1986) pp. 29–44; S. Wallech, 'Class versus Rank: the Transformation of Eighteenth-Century English Social Terms and Theories of Production', *Journal of the History of Ideas*, 47 (1986) pp. 409–31; J. Seed, 'From "Middling Sort" to Middle Class in Late Eighteenth-Century and Early Nineteenth-Century England', in M. L. Bush (ed.), *Social Orders and Social Classes in Europe since 1500* (Harlow, 1992) pp. 114–35.

7. A Briggs, 'Middle-Class Consciousness in English Politics 1780–1846', *Past and Present*, 9 (1956) pp. 65–74; A. Briggs, 'The Language of Class in Early Nineteenth-Century England', in A. Briggs and J. Saville (eds), *Essays in Labour History* (1960) pp. 43–73; R. S. Neale, *Class in English History 1680–1850* (Oxford, 1981). Neale's distinction is developed in D. Wahrman, 'National Society, Communal Culture: An Argument about the Recent Historiography of Eighteenth-Century Britain', *Social History*, 17 (1992) pp. 43–72, while the same author provides a splendid account of the politics of class language in 'Virtual Representation: Parliamentary Reporting and the Languages of Class in the 1790s', *Past and Present*, 136 (1992) pp. 83–113. The coexistence of class with other social classifica-

tions in the nineteenth century is emphasised in G. Crossick, 'From Gentlemen to the Residuum: Languages of Social Description in Victorian Britain', in Corfield (ed.), *Language, History and Class,* pp. 150–78.

8. Convenient introductions can be found in J. Barry (ed.), *The Tudor and Stuart Town* (Harlow, 1990), and P. Borsay (ed.), *The Eighteenth-Century Town* (Harlow, 1990).

9. In this respect G. Holmes 'The Professions and Social Change', *Proceedings of the British Academy,* 65 (1979) pp. 313–54, and Holmes, *Augustan England: Professions, State and Society, 1680–1730* (1982), should be read in the light of W. Prest (ed.), *The Professions in Early Modern England* (1987), especially Margaret Pelling's essay on medicine.

10. M. Campbell, *The English Yeoman under Elizabeth and the Early Stuarts* (1960); see also J. Thirsk, *English Peasant Farming* (1957); G. E. Mingay, *English Landed Society in the Eighteenth Century* (1963). Despite its championing of yeoman agriculture, there is no picture of yeoman society in R. C. Allen, *Enclosure and the Yeoman* (Oxford, 1992). The classic local studies are: W. G. Hoskins, *The Midland Peasant* (1957); M. Spufford, *Contrasting Communities: English Villages in the Sixteenth and Seventeenth Centuries* (Cambridge, 1974); D. Hey, *An English Rural Community: Myddle under the Tudors and Stuarts* (Leicester, 1974); K. Wrightson and D. Levine, *Poverty and Piety in an English Village: Terling 1525–1700* (1979); C. Howell, *Land, Family and Inheritance in Transition: Kibworth Harcourt 1280–1700* (Cambridge, 1983); M. K. McIntosh, *A Community Transformed: The Manor and Liberties of Havering 1500–1620* (Cambridge, 1991), together with the regional studies in J. Thirsk (gen. ed.), *Agrarian History of England and Wales,* vols IV–VI (Cambridge, 1967, 1985, 1989). Yeomen and husbandmen feature prominently in many collections and studies of probate inventories, notably J. D. Marshall, 'The Domestic Economy of the Lakeland Yeoman 1660–1749', *Transactions of the Cumberland and Westmoreland Antiquarian and Archaeological Society,* 73 (1973) pp. 190–219, and Marshall, 'Agrarian Wealth and Social Structure in Pre-Industrial Cumbria', *Economic History Review,* 33 (1980) pp. 503–21, and for general comments on this material see Weatherill, *Consumer Behaviour,* pp. 191–4. For the current research in this area see J. Chartres and D. Hey (eds), *English Rural Society 1500–1800* (Cambridge, 1991).

11. D. Hirst, *The Representative of the People? Voters and Voting in England under the Early Stuarts* (Cambridge, 1976); Wrightson and Levine, *Poverty and Piety;* D. Underdown, *Revel, Riot and Rebellion: Popular Politics and Culture in England 1603–1660* (Oxford, 1985); C. Holmes, 'The County Community in Stuart Historiography', *Journal of British Studies,* 19 (1980) pp. 54–73; C. Herrup, 'The Counties and the Country', *Social History,* 8 (1983) pp. 169–82; C. Herrup, *The Common Peace: Participation and the Common Law in Seventeenth-Century England* (Cambridge, 1987); R. Cust, *The Forced Loan in English Politics 1626–8* (Oxford, 1987).

12. D. Read, *The English Provinces* (1964); J. Torrance, 'Social Class and Bureaucratic Innovation, 1780–87', *Past and Present,* 78 (1978) pp. 56–81; J. Brewer, 'The Commercialization of Politics', in N. McKendrick et al., *Birth of a Consumer Society* (1982) pp. 197–262; J. Brewer, *The Sinews of Power*

(1989); P. Langford, 'Property and "Virtual Representation" in Eighteenth-Century England', *Historical Journal*, 31 (1988) pp. 83–115; P. Langford, *A Polite and Commercial People: England 1727–83* (Oxford, 1989); P. Langford, *Public Life and the Propertied Englishman 1689–1798* (Oxford, 1991). For comments on this work, see N. Rogers, 'Paul Langford's "Age of Improvement"', *Past and Present*, 130 (1991) pp. 201–9; J. Barry, 'The State and the Middle Classes in Eighteenth-Century England', *Journal of Historical Sociology*, 4 (1991) pp. 75–86; L. Davison et al., 'Introduction: The Reactive State', in *Stilling the Grumbling Hive: The Response to Social and Economic Problems in England 1689–1750* (Stroud, 1992) pp. xi–liv. This contrasts with the emphasis on continued aristocratic domination of the state in P. Corrigan and D. Sayer, *The Great Arch: English State Formation as Cultural Revolution* (Oxford, 1985), especially p. 88.

13. The literature on land purchase is vast, but the most relevant items are: L. Stone, 'Social Mobility in England 1500–1700', *Past and Present*, 33 (1966) pp. 16–55; A. Everitt, 'Social Mobility in Early Modern England', *Past and Present*, 33 (1966) pp. 56–73; R. G. Wilson, *Gentlemen Merchants: The Merchant Community in Leeds 1700–1830* (Manchester, 1971); R. G. Lang, 'Social Origins and Social Aspirations of Jacobean London Merchants', *Economic History Review*, 27 (1974) pp. 28–47; G. Ramsay, 'The Recruitment and Fortunes of Some London Freemen in the Mid-Sixteenth Century', *Economic History Review*, 31 (1978) pp. 526–40; R. Grassby, 'Social Mobility and Business Enterprise in Seventeenth-Century England', in D. Pennington and K. Thomas (eds), *Puritans and Revolutionaries* (Oxford, 1978) pp. 355–81; H. J. Habbakuk, 'The Rise and Fall of Landed Families 1600–1800', *Transactions of the Royal Historical Society*, 29 (1979) pp. 187–207, 30 (1980) pp. 199–221, and 31 (1981) pp. 195–217; N. Rogers, 'Money, Land and Lineage in Hanoverian London', *Social History*, 4 (1979) pp. 437–54, and 6 (1981) pp. 365–9; D. T. Andrew, 'Aldermen and Big Bourgeoisie of London Reconsidered', *Social History*, 6 (1981) pp. 359–64; L. and J. C. F. Stone, *An Open Elite? England 1540–1880* (Oxford, 1984); A. Everitt, 'Dynasties and Communities since the Seventeenth Century', in his *Landscape and Community in England* (1985) pp. 309–30; H. Horwitz, 'The Mess of the Middle Class Revisited', *Continuity and Change*, 2 (1987) pp. 263–96; R. G. Wilson, 'Merchants and Land', *Northern History*, 24 (1988) pp. 75–100; R. C. Allen, 'The Price of Freehold Land and the Interest Rate in the Seventeenth and Eighteenth Centuries', *Economic History Review*, 41 (1988) pp. 33–50; C. Clay (ed.), *Rural Society: Landowners, Peasants and Labourers 1500–1750* (Cambridge, 1990). For an overall perspective on mobility see P. Clark and D. Souden (eds), *Migration and Society in Early Modern England* (1987).

14. E. A. Wrigley, 'A Simple Model of London's Importance in Changing English Society and Economy 1675–1750', *Past and Present*, 37 (1967) pp. 45–70; A. Everitt, *Change in the Provinces* (Leicester, 1969); R. Emerson, 'The Enlightenment and Social Structures', in P. Fritz and D. Williams (eds), *City and Society in the Eighteenth Century* (Toronto, 1973) pp. 99–124; R. Williams, *The Country and the City* (1973); P. Abrams and E. A. Wrigley (eds), *Towns in Societies* (Cambridge, 1978); L. Stone, 'Residential Development in the West End of London', in B. C. Malament (ed.), *After the*

Reformation (Manchester, 1980) pp. 167–212; P. Corfield, *The Impact of English Towns 1700–1800* (Oxford, 1982); McKendrick et al., *Birth of a Consumer Society;* P. Clark (ed.), *Country Towns in Pre-Industrial England* (Leicester, 1982); P. Clark (ed.), *The Transformation of English Provincial Towns 1600–1800* (1984); P. Borsay, 'Urban Development in the Age of Defoe' in C. Jones (ed.), *Britain in the First Age of Party* (1987) pp. 195–219; P. Borsay, *The English Urban Renaissance* (Oxford, 1989).

15. E. Kamenka and R. S. Neale (eds), *Feudalism, Capitalism and Beyond* (1975); E. P. Thompson, *Whigs and Hunters* (Harmondsworth, 1975); G. E. Mingay, *The Gentry* (1976); J. P. Jenkins, *The Making of a Ruling Class: The Glamorgan Gentry 1640–1790* (Cambridge, 1983); M. L. Bush, *The English Aristocracy* (Manchester, 1984); J. Cannon, *Aristocratic Century* (Cambridge, 1984); Wrigley, 'Urban Growth and Agricultural Change'; J. V. Beckett, *The Aristocracy in England, 1660–1914* (Oxford, 1986); T. H. Aston and E. Philpin (eds), *The Brenner Debate* (Cambridge, 1987); R. Brenner, 'Bourgeois Revolution and Transition to Capitalism', in A. L. Beier et al. (eds), *The First Modern Society* (Cambridge, 1989) pp. 271–303; C. W. Chalklin and J. Wordie (eds), *Town and Countryside: The English Landowner in the National Economy 1660–1860* (1989); F. Heal, *Hospitality in Early Modern England* (Oxford, 1990); T. Koditschek, *Class Formation and Urban Industrial Society: Bradford, 1750–1850* (Cambridge, 1990) pp. 1–78. No English historian has essayed a study of the entrepreneur since J. W. Gough, *The Rise of the Entrepreneur* (1969), but for the end of our period see F. Crouzet, *The First Industrialists* (Cambridge, 1985).

16. See Stone, *An Open Elite?* and Borsay, *English Urban Renaissance.* For a critique of the cultural side of this analysis, see J. Barry, 'Provincial Town Culture 1640–1780: Urbane or Civic?', in J. H. Pittock and A. Wear (eds), *Interpretation and Cultural History* (Basingstoke, 1990) pp. 198–234.

17. P. Zagorin, *The Court and the Country* (1969); J. G. A. Pocock, *The Machiavellian Moment* (Princeton, 1975); J. Morrill, *The Revolt of the Provinces* (1976); J. J. Murrin, 'The Great Inversion or Court Versus Country 1688–1776', in Pocock (ed.), *Three British Revolutions,* pp. 368–453; L. Colley, 'Eighteenth-Century English Radicalism before Wilkes', *Transactions of the Royal Historical Society,* 31 (1981) pp. 1–20; N. Rogers, 'Urban Opposition to Whig Oligarchy', in M. C. and J. Jacob (eds), *The Origins of Anglo-American Radicalism* (1984) pp. 132–48; J. G. A. Pocock, *Virtue, Commerce and History* (Cambridge, 1985); J. C. D. Clark, *Revolution and Rebellion: State and Society in England in the Seventeenth and Eighteenth Centuries* (Cambridge, 1986); J. Hoppit, 'Attitudes to Credit in Britain 1660–1790', *Historical Journal,* 33 (1990) pp. 305–22. For the continued vitality of the language of this type of politics, compare G. Stedman Jones, *Languages of Class* (Cambridge, 1983) and I. Kramnick, *Republicanism and Bourgeois Radicalism: Political Identity in Late Eighteenth-Century England* (Cornell, 1990).

18. The liveliest, if most polemical, review of this revisionism is found in Clark, *Revolution and Rebellion.* See also: Pocock (ed.), *Three British Revolutions;* G. Holmes, 'The Achievement of Stability', in J. Cannon (ed.), *The Whig Ascendancy* (1981) pp. 1–23; A. McInnes, 'When was the English Revolution?' *History,* 67 (1982) pp. 377–92; R. Porter, 'The Enlightenment in England', in

R. Porter and M. Teich (eds), *The Enlightenment in National Context* (Cambridge, 1981) pp. 1–18; L. Stone, 'The Bourgeois Revolution of Seventeenth-Century England Revisited', *Past and Present*, 109 (1985) pp. 44–54; B. Coward, 'Was there an English Revolution in the Middle of the Seventeenth Century?', in C. Jones et al. (eds), *Politics and People in Revolutionary England* (Oxford, 1986) pp. 9–40, especially pp. 35–6; C. Coleman and D. Starkey (eds), *Revolution Reassessed* (Oxford, 1986); C. Haigh (ed.), *The Reformation Revised* (Cambridge, 1987); Jones (ed.), *Britain in the First Age of Party*: P. Monod, *Jacobitism and the English People* (Cambridge, 1989).

19. In addition to Thompson's works cited in notes 3 and 15, see D. Hay, P. Linebaugh and E. P. Thompson (eds), *Albion's Fatal Tree* (Harmondsworth, 1975); E. and S. Yeo (eds), *Popular Culture and Class Conflict 1590–1914* (Hassocks, 1981); R. W. Malcolmson, *Life and Labour in England, 1700–1780* (1981); H. Medick, 'Plebeian Culture in the Transition to Capitalism', in R. Samuel and G. S. Jones (eds), *Culture, Ideology and Politics* (1982) pp. 84–113; B. Reay (ed.), *Popular Culture in Seventeenth-Century England* (Beckenham, 1985); M. Mullett, 'Popular Culture and Popular Politics: Some Regional Case Studies', in Jones (ed.), *Britain in the First Age of Party*, pp. 129–50. For crime see J. Innes and J. Styles, 'The Crime Wave', *Journal of British Studies*, 25 (1986) pp. 380–435. This tradition owes much to the European perspective of P. Burke, *Popular Culture in Early Modern Europe* (1978), on which see M. Mullett, *Popular Culture and Popular Protest in Late Medieval and Early Modern Europe* (Beckenham, 1987).

20. C. S. L. Davies, 'Peasant Revolts in England and France', *Agricultural History Review*, 21 (1973) pp. 122–34; S. Clark, 'French Historians and Early Modern Popular Culture', *Past and Present*, 100 (1983) pp. 62–99; A. Fletcher and J. Stevenson (eds), *Order and Disorder in Early Modern England* (1985); T. Harris, *London Crowds in the Reign of Charles II* (Cambridge, 1987); M. Harrison, *Crowds and History: Mass Phenomena in English Towns 1790–1835* (Cambridge, 1988); N. Rogers, *Whigs and Cities: Popular Politics in the Age of Walpole and Pitt* (Oxford, 1989); M. Shiach, *Discourse on Popular Culture: Class, Gender and History in Cultural Analysis, 1730 to the Present* (Cambridge, 1989).

21. Williams, *Keywords*, pp. 198–9; Hirst, *Representative of the People;* C. Hill, 'The Poor and the People', in his *Collected Essays*, vol. 3 (Brighton, 1986) pp. 247–73, especially pp. 260–1; E. S. Morgan, *Inventing the People* (New York, 1988). P. Joyce, *Visions of the People* (Cambridge, 1991) argues for the continued force of the term in the nineteenth century.

22. For recent studies of the boundaries of poverty see: K. D. M. Snell, *Annals of the Labouring Poor: 1600–1900* (Cambridge, 1985); J. G. Rule, *The Labouring Classes in Early Industrial England* (1986); R. M. Smith (ed.), *Land, Kinship and Life-Cycle* (Cambridge, 1986) pp. 351–422; T. Arkell, 'The Incidence of Poverty in the Late Seventeenth Century', *Social History*, 12 (1987) pp. 1–22; M. K. McIntosh, 'Local Responses to the Poor in Late Medieval and Tudor England', *Continuity and Change*, 3 (1988) pp. 209–45; P. Slack, *Poverty and Policy in Tudor and Stuart England* (Harlow, 1988); A. Hassell Smith, 'Labourers in the Late Sixteenth Century', *Continuity and Change*, 4 (1989) pp. 11–52 and 367–94.

23. For land tenure, in addition to the works cited in note 10, see: D. Hirst, 'The Seventeenth-Century Freeholder', *Economic History Review*, 29 (1976) pp. 306–11; Clay (ed.), *Rural Society*, pp. 325–57. On towns see: J. Patten, 'Urban Occupations in Pre-Industrial England', *Transactions of the Institute of British Geographers*, 3 (1977) pp. 296–313; J. F. Pound, 'The Validity of the Freemen's Lists: Some Norwich Evidence', *Economic History Review*, 34 (1981) pp. 48–59; M. C. Burrage and D. Curry, 'At Sixes and Sevens: Occupation and Status in the City of London from the Fourteenth to the Seventeenth Centuries', *American Sociological Review*, 46 (1981) pp. 375–93; M. Pelling, 'Occupational Diversity: Barber-Surgeons and Trades of Norwich 1550–1640', *Bulletin of the History of Medicine*, 56 (1982) pp. 484–511; I. K. Ben-Amos, 'Failure to Become Freemen: Urban Apprentices in Early Modern England', *Social History*, 16 (1991) pp. 154–72. For similar medieval problems see H. Swanson, 'The Illusion of Economic Structure: Craft Guilds in Late Medieval English Towns', *Past and Present*, 121 (1988) pp. 29–48.

24. See Holmes, 'Gregory King', J. V. Beckett, 'Land Tax or Excise?', *English Historical Review*, 100 (1985) pp. 285–308; M. Turner and D. Mills (eds), *Land and Property: English Land Tax 1692–1832* (Gloucester, 1986); N. Alldridge (ed.), *Hearth Tax: Problems and Possibilities* (Hull, 1987); R. Schofield, 'Taxation and the Limits of the Tudor State', in C. Cross et al. (eds), *Law and Government under the Tudors* (Cambridge, 1988) pp. 227–55; P. O'Brien, 'Political Economy of British Taxation 1660–1815', *Economic History Review*, 41 (1988) pp. 1–32; Brewer, *Sinews of Power;* J. V. Beckett and M. Turner, 'Tax and Economic Growth in Eighteenth-Century England', *Economic History Review*, 43 (1990) pp. 377–403; H. Roseveare, *The Financial Revolution 1660–1760* (1992); K. Schurer and T. Arkell (eds), *Surveying the People* (Oxford, 1992); Barry, *Tudor and Stuart Town*, pp. 18–20, 25 and works cited there. See also, for examples of studies using tax sources: D. V. Glass, 'Socio-Economic Status and Occupations in London at the End of the Seventeenth Century', in A. E. J. Hollaender and W. Kellaway (eds), *Studies in London History* (1969) pp. 373–92; R. Grassby, 'The Personal Wealth of the Business Community in Seventeenth-Century England', *Economic History Review*, 23 (1970) pp. 220–34; L. D. Schwarz, 'Income Distribution and Social Structure in London in Late Eighteenth Century', *Economic History Review*, 32 (1979) pp. 250–9; L. D. Schwarz, 'Social Class and Social Geography: The Middle Classes in London at the End of the Eighteenth Century', *Social History*, 7 (1982) pp. 167–85; J. Hindson, 'The Marriage Duty Acts and the Social Topography of the Early Modern Town: Shrewsbury 1695–8', *Local Population Studies*, 31 (1983) pp. 21–8; S. J. Wright, 'Easter Books and Parish-Rate Books', *Urban History Yearbook*, 12 (1985) pp. 30–45; J. Cornwall, *Wealth and Society in Early Sixteenth-Century England* (1988); E. Baigent, 'Assessed Taxes as Sources for the Study of Urban Wealth: Bristol in the Late Eighteenth Century', *Urban History Yearbook*, 15 (1888) pp. 31–48; E. Baigent, 'Economy and Society in Eighteenth-Century English Towns: Bristol in the 1770s', in D. Denecke and G. Shaw (eds), *Urban Historical Geography* (Cambridge, 1988) pp. 109–24, 366–7; J. Alexander, 'The Economic Structure of the

City of London at the End of the Seventeenth Century', *Urban History Yearbook*, 16 (1989) pp. 47–62; H-C. and L. H. Mui, *Shops and Shopkeeping in Eighteenth-Century England* (1989) pp. 106–47.

25. For recent comments on this subject see: S. Smith, 'The Ideal and the Real: Apprentice–Master Relationships in Seventeenth-Century London', *History of Education Quarterly*, 21 (1981) pp. 449–60; A. Kussmaul, *Servants in Husbandry in Early Modern England* (Cambridge, 1981); M. K. McIntosh, 'Servants and the Household Unit in an Elizabethan English Community', *Journal of Family History*, 9 (1984) pp. 3–23; Everitt, 'Dynasty and Community', pp. 323–4; P. J. P. Goldberg, 'Marriage, Migration, Servanthood and Life-Cycle in Yorkshire Towns of the Later Middle Ages', *Continuity and Change*, 1 (1986) pp. 141–69; Smith (ed.), *Land, Kinship and Life-Cycle*, especially R. Wall, 'Real Property, Marriage and Children', pp. 443–80; P. Earle, 'Age and Accumulation in the London Business Community', in N. McKendrick and R. B. Outhwaite (eds), *Business Life and Public Policy* (Cambridge, 1986) pp. 38–63; S. Rappaport, *Worlds within Worlds: Structures of Life in Sixteenth-Century London* (Cambridge, 1989); I. K. Ben-Amos, 'Service and the Coming of Age of Young Men in Seventeenth-Century England', *Continuity and Change*, 3 (1988) pp. 41–64; I. K. Ben-Amos, 'Women Apprentices in the Trades and Crafts of Early Modern Bristol', *Continuity and Change*, 6 (1991) pp. 227–53; G. Mayhew, 'Life-Cycle Service and the Family Unit in Early Modern Rye', *Continuity and Change*, 6 (1991) pp. 201–27. The best introduction to the growing role of schools in the eighteenth century is still J. H. Plumb, 'The New World of Children in Eighteenth-Century England', reprinted in McKendrick et al., *Birth of a Consumer Society*, pp. 286–315.

26. The classic expositions can be found in L. B. Wright, *Middle-Class Culture in Elizabethan England* (new edn, Cornell, 1958), and C. Hill, *Society and Puritanism in Pre-Revolutionary England* (1964). For recent comments on the social significance of morality see P. Seaver, 'The Puritan Work Ethic Revisited', *Journal of British Studies*, 19 (2) (Spring 1980) pp. 35–53; P. Seaver, *Wallington's World: A Puritan Artisan in Seventeenth-Century London* (1985); M. Spufford, 'Puritanism and Social Control?', in Fletcher and Stevenson (eds), *Order and Disorder*, pp. 41–57; E. Duffy, 'The Godly and the Multitude in Seventeenth-Century England', *The Seventeenth Century*, 1 (1986) pp. 31–55; J. Innes, 'Politics and Morals', in E. Hellmuth (ed.), *The Transformation of Political Culture in Britain and Germany in the Late Eighteenth Century* (Oxford, 1990) pp. 165–84; Davison *et al.*, *Stilling the Grumbling Hive*.

27. L. Davidoff and C. Hall, *Family Fortunes: Men and Women of the English Middle Class 1780–1850* (1987). The most direct account of the class significance of gender before 1750 is S. Amussen, *An Ordered Society: Gender and Class in Early Modern England* (Oxford, 1988), but for a critique of most recent work see A. Vickery, 'Golden Age to Separate Spheres?; A Review of the Categories and Chronologies of English Women's History', *Historical Journal*, 36 (1993) pp. 383–414.

28. There has been a welcome explosion of work on these subjects since 1980, including: V. Brodsky, 'Single Women in the London Marriage Market 1580–1619', in R. B. Outhwaite (ed.), *Marriage and Society* (1981)

pp. 87–100; R. A. Houlbrooke, *The English Family 1450–1700* (1984); L. Charles and L. Duffin (eds), *Women and Work in Pre-Industrial England* (1985); M. Prior (ed.), *Women in English Society 1500–1800* (1985); D. Underdown, 'The Taming of the Scold: the Enforcement of Patriarchal Authority in Early Modern England', in Fletcher and Stevenson (eds), *Order and Disorder,* pp. 116–36; V. Brodsky, 'Widows in Late Elizabethan London', in Bonfield et al. (eds), *The World We Have Gained,* pp. 122–54; M. Ezell, *The Patriarch's Wife* (Chapel Hill, 1987); P. Earle, 'Female Labour Market in London', *Economic History Review,* 42 (1989) pp. 328–52; B. Hill, *Women, Work and Sexual Politics in Eighteenth-Century England* (Oxford, 1989); D. Kent, 'Female Domestic Servants in Eighteenth-Century London', *History Workshop Journal,* 28 (1989); D. Kent, 'Family Breakdown 1750–91', *Local Population Studies,* 45 (1990); M. Roberts, 'Women and Work in Sixteenth-Century England', in P. Corfield and D. Keene (eds), *Work in Towns 850–1850* (Leicester, 1990) pp. 86–102; A. Erickson, 'Common Law versus Common Practice: the Use of Marriage Settlements in Early Modern England', *Economic History Review,* 43 (1990) pp. 21–39.

29. On this claim see J. Barrell, *English Literature in History 1730–80: An Equal, Wide Survey* (1983).

30. L. S. O'Connell, 'The Elizabethan Bourgeois Hero-Tale', in B. C. Malament (ed.), *After the Reformation* (Manchester, 1980) pp. 267–90, expanded in L. Stevenson, *Praise and Paradox: Merchants and Craftsmen in Elizabethan Popular Literature* (Cambridge, 1984); J. McVeagh, *Tradeful Merchants: The Portrayal of the Capitalist in Literature* (1981); J. Raven, *Judging New Wealth* (Cambridge, 1992).

31. The basic texts for the growth of consumer society are McKendrick et al., *Birth of a Consumer Society,* and Borsay, *English Urban Renaissance.* For critiques see A. McInnes, 'The Emergence of a Leisure Town: Shrewsbury 1660–1760', *Past and Present,* 120 (1988) pp. 53–87, and debate in ibid., 126 (1990) pp. 189–202; Weatherill, *Consumer Behaviour;* B. Fine and E. Leopold, 'Consumerism and the Industrial Revolution', *Social History,* 15 (1990) pp. 151–79; C. Shammas, *The Pre-Industrial Consumer in England and American* (Oxford, 1990); J. Barry, 'Consuming Passions', *Historical Journal,* 34 (1991) pp. 207–16. Useful comparisons can be made with S. Schama, *The Embarrassment of Riches* (1988), on contemporary Dutch responses, and J. Wolff and J. Seed (eds), *The Culture of Capital* (Manchester, 1988), on the nineteenth century.

32. J. Brewer, *Party Ideology and Popular Politics at the Accession of George III* (Cambridge, 1976); J. Money, *Experience and Identity: Birmingham and the West Midlands 1760–1800* (Manchester, 1977); V. Pearl, 'Change and Stability in Seventeenth-Century London', *London Journal,* 5 (1979) pp. 3–34; J. T. Evans, *Seventeenth-Century Norwich: Politics, Religion and Government 1620–90* (Oxford, 1979); J. Brewer, 'English Radicalism in the Age of George III', in Pocock (ed.), *Three British Revolutions,* pp. 323–67; J. A. Phillips, *Electoral Behavior in Unreformed England* (Princeton, 1982); W. Speck, 'The Electorate in the First Age of Party', and H. Horwitz, 'Party in a Civic Context: London from the Exclusion Crisis to the Fall of Walpole', both in Jones (ed.), *Britain in the First Age of Party,* pp. 45–62 and 173–94; J. Barry,

'The Parish in Civic Life', in S. Wright (ed.), *Parish, Church and People* (1988) pp. 152–78; F. O'Gorman, *Voters, Patrons and Parties* (Oxford, 1989); J. E. Bradley, *Religion, Revolution and English Radicalism: Nonconformity in Eighteenth-Century Politics and Society* (Cambridge, 1990); K. Wilson, 'Urban Culture and Political Activism in Hanoverian England', in Hellmuth (ed.), *Transformation of Political Culture*, pp. 165–84; J. Barry, 'The Politics of Religion in Restoration Bristol', in T. Harris, P. Seaward and M. Goldie (eds), *The Politics of Religion in Restoration England* (Oxford, 1990) pp. 163–90; J. Barry, 'The Press and the Politics of Culture in Bristol, 1660–1775', in J. Black and J. Gregory (eds), *Culture, Politics and Society in Britain 1660–1800* (Manchester, 1991) pp. 49–81; I. Archer, *The Pursuit of Stability: Social Relations in Elizabethan London* (Cambridge, 1991); R. Tittler, *Architecture and Power: The Town Hall and the English Urban Community c.1500–1640* (Oxford, 1991).

33. C. Holmes, 'Drainers and Fenmen: the Problem of Popular Political Consciousness in the Seventeenth Century', in Fletcher and Stevenson (eds), *Order and Disorder*, pp. 166–95. See also: K. Wrightson, 'Two Concepts of Order', in J. Brewer and J. Styles (eds), *An Ungovernable People* (1980) pp. 21–46; W. King, 'Leet Jurors', *Histoire Sociale/Social History*, 13 (1980) pp. 305–23; J. A. Sharpe, *Crime in Early Modern England* (1984); P. J. King, 'Decision-Makers and Decision-Making in English Criminal Law 1750–1800', *Historical Journal*, 27 (1984) pp. 25–58; J. Kent, *The English Village Constable 1580–1642* (Oxford, 1986); J. M. Beattie, *Crime and the Courts in England 1660–1800* (Oxford, 1986); Herrup, *The Common Peace*.

34. P. Laslett, *The World We Have Lost* (1965), revised as *The World We Have Lost – Further Explored* (1983).

35. For this phase, see D. Nicholls, 'The English Middle-Class and the Ideological Significance of Radicalism 1760–1886', *Journal of British Studies*, 24 (1985) pp. 415–33.

36. R. Tittler, 'The Emergence of Urban Policy 1536–58', in J. Loach and R. Tittler (eds), *The Mid-Tudor Policy* (1980) pp. 74–93; R. Howell, 'Newcastle and the Nation: the Seventeenth-Century Experience', *Archaeologia Aeliana*, 8 (1980) pp. 17–34, reprinted in his *Puritans and Radicals in North England* (1984) pp. 16–44; D. Underdown, 'Community and Class: Theories of Local Politics in the English Revolution', in Malament (ed.), *After the Reformation*, pp. 147–66; J. Triffitt, 'Politics and the Urban Community: Parliamentary Boroughs in the South West 1710–30' (University of Oxford, D.Phil thesis, 1985); D. Sacks, 'The Corporate Town and the British State: Bristol's Little Businesses 1625–41', *Past and Present*, 110 (1986) pp. 69–105; L. Colley, 'Whose Nation? Class and National Consciousness in Britain, 1760–1820', *Past and Present*, 113 (1986) pp. 97–117; A. Hughes, 'Local History and the Origins of the Civil War', in R. Cust and A. Hughes (eds), *Conflict in Early Stuart England* (1989) pp. 224–53.

37. A. Mayer, 'The Lower Middle Class as a Historical Problem', *Journal of Modern History*, 47 (1975) pp. 409–36; C. R. Dobson, *Masters and Journeymen* (1980); J. G. Rule, *The Experience of Labour in Eighteenth-Century Industry* (1981); J. G. Rule, 'The Property of Skill in the Period of Manufacture', in P. Joyce (ed.), *Historical Meanings of Work* (Cambridge, 1987) pp. 99–118;

J. Smail, 'Manufacturer or Artisan? The Relationship between Economic and Cultural Change in the Early Stages of Eighteenth-Century Industrialization', *Journal of Social History*, 25 (1991–2) pp. 791–814.

38. Allen, *Enclosure and the Yeoman;* D. Rollison, *The Local Origins of Modern Society: Gloucestershire 1500–1800* (1992).

39. See Wrightson and Levine, *Poverty and Piety*, for the pre-1660 period, and Snell, *Annals of the Labouring Poor*, for the later period, but especially for post-1760; a close study of the intervening century is much needed.

40. A critical review of the work of Everitt, Thirsk, Underdown and others on rural regions can be found in N. Davie, 'Chalk and Cheese? "Fielden" and "Forest" Communities in Early Modern England', *Journal of Historical Sociology*, 4 (1991) pp. 1–31.

41. R. Gough, *The History of Myddle*, ed. D. Hey (Harmondsworth, 1981), which should be supplemented by Hey's own study of the parish, *An English Rural Community*. For analysis of the diary of a yeoman clergyman, see A. MacFarlane, *The Family Life of Ralph Josselin* (Cambridge, 1970).

42. For inheritance among the agrarian middling sort, see the works cited in note 10, plus the essays by Howell and Spufford in J. Goody, J. Thirsk and E. P. Thompson (eds), *Family, Inheritance and Rural Society in Western Europe 1200–1800* (Cambridge, 1976), and L. Bonfield, 'Normative Roles and Property Transmission', in Bonfield et al. (eds), *World We Have Gained*, pp. 155–76. For the urban context see S. M. Cooper, 'Intergenerational Social Mobility in Late Seventeenth-Century and Early Eighteenth-Century England', *Continuity and Change*, 7 (1992) pp. 283–302, on King's Lynn.

43. A pioneering study of rural education was offered by M. Spufford, 'Schooling of the Peasantry in Cambridgeshire 1575–1700', in J. Thirsk (ed.), *Land, Church and People* (Reading, 1970) pp. 112–47. The only overview of education is provided by R. O'Day, *Education and Society 1500–1800* (1982), and for an update of work on literacy see W. B. Stephens, 'Literacy in England, Scotland and Wales 1500–1900', *History of Education Quarterly*, 30 (1990) pp. 545–71, and on the post-1750 period, David Vincent's brilliant *Literacy and Popular Culture* (Cambridge, 1989). On the equally vital subject of numeracy see K. Thomas, 'Numeracy in Early Modern England', *Transactions of the Royal Historical Society*, 37 (1987) pp. 110–32. A valuable collection of sources on family life is provided in R. Houlbrooke (ed.), *English Family Life 1576–1716* (Oxford, 1988).

1. 'SORTS OF PEOPLE' IN TUDOR AND STUART ENGLAND   *Keith Wrightson*

1. S. C. Lomas (ed.), *The Letters and Speeches of Oliver Cromwell, with Elucidations by Thomas Carlyle*, 3 vols (1904) vol. II, p. 342.

2. W. G. Hoskins, *Provincial England: Essays in Social and Economic History* (1965) p. 209. I have discussed the emergence of the classical social hierarchy in 'Estates, Degrees and Sorts: changing perceptions of society in

Tudor and Stuart England', in P. Corfield (ed.), *Language, History and Class* (Oxford, 1991) pp. 29–51. In stating that the mature formulation of this account of the social order was achieved in the later sixteenth century, I recognise that this development was the culmination of a gradual evolution of a more complex and precise terminology of social differentiation, which can be traced back deep into the later Middle Ages. The dominant medieval conception of society as being composed of three functionally distinct but interdependent 'estates' or 'orders' – those who pray, those who fight, and those who work – had long been inadequate as an account of a society of growing complexity and diversity. Elaboration of the 'degrees' observable within each of the three estates, and the establishment of rough and ready 'equivalences' between them, paved the way for their eventual shuffling together into a single hierarchy of status. Nevertheless, the model of the three estates remained current into the early sixteenth century and Dr Keen, who fully recognises the complexities of the situation, still finds it a useful organising device for his account of late medieval society. See, for example, S. L. Thrupp, *The Merchant Class of Medieval London 1300–1500* (Chicago, 1948) ch. 7; M. Keen, *English Society in the Later Middle Ages, 1348–1500* (1990) ch. 1 and *passim;* L. R. Poos, *A Rural Society after the Black Death: Essex 1350–1525* (Cambridge, 1991) pp. 21–2. For two broader discussions of the 'society of orders', which reach different conclusions regarding its appropriateness as a model for early modern social structures, see P. Burke, 'The Language of Orders in Early Modern Europe', and W. Doyle, 'Myths of Order and Ordering Myths', both in M. L. Bush (ed.), *Social Orders and Social Classes in Europe since 1500: Studies in Social Stratification* (1992) pp. 1–12, 218–29.

3. Quoting from orders regarding the allocation of pews in Swavesey, Cambs (1635), Tisbury, Wilts (1637) and West Walton, Norfolk (1633). Sources: Cambridge University Library, Palmer Papers B/58 (I must thank Dr Michael Cross for this reference); D. Underdown, *Revel, Riot and Rebellion, Popular Politics and Culture in England, 1603–1660* (Oxford, 1985) p. 33; S. D. Amussen, *An Ordered Society, Gender and Class in Early Modern England* (Oxford, 1988) pp. 137–8.

4. Richard Gough, *The History of Myddle,* ed. D. Hey (Harmondsworth, 1981) *passim.*

5. These included, for example, 'the common people', 'rich men', 'the poor', 'sufficient men', 'poore labouring people', 'worshipful men', 'the best of the parish', the 'principal' or 'chief inhabitants', 'persons of credit', 'mean personages', 'the quality', 'the vulgar', 'the multitude', 'the rascality'.

6. A preliminary discussion of the language of 'sorts' can be found in my 'Estates, Degrees, and Sorts'. This chapter is an extension and considerable elaboration of arguments first sketched there.

7. See *Oxford English Dictionary* under 'sort'.

8. Ibid.; T. F. Mayer (ed.), *Thomas Starkey: A Dialogue between Pole and Lupset* (Camden 4th Series, 37, 1989) p. 36; T. Elyot, *The Book Named the Governor (1531),* Facsimile reprint (Menston, 1970) fo. 228. Cf. W. Marshall [trans.], *The Defence of Peace: Lately Translated out of Laten in to Englysshe*

(1535) fo. 14v; E. Lamond (ed.), *A Discourse of the Common Weal of this Realm of England* (Cambridge, 1929) pp. 38, 80–1, 127. These works, like other contemporary works to be cited below, have been systematically searched for all instances of socially descriptive language.

9. Numerous examples can be found throughout the sixteenth and seventeenth centuries, and the usage, of course, continues to this day.

10. J. Griffiths (ed.), *The Two Books of Homilies* (Oxford, 1859) pp. 4, 105, 135, 172, 213, 239, 242, 251, 294, 503, 541, 579, 585, 590, 591.

11. Instances of the language of 'sorts' in the Authorised Version of the English Bible (1611) were identified with the aid of J. Strong (ed.), *The Exhaustive Concordance of the Bible* (1894), and C. H. Irwin and A. D. Adams (eds), *Cruden's Complete Concordance to the Old and New Testaments* (1941). The relevant texts were then traced through the following translations of the Bible: J. Lewis (ed.), *The New Testament ... Translated out of the Latin Vulgat by John Wiclif* (1731); Tyndale's New Testament (1552 edn); the 'Matthew Bible' (1537); the 'Great Bible' (1539); the 'Bishops' Bible' (1585 edn); the 'Geneva Bible' (1583 edn); the 'Authorised Version' (1613 edn); W. Fulke (ed.), *The Text of the New Testament ... Translated ... by the Papists* (1617). As a matter of interest, the *New English Bible* (1970) renders the passage from 2 Kings 24:14 as 'the weakest class of people' and that from Acts 17:5 as 'the dregs of the populace' and 'the rabble'.

12. What follows is based upon a large collection of examples of the language of 'sorts' built up over a number of years by systematically noting examples in both primary and secondary sources. However, it should be stressed that there is no foolproof method of pursuing research of this kind and the account given of its chronological development inevitably remains open to modification and correction in the light of further evidence. I owe some of the specific examples cited to the generous assistance of C. W. Brooks, Adam Fox, Paul Griffiths, Christine Issa, R. B. Outhwaite, William Sherman, Paul Slack and Andrew Wood.

13. Mayer (ed.), *Thomas Starkey*, p. 124; Lamond (ed.), *Discourse*, p. xlvi.

14. P. Slack, *Poverty and Policy in Tudor and Stuart England* (1988) p. 66; Durham University Dept of Palaeography and Diplomatic DR V/9 unfol., R. B. Manning, *Village Revolts: Social Protest and Popular Disturbances in England, 1509–1640* (Oxford, 1988) p. 105.

15. A. Dent, *The Plaine Man's Path-way to Heaven* (1601), 'To the Reader'. Cf. R. Sherrard, *The Country-man with his Household* (1620) 'To the Reader'. For catechisms, see I. Green, ' "For Children in Yeeres and Children in Understanding": The Emergence of the English Catechism under Elizabeth and the Early Stuarts', *Journal of Ecclesiastical History*, 37 (1986) pp. 409–10.

16. Bourne and Record, quoted in L. B. Wright, *Middle-Class Culture in Elizabethan England* (Chapel Hill, 1935) pp. 156, 159, cf. p. 243; H. Swinburne, *A Treatise of Testaments and Last Wills* (1635) p. 176; P[ublic] R[ecord] O[ffice], STAC 8/53/7; Underdown, *Revel, Riot and Rebellion*, p. 263.

17. P. Lawson, 'Lawless Juries? The Composition and Behaviour of Hertfordshire Juries, 1573–1624', in J. S. Cockburn and T. A. Green (eds), *Twelve Good Men and True: The Criminal Trial Jury in England, 1200–1800*

(Princeton, 1988) pp. 124–5; C. Gittings, *Death, Burial and the Individual in Early Modern England* (1984) p. 141; Amussen, *Ordered Society*, p. 156; J. O. Halliwell (ed.), *The Social Condition of the People of Anglesey* (1880) p. 36; P.R.O. STAC 8/153/5; G. W. Robinson (ed.), *The Winthrop Papers*, 3 vols (Boston, Mass., 1929–31) vol. I, pp. 307–8; I. W. Archer, *The Pursuit of Stability: Social Relations in Elizabethan London* (Cambridge, 1991) p. 235, cf. p. 93; P. Slack, *The Impact of Plague in Tudor and Stuart England* (1985) p. 306; D. Hirst, *The Representative of the People? Voters and Voting in England under the Early Stuarts* (Cambridge, 1976) p. 70.

18. Archer, *Pursuit of Stability*, pp. 4–5; B. Reay, 'Popular Religion', in B. Reay (ed.), *Popular Culture in Seventeenth-Century England* (1985) p. 94; W. Gouge, *God's Three Arrowes; Plague, Famine, Sword* (1631) p. 152; Slack, *Impact of Plague*, pp. 239, 306; S. J. and S. J. Watts, *From Border to Middle Shire: Northumberland, 1586–1625* (Leicester, 1975) p. 203; *Winthrop Papers*, vol. II, pp. 62–3; K. Lindley, *Fenland Riots and the English Revolution* (1982) pp 28, 61, 92, 97, 107, 109, 149, 179; T. Harris, *London Crowds in the Reign of Charles II: Propaganda and Politics from the Restoration until the Exclusion Crisis* (Cambridge, 1987) p. 34.

19. See, for example, *Acts of the Privy Council 1596–7*, pp. 15, 81, 92, 95, 154, 281, 380, 399, 505, 534; *Calendar of State Papers Domestic 1595–7*, p. 420; *Historical Manuscript Commission, Somerset Mss*, p. 20.

20. Hirst, *Representative of the People?*, pp. 69–70, 101, 102, 115–16, 169, 207, 211, 212.

21. Lindley, *Fenland Riots*, pp. 24, 28, 32, 38, 39, 40, 61, 179, 201, 202.

22. For a discussion, for example, of the Ramist method of presentation and its use of dichotomies, see C. B. Schmitt, *John Case and Aristotelianism in Renaissance England* (Kingston and Montreal, 1983) p. 145. For examples see Griffiths (ed.), *Books of Homilies*, pp. 88, 280, 341, 353–5, 377; M. MacDonald, *Mystical Bedlam, Madness, Anxiety, and Healing in Seventeenth-Century England* (Cambridge, 1981) p. 3; Gouge, *God's Three Arrowes*, p. 80. The implications of the rhetorical conventions of the day are explored in a related context in P. Collinson, *The Birthpangs of Protestant England: Religious and Cultural Change in the Sixteenth and Seventeenth Centuries* (1988) pp. 147–8.

23. See, for example, S. Reynolds, *Kingdoms and Communities in Western Europe, 900–1300* (Oxford, 1984) pp. 100, 146: Thrupp, *Merchant Class*, p. 15.

24. Collinson, *Birthpangs*, p. 147.

25. See, for example, K. Wrightson, *English Society 1580–1680* (1982) ch. 5 and conclusion; Slack, *Poverty and Policy*, ch. 3.

26. See, for example, K. Thomas, *Religion and the Decline of Magic: Studies in Popular Beliefs in Sixteenth and Seventeenth-Century England* (1971) chs. 2–6; P. Collinson, *The Religion of Protestants: The Church in English Society, 1559–1625* (Oxford, 1982) ch. 5; Wrightson, *English Society*, ch. 7; C. Haigh, 'The Church of England, the Catholics and the People', in C. Haigh (ed.), *The Reign of Elizabeth I* (1984) pp. 195–219; Reay, 'Popular Religion'; Underdown, *Revel, Riot and Rebellion*, ch. 3; Collinson, *Birthpangs*, ch. 5.

27. See, for example, F. Heal, *Hospitality in Early Modern England* (Oxford, 1990) pp. 99ff., quoting p. 103. For developments from the mid-seventeenth century, P. Borsay, *The English Urban Renaissance: Culture*

and Society in the Provincial Town 1660–1770 (Oxford, 1989) especially pp. 226–8 and chs 10–11.

28. See, for example, P. Williams, *The Tudor Regime* (Oxford, 1979); A. Fletcher, *Reform in the Provinces: The Government of Stuart England* (1986); Wrightson, *English Society*, ch. 6; C. B. Herrup, *The Common Peace, Participation and the Criminal Law in Seventeenth-Century England* (Cambridge, 1987).

29. F. J. Furnival (ed.), *Harrison's Description of England, Part I* (New Shakespeare Society, 6th Series 1877) pp. 132–3, 137; H. J. Carpenter, 'Furse of Moreshead: A Family Record of the Sixteenth Century', *Devonshire Association Transactions*, XXVI (1894) p. 179.

30. Essex Record Office Q/SR 191/103, 259/10, cf. T/A 278, fo. 503; D. G. Allen, *In English Ways: The Movement of Societies and the Transferal of English Local Law and Custom to Massachusetts Bay in the Seventeenth Century* (Chapel Hill, 1981) pp. 146–7.

31. See, for example, Borsay, *English Urban Renaissance*, pp. 96, 166, 293; J. Brand, *Observations on Popular Antiquities: Including the Whole of Mr Bourne's Antiquitates Vulgares* (Newcastle, 1777) pp. ix, 18, 37, 41, 54, 87, 99, 101, 113, 187, 225, 241, 253, 314, 355.

32. P. Laslett, *The World We Have Lost – Further Explored* (1983) pp. 46–7; S. Reynolds, *An Introduction to the History of English Medieval Towns* (Oxford, 1977) pp. 76, 78, 79, 133–5, 163, 185; Thrupp, *Merchant Class*, pp. 26, 32, 89, 292, 299; T. Smith (ed.), *English Gilds: The Original Ordinances* (1870) p. 178. The broader significance of the occasional use of such terms in medieval English towns has been questioned by Dr Reynolds (p. 185), who suggests that 'Urban society, while undoubtedly stratified, resembled a trifle rather than a cake: its layers were blurred and the sherry of accepted values soaked through them.' For the more consistent use of such terminology in Italian cities, see Burke, 'The Language of Orders', p. 7.

33. J. Meadows (ed.), *Henry Brinklow's Complaynt of Roderyck Mors* (1874) p. 51; R. Mulcaster, *Positions Wherein Those Primitive Circumstances be Examined which are Necessarie for the Training Up of Children* (1581) p. 140; J. Stow, *The Survey of London*, Everyman edn (1956) pp. 492–3.

34. Ibid., pp. 46, 76, 86, 140, 187, 190, 210, 268, 293, 349, 383, 481. For London, see, for example, A. L. Beier and R. Finlay, *London 1500–1700: The Making of the Metropolis* (1986); J. Boulton, *Neighbourhood and Society: A London Suburb in the Seventeenth Century* (Cambridge, 1987); S. Rappaport, *Worlds within Worlds: Structures of Life in Sixteenth-Century London* (Cambridge, 1989); Archer, *Pursuit of Stability*; V. Brodsky Elliott, 'Mobility and Marriage in Pre-industrial England' (unpub. Ph.D. thesis, University of Cambridge, 1978). For provincial towns, see Hirst, *Representative of the People, passim*.

35. This paragraph is based upon the following literary concordances (an invaluable resource in studies of this kind): J. S. P. Tatlock and A. E. Kennedy (eds), *A Concordance of the Complete Works of Geoffrey Chaucer* (Washington, D.C., 1927); A. Fox and G. Waite (eds), *A Concordance of the Complete English Poems of John Skelton* (1987); H. S. Donow (ed.), *A Concordance to the Poems of Sir Philip Sidney* (1975); C. G. Osgood (ed.), *A Concordance to the Poems of Edmund Spenser* (Washington, D.C., 1915); J. Bartlett

(ed.), *A New and Complete Concordance or Verbal Index to Words, Phrases and Passages in the Dramatic Works of Shakespeare* (1894); M. A. Di Cesare and R. Mignani (eds) *A Concordance to the Complete Writings of George Herbert* (1977); L. Sterne and H. H. Kollmeier (eds), *A Concordance to the English Prose of John Milton* (Binghamton, 1985).

36. Schmitt, *John Case and Aristotelianism*, pp. 26–8, 87; Anon [trans.], *Aristotles Politiques or Discourses of Government by Loys Le Roy, called Regius: Translated out of French into English* (1598) pp. 156, 157, 219, 220, 222, 345, 346, 347.

37. *Oxford English Dictionary*; British Library Lansdowne MS 67, no. 22; W. W. Skeat (ed.), *The Book of Husbandry by Master Fitzherbert* (1882) p. 86; J. Dee, *General and Rare Memorials Pertayning to the Perfect Arte of Navigation* (1577) marginal note, Sig. F. ii R; T. S. Willan (ed.), *A Tudor Book of Rates* (Manchester 1962) pp. 48, 71; *The Rates of Marchandizes 1609*, Facsimile reprint (Amsterdam and New York, 1969) E2v, E3, G3v and unpag.

38. C. Read (ed.), *William Lambarde and Local Government* (Ithaca, N.Y., 1962) p. 167.

39. Underdown, *Revel, Riot and Rebellion*, pp. 85–6; *Winthrop Papers*, I, p. 293; D. W. Davies and E. S. Wrigley (eds), *A Concordance to the Essays of Francis Bacon* (Detroit, 1973); M. Campbell, *The English Yeoman under Elizabeth and the Early Stuarts* (New Haven, Conn., 1942) p. 61; R. Rawlidge, *A Monster Late Found Out* (1628) p. 17; Wright, *Middle-Class Culture*, p. 237; B. Manning, *The English People and the English Revolution 1640–1649* (1976) p. 154.

40. Manning, *English People*, pp. 154, 203, 205, 241; Underdown, *Revel, Riot and Rebellion*, p. 169.

41. R. Clifton, *The Last Popular Rebellion: The Western Rising of 1685* (1984) p. 33; Underdown, *Revel, Riot and Rebellion*, p. 169; J. Hutchinson (ed.), *Lucy Hutchinson: Memoirs of the Life of Colonel Hutchinson*, Everyman edn (1908) p. 80; J. M. Lloyd Thomas (ed.), *The Autobiography of Richard Baxter*, Everyman edn. (1931) p. 34.

42. J. Lilburne, 'England's Birth-Right Justified' (1645), in W. Haller (ed.), *Tracts on Liberty in the Puritan Revolution, 1638–1647*, 3 vols (New York, 1934) vol. III, p. 303; J. Lilburne, 'England's New Chains Discovered' (1649), in W. Haller and G. Davies (eds), *The Leveller Tracts, 1647–1653* (New York, 1944) p. 159; J. Wildman, *A Call to All the Soldiers of the Army by the Free People of England* (1647) p. 2; Anon, *The Standard of Equality* (London, 1647); H. N. Brailsford, *The Levellers and the English Revolution* (1961) pp. 447, 603; G. Foster, *The Sounding of the Last Trumpet* (1650) pp. 17–18. I am grateful to Andrew Wood for his advice on the radical literature of the period.

43. See, for example, T. Harris, *London Crowds in the Reign of Charles II. Propaganda and Politics from the Restoration until the Exclusion Crisis* (Cambridge, 1987); G. S. De Krey, *A Fractured Society: The Politics of London in the First Age of Party, 1688–1715* (Oxford, 1985); N. Rogers, *Whigs and Cities: Popular Politics in the Age of Walpole and Pitt* (Oxford, 1989). For a stimulating recent attempt to conceptualise the place of the 'middle sort of people' in eighteenth-century society, and discussion of the subsequent development

of 'middle-class' identities, see D. Wahrman, 'National Society, Communal Culture', *Social History*, 17 (1992) pp. 43–72, and J. Seed, 'From "Middling Sort" to Middle Class in Late Eighteenth and Early Nineteenth Century England', in Bush (ed.), *Social Orders and Social Classes*, pp. 114–35.

44. C. Hill, *A Turbulent, Seditious, and Factious People: John Bunyan and his Church* (Oxford, 1988) p. 115; R. Baxter, *The Poor Husbandman's Advocate and Christian Directory*, 4 parts (1673) part IV, p. 19; Borsay, *English Urban Renaissance*, p. 242.

45. J. Thirsk, and J. P. Cooper (eds), *Seventeenth-Century Economic Documents* (Oxford, 1972) pp. 780–1, 795; Defoe, quoted in R. W. Malcolmson, *Life and Labour in England 1700–1780* (1981) p. 11; G. Miège, 'The Present State of Great Britain: An Eighteenth-Century Self-Portrait', in D. A. Baugh (ed.), *Aristocratic Government and Society in Eighteenth-Century England: The Foundations of Stability* (New York, 1975) pp. 46–8; P. Mathias, 'The Social Structure in the Eighteenth Century: A Calculation by Joseph Massie', in *The Transformation of England: Essays in the Economic and Social History of England in the Eighteenth Century* (1979) pp. 171–89; P. Corfield, 'Class by Name and Number in Eighteenth-Century Britain', *History*, 72 (1987) pp. 48, 50. It has been pointed out to me by Dr Paul Slack that the work of Guy Miège provides a particularly good instance of the adoption of a tripartite perception of society expressed in the language of 'sorts' of people. In the sixth and final edition of his *The New State of England* (1707), Miège devoted separate chapters to 'the Gentry of England' and 'the Commonalty of England', the latter including 'Yeomen, Merchants, Artificers, Tradesmen, Mariners and all others getting their livelihood after a mechanic way'. Revising his work for the first edition of *The Present State of Great Britain* (1707), Miège introduced a single chapter on the social order, distinguishing 'Gentlemen', 'the Inferiour Sort of people ... such as get their livelihood in a mechanick, or servile way', and 'a middle sort of people between the Degree of a Gentleman and them' (pp. 263–4).

46. P. Earle, *The Making of the English Middle Class: Business, Society and Family Life in London 1660–1750* (1989) ch. 1; P. Langford, *A Polite and Commercial People, England 1727–1783* (Oxford, 1989) ch. 3; Corfield, 'Class by Name and Number', pp. 53–5 and *passim*.

47. Paraphrasing MacDonald, *Mystical Bedlam*, p. 113.

48. L. C. Stevenson, *Praise and Paradox, Merchants and Craftsmen in Elizabethan Popular Literature* (Cambridge, 1984) p. 5.

2. APPRENTICESHIP, SOCIAL MOBILITY AND THE MIDDLING SORT,
1550–1800   *Christopher Brooks*

1. For a similar view, which is based on largely different sources, see M. J. Mascuch, 'Social Mobility in English Autobiography 1600–1750' (Cambridge University Ph.D. thesis, 1989).

2. G. Mayhew, 'Life-cycle Service and the Family Unit in Early Modern Rye', *Continuity and Change*, 6(2) (1991) pp. 201–27, argues that appren-

ticeship may have been less common for eldest sons of urban families than has previously been thought. However, this seems more characteristic of the later rather than the earlier seventeenth century.

3. A. Kussmaul, *Servants in Husbandry in Early Modern England* (Cambridge, 1981).

4. M. Spufford, *Contrasting Communities: English Villages in the Sixteenth and Seventeenth Centuries* (Cambridge, 1974) pp. 111–12; C. W. Brooks, *Pettyfoggers and Vipers of the Commonwealth: The 'Lower Branch' of the Legal Profession in Early Modern England* (Cambridge, 1986) pp. 258, 261–2; Vivien Brodsky Elliot, 'Single Women in the London Marriage Market: Age, Status and Mobility, 1598–1619', in R. B. Outhwaite (ed.), *Marriage and Society: Studies in the Social History of Marriage* (1981) pp. 81–100.

5. See I. K. Ben-Amos, 'Women Apprentices in Trades and Crafts of Early Modern Bristol', *Continuity and Change,* 6(2) (1991) pp. 227–253; P. Earle, 'The Female Labour Market in London in the Late Seventeenth and Early Eighteenth Centuries', *Economic History Review,* xliv (3) (1989) pp. 328–53. Women apprentices may, in fact, appear more frequently in the sources for the eighteenth century than they do for the seventeenth.

6. W. West, *The First Part of Symboleography: Which May Be Termed the Art, or Description of Instruments and Presidents* (1605 edn), Sec. 582–3.

7. Most notably G. Holmes, *Augustan England: Professions, State and Society, 1680–1730* (1982), and P. Borsay, *The English Urban Renaissance: Culture and Society in the Provincial Town 1660–1770* (Oxford, 1989) especially pp. 19–20, 37, 200–211, 231.

8. See below p. 249n.4, and E. Shelton-Jones, 'The Barber-Surgeons Company of London and Medical Education, 1540–1660' (Univ. of London, M. Phil thesis, 1981). For attorneys and solicitors see Brooks, *Pettyfoggers and Vipers of the Commonwealth,* ch. 8.

9. In 1669, it was noted that the judges had stated they would never extend the Statute of Artificers to villages. *The E[nglish] R[eports]* (1908) vol. 86, 1 Modern 26.

10. E. A. Wrigley, 'Urban Growth and Agricultural Change: England and the Continent in the Early Modern Period', *Journal of Interdisciplinary History,* xv (4) (1985) pp. 684–95.

11. Women migrated to towns to take up places in domestic service, and a significant number of 'subsistance' migrants, came to towns outside the apprenticeship system in search of work for wages. P. Clark, 'The Migrant in Kentish Towns 1580–1640', in P. Clark and P. Slack (eds), *Crisis and Order in English Towns 1500–1700* (1972) pp. 117–63.

12. G[uildhall] L[ibrary], London, MS 11,592 (Grocers' Co.) fols 179, 670; S. R. Smith, 'The Social and Geographical Origins of the London Apprentices, 1630–1660', *Guildhall Miscellany,* IV (4) (1973) pp. 200–3; P. E. Jones, *The Butchers of London* (1976) p. 15; R. Finlay, *Population and Metropolis: The Demography of London 1580–1650* (Cambridge, 1981) pp. 9, 63–7.

13. D. Hollis (ed.), *Calendar of the Bristol Apprenticeship Book 1532–1562, part 1: 1532–1542* (Bristol Record Society, vol. XIV, 1949) pp. 11, 199;

B[ristol] C[ity] A[rchives] O[ffice], Apprentice Books, 1605, 1606–7, 1670–71, 1690–92.

14. J. Youings, *Tuckers Hall Exeter: The History of a Provincial Company Through Five Centuries* (Exeter, 1968) p. 62; F. W. Dendy (ed.), *Extracts from the Records of the Merchant Adventurers of Newcastle-upon-Tyne*, Vol. II (Surtees Society, ci, 1899) pp. 185–381; T[yne] [and] W[ear] A[rchives] D[epartment], Newcastle, MS 786/1, Barber Surgeons Company; R. A. Houston, 'Aspects of Society in Scotland and North-east England, c.1550–c.1750: Social Structure, Literacy and Geographical Mobility' (Cambridge University Ph.D thesis, 1981) p. 64, Table 2; R. Howell, *Newcastle upon Tyne During the Puritan Revolution* (Oxford, 1967) p. 19; J. Patten, 'Patterns of Migration and Movement of Labour to Three Pre-industrial East Anglian Towns', *Journal of Historical Geography*, 2 (2) (1976) p. 119; B. Taylor, *The Acts and Ordinances of the Merchant Taylors in the City of York* (1949) pp. 54–9. See also A. J. Willis and A. L. Merson (eds), *A Calendar of Southampton Apprenticeship Registers 1609–1740* (Southampton Record Series, xii, 1968) p. xli.

15. Dendy (ed.), *Merchant Adventurers of Newcastle* Vol. II, pp. 185–381; Finlay, *Population and Metropolis*, Table 3.6, p. 65; G. D. Ramsay, 'The Recruitment and Fortunes of some London Freemen', *Economic History Review*, 2nd series, XXXI (4) (1978) p. 529; Smith, 'Social and Geographical Origins of London Apprentices', p. 206.

16. John Stow, in C. L. Kingsford (ed.), *A Survey of London* (2 vols, Oxford, 1971 edn) vol. II, pp. 207–8; R. G. Lang, 'London's Aldermen in Business 1600–1625', *Guildhall Miscellany*, III (4) (1971) pp. 240–64; R. G. Lang, 'The Greater Merchants of London in the Early Seventeenth Century' (Oxford University D.Phil. thesis, 1963) pp. 79–83.

17. Howell, *Newcastle Upon Tyne*, pp. 35–62; J. T. Evans, *Seventeenth-Century Norwich* (Oxford, 1979) p. 32; W. T. MacCaffrey, *Exeter, 1540–1640: The Growth of an English County Town* (Cambridge, Mass., 1958) pp. 136ff, 253–5.

18. Houston, 'Aspects of Society in Scotland and North-east England', p. 85; W. B. Stephens, *Seventeenth-Century Exeter: A Study of Industrial and Commercial Development 1625–1688* (Exeter, 1958) p. 41.

19. Lang, 'Greater Merchants of London', p. 78, for Haberdashers; GL MS 4329/3 for Carpenters' Company, 1600–1603.

20. My calculations from Dendy, *Merchant Adventurers of Newcastle*, Vol. II, pp. 185–381; TWAD MS 903/2, Housecarpenters, Millwrights, and Trunkmakers. For other places see Houston, 'Aspects of Society in Scotland and North-east England', p. 63; Willis and Merson, *Southampton Apprenticeship Registers*, pp. xxxii–xxxiii; P. J. Stiff, 'Apprenticeship Migration to Three Pre-industrial English Towns' (Liverpool University Ph.D. thesis, 1981) p. 202.

21. Ramsay, 'Recruitment and Fortunes of London Freemen', pp. 530–1.

22. Lang, 'Greater Merchants of London', p. 78; my conclusion from figures for each of the four companies given by Lang. See also Smith, 'Social and Geographical Origins of London Apprentices', p. 199.

23. A detailed analysis of the 'gent' entrants to the Haberdashers' and Grocers' Companies of London in the 1580s and 1630s indicates that at both dates about 20 per cent of those listed as sons of 'gents' were in fact the offspring of townsmen. Haberdashers, April 1583–April 1584, GL MS 15,860/1. Grocers, November 1629–November 1632, GL MS 11,593/1.

24. GL MS 11,593/1, fols 1–31; Smith, 'Social and Geographical Origins of London Apprentices', p. 199.

25. K. Wrightson, *English Society 1580–1680* (1982) pp. 25, 31–2. Internal evidence suggests that guild apprenticeship registers were reasonably accurate in the way they styled fathers. Nothing was to be gained in the way of special concessions from giving a false style, and since they were probably copied into registers from indentures of apprenticeship, which were legal documents, both masters and apprentices would have had an interest in accuracy, because the mis-use of styles was grounds for throwing out suits at law. Finally, although some townsmen used the ambiguous style, 'gent', most of them, even in the late seventeenth century, were described in guild records according to their occupation, especially outside London. For example, of the 'gents' admitted to the Grocers' Company of London in the years 1690–93, only 2 of 56 came from a major town with a population of over 3000, but 18 per cent of them were from London and its suburbs. In these records, the only major occupational label which never appears is that of 'attorney', but, even in the sixteenth century, and in wills, these lawyers inevitably described themselves as 'gents'. Overall, it would appear likely that the styles given in apprenticeship records are a good deal more reliable than those found in the admissions registers of the universities or the Inns of Court. For an important discussion of the significant of gent entries in the records of the universities, see L. Stone, 'The Size and Composition of the Oxford Student Body 1580–1909', in Stone (ed.), *The University in Society* (2 vols, Princeton, 1975) vol. i, pp. 12–14, 48.

26. E. A. Wrigley and R. S. Schofield, *The Population History of England 1541–1871* (1981) Table 7.8; Wrigley, 'Urban Growth and Agricultural Change', p. 688.

27. Daniel Defoe, *A Tour Through the Whole Island of Great Britain* (1724–6, Penguin edn, 1971) p. 362; BCAO, Apprenticeship Books, 1605–6, 1629–31, 1670–71, 1690–92; J. R. Holman, 'Apprenticeship as a Factor in Migration: Bristol 1675–1726', *Trans. Bristol and Glouc. Archaeological Society*, XCVII (1979) pp. 91–2.

28. Youings, *Tuckers Hall Exeter*, pp. 86, 89; J. Ellis, 'A Dynamic Society: Social Relations in Newcastle-upon-Tyne 1660–1760', in P. Clark (ed.), *The Transformation of English Provincial Towns 1600–1800* (1984) p. 201.

29. Patten, 'Patterns of Migration and Movement of Labour', p. 119; P. Corfield, 'A Provincial Capital in the Late Seventeenth Century: The Case of Norwich', in Clark and Slack (eds), *Crisis and Order*, p. 273.

30. E. A. Wrigley, 'A Simple Model of London's Importance in Changing English Society and Economy 1650–1700', *Past and Present*, 37 (1967) p. 46; R. Finlay and B. Shearer, 'Population Growth and Suburban Expansion', in A. L. Beier and R. Finlay (eds), *London 1500–1700: The Making of the Metropolis* (1986) pp. 37–59.

31. D. V. Glass, 'Socio-economic Status and Occupations in the City of London at the End of the Seventeenth Century', in A. E. J. Hollaender and W. Kellaway (eds), *Studies in London History* (1969) pp. 386–7.

32. Dendy (ed.), *Merchant Adventurers of Newcastle* Vol. II, pp. 185–323; TWAD MS 786/2, Barber-Surgeons' Co., 1690–93; D. J. Rowe (ed.) *Records of the Company of Shipwrights of Newcastle upon Tyne, 1622–1967,* Vol. II (Surtees Soc., vol. CLXXXIV, 1971) pp. 240–5.

33. W. F. Kahl, 'Apprenticeship and the Freedom of the London Livery Companies, 1690–1750', *Guildhall Miscellany,* 7 (1956) pp. 17–19.

34. Interestingly, an early-seventeenth-century client of the Duke of Buckingham also had the idea, which came to nothing, of establishing an office to enroll apprenticeship. The proposal came before Attorney General Sir Francis Bacon, who could find no grounds for it in law. Sir Francis Bacon, *Works,* (eds) J. Spedding *et al.* (14 vols, 1857–74) vol. VI, p. 269.

35. As compared with 24 in 1716, P[ublic] R[ecord] O[ffice], London, IR1/44, 51.

36. These were also the occupations which brought apprenticeship premiums well in excess of £100; PRO IR 1 *passim.*

37. PRO IR 1/4-6, 44–5, 51.

38. N. Rogers, *Whigs and Cities: Popular Politics in the Age of Walpole and Pitt* (Oxford, 1989) ch. 5, notes charity apprentices may have accounted for as many as one-third of all apprenticeships in early-eighteenth-century Bristol.

39. PRO IR 1/4, 44.

40. R. A. Pelham, 'The Immigrant Population of Birmingham, 1686–1726', *Transactions and Proceedings of the Birmingham Archeaological Society,* 61 (1940) pp. 45–80.

41. *ER,* vol. 88, 8 Modern 285.

42. W. Hutton, *Courts of Requests: Their Nature, Utility and Power Described, with a Variety of Cases Determined in that of Birmingham* (Birmingham, 1787) pp. 25, 53. See also K. D. M. Snell, *Annals of the Labouring Poor: Social Change and Agrarian England 1660–1900* (Cambridge, 1985) ch. 5, for a discussion of the change in apprenticeship, although most of the evidence adduced relates to poor apprentices rather than those from the middling sort.

43. H. Jenkinson (ed.), *Surrey Apprenticeships from the Registers in the Public Record Office 1711–1731* (Surrey Record Society, vol. X, 1929); Paul Langford, *A Polite and Commercial People: England 1727–1783* (Oxford, 1989) p. 62.

44. R. G. Wilson, *Gentleman Merchants: The Merchant Community in Leeds 1700–1830* (Manchester, 1971) p. 27; M. B. Rowlands, *Masters and Men in the West Midlands Metalware Trades Before the Industrial Revolution* (Manchester, 1975) p. 147.

45. D. Defoe, *The Complete English Tradesman* (4th edn, 1738) pp. 143–51.

46. Arthur Redford, *Labour Migration in England 1800–1850* (Manchester University Press, 3rd edn, 1976; first edition, 1926) ch. II.

47. Wrigley, 'Urban Growth and Agricultural Change', may place too much emphasis on high urban real wages.

48. S. Rappaport, 'Social Structure and Mobility in Sixteenth-Century London. Part 1', *London Journal*, 9 (2) (1983) pp. 113–131; N. R. Goose, 'In Search of the Urban Variable: Towns and the English Economy, 1500–1650', *Economic History Review*, 2nd series, XXXIX (2) (1986) pp. 165–85.

49. J. Thirsk (ed.), *The Agrarian History of England and Wales*, Vol. IV. *1500–1640* (Cambridge, 1967) pp. 304–5.

50. Wrightson, *English Society*, pp. 132–9, 142–5; C. Wilson, *England's Apprenticeship 1603–1763* (1965) ch. 3; B. E. Supple, *Commercial Crisis and Change in England 1600–1649* (1959) chs 1–6; A. H. Johnson (ed.), *The History of the Worshipful Company of Drapers of London* (5 vols, Oxford, 1914–22) vol. III, pp. 171–2, for hardship caused by the dislocation of trade in the 1620s.

51. See generally O. J. Dunlop and R. D. Denman, *English Apprenticeship and Child Labour* (1912) ch. XII. For examples of seventeenth-century premiums see A. Simpson, 'Thomas Cullum, Draper, 1587–1664', *Economic History Review*, 2nd series, XI (1) (1958) pp. 21–3; R. Grassby, 'Social Mobility and Business Enterprise in Seventeenth-century England', in D. Pennington and K. Thomas (eds), *Puritans and Revolutionaries: Essays in Seventeenth-Century History Presented to Christopher Hill* (Oxford, 1978) pp. 364–5; R. Davis, *Aleppo and Devonshire Square: English Traders in the Levant in the Eighteenth Century* (1967) pp. 10–11, 64–5, 69.

52. E. A. Wrigley and R. S. Schofield, *The Population History of England, 1541–1871: A Reconstruction* (1981) pp. 215–18, 410, 418, 441; D. Souden, 'Migrants and the Population Structure of Later Seventeenth-century Provincial Cities and Market Towns', in Clark (ed.), *The Transformation of English Provincial Towns*, pp. 147–60.

53. J. P. Cooper, *Land, Men and Beliefs: Studies in Early Modern History* (1983) p. 28; J. Thirsk (ed.), *The Agrarian History of England and Wales, Vol. v(ii); 1640–1750* (Cambridge, 1985) p. 163.

54. L. Stone and J. C. F. Stone, *An Open Elite? England 1540–1880* (Oxford, 1984) pp. 181–4, 258–9, 400.

55. P. Aylett, 'Attorneys in the Market Place: The Distribution of Attorneys in England and Wales 1730–1800', *Law and History Review* 5 (1) (1987) pp. 1–30; David Lemmings, *Gentlemen and Barristers: The Inns of Court and The English Bar 1680–1730* (Oxford, 1990) p. 123.

56. Compare N. McKendrick, J. Brewer and J. H. Plumb, *The Birth of a Consumer Society: The Commercialization of Eighteenth-Century England* (1982) pp. 1–33, with J. F. Pound, 'Government and Society in Tudor and Stuart Norwich 1525–1675' (Leicester University Ph.D thesis, 1974), pp. 45–6.

57. S. Macfarlane, 'Social Policy and the Poor in the Later Seventeenth Century', in Beier and Finlay (eds), *London 1500–1700*, pp. 252–78.

58. *The Gentlemans Magazine*, 17 (1747) p. 540.

59. 6 George III, c. 25; Snell, *Annals of the Labouring Poor*, ch. 5.

60. Especially L. Stone, *The Family, Sex and Marriage in England* (1977) p. 167.

61. *The Works of Richard Brownlow, Esquire, Late one of the Prothonotaries of the Court of Common Pleas* (1654) p. 67; *The Reports of That Learned Sir Henry*

Hobart Knight: Late Lord Chief Justice of his Majesties Court of Common Pleas at Westminster (1641) p. 134.

62. John Dod and Robert Cleaver, *A Plaine and Familiar Exposition of the Ten Commandments* (1607 edn) pp. 202–5.

63. GL MS 15, 860/1.

64. See generally, I. K. Ben-Amos, 'Service and the Coming of Age of Young Men in Early Modern England, *Continuity and Change*, 3 (1) (1988) pp. 53–6; Jones, *Butchers of London*, pp. 16–17; B. Marsh (ed.), *Records of the Worshipful Company of Carpenters* (7 vols, Oxford, 1913) vol. i, p. x; Glass, 'Socio-economic Status and Occupations', pp. 373–89; Rappaport, 'Social Structure and Mobility, Part I', p. 117. Pound, 'Government and Society in Tudor and Stuart Norwich', p. 55, found that only 20 per cent of registered apprentices ever took up the freedom in the late sixteenth century. At Bristol, in the late seventeenth century, the percentage was between 40 and 50 per cent. Holman, 'Apprenticeship as a Factor in Migration', p. 90.

65. I. K. Ben-Amos, 'Failure to Become Freemen: Urban Apprentices in Early Modern England', *Social History* 16 (2) (1991) pp. 154–172.

66. K. M. Briggs (ed.), *The Last of the Astrologers: Mr William Lilly's History of his Life and Times from the Year 1602–1681* (reprint of 2nd edn of 1715, Mistletoe Books, no. 1, Ilkley, Yorks, 1974) pp. 26–7; Brooks, *Pettyfoggers and Vipers of the Commonwealth*, p. 136; W. Scott, *An Essay of Drapery (1635)*, (ed.) S. Thrupp (Kress Library of Business and Economics, 9, Boston, Mass. 1953) p. 57; A. L. Beier, 'Social Problems in Elizabethan London', *Journal of Interdisciplinary History*, IX (2) (1978) pp. 214–17.

67. Philip Jones and R. Smith, *A Guide to the Records of the Corporation of London Records Office and Guildhall Library Muniment Room* (1951) p. 66, notes that about 200 apprenticeship indentures were exhibited in the Mayor's Court during the seventeenth century, a figure which probably represents many of the cases. Corporation of London Record Office, London, Large Suits Box 1.11 for examples. Also 'Mayor's Court Original Bills. List of Schedules of Goods among the Common Law Original Bills in the Mayor's Court' (typescript) p. xix. A judicial decision (Berwick v. Johnson) at Newcastle in 1701, which confirmed the power of JPs to discharge apprentices on the first complaint of either master or apprentice, suggests that by then terminations which alleged a fictitious breach of the relationship were becoming common. Folger Shakespeare Library, Washington DC, MS Va 487, fol. 21.

68. Greater London Record Office, Calendars of Sessions Rolls, 1610–1727.

69. D. M. Palliser, 'The Trade Gilds of Tudor York', in Clark and Slack (eds), *Crisis and Order*, p. 95.

70. B[ritish] L[ibrary] Add. MS 10,407, Accounts and Memoranda Relating to the Co. of Silkweavers of York, fol. 16ᵛ GL MS 3969, fol. 3. See also Charles Welch, *History of the Cutlers' Company of London and of the Minor Cutlery Crafts* (2 vols, 1916, 1923) vol. II, p. 68.

71. P. McGrath (ed.), *The Marchants Avizo By I[ohn] B[rowne], Marchant 1589* (Kress Library of Business and Economics, no. 11, Boston, Mass.,

1957); Goldsmiths' Company, Goldsmiths' Hall, London, MS C. II. 2; Scott, *An Essay of Drapery,* p. 24.

72. Willis and Merson, *Southampton Apprenticeship Registers,* p. xxii; Palliser, 'Trade Gilds of Tudor York', p. 99.

73. J. J. Lambert (ed.), *Records of the Skinners of London* (1933) p. 177; Welch, *History of Cutlers' Company of London,* pp. 169–70; C. M. Clode, *The Early History of the Guild of Merchant Taylors of the Fraternity of St John the Baptist* (2 vols, 1888) vol. ii, pp. 158–67, 176, 187; B. W. E. Alford and T. C. Barker, *A History of the Carpenters' Company* (1968) p. 110–11.

74. John Ward, *The Lives of the Professors of Gresham College to which is prefixed the Life of the Founder, Sir Thomas Gresham* (1740) pp. ii, v, 19, 26, 34.

75. Thomas Dekker, 'Troia-Nova Triumphans', in F. Fairholt (ed.), *Lord Mayor's Pageants: Being Collections Towards a History of These Annual Celebrations, Part II* (Percy Society, vol. x, 1844) pp. 17–19.

76. See, for example, Lambert (ed.), *Records of the Skinners,* pp. 85–91; Welch, *History of the Cutlers' Company,* vol. i, pp. 15–17; Palliser, 'Trade Gilds of Tudor York', p. 95; Johnson, *History of Drapers,* vol. 1, pp. 196–201, 256, 263; vol. ii, p. 73; Toulmin Smith (ed.), *English Gilds. The Original Ordinances of more than One Hundred Early English Gilds: Together with Ye old Usages of Ye City of Wynchestre: The Ordinances of Worcester ...* (Early English Text Society, vol. 40, 1870) *passim.* Most original guild ordinances date from the late fourteenth and fifteenth centuries.

77. S. Brigden, 'Religion and Social Obligation in Early Sixteenth-Century London', *Past and Present,* 103 (1984), p. 79.

78. Marsh (ed.), *Records of the Worshipful Company of Carpenters,* vol. IV, p. xvii; Embleton, 'Incorporated Company of Barber-Surgeons', p. 237.

79. Marsh (ed.), *Records of the Worshipful Company of Carpenters,* vol. III, p. xvii; Dendy (ed.), *Merchant Adventurers of Newcastle,* Vol. I, p. 93. According to an ordinance of 1564, those who committed perjury were to be expelled from the company, p. 70.

80. Johnson, *History of Drapers,* vol. I pp. 197, 265; Welch, *History of the Cutlers' Company,* vol. I, pp. 16–17.

81. Quoted in Lambert (ed.), *Records of the Skinners,* p. 213.

82. Johnson, *History of Drapers,* vol. II, p. 65–7. The Drapers bought Thomas Cromwell's house in Throgmorton Street in the 1540s. For their elaborate garden regulations dated 1674, see *Ibid.,* vol. IV, pp. 294–5. A description of the Pewterers' Hall in 1589 is given in their minute book, GL MS 7090/3, fols 2–4v. The hall contained a long table and a 'frame wherein is wrytten a comendation of Love *and* Justyce'. See G. Unwin, *Gilds and Companies of London* (1908) ch. XII.

83. Ibid., p. 195. By the mid-sixteenth century, the Carpenters of London decorated their tables with cut flowers, and in 1571 the members of the livery asked that for 'the worshipp of this mysterie those that nowe are and those that here after shalbe called unto the Clothinge ... to be knowen from the reste of the yeomanrie' by having their own table napkins. Marsh (ed.), *Records of the Worshipful Company of Carpenters,* vol. III, p. 140; vol. IV, p. xvii.

84. M. Spufford, *Small Books and Pleasant Histories* (1981) pp. 50, 54, 72–4. Though she draws a different conclusion, much of the Elizabethan material is discussed in L. C. Stevenson, *Praise and Paradox: Merchants and Craftsmen in Elizabethan Popular Literature* (Cambridge, 1984). The assumption that there was no bourgeois culture before 1660 is based mainly on a lack of study of previous periods. An analysis of popular literature without establishing a detailed context from other sources can lead to misunderstanding. For gentry values, see John Ferne, *The Blazon of Gentrie Devided into Two Parts. The First Named the Glorie of Generositie. The Second Lacyes Nobilite* (1586) pp. 24–31, and R. Kelso, *The Doctrine of the English Gentleman in the Sixteenth Century* (Urbana, Ill., 1929) pp. 67–76.

85. Fairholt, *Lord Mayor's Pageants, passim.*

86. See, for example, T. Nash, *Quarternio: or a Fourfold Way to a Happie Life, set forth in a Dialogue between a Countryman and a Citizen, a Divine and a Lawyer* (1633), 'To the Reader'; William Martyn, *Youths Instruction* (1612); R. Brathwait, *The English Gentleman* (1630) pp. 107, 136ff.

87. Sir Thomas Elyot, *The Boke Named the Governour,* (ed.) H. H. S. Croft (2 vols, 1880) vol. i, pp. 7ff.; *Aristotle's Politics and the Athenian Constitution,* (ed.) J. Warrington (1959) pp. 21, note 3, 74. See also Sir Thomas Smith's account of artificers in *De Republica Anglorum (1583),* (ed.) Mary Dewar (Cambridge, 1982) p. 76.

88. Brooks, *Pettyfoggers and Vipers of the Commonwealth,* pp. 179–81; Smith, *De Republica,* pp. 140–1.

89. Ferne, *Blazon of Gentrie,* pp. [Sig. A. vi]. 7–9, 32–4, 70ff. Cooper, *Land, Men and Beliefs,* pp. 63–73. See also Edmund Bolton, *The Cities Advocate. In this Case or Question of Honour and Armes: Whether Apprenticeship Extinguisheth Gentry? Containing a Cleare Refutation of the Pernicious Common Errour Affirming it, Swallowed by Erasmus of Roterdam, Sir Thomas Smith in his Common-weal, Sir John Fern in his Blazon, Raphe Broke and Others* (1628). It is of interest that this book was one of the few kept by the Goldsmiths of London in their Library. Goldsmiths' Company MS E. III, Inventory of books and writings in the Custody of the Wardens. Bolton himself constantly sought financial support for his antiquarian efforts from the City authorities. BL Harleian MS 6521, fol. 243.

90. M. Shinagel, *Daniel Defoe and Middle-Class Gentility* (Cambridge, Mass., 1968) pp. 109–10.

91. Dendy, *Merchant Adventurers of Newcastle,* Vol. I, pp. 20–5.

92. Lambert (ed.), *Records of the Skinners,* p. 213. Thrupp, *Short History of the Worshipful Company of Bakers,* p. 90.

93. Bolton, *The Cities Advocate,* pp. 38–9; B. P., *The Prentises Practice in Godlinesse, and his true Freedome. Divided into Ten Chapters* (1608) p. 42v; *The Works of William Gouge in Two Volumes. The First Domestical Duties. The Second, the Whole Armour of God* (1627) vol. I, p. 346; A. Dent, *The Plaine Man's Path-Way to Heaven* (1612 edn) pp. 16–18, 80, 92. See also the treatise of Thomas Cooper, who received support from the Fishmongers' Company, *The Estate of the Hypocrite and Syncere Christian* (1613), Preface, p. 1, p. 337.

94. Jones, *The Butchers of London,* p. 16; Welch, *History of the Cutlers' Company,* vol. II, p. 208.

95. Gouge, *Domesticall Duties,* vol. I, pp. 334–5.

96. Robert Green, *A Quip for an Upstart Courtier: or a Quaint Dispute between Velvet-Breeches and Cloth-Breeches. Wherein is Plainely Set Down the Disorders in all Estates and Trades*, in W. Oldys and T. Park (eds) *The Harleian Miscellany* (10 vols, 1808–12) vol. v, pp. 400–6. Green himself is reported to have lost favour with 'honourable' Londoners because of his dissipations and licentiousness.

97. M. Heineman, *Puritanism and Theatre: Thomas Middleton and Opposition Drama Under the Early Stuarts* (Cambridge, 1980) pp. 52, 55, 64, 88, 114, 116–17, 172.

98. Shinagel, *Defoe and Middle-Class Gentility*, pp. 124, 188, 195, 210–11, 228–9, although the conclusion here is quite different from that presented by this author.

99. J. D. Marshall (ed.), *The Autobiography of William Stout of Lancaster 1655–1752* (Chetham Soc., 3rd series, vol. xiv, 1967) p. 206.

100. Langford, *Polite and Commercial People*, pp. 66–7, 653.

101. For the biographical details see *Dictionary of National Biography*.

102. C. R. Dobson, *Masters and Journeymen: A Prehistory of Industrial Relations 1717–1800* (1980) pp. 47–9; J. Rule, *The Experience of Labour in Eighteenth-Century Industry* (1981) p. 111.

103. *Parliamentary Papers: Report 1812–13*, 'Apprenticeship Laws'.

104. Thomas Gisbourne, *An Enquiry into the Duties of Men in the Higher and Middle Classes of Society in Great Britain, Resulting from their Respective Stations, Profession, and Employments* (Dublin, 1795) pp. 476–91. See also the emphasis on education in John Wade, *History of the Middle and Working Classes: with a Popular Exposition of the Economical and Political Principles which have Influenced the Past and Present Condition of the Industrious Orders* (1833).

3. BOURGEOIS COLLECTIVISM? URBAN ASSOCIATION AND THE MIDDLING SORT   *Jonathan Barry*

1. I would like to express my thanks for helpful discussion of the ideas expressed here to Christopher Brooks, Sandra Cavallo, David Cullum, Colin Jones, John Triffitt and all those who responded to papers given a the Institute of Historical Research, the University of St Andrews, the Maison des Sciences des Hommes and the ESRC colloquium on urban history at the University of Essex. Many of the conclusions about associations are drawn from my research on Bristol, summarised in J. Barry, 'The Cultural Life of Bristol, 1640–1775' (University of Oxford D.Phil. thesis, 1985).

2. Recent examples include: I. Kramnick, *Republicanism and Bourgeois Radicalism: Political Identity in Late Eighteenth-Century England* (Cornell, 1990); M. Billinge, 'Hegemony, Class and Power in Late Georgian and Early Victorian England', in A. R. H. Baker and D. Gregory (eds), *Explorations in Historical Geography* (Cambridge, 1984) pp. 28–67; T. Koditschek, *Class Formation and Urban Industrial Society: Bradford, 1750–1850* (Cambridge, 1990).

3. For this debate see R. G. Lang, 'Social Origins and Social Aspirations of Jacobean London Merchants', *Economic History Review*, 27 (1974)

pp. 28–47; R. Grassby, 'Social Mobility and Business Enterprise in Seventeenth-Century England', in D. Pennington and K. Thomas (eds), *Puritans and Revolutionaries* (Oxford, 1978) pp. 355–81; N. Rogers, 'Money, Land and Lineage in Hanoverian London', *Social History*, 4 (1979) pp. 437–54; D. T. Andrew and N. Rogers, 'Aldermen and Big Bourgeoisie of London Reconsidered', *Social History*, 6 (1981) pp. 359–69; L. and J. C. F. Stone, *An Open Elite? England 1540–1880* (Oxford, 1984); H. Horwitz, 'The Mess of the Middle Class Revisited', *Continuity and Change*, 2 (1987) pp. 263–96; R. G. Wilson, 'Merchants and Land', *Northern History*, 24 (1988) pp. 75–100; R. C. Allen, 'The Price of Freehold Land and the Interest Rate in the Seventeenth and Eighteenth Centuries', *Economic History Review*, 41 (1988) pp. 33–50.

4. A. Black, *Guilds and Civil Society in European Political Thought from the Twelfth Century to the Present* (1984); E. Kamenka and R. S. Neale (eds), *Feudalism, Capitalism and Beyond* (1975); A. MacFarlane, *The Origins of English Individualism* (Oxford, 1978); R. S. Neale, *Class in English History 1680–1850* (Oxford, 1981); P. Corrigan and D. Seyer, *The Great Arch: English State Formation as Cultural Revolution* (Oxford, 1985); T. H. Aston and E. Philpin (eds), *The Brenner Debate* (Cambridge, 1987); C. Mooers, *The Making of Bourgeois Europe* (1991) pp. 155–85.

5. D. Fraser, *Urban Politics in Victorian England* (Leicester, 1976); D. Fraser, *Power and Authority in the Victorian City* (Oxford, 1979); R. J. Morris, 'Voluntary Societies and the British Urban Elite 1780–1850', *Historical Journal*, 26 (1983) pp. 95–118; R. J. Morris (ed.), *Class, Power and Social Structure in British Nineteenth-Century Towns* (Leicester, 1986); L. Davidoff and C. Hall, *Family Fortunes: Men and Women of the English Middle Class 1780–1850* (1987); P. Jones, S. Nenadic and P. Hills, 'Studying the Middle Class in Nineteenth-Century Britain', *Urban History Yearbook*, 14 (1987) pp. 22–50; R. J. Morris, *Class, Sect and Party: The Making of the British Middle Class, Leeds 1820–1850* (Manchester, 1990); S. Nenadic, 'Businessmen, the Urban Middle Class and the "Dominance" of Manufacturers in Nineteenth-Century Britain', *Economic History Review*, 44 (1991) pp. 66–85.

6. P. Clark, *Sociability and Urbanity: Clubs and Societies in the Eighteenth-Century City* (Leicester, 1986) p. 4. The general case is made in P. Clark and P. Slack, *English Towns in Transition 1500–1700* (Oxford, 1976), and C. Phythian-Adams, *Desolation of a City: Coventry and the Urban Crisis of the Late Middle Ages* (Cambridge, 1979). Critiques include V. Pearl, 'Change and Stability in Seventeenth-Century London', *London Journal*, 5 (1979) pp. 3–34; J. Boulton, *Neighbourhood and Society: London Suburb in the Seventeenth Century* (Cambridge, 1987); A. Dyer, *Decline and Growth in English Towns 1400–1640* (Basingstoke, 1991); I. Archer, *The Pursuit of Stability: Social Relations in Elizabethan London* (Cambridge, 1991).

7. P. Borsay, 'The English Urban Renaissance', *Social History*, 2 (1977) pp. 581–603; G. Holmes, 'The Achievement of Stability', in J. Cannon (ed.), *The Whig Ascendancy* (1981) pp. 1–23; P. Clark (ed.), *The Transformation of English Provincial Towns 1600–1800* (1984); P. Borsay, 'Urban Development in the Age of Defoe', in C. Jones (ed.), *Britain in First Age of Party* (1987) pp. 195–219; P. Borsay, *The English Urban Renaissance* (Oxford,

1989). For a critique see J. Barry, 'Provincial Town Culture 1640–1780: Urbane or Civic?', in A. Wear and J. H. Pittock (eds), *Interpretation and Cultural History* (Basingstoke, 1991) pp. 198–234. Dror Wahrman, in 'National Society, Communal Culture', *Social History*, 17 (1992) pp. 43–72, argues that the middling sort was divided by this urban renaissance, one part accepting its national values, and the other rejecting them in favour of a 'provincial–communal alternative', but this valuable suggestion overlooks the characteristic ambivalence towards both cultures felt by the middling sort as a whole, while exaggerating the gulf between these two cultures.

8. J. H. Hexter, 'The Myth of the Middle Class in Tudor England', in his *Reappraisals in History* (1961) pp. 71–116; H. Perkin, *The Origins of Modern English Society 1780–1880* (1969); E. P. Thompson, 'Patrician Society, Plebeian Culture', *Journal of Social History*, 7 (1974) pp. 382–405; E. P. Thompson, 'Eighteenth-Century Society: Class Struggle without Class?', *Social History*, 3 (1978) pp. 133–65; K. Wrightson, *English Society 1580–1680* (1982); M. L. Bush, *The English Aristocracy* (Manchester, 1984); J. Cannon, *Aristocratic Century* (Cambridge, 1984); J. C. D. Clark, *English Society, 1688–1832* (Cambridge, 1985); J. V. Beckett, *The Aristocracy in England, 1660–1914* (Oxford, 1986). For critical reviews of this approach, see C. Hill, 'A Bourgeois Revolution?', in J. G. A. Pocock (ed.), *Three British Revolutions* (Princeton, 1908) pp. 109–39; K. Wrightson, 'The Social Order of Early Modern England: Three Approaches', in L. Bonfield et al. (eds), *The World We Have Gained* (Oxford, 1979) pp. 177–202; P. Corfield (ed.), *Language, History and Class* (Oxford, 1991); J. G. Rule, *Albion's People: English Society 1714–1815* (Harlow, 1992); J. Seed, 'From "Middling Sort" to Middle Class in Late Eighteenth-Century and Early Nineteenth-Century England', in M. L. Bush (ed.), *Social Orders and Social Classes in Europe since 1500* (Harlow, 1992) pp. 114–35.

9. E. and S. Yeo (eds), *Popular Culture and Class Conflict 1590–1914* (Hassocks, 1981); A. Fletcher and J. Stevenson (eds), *Order and Disorder in Early Modern England* (Cambridge, 1985); D. Underdown, *Revel, Riot and Rebellion: Popular Politics and Culture in England 1603–1660* (Oxford, 1985); M. Mullett, 'Popular Culture and Popular Politics: Some Regional Case Studies', in Jones (ed.), *Britain*, pp. 129–50.

10. A similar point is made in R. Weissman, 'The Importance of Being Ambiguous: Social Relations, Individualism and Identity in Renaissance Florence', in S. Zimmerman and R. Weissman (eds), *Urban Life in the Renaissance* (Newark, 1989) pp. 269–80.

11. D. Sacks, 'The Corporate Town and the British State: Bristol's Little Businesses 1625–41'. *Past and Present*, 110 (1986) pp. 69–105; D. Sacks, *The Widening Gate: Bristol and the Atlantic Economy, 1450–1700* (Berkeley, 1991). See also: J. Money, *Experience and Identity: Birmingham and the West Midlands 1760–1800* (Manchester, 1977); J. Evans, *Seventeenth-Century Norwich: Politics, Religion and Government 1620–90* (Oxford, 1979); R. Howell, 'Newcastle and the Nation', *Archaeologia Aeliana*, 8 (1980) pp. 17–34; N. Rogers, *Whigs and Cities: Popular Politics in the Age of Walpole and Pitt* (Oxford, 1989); P. Langford, *Public Life and the Propertied Englishman 1689–1798* (Oxford, 1991).

12. A. Everitt, 'Social Mobility in Early Modern England', *Past and Present*, 33 (1966); Rogers, 'Money, Land and Lineage'; D. Souden, 'Migrants and the Population Structure of Later Seventeenth-Century Provincial Cities and Market Towns', in P. Clark (ed.), *Transformation of English Provincial Towns*, pp. 133–68; A. Everitt, 'Dynasty and Community since the Seventeenth Century', in his *Landscape and Community in England* (1985) pp.309–30; A. L. Beier and R. Finlay (eds), *The Making of the Metropolis: London 1500–1700* (Harlow, 1986); P. Clark and D. Souden (eds), *Migration and Society in Early Modern England* (1987); Horwitz, 'Mess of the Middle Class'.

13. G. E. Mingay, *The Gentry* (1976); P. Jenkins, *The Making of a Ruling Class: the Glamorgan Gentry 1640–1790* (Cambridge, 1983); Stones, *An Open Elite;* Morris (ed.), *Class, Power and Social Structure.*

14. C. W. Chalklin, 'Capital Expenditure on Building for Cultural Purposes', *Business History,* 22 (1980) pp. 51–70; Borsay, *English Urban Renaissance;* K. Wilson, 'Urban Culture and Political Activism in Hanoverian England', in E. Hellmuth (ed.), *The Transformation of Political Culture in Britain and Germany in the Late Eighteenth Century* (Oxford, 1990) pp. 165–84. For the medieval antecedents of collective association to promote continuity, see S. Reynolds, *Kingdoms and Communities in Western Europe 900–1300* (Oxford, 1984).

15. Clark and Slack, *Towns;* N. Rogers, 'Urban Opposition to Whig Oligarchy', in M. C. and J. Jacob (eds), *The Origins of Anglo-American Radicalism* (1984) pp. 132–48; Neale, *Class;* Borsay, *English Urban Renaissance.* The fullest critique of the oligarchy theory is in Evans, *Seventeenth-Century Norwich.*

16. Morris, *Class, Sect and Party.* For the gentry see C. Holmes, 'The County Community in Stuart Historiography', *Journal of British Studies,* 19 (1980) pp. 54–73; Bush, *English Aristocracy;* and Mingay, *Gentry.*

17. A. Mayer, 'The Lower Middle Class as a Historical Problem', *Journal of Modern History,* 47 (1975) pp. 409–36. For London see: R. Brenner, 'The Civil War Politics of London's Merchant Community', *Past and Present,* 58 (1973) pp. 53–107; J. Brewer, *Party Ideology and Popular Politics at the Accession of George III* (Cambridge, 1976); J. Stevenson (ed.), *London in the Age of Reform* (Oxford, 1977); G. S. De Krey, *A Fractured Society: The Politics of London in the First Age of Party, 1688–1715* (Oxford, 1985); T. Harris, *London Crowds in the Reign of Charles II* (Cambridge, 1987); H Horwitz, 'Party in a Civic Context: London from the Exclusion Crisis to the Fall of Walpole', in Jones (ed.), *Britain;* T. Liu, *Puritan London* (Newark, 1989); P. Earle, *The Making of the English Middle Class: Business, Society and Family Life in London 1660–1730* (1989); Rogers, *Whigs and Cities;* Archer, *Pursuit of Stability;* R. Brenner, *Merchants and Revolution: Commercial Change, Political Conflict and London's Overseas Traders 1550–1653* (Cambridge, 1993).

18. E. P. Thompson, *The Making of the English Working Class* (revised edition, Harmondsworth, 1968).

19. S. Smith, 'The Ideal and the Real: Apprentice–Master Relationships in Seventeenth-Century London', *History of Education Quarterly,* 21 (1981) pp. 449–60; J. G. Rule, 'The Property of Skill in the Period of Manufacture', in P. Joyce (ed.), *Historical Meanings of Work* (Cambridge, 1987)

pp. 99–118; M. Pelling, 'Child Health as a Social Value in Early Modern England', *Social History of Medicine,* 1 (1988) pp. 135–64; I. K. Ben-Amos, 'Service and the Coming of Age of Young Men in Seventeenth-Century England', *Continuity and Change,* 3 (1988) pp. 41–64; H. Cunningham, 'The Employment and Unemployment of Children in England c. 1680–1851', *Past and Present,* 126 (1990) pp. 115–50; G. Mayhew, 'Life-Cycle Service and the Family Unit in Early Modern Rye', *Continuity and Change,* 6 (1991) pp. 201–27.

20. F. G. James, 'Charity Endowments as Sources of Local Credit in Seventeenth and Eighteenth-Century England'. *Journal of Economic History,* 8 (1948); C. Carlton, *The Court of Orphans* (Leicester, 1974); J. R. Holman, 'Orphans in Pre-Industrial Towns: the Case of Bristol', *Local Population Studies,* 15 (1975) pp. 40–4; R. J. Morris, 'The Middle Class and the Property Cycle during the Industrial Revolution', in T. Smout (ed.), *The Search for Wealth and Stability* (1979) pp. 91–113; P. Earle, 'Age and Accumulation in the London Business Community', in N. McKendrick and R. B. Outhwaite (eds), *Business Life and Public Policy* (Cambridge, 1986) pp. 38–63; G. Rosser, 'Communities of Parish and Guild in the Later Middle Ages', in S. J. Wright (ed.), *Parish, Church and People* (1988) pp. 29–55; M. Pelling and R. M. Smith (eds), *Life, Death and the Elderly* (1991).

21. For apprentices' public actions, see notes 17 and 19, together with the essays collected or cited in P. Slack (ed.), *Rebellion, Popular Protest and the Social Order in Early Modern England* (Cambridge, 1984), especially pp. 4–5. For women see L. Davidoff and C. Hall, *Family Fortunes* (1987), and the critique offered in A. Vickery, 'Golden Age to Separate Spheres?: A Review of the Categories and Chronology of English Women's History', *Historical Journal,* 36 (1993) pp. 383–414.

22. C. Phythian-Adams, 'Ceremony and the Citizen: the Ceremonial Year at Coventry 1450–1550', in P. Clark and P. Slack (eds), *Crisis and Order in English Towns 1500–1700* (1972); Morris, 'Voluntary Associations'; M. James, *Society, Politics and Culture* (Cambridge, 1986); D. H. Sacks, 'The Demise of the Martyrs: the Feasts of St Clement and St Katherine in Bristol 1400–1600', *Social History,* 11 (1986) pp. 141–96; Clark, *Sociability and Urbanity;* Borsay, *English Urban Renaissance;* R. J. Morris, 'Clubs, Societies and Associations', in F. M. L. Thompson (ed.), *The Cambridge Social History of Britain, 1750–1950,* vol. 3 (Cambridge, 1990) pp. 395–443. For a revisionist account, emphasising guild vitality into the eighteenth century, see M. J. Walker, 'The Extent of the Guild Control in Trades in England, 1660–1820' (University of Cambridge, Ph.D thesis, 1985).

23. For recent consideration of these topics, see: P. Seaver, 'The Puritan Work Ethic Revisited', *Journal of British Studies,* 19:2 (1980) pp. 35–53; D. Rollison, 'The Bourgeois Soul of John Smyth of Nibley', *Social History,* 12 (1987) pp. 309–30: J. Innes, 'Politics and Morals: the Reformation of Manners Movements in the Late Eighteenth Century', in Hellmuth (ed.), *Transformation of Political Culture,* pp. 165–84; Sacks, *Widening Gate,* pp. 304–29; L. Davison et al. (eds), *Stilling the Grumbling Hive: The Response to Social and Economic Problems in England, 1689–1750* (Stroud, 1992).

24. W. K. Jordan, *Philanthropy in England 1480–1640* (1959); W. K. Jordan, *The Charities of London 1480–1660* (1960); D. Owen, *English Philanthropy* (Cambridge, Mass., 1964); D. Andrew, *Philanthropy and Police: London Charity in the Eighteenth Century* (Princeton, 1989); R. Porter, 'The Gift Relation: Philanthropy in Provincial Hospitals in Eighteenth-Century England', in L. Granshaw and R. Porter (eds), *The Hospital in History* (1989). Recent work has emphasised the need to see charity and mutualism in the same context. See, for example, J. Barry and C. Jones (eds), *Medicine and Charity before the Welfare State* (1991), especially S. Cavallo, 'The Motives of Benefactors: an Overview of Approaches', pp. 46–62, and F. Prochaska, 'Philanthropy', in Thompson (ed.), *Cambridge Social History*, vol. 3, pp. 357–93. The standard works on friendly societies by Gosden only sketch an eighteenth-century background, but for a regional study, which, despite its subtitle, deals extensively with small-town societies, see M. D. Fuller, *West Country Friendly Societies: an Account of Village Benefit Clubs and their Brass Pole Heads* (Reading, 1964).

25. I owe this point to J. Triffitt, 'Believing and Belonging', in Wright (ed.), *Parish, Church and People*, pp. 179–202.

26. This is the crucial point made by Morris in his nineteenth-century work.

27. Triffitt, 'Believing and Belonging'; J. Barry, 'The Parish in Civic Life', in Wright (ed.), *Parish, Church and People*, pp. 152–78. On the notion of trust and its significance for the bourgeoisie, see the penetrating observations in J. Torrance, 'Social Class and Bureaucratic Innovation, 1780–87', *Past and Present*, 78 (1978) pp. 56–81.

28. J. McVeagh, *Tradefull Merchants: The Portrayal of the Capitalist in Literature* (1981); L. S. O'Connell, 'The Elizabethan Bourgeois Hero-Tale', in B. C. Malament (ed.), *After the Reformation* (Manchester, 1980) pp. 267–90; P. Clark, 'Visions of the Urban Community: Antiquarians and the English City before 1800', in D. Fraser and A. Sutcliffe (eds), *The Pursuit of Urban History* (1983) pp. 105–24; L. Stevenson, *Praise and Paradox: Merchants and Craftsmen in Elizabethan Popular Literature* (Cambridge, 1984); J. G. A. Pocock, *Virtue, Commerce and History* (Cambridge, 1985); Clark, *English Society;* Stones, *An Open Elite;* Borsay, *English Urban Renaissance;* D. Wahrman, 'National Society'.

29. For the nineteenth-century literature on these themes see: D. Blackbourn and G. Eley, *The Peculiarities of German History* (Oxford, 1984); J. Wolff and J. Seed (eds), *The Culture of Capital: Art, Power and the Nineteenth-Century Middle Class* (Manchester, 1988); M. J. Daunton, '"Gentlemanly Capitalism" and British Industry 1820–1914' *Past and Present*, 122 (1989) pp. 119–58 (and debate in ibid., 132 (1991) pp. 150–87).

30. D. F. Allen, 'The Role of the London Trained Bands in the Exclusion Crisis, 1678–81', *English Historical Review*, 87 (1972) pp. 287–303; J. Brewer, 'The Commercialization of Politics', in N. McKendrick et al., *Birth of a Consumer Society* (Cambridge, 1980) pp. 197–262; P. O'Malley, 'From Feudal Honour to Bourgeois Reputation', *Sociology*, 15 (1981) pp. 79–93; J. Hoppit, 'The Use and Abuse of Credit in Eighteenth-Century England', in McKendrick and Outhwaite (eds), *Business Life*, pp. 64–78; J. Hoppit, *Risk*

and Failure in English Business 1700–1800 (Cambridge, 1987); P. O'Brien, 'The Political Economy of British Taxation 1660–1815', *Economic History Review,* 41 (1988) pp. 1–32; Sacks, *Widening Gate,* pp. 65–84; R. C. Richardson (ed.), *Town and Countryside in the English Revolution* (Manchester, 1992), especially the essays by Hughes and Roy; C. Muldrew, 'Credit and the Courts: Debt Litigation in a Seventeenth-Century Urban Community', *Economic History Review,* 46 (1993) pp. 23–38; C. Muldrew, 'Interpreting the Market', *Social History,* 18 (1993) pp. 163–83.

31. N. Elias, *The Civilizing Process* (Oxford, 1978).

32. D. Palliser, 'The Trade Gilds of Tudor York', in Clark and Slack (eds), *Crisis and Order;* Clark and Slack, *Towns;* Rosser, 'Communities of Parish and Guild'; N. J. Alldridge, 'Loyalty and Identity in Chester Parishes 1540–1640', in Wright (ed.), *Parish, Church and People,* pp. 85–124; P. Collinson, *The Birthpangs of Protestant England* (1988); Archer, *Pursuit of Stability.*

33. L. B. Wright, *Middle-Class Culture in Elizabethan England* (new edition, Ithaca, 1958); M. Heinemann, *Puritanism and Theatre* (Cambridge, 1980); M. Butler, *Theatre and Crisis 1632–42* (Cambridge, 1984); A. Gurr, *Playgoing in Shakespeare's London* (Cambridge, 1987); J. C. Agnew, *Worlds Apart: The Market and the Theatre in Anglo-American Thought 1550–1750* (Cambridge, 1986). The best overview of 'popular literature' in this period is given by T. Watt, *Cheap Print and Popular Piety* (Cambridge, 1991).

34. Holmes, 'Achievement of Stability'; Barry, 'Parish in Civic Life'; Borsay, *English Urban Renaissance;* J. Barry, 'The Politics of Religion in Restoration Bristol', in T. Harris, P. Seaward and M. Goldie (eds), *The Politics of Religion in Restoration England* (Oxford, 1990) pp. 163–90; J. Barry, 'The Press and the Politics of Culture in Bristol, 1660–1775', in J. Black and J. Gregory (eds), *Culture, Politics and Society in Britain 1660–1800* (Manchester, 1991) pp. 49–81.

35. J. Brewer, 'English Radicalism in the Age of George III', in Pocock (ed.), *Three British Revolutions,* pp. 323–67; J. A. Phillips, *Electoral Behavior in Unreformed England* (Princeton, 1982); K. Wilson, 'Empire, Trade and Popular Politics in Mid-Hanoverian Britain', *Past and Present,* 121 (1988) pp. 74–109; P. Monod, *Jacobitism and English People* (Cambridge, 1989); F. O'Gorman, *Voters, Patrons and Parties* (Oxford, 1989); Rogers, *Whigs and Cities;* J. E. Bradley, *Religion, Revolution and English Radicalism: Nonconformity in 18C Politics and Society* (Cambridge, 1990); Langford, *Public Life.*

36. The most illuminating work on this theme so far is: N. Rogers, 'Aristocratic Clientage, Trade and Independency: Popular Politics in Pre-Radical Westminster', *Past and Present,* 61 (1973) pp. 70–106; C. Hill, 'Pottage for Freeborn Englishmen: Attitudes to Wage-Labour', in his *Change and Continuity in Seventeenth-Century England* (1974) pp. 219–38; H. Cunningham, 'The Language of Patriotism', *History Workshop Journal,* 12 (1981) pp. 8–33; G. Stedman Jones, *Languages of Class* (Cambridge, 1983); L. Colley, 'Whose Nation? Class and National Consciousness in Britain, 1760–1820', *Past and Present,* 113 (1986) pp. 97–117; Neale, *Class;* H. Dickinson, 'Precursors of Political Radicalism in Augustan Britain', in Jones (ed.), *Britain,* pp. 63–84; J. Epstein, 'Understanding the Cap of

Liberty: Symbolic Practice and Social Conflict in Early Nineteenth-Century England', *Past and Present*, 122 (1989) pp. 75–118; Rogers, *Whigs and Cities;* Davison et al., *Stilling the Grumbling Hive*, pp. xii–liv. See also J. Barry, 'The State and the Middle Classes in Eighteenth-Century England', *Journal of Historical Sociology*, 4 (1991) pp. 75–86.

37. J. Triffitt, 'Politics and the Urban Community: Parliamentary Boroughs in the South West 1710–30' (University of Oxford D.Phil. thesis, 1985).

38. L. Colley, 'The Apotheosis of George III: Loyalty, Royalty and the British Nation 1760–1820', *Past and Present*, 102 (1984) pp. 94–129; D. Nicholls, 'The English Middle Class and the Ideological Significance of Radicalism 1760–1886', *Journal of British Studies*, 24 (1985) pp. 415–33; Colley, 'Whose Nation?'; Kramnick, *Republicanism and Bourgeois Radicalism;* J. Money, 'Freemasonry and the Fabric of Loyalism in Hanoverian England', in Hellmuth (ed.), *Transformation of Political Culture*, pp. 235–71; Bradley, *Religion, Revolution and English Radicalism;* Seed, 'From "Middling Sort" '; Wahrman, 'National Society'; D. Wahrman, 'Virtual Representation: Parliamentary Reporting and the Language of Class in the 1790s', *Past and Present*, 136 (1992) pp. 83–113.

4. PROFESSIONS, IDEOLOGY AND MIDDLING THE SORT IN THE LATE SIXTEENTH AND EARLY SEVENTEENTH CENTURIES   *Christopher Brooks*

1. For two recent examples see Harold Perkin *The Rise of Professional Society: England since 1880* (1989); Anthony Giddens, *The Consequences of Modernity* (Stanford, 1990) chapter III. For an alternative view see W. R. Prest, 'Why the History of the Professions is Not Written', in G. R. Rubin and David Sugarman (eds), *Law, Economy and Society. Essays in the History of English Law 1750–1914* (1984) pp. 300–20.

2. C. W. Brooks, *Pettyfoggers and Vipers of the Commonwealth: The 'Lower Branch' of the Legal Profession in Early Modern England* (Cambridge, 1986) pp. 112–14.

3. See this volume, Chapter 2, Table 2.1, pp. 56–9.

4. S. R. Roberts, 'The Personnel and Practice of Medicine in Tudor and Stuart England. Part I. The Provinces', *Medical History*, 6 (1962) pp. 363–82; M. Pelling and C. Webster, 'Medical Practitioners', in C. Webster (ed.), *Health, Medicine, and Mortality in the Sixteenth Century* (Cambridge, 1979) pp. 166–7, 183, 225; M. Pelling, 'Appearance and Reality: Barber-Surgeons, the Body, and Disease', in A. L. Beier and Roger Finlay (eds), *London, 1500–1700: The Making of the Metropolis* (1986) pp. 82–112; E. Shelton-Jones, 'The Barber-Surgeons Company of London and Medical Education, 1540–1660' (University of London M.Phil. thesis, 1981); T. D. Whittet, 'The Apothecary in Provincial Guilds', *Medical History*, 8 (1964) pp. 245–73; C. Wall, H. C. Cameron and E. A. Underwood, *A History of the Worshipful Society of Apothecaries of London* (2 vols, Oxford, 1963) vol. 1, ch. 2; S. R. Roberts, 'The London Apothecaries and Medical Practice in

Tudor and Stuart England' (London University Ph.D thesis, 1964) pp. 201ff.; G. Holmes, *Augustan England: Professions, State and Society, 1680–1730* (1982) pp. 191–2; D. Embleton, 'The Incorporated Company of Barber-Surgeons and Wax and Tallow Chandlers of Newcastle-upon-Tyne', *Archaeologia Aeliana*, XV (1892) pp. 228–69; M. C. Barnet, 'The Barber-Surgeons of York', *Medical History*, 12 (1968) pp. 19–30.

5. William Birken, 'The Social Problem of the English Physicians in the Early Seventeenth Century', *Medical History*, 31 (2) (1987) pp. 205–9, 216; L. Stone, 'Social Mobility in England 1500–1700', *Past and Present*, 33 (1966) pp. 19, 48.

6. Wilfrid R. Prest, *The Rise of the Barristers: A Social History of the English Bar 1590–1640* (Oxford, 1986) pp. 87–95; Brooks, *Pettyfoggers and Vipers*, pp. 242–7.

7. Prest, *Barristers*, ch. 5; Brooks, *Pettyfoggers and Vipers*, pp. 272–8.

8. For some concise comments on the political use of images of the body see Kevin Sharpe, *Politics and Ideas in Early Stuart England: Essays and Studies* (1989) pp. 61–3. Lack of space and the inadequate knowledge of the present author are the reasons why the politics of the body have not been pursued further in this essay, but, for some perceptive and suggestive work, see R. Porter (ed.), *Patients and Practitioners: Lay Perceptions of Medicine in Pre-industrial Society* (Cambridge, 1985).

9. Sharpe, *Politics and Ideas*, pp. 3–9, usefully explains some of the reasons for the failure of recent early modern historians to pursue the connection between 'ideas and events'.

10. Extreme statements of what is now commonly described as the 'revisionist' view of seventeenth-century political history are, for example, A. Everitt, *The Community of Kent and the Great Rebellion* (1966), and J. S. Morrill, *The Revolt of the Provinces* (1976). However, religion is now widely accepted as a crucial determinant of political allegiance. See, for example, J. S. Morrill, 'The Religious Context of the English Civil War', *Transactions of the Royal Historical Society*, 5th series, 34 (1984) pp. 155–78, and a number of the writers in Richard Cust and Ann Hughes (eds), *Conflict in Early Stuart England* (1989), make strong cases for the importance of ideological conflict. But none of these works looks at sections of the population who dwelt beyond the studies of the learned or the social milieu of the gentry.

11. This case is put in K. Wrightson, 'Two Concepts of Order: Justices, Constables, and Jurymen in Seventeenth-Century England', in J. Brewer and J. Styles (eds), *An Ungovernable People: The English and their Law in the Seventeenth and Eighteenth Centuries* (1980) pp. 21–46. See also Cynthia B. Herrup, *The Common Peace: Participation and the Criminal Law in Seventeenth-century England* (Cambridge, 1987) ch. 1. However, there have been dissenting voices. See, for example, James Sharpe, 'The People and the Law', in Barry Reay (ed.), *Popular Culture in Seventeenth-Century England* (1985) pp. 244–70, and Eamon Duffy, 'The Godly and the Multitude in Stuart England', *The Seventeenth Century*, I (1) (1986) pp. 31–55.

12. For a subtle statement of this view, which does, nevertheless, acknowledge the importance of the middling sort, see K. Wrightson, *English Society 1580–1680* (1982) Conclusion.

13. This issue is put in historiographical context by Cust and Hughes, *Conflict*, pp. 33–8.

14. Stephen Greenblatt, 'Murdering Peasants: Status, Genre, and the Representation of Rebellion', in Greenblatt (ed.), *Representing the English Renaissance* (Berkeley, Cal., 1988) pp. 18–19, 29.

15. J. Griffiths (ed.), *Homilies Appointed to be Read in Churches in the Time of Queen Elizabeth* (1857) pp. 95–9; Patrick Collinson, *The Religion of Protestants: The Church in English Society 1559–1625* (Oxford, 1982) ch. 4.

16. B[ritish] L[ibrary], Add[itional] MS 48, 047, fols 59–61v.

17. Richard Crompton, *A Short Declaration of the Ende of Traytors and False Conspirators against the State and the Duetie of Subjectes to Theyr Soueraigne Gouernour* ... (1587).

18. Sir Edward Coke, Eleventh Report 70. Coke's reports were originally published in separate volumes in Law French between 1600 and 1615. This paper follows the standard convention of referring to the original volume and page numbers. Apart from the earliest editions, the references can be used in connection with *The English Reports* (1900–30), a multi-volume collection of most of the printed law reports from the mid-sixteenth to the nineteenth centuries, or other editions of Coke, such as J. H. Thomas and J. F. Fraser (eds), *The Reports of Sir Edward Coke in Thirteen Parts* (6 vols, 1827). For more on the sixteenth century legal thought, see Christopher W. Brooks, 'The Place of Magna Carta and the Ancient Constitution in Sixteenth-Century English Legal Thought', in Ellis Sandoz (ed.), *The Roots of Liberty: Magna Carta, Ancient Constitution, and the Anglo-American Tradition of the Rule of Law* (Columbia, Missouri, 1993) pp. 57–88.

19. See, for example, Everitt, *Community of Kent*, pp. 33–55.

20. Prest, *Rise of the Barristers*, ch. 5.

21. L. Stone, 'The Education Revolution in England 1500–1640', *Past and Present*, 28 (1964) pp. 41–80.

22. For a telling contemporary observation, see John Edward Jackson (ed.), *Wiltshire: The Topographical Collections of John Aubrey* (Devizes, 1862) p. 16. For examples, see V. M. Larminie, *The Godly Magistrate: The Private Philosophy and Public Life of Sir John Newdigate 1571–1610* (Dugdale Society Occasional Papers, no. 28, Oxford, 1982); BL Add MS 34,239, Rodney of Stoke Rodney papers, fols 15, 21–27, 52ff; and Sir Edward Dering's concern for the education his sons were getting at Cambridge in the 1630s: P. A. Salt, 'The Origins of Sir Edward Dering's Attack on the Ecclesiastical Hierarchy, c.1625–1640', *Historical Journal*, 30 (1) (1987) p. 41. Elizabeth Brereton owned a copy of Ferdinando Pulton, *De Pace Regis et Regni viz A Treatise Declaring which be the Great and Generall Offences of the Realme and the Chiefe Impediments of the Peace of the King and the Kingdome* ... (1609) [Bodleian Law Library, Oxford, Shelf mark 35 e. 26]. See also W. R. Prest, 'Law and Women's Rights in Early Modern England', *The Seventeenth Century*, VI (2) (1991) pp. 169–87. There are thought-provoking analyses of the significance of gentry education in M. E. James, *Family, Lineage, and Civil Society: A Study of Society, Politics, and Mentality in the Durham Region, 1500–1640* (Oxford, 1974) pp. 177–98, and *Society, Politics and Culture: Studies in Early Modern England* (Cambridge, 1986) pp. 375–413.

23. Wrightson, *English Society*, ch. 1.

24. Brooks, *Pettyfoggers and Vipers*, pp. 270–2.

25. W. Perkins, 'A Treatise of the Vocations or Callings of Men', in *The Works ... of W. Perkins* (Cambridge, 1605) p. 915.

26. Henry E. Huntington Library, San Marino, Calif., Hastings MSS, Legal Box 5/8.

27. BL Add. MS 48, 109, fols 12v–13v.

28. Brooks, *Pettyfoggers and Vipers*, pp. 173–81.

29. Wall, Cameron, Ashworth and Underwood, *Worshipful Society of Apothecaries*, vol. I, pp. 82–192.

30. Brooks, *Pettyfoggers and Vipers*, ch. 3, pp. 141–5; Margaret Pelling and Charles Webster, 'Medical Practitioners', in Webster (ed.), *Health, Medicine and Mortality in the Sixteenth Century* (Cambridge, 1979) pp. 165–235.

31. Norfolk Record Office, King's Lynn Borough Records, Book of Francis Parlett, recorder, fols 69vff.; John Cotta, *A Short Discoverie of the Un-Observed Dangers of Seuerall Sorts of Ignorant and Unconsiderate Practisers of Physicke in Englande Profitable not onely for the Deceived Multitude, and Easie for their Meane Capacities, but Raising Reformed and More Advised Thoughts in the Best Understanding ...* (1612) pp. 25–30, expresses the mutual suspicion which apparently characterised the relationship between physicians and women.

32. The London Barber-Surgeons' Company carried out public dissections and the Apothecaries tested entrants to the company on their ability to read Latin. See Shelton-Jones, 'Barber-Surgeons of London', pp. 25–55, 64–8, 92, 97, 173–91; G[uildhall] L[ibrary], London, MS 8200/1, p. 209. For attorneys, see Brooks, *Pettyfoggers and Vipers*, pp. 173–81.

33. See, for example, Cotta, *A Short Discoverie*, especially pp. A3, 10, 21, 25. Wylliam Clowes, *A Prooued Practise for All Young Chirurgians ...* (1588) p. 1, praises a Derbyshire attorney who had an allegedly unskilful surgeon banished from the county.

34. Thomas Phaer, *The Regiment of Life, Wherunto is Added a Treatise of the Pestilence, with the Boke of Children, New Corrected and Enlarged ...* (1545) Sig. Aii–Aiii. For a fuller account see, C. W. Brooks, R. H. Helmholz and P. G. Stein, *Notaries Public in England since the Reformation* (Norwich, 1991) pp. 85–8.

35. L. B. Wright, *Middle Class Culture in Elizabethan England* (1935) pp. 160ff.

36. Clowes, *A Prooved Practise ...*, Sig. A3.

37. Measures to make the English Bible available in the 1530s were followed by a statute of 1542, which restricted its readership. 34 and 35 Henry VIII, c. 1 'An Act for the Advancement of True Religion and for Abolishing False Doctrines', was repealed under Edward VI.

38. Brooks, 'The Place of Magna Carta', p. 67. It is worth noticing also Margaret Spufford's observation that the need to understand legal documents, such as bills and bonds, must have been as powerful an incentive for ordinary people to learn to read as Protestant emphasis on knowledge of the Bible. 'The Limitations of the Probate Inventory' in John Chartres and David Hey (eds), *English Rural Society, 1500–1800. Essays in Honour of*

Joan Thirsk (Cambridge, 1990) p. 173. See also H. J. Graham, '"Our Tong Maternall Maruellously Amendyed and Augmented": The First Englishing and Printing of the Medieval Statutes at Large, 1530–33', *UCLA Law Review,* 13 (1965) pp. 58–98.

39. *The Two Bookes of Francis Bacon. Of the Proficience and Advancement of Learning, Divine and Humane* (1605) pp. 10–11. See also Margo Todd, *Christian Humanism and the Puritan Social Order* (Cambridge, 1987) chapter 6.

40. See below, pp. 139–40, although it is notable that in 1609 James I advocated making the law available in more systematic English works. C. H. McIlwain (ed.), *The Political Works of James I Reprinted from the Edition of 1616* (Cambridge, Mass., 1918) pp. 307, 311.

41. Brooks, *Pettyfoggers and Vipers,* pp. 135, 200.

42. Ibid., ch. 4, 5, 9; M. Pelling, 'Child Health as a Social Value in Early Modern England', *Social History of Medicine,* 1 (1988) pp. 135–64.

43. Joan R. Kent, *The English Village Constable 1580–1642. A Social and Administrative Study* (Oxford, 1986); Herrup, *The Common Peace.*

44. Brooks, *Pettyfoggers and Vipers,* pp. 189–91; W. P. Baildon (ed.), *Les Reportes del Cases in Camera Stellata 1593–1609 . . .* (1894) pp. 234–5.

45. National Library of Wales, Aberystwyth, MS 5932A; anonymous notebook of sermons written about 1635, no pagination.

46. *The Workes of William Gouge In Two Volumes, The First Domesticall Duties. The Second, The Whole Armour of God* (1627); Epistle, Sig. A3.

47. Perkins, 'A Treatise of the Vocations or Callings of Men', pp. 747–50; P. Seaver, 'The Puritan Work Ethic Revisited', *Journal of British Studies,* XIX (2) (1980) pp. 35–53, and his *Wallington's World. A Puritan Artisan in Seventeenth-Century London* (Stanford, Cal., 1985).

48. John Stow, *A Survey of London,* (ed.) C. L. Kingsford (2 vols, Oxford, 1971) vol. I, p. 272.

49. For clerical patriarchalism see Gordon J. Schochet, *Patriarchalism in Political Thought: The Authoritarian Family and Political Speculation and Attitudes Especially in Seventeenth Century England* (Oxford, 1975); D. E. Underdown, 'The Taming of the Scold: the Enforcement of Patriarchal Authority in Early Modern England', in Anthony Fletcher and John Stevenson (eds), *Order and Disorder in Early Modern England* (Cambridge, 1985) pp. 116–36; Prest, *Rise of the Barristers,* pp. 123–6.

50. See Chapter 2 of this volume, pp. 76–7; Wrightson, *English Society,* pp. 51–7, 61–5. However, institutionalised forms of conflict resolution were also traditional features of both urban and rural communities. Steve Rappaport, *Worlds Within Worlds: Structures of Life in Sixteenth-century London* (Cambridge, 1989) pp. 201–14; Brooks, *Pettyfoggers and Vipers,* pp. 33–6.

51. As David Underdown, *Revel, Riot and Rebellion: Popular Politics and Culture in England 1603–1660* (Oxford, 1985) pp. 63, 66 reminds us, many popular customs were supported by the elite precisely because they were associated with hierarchy and deference.

52. Crompton, *Short Declaration of the End of Traitors,* Sig. E4v–F; Brooks, 'The Place of Magna Carta', pp. 74–83.

53. BL Harleian MS 4841.

54. Todd, *Christian Humanism,* pp. 196ff.; Fritz Caspari, *Humanism and the Social Order in Tudor England* (Chicago, 1954).

55. Hampshire Record Office, Winchester, MS 107 M88/W23.

56. BL Add MS 48, 109, fols 37–8, 42.

57. Apart from sitting in the House of Lords, the most significant privileges of the nobility were probably exemption from imprisonment for debt, torture, and jury service. See *Coke's Reports,* vol. 12, p. 96.

58. B[edfordshire] R[ecord] O[ffice], Bedford, L28/49, 'God before all and all after the King, by Sir Anthony Benn, knt, Recorder of London' (c.1610) fol. 2.

59. According to the Gloucestershire clergyman, John Corbet, many of these same values characterised those of the middling sort who supported the parliamentary cause in the 1640s. David Rollison, 'The Bourgeois Soul of John Smyth of Nibley', *Social History,* 12 (3) (1987) pp. 325–6.

60. Conyers Read (ed.), *William Lambarde and Local Government: His 'Ephemeris' and Twenty-nine Charges to Juries and Commissions* (Ithaca, N.Y., 1962) p. 167 (I am grateful to Keith Wrightson for this reference).

61. H[ertfordshire] R[ecord] O[ffice], Hertford, Gorhambury MS VIII. B. 108, 'A Treatise of Knighthood' [no pagination]. This reference to yeoman farmers appears to be in the tradition of the well-known fifteenth-century judge, Sir John Fortescue, *De Laudibus Legum Angliae,* (ed.) S. B. Crimes (Cambridge, 1942) p. 67–71, who stressed the unique character of England because there were large numbers of men of modest landed wealth who constituted juries.

62. G. E. M. De Ste Croix, *The Class Struggle in the Ancient Greek World* (1981) pp. 70–6; Ernest Barker (ed.), *The Politics of Aristotle* (Oxford, 1958) Books IV–V.

63. Folger Shakespeare Library, Washington, DC, MS Va 197, fol. 59v, where the speaker in 1575 is described as having given a lengthy account of sundry kinds of government; BL Add MS 48, 109, fols 18v–20, Sir Christopher Yelverton, 1597; E. S. Cope and W. H. Coates (eds), *Proceedings of the Short Parliament of 1640* (Royal Hist. Soc., Camden Fourth Series, vol. 19, 1977) p. 127: John Glanvill, 15 April 1640.

64. HRO Gorhambury MS VIII. B. 108.

65. 'A true List of the Jury impanneled at Huntingdon Assizes before Judge Dodderidge', in J. Malham (eds), *The Harleian Miscellany: A Collection of Scarce Curious and Entertaining Tracts* (12 vols, 1808–11) vol. III, p. 396.

66. North[amptonshire] R[ecord] O[ffice], Northampton, Finch-Hatton MS 3467. Opinions concerning the Higham election to the Short Parliament. Inner Temple Library, London, Petyt MS 511(23), fol. 1.

67. For example, unless they held local offices, many urban attorneys were not necessarily likely to be amongst the ruling councillors or aldermen. Brooks, *Pettyfoggers and Vipers,* pp. 209–17.

68. Brooks, 'The Place of Magna Carta', pp. 71–3; John Selden, *Titles of Honour* (1614) pp. 1–15 (although later editions of this work place less emphasis on the popular origins of government, it seems unlikely that Selden fundamentally changed his opinions); J. P. Sommerville, 'John

Selden, the Law of Nature and the Origins of Government', *Historical Journal*, 27 (2) (1984) pp. 437–48; D. S. Berkowitz, *John Selden's Formative Years. Politics and Society in Early Seventeenth-Century England* (Washington, DC, 1988) pp. 294–5.

69. Brooks, 'The Place of Magna Carta', pp. 73–4.

70. BRO L28/46, 'Essays of Sir Anthony Benn, knt, Recorder of London', fol. 44v–45; L28/49, 'God before all and all after the King'.

71. Bartholomew Parsons, *The Magistrates Charter Examined or His Duty and Dignity Opened in a Sermon Preached at an Assizes, held at Sarum in the County of Wiltes on the ninth day of March, last past, 1614* (1616) pp. 8–20. The work was dedicated to the judges Sir Henry Hobart and Laurence Tanfield, who had apparently approved of the sermon when they heard it delivered.

72. Samuel Burton, *A Sermon Preached at the Generall Assises in Warwicke, the third of March, being the first Friday in Lent, 1619* (1620) pp. 1–20.

73. NRO, 'Book of Francis Parlett', fols 6v–8, 11v, 72, 99–100. This kind of political rhetoric was also characteristic of the Caroline court. See Kevin Sharpe, *Criticism and Compliment: The Politics of Literature in the England of Charles I* (Cambridge, 1987) ch. 6.

74. *Coke's Reports*, vol. 4, 77b–78a.

75. A number of examples are given in Brooks, *Pettyfoggers and Vipers*, pp. 220–3.

76. Goldsmiths' Company, Goldsmiths' Hall, London, Court Minute Book N, pt. 1, pp. 109–10: Attorney General Coke requests severe penalties against two men for making false plate, 1597; Minute Book Q, pt 1, pp.57, 80: consultations with John Selden, William Noy and Sir Edward Coke about the threat of the establishment of a new royal exchange, 1627–8. GL MS 8200/1, pp. 283–4: two apothecaries, represented by counsel, in a dispute concerning precedence within the Apothecaries Company, 1631.

77. *Coke's Reports*, vol. 5, 62b: 'Chamberlain of London's Case' (1590); vol. 8, 113b: 'Dr Bonham's Case' (1610); and ibid., 121b: 'Case of the City of London (1610), where the usefulness of guilds for establishing 'good order and rule' is acknowledged.

78. *Coke's Reports*, vol. 11, 53a.

79. This James Bagg seems to have been the father of the James Bagg who was a client of the Duke of Buckingham, and who told Buckingham that it was dangerous for Sir John Elyot's petition against the forced loan of 1626 to be circulated amongst the many-headed people. H. E. Hulme, *The Life of Sir John Eliot* (1957), pp. 43, 62, 97, 170. Bagg, senior had served as a mayor of the town, and refused to contribute to the 'free gift' to the king in 1615. R. N. Worth, *Calendar of the Plymouth Municipal Records* (Plymouth, 1893) pp. 21, 148. Nevertheless, he had friends in London, to whom he complained about the injustices done to him by the mayor of Plymouth. *Acts of the Privy Council of England*, vol. 33, p. 411.

80. *Coke's Reports*, vol. 11, 93b.

81. Brooks, Helmholz and Stein, *Notaries Public*, pp. 82–91.

82. There is a long tradition, of which J. G. A. Pocock, *The Ancient Constitution and the Feudal Law. A Study of English Historical Thought in the Seven-*

teenth Century. A Reissue with a Retrospect (Cambridge, 1987, but 1st edn 1957), has probably been the most influential in modern times. J. P. Sommerville, *Politics and Ideology in England 1603–1640* (1986) ch. 3, discusses some formal aspects of common-law thought and refines Pocock. But while he achieves a great deal in systematising legal thought, he oversimplifies its political impact. The works of Christopher Hill, especially *Puritanism and Revolution. Studies in Interpretation of the English Revolution of the 17th Century* (1958), and *Society and Puritanism in Pre-Revolutionary England* (1964), make the case for religion. See also G. Burgess, *The Politics of the Ancient Constitution: An Introduction to English Political Thought, 1603–1642* (1992).

83. John Rushworth, *Historical Collections. The Third Part: in Two Volumes, Containing the Principal Matters Which happened from the Meeting of the Parliament, November the 3rd 1640 To the End of the Year 1644 ...* (London, 1692) vol. I, p. 294. Lord Keeper Coventry reminded the judges as they were about to go on circuit in June 1635 that one of the purposes of assizes was to give the 'People a better knowledge of Justice ... that they may bless God and the King for the same'. See also Collinson, *Religion of Protestants*, ch. 4.

84. For references and criticisms of the relevant historiography, see Cust and Hughes, 'Introduction', in *Conflict* pp.4–6. For a sophisticated argument in favour of a more consensual view, see Sharpe, *Politics and Ideas*, pp. 3–75.

85. N. Tyacke, *Anti-Calvinists: The Rise of English Arminianism c.1590–1640* (Oxford, 1987).

86. *Cobbett's Complete Collection of States Trials and Proceedings for High Treason and Other Crimes and Misdemeanors From the Earliest Period to the Present Time* (42 vols, 1809–98), vol. III, pp. 1369–76. See also W. R. Prest (ed.), *The Diary of Sir Richard Hutton*, Seldon Society, Supp. Ser. (1991).

87. BL Hargrave MS 206, fol. 2v. Harleian MS 1222, fols 108–9; *A Just Vindication of the Questioned Part of the Reading of Edward Bagshaw ...* (1660) pp. 1–7, explains his eventual disillusionment with the parliamentary cause. See also the comments Justice Croke made about the political ideas of the clergy during the Ship Money trial. *State Trials*, vol. III, p. 1186.

88. J. Guy, *Tudor England* (Oxford, 1986) p. 372; Sommerville, *Politics and Ideology*, pp. 118–19.

89. Ibid., chs 1, 4, 6. See also P. Lake, *Anglican and Puritans? Presbyterianism and English Conformist Thought from Whitgift to Hooker* (1988), especially pp. 245–6.

90. The critical source of this view was a work of Continental jurisprudence which was widely known to English lawyers, *Jean Bodin the Six Bookes of a Commonweale. A Facsimile Reprint of the English Translation of 1606 Corrected and Supplemented in the Light of a New Comparision with the French and Latin Texts,* (ed.) Kenneth D. McRae (Cambridge, Mass., 1962), especially pp. 199–201, 210–12, but many also found it implicit in the thought of the thirteenth-century judge, Henry de Bracton. See also Brooks, 'The Place of Magna Carta', pp. 73–4; and Sommerville, *Politics and Ideology*, pp. 145–51. I will deal with this point in more detail in my forthcoming book.

91. M. F. Keeler, M. J. Cole and W. B. Bidwell (eds), *Proceedings in Parliament 1628* (6 vols, 1984) vol. II, pp. 64, 66, 358; vol. III, p. 494.

92. Brooks, *Pettyfoggers and Vipers,* pp. 86, 89.

93. *Coke's Reports,* vol. 4, 27b: Hobart v. Hammond. See also vol. 4, 36b, 46; vol. 11, 42; vol. 13, 1.

94. BL Harleian MS 4841, p. 50.

95. An anonymous quarter sessions charge, which probably dates from the 1620s, declares, 'Had we not this Guardian Angell of the Law to protect us we should be exposed to every Insulting and uncontrolled power ... our goods ... Ravished and snatched from us by violent exactions.' Cambridge University Library MS Dd. xiv. 3, fol. 213. Interestingly, in June 1632, Richard Neile, Archbishop of York, expressed the concern of the privy council that clergymen of ill disposition to the government were allowed to give assize sermons. *Historical Manuscripts Commission Fourteenth Report, Appendix, Part IV. The Manuscripts of Lord Kenyon,* p. 49.

96. BL Hargrave MS 132, fol. 68v. The words are attributed to James.

97. Printed in *Cases Collect and Report per Sir Francis Moore, Chivaler, Serjeant del Ley* (1663) p. 827. There are several surviving manuscript copies.

98. Somerset Record Office, Taunton, MS DD/PH 212/12. For an account of Noy's career see W. J. Jones, ' "The Great Gamaliel of the Law": Mr. Attorney Noye', *Huntington Library Quarterly,* xl (3) (1977) pp. 197–226.

99. *State Trials,* vol. III, p. 1374. For examples of grand jury presentments see E. S. Cope, *Politics Without Parliaments 1629–1640* (1987) pp. 101–6, 150–1, 185–6, 194–5.

100. BL Egerton MS 2982, fols 81–3.

101. For more detail on Hurste's career, see Clive Holmes, *Seventeenth Century Lincolnshire* (Lincoln, 1980) pp. 112, 195.

102. Thomas Hurste, *The Descent of Authoritie: or the Magistrates Patent From Heaven. Manifested in a Sermon preached at Lincoln Assizes, March 13 1636* (1637) pp. 1–3, 5, 26, 32.

103. Cope and Coates (eds), *Proceedings of the Short Parliament of 1640,* pp. 136, 141, 153–4, 172, 178; Wallace Notestein (ed.), *The Journal of Sir Simonds D'Ewes, from the Beginning of the Long Parliament to the Opening of the Trial of the Earl of Strafford* (New Haven, Conn., 1923) pp. 6, 7, 8–11. For the period generally see Anthony Fletcher, *The Outbreak of the English Civil War* (1981).

104. S. R. Gardiner, *History of England from the Accession of James I to the Outbreak of the Civil War 1603–1642* (10 vols, 1884) vol. x, pp. 10–12, 59; Morrill, *Revolt of the Provinces,* p. 13.

105. K. V. Thomas, 'Women and the Civil War Sects', in Trevor Aston (ed.), *Crisis in Europe 1560–1600* (New York, 1967 edn) pp. 332–57.

106. W. H. Coates (ed.), *The Journal of Sir Simonds D'Ewes, from the First Recess of the Long Parliament to the Withdrawal of King Charles from London* (New Haven, Conn., 1942) pp. 14–15, 21, 24, 30, 44, 51, 112, 117, 133, 150–1, 165, 183, 187, 290, 327, 337.

107. *A Collection of Sundry Petitions Presented to the King's Most Excellent Majestie as Also to the Two Most Honourable Houses, Now Assembled in Parliament. And Others, Already Signed, by Most of the Gentry, Ministers, and Free-holders of Several Counties, in Behalfe of Episcopacie, Liturgie, and Supportation of Church-*

Revenues, and Suppression of Schismaticks. Collected by a Faithful Lover of the Church, for the Comfort of the Dejected Clergy, and all Moderately Affected Protestants. Published by his Majesties Special Command (1642) pp. 2–3; *His Majesties Answer to the xix Propositions of Both Houses of Parliament* (1642) pp. 11, 18, 22.

108. [Henry Parker], *Some Few Observations upon his Majesties late Answer to the Declaration, or Remonstrance of the Lords and Commons of the 19 of May 1642* (1642) pp. 7, 8, 12, 15; North. R.O., Finch Hatton MS 4132, Anonymous, undated, and unpaginated.

109. Conrad Russell, *The Causes of the English Civil War* (Oxford, 1990), especially ch. 6.

110. Ibid., pp. 131–3. Juan de Santa Maria, *Policie Vnveiled: Wherein May Be Learned, The Order of True Policy in Kingdomes and Common-wealths* ... (London, 1634) was translated by the Spanish scholar and sometime fellow of Magdalen College, Oxford, James Mabbe, who lived in Strangewayes's house from 1627 until his death in 1642. See also *Dictionary of National Biography*; Coates (ed.), *The Journal of Sir Simonds D'Ewes, From the First Recess of the Long Parliament to the Withdrawal of King Charles from London*, p. 214.

111. Prest, *Rise of the Barristers*, pp. 276–80; Brooks, *Pettyfoggers and Vipers*, pp. 223–4.

112. W. J. Jones, *Politics and the Bench. The Judges and the Origins of the English Civil War* (1971) pp. 137–48, 209–15.

113. See generally D. Veall, *The Popular Movement for Law Reform 1640–1660* (Oxford, 1970).

114. John Warr, 'The Corruption and Deficiency of the Laws of England, Soberly Discovered: Or, Liberty Working up to its Just Height ...' (1649), *Harleian Miscellany*, vol. III, pp. 240–49.

115. Veall, *Popular Movement*. For the 1650s, see N. L. Matthews, *William Sheppard. Cromwell's Law Reformer* (Cambridge, 1984).

116. C. Webster, *The Great Instauration: Science, Medicine and Reform 1626–1660* (1975) pp. 131, 180, 256–61, 285.

117. Brian Manning, *The English People and the English Revolution* (1978 edn) pp. 331, 339.

5. THE MIDDLING SORT IN LONDON   *Peter Earle*

1. Daniel Defoe, *A Plan of the English Commerce* (1728) p. 103.

2. Daniel Defoe, *Robinson Crusoe* (1719), ed. J. D. Crowley (1972) pp. 4–5.

3. *A Review of the Affairs of France*, V (1709) pp. 516–17 and VI (1709) p. 142.

4. Henri Misson, *Memoirs and Observations in his Travels over England* (1719) pp. 69, 92, 314, 349. The words quoted here are in fact those of Misson's translator, John Ozell. In the original French edition (of 1698) the expression usually translated as 'middling people' was 'gens de médiocre condition', whose social position lay between 'gens de qualité' and 'gens du commun' or 'le commun peuple'. Henri Misson, *Mémoires et observations faites par un voyageur en Angleterre* (The Hague, 1698).

5. Jacob Vanderlint, *Money Answers All Things* (1734), p. 22; Joseph Massie, *Calculations of the Present Taxes* (1761).

6. Joseph Massie, *To the Printer of the Gazetteer* (1760).

7. The inventories mentioned here and elsewhere in the chapter are those used for my book, *The Making of the English Middle Class: Business, Society and Family Life in London, 1660–1730* (1989). Much of this was based on a sample of 375 inventories of London citizens whose estates were valued by the Orphans' Court. By one of those nice historical accidents (or truths?), their median value was almost exactly the £2000 mentioned in the text as a 'middling' mean wealth.

8. The Marriage Duties and Poll Tax respectively. For these taxes see 3 W & M c.6, and 6 and 7 W & M c.6.

9. J. Collyer, *Parents and Guardians Directory* (1761); R. Campbell, *The London Tradesman* (1747).

10. Collyer, *Directory* pp. 45, 250. Some occupations, which were not themselves genteel, still required their practitioners to have a 'genteel person', such as barbers and haberdashers.

11. Earle, *Middle Class*, p. 292.

12. Guy Miège, *New State of England under our Sovereign Queen Anne* (1703) p. 264.

13. Richard Steele, *The Conscious Lovers* (1722), Act IV, Scene 2.

14. For investment, see Earle, *Middle Class*, ch. 6.

15. The evidence for this statement and what follows comes from depositions in the London church courts, where many witnesses styled themselves gentlemen but later gave evidence as to what they actually did for a living.

16. Steve Rappaport, *Worlds within Worlds: Structures of Life in Sixteenth-Century London* (Cambridge, 1989) especially ch. 8.

17. On adult mortality in London, and the entry costs to business, see Earle, *Middle Class*, pp. 106–12, 306–10.

18. On this, see Peter Earle, 'Age and Accumulation in the London Business Community', in Neil McKendrick and R. B. Outhwaite (eds), *Business Life and Public Policy* (Cambridge, 1986).

19. *Review*, IV (3 April 1707) p. 91.

20. Earle, *Middle Class*, pp. 129–30. On bankruptcy, see Julian Hoppit, *Risk and Failure in English Business, 1700–1800* (Cambridge, 1987).

21. This section draws mainly on material from the London church courts which has been presented in Peter Earle, 'The Female Labour Force in Late Seventeenth and Early Eighteenth-Century London', *Economic History Review*, 2nd. series, XLII (1989).

22. Greater London Record Office DLC 252, f. 443. Widows, like other witnesses to the church courts, were often required to give information on their source of maintenance for some period of years before they gave their evidence, and these provide many other examples of such slides into poverty.

23. Joan Thirsk and J. P. Cooper (eds), *Seventeenth-century Economic Documents* (Oxford, 1972) p. 773, where King's figures show widows as 27.5 per cent of the combined total of wives and widows. The sample of

church-court witnesses used in Earle, 'Female Labour Force', produces a figure of 35 per cent.

24. This phrase is used by some modern writers to refer to those who would later be called 'the City'.

25. For the evolution of this terminology, see P. J. Corfield, 'Class by Name and Number in Eighteenth-Century Britain', *History*, LXXII (1987) pp. 38–61.

26. Gilbert Burnet, *History of my Own Times* (1969 edn) vol. VI, p. 215.

27. Walter Houghton, *The Victorian Frame of Mind* (New Haven, 1957).

28. See, for example, Michael Shinagel, *Daniel Defoe and Middle-Class Gentility* (Harvard, 1968), and Hans H. Andersen, 'The Paradox of Trade and Morality in Defoe', *Modern Philology*, XXXIX (1941), for a discussion of these two paradoxes in the earlier period.

29. Daniel Defoe, *The Farther Adventures of Robinson Crusoe* (1719) p. 228.

6. THE MIDDLING SORT IN EIGHTEENTH-CENTURY POLITICS *Nicholas Rogers*

1. Peter Earle, *The Making of the English Middle Class: Business, Society and Family Life in London 1660–1730* (1989); Paul Langford, *A Polite and Commercial People. England 1727–1783* (Oxford, 1989), especially ch. 3.

2. E. J. Hobsbawm, *Industry and Empire* (Harmondsworth, 1969) p. 32.

3. For a useful discussion of the genealogy of the term, see Raymond Williams, *Keywords* (1976) pp. 60–9.

4. Brian Manning, *The English People and the English Revolution, 1640–49* (1976) pp. 152–62; Keith Wrightson, 'Estates, Degrees and Sorts: Changing Perceptions of Society in Tudor and Stuart England', in Penelope J. Corfield (ed.), *Language, History and Class* (Oxford, 1991) pp. 45–52.

5. See P. J. Corfield, 'Class by Name and Number in Eighteenth-Century Britain', *History*, LXXII (1987) pp. 38–61, reprinted in Corfield (ed.), *Language, History and Class*, pp. 101–30.

6. Harold Perkin, comparing the figures of Gregory King and Patrick Colquhoun, suggested that the wealth and numbers of the middling ranks in society remained proportionately the same from 1688 to 1803. But J. A. Cannon has noted the marked increase in urban wealth. See Harold Perkin, *The Origins of Modern English Society, 1780–1880* (1969) pp. 20–21; J. A. Cannon, *Parliamentary Reform 1640–1832* (Cambridge, 1973) p. 49n. For some appreciation of the difficulties in comparing the figures of King, Massie and Colquhoun, see Peter Mathias, 'The Social Structure in the Eighteenth Century: A Calculation by Joseph Massie', *Economic History Review*, 2nd series, X (1957) pp. 30–45, and Peter H. Lindert and Jeffrey G. Williamson, 'Revising England Social Tables 1688–1812', *Explorations in Economic History*, XIX (1982) pp. 385–408.

7. See, for example, the *Protester,* 9 June 1753. Among historians, John Cannon included the gentry within the middling sort. See John Cannon, *Aristocratic Century* (Cambridge, 1984) p. 178.

8. Paul Langford has recently shown that if £50 per annum constituted the minimum income requirement for membership, then one in five families in 1750 would have belonged to the middling sort. If £40 per annum is taken as the base line, then the number of middling families would double. See Langford, *Polite and Commercial People*, pp. 62–3.

9. See Nicholas Rogers, 'Money, Land and Lineage: the Big Bourgeoisie of Hanoverian London', *Social History*, IV (1979) pp. 437–54.

10. See Jacob Price, 'The Excise Affair Revisited', in Stephen B. Baxter (ed.), *England's Rise to Greatness, 1660–1763* (Berkeley and Los Angeles, 1983) p. 293; Hon-Cheung and Lorna H. Mui, *Shops and Shopkeeping in Eighteenth-Century England* (1989) pp. 73–85; John Brewer, *The Sinews of Power: War, Money and the English State, 1688–1783* (1989) p. 233.

11. Quoted by R. G. Wilson. 'Newspapers and the Business Community in the Eighteenth Century' (unpublished paper, 1982) p. 27.

12. See *Gentleman's Magazine*, XXII (1752) pp. 358–9.

13. J. M. Norris, 'Samuel Garbett and the Early Development of Industrial Lobbying in Great Britain', *Economic History Review*, X (1958) pp. 450–60.

14. See Langford, *Polite and Commercial People*, ch. 9, and his 'Property and "Virtual Representation" in Eighteenth-Century England', *Historical Journal*, XXXI (1988) p. 84.

15. Paul Langford, *Public Life and the Propertied Englishman 1689–1798* (Oxford, 1991) ch. 4.

16. Kathleen Wilson, 'Urban Culture and Political Activism in Hanoverian England: The Example of Voluntary Hospitals', in Eckhart Hellmuth (ed.), *The Transformation of Political Culture. England and Germany in the Late Eighteenth Century* (Oxford, 1990) p. 174.

17. P[ublic] R[ecord] O[ffice] SP 37/5/31a, cited by Norris, 'Samuel Garbett and Industrial Lobbying', p. 451n.

18. Avon County Library, Edward Southwell Papers, V, Southwell to John Berrow, 11 December 1740.

19. A. Temple Patterson, *A History of Southampton 1700–1914*, 2 vols (Southampton, 1976) vol. I, pp. 46–8.

20. Langford, *Public Life*, pp. 263–4.

21. *Cobbett's Parliamentary History*, vol. XV, pp. 480–6.

22. Wilson, 'Urban Culture and Political Activism', pp. 180–1.

23. These figures are taken from Frank O'Gorman, *Voters, Patrons, and Parties. The Unreformed Electoral System of Hanoverian England 1734–1832* (Oxford, 1989) p. 179.

24. See O'Gorman, ibid., pp. 202–17, and John A. Phillips, *Electoral Behaviour in Unreformed England* (Princeton, 1982) pp. 205–11, especially Table 5.11.

25. L. B. Namier, *The Structure of Politics at the Accession of George III*, 2nd edn (1957) p. 73.

26. L. B. Namier and John Brooke (eds), *The History of Parliament; The House of Commons 1754–1790*, 3 vols (1960).

27. J. H. Plumb, 'Political Man', in James L. Clifford (ed.), *Man Versus Society in Eighteenth-Century Britain* (Cambridge, 1968) pp. 1–21.

28. John A. Phillips, 'The Structure of Electoral Politics in Unreformed England', *Journal of British Studies*, XIX (February 1979) pp. 76–100.

29. The county electorate probably numbered 160,000 in 1750, but about 30,000 were urban freeholders or gentry. Inflation meant that some of the freeholders who qualified to vote were quite poor and questionably middling, but Acts of 1745 and 1780 required that voters be assessed by the land tax, which probably excluded considerable numbers of small freeholders.

30. G. E. Mingay, *English Landed Society in the Eighteenth Century* (1963) pp. 111, 121.

31. D. C. Moore, *The Politics of Deference* (New York, 1976) pp. 5–12.

32. Frank O'Gorman, 'Electoral Deference in "Unreformed" England: 1760–1832', *Journal of Modern History*, LVI (1984) pp. 418–19.

33. Cited by Linda Colley, *In Defiance of Oligarchy: The Tory Party 1714–1760* (Cambridge, 1982) p. 129.

34. Mingay, *English Landed Society*, pp. 125–6.

35. Namier and Brooke (eds), *The History of Parliament*, vol. I, p. 282.

36. See *A Copy of the Poll for the Knights of the Shire For the County of Norfolk, taken at Norwich, May 22 1734* (Norwich, 1734). The rate of dissidence in squire-resident parishes (n = 60) was 26 per cent for the Whigs and 19.5 per cent for the Tories.

37. *Public Advertiser*, 7 April 1784.

38. The Bristol and Norwich figures are based on the extant poll books; for post-1754 figures, see Phillips, *Electoral Behavior*, pp. 86–96, 212–52; O'Gorman, *Voters, Patrons and Parties*, pp. 183–99, 350–8; and James E. Bradley, *Religion, Revolution and English Radicalism. Nonconformity in Eighteenth-Century Politics and Society* (Cambridge, 1990) chs 7 and 8.

39. Of the new voters admitted to the freedom in the month prior to the election, the participation rates were 64 per cent in 1734, 80 per cent in 1739, and 63 per cent in 1754. The participation rates of nonconformists were as follows: Lewin's Mead Presbyterian, 66 per cent (1722), 44 per cent (1734–39), 60 per cent (1754); Quakers registering as burgesses 1732–4, 54 per cent (1734); Broadmead Baptist 50 per cent (1754). The figures are derived from the poll books and the pertinent records in the Bristol Record Office. The importers and exporters are taken from the Bristol port books, PRO, E 190/1215/4.

40. The participation rates in 1754 were as follows: vestrymen – St Stephen's (73 per cent) – All Saints (66 per cent) – Christchurch (90 per cent); Quaker trustees (78 per cent); churchwardens, all parishes (91 per cent).

41. See Phillips's figures for Maidstone, Norwich and Northampton, 1774–1802, in *Electoral Behavior*, p. 269, Table 7.5.

42. PRO, TS 11/962/3509 f. 181.

43. See Nicholas Rogers, 'Aristocratic Clientage, Trade and Independency: Popular Politics in Pre-radical Westminster', *Past and Present*, 61 (1973) pp. 70–106.

44. Phillips, *Electoral Behavior*, ch. 7. See also J. C. D. Clark, *English Society 1688–1832*, pp. 64–93, 277–348.

45. Langford, *Public Life*, p. 93.

46. Nicholas Rogers, *Whigs and Cities. Popular Politics in the Age of Walpole and Pitt* (Oxford, 1989) ch. 7.

47. See John Brewer, *Party Ideology and Popular Politics at the Accession of George III* (Cambridge, 1976) ch. 9.

48. Jurgen Habermas, 'The Public Sphere', *New German Critique*, I, no. 3 (1974) p. 49.

49. See John Brewer, 'Commercialization and Politics', in Neil McKendrick, John Brewer and J. H. Plumb, *The Birth of a Consumer Society* (1982) pp. 197–262.

50. For the 1733–56 instructions, see Rogers, *Whigs and Cities*, p. 244. The petitions and addresses of the period 1769–84, over Wilkes, America, economic and parliamentary reform, and the dismissal of the Fox–North coalition and subsequent dissolution of Parliament, have been reconstructed from a variety of sources: among them, George Rudé, *Wilkes and Liberty* (Oxford, 1962) pp. 133, 211; James E. Bradley, *Popular Politics and the American Revolution in England* (Macon, Georgia, 1986) passim; *Cobbett's Parliamentary History of England*, (36 vols, 1806–20) vol. XX, columns c1370–2; Ian Christie, *Wilkes, Wyvill and Reform* (1962) p. 169; *London Gazette*, January–May 1784.

51. Bradley, *Popular Politics and the American Revolution*, pp. 138–41, and *Religion, Revolution and English Radicalism*, pp. 319, 371–85.

52. Vicesimus Knox, *Essays, Moral and Literary*, 3 vols (1778, 9th edition) vol. I, pp. 102–5; 17 editions of these essays had been published by 1815.

53. Richard Price, *A Sermon Delivered to a Congregation of Protestant Dissenters at Hackney, on the 10 of February Last, Being the Day Appointed for a General Fast* (1779). For contemporary concern about such profligacy, see John Thornton's letters to John Newton in 1778. Cambridge University Library, Add. Ms. 7674/1/x/44, pp. 51–5. I am indebted to Susan Foote of York University for this reference.

54. See Joanna Innes, 'Politics and Morals. The Reformation of Manners Movement in Later Eighteenth-Century England', in Hellmuth (ed.), *The Transformation of Political Culture*, pp. 57–118.

55. William Clements Library, Ann Arbor, Michigan, Wilkes MSS, vol. 2, f. 95. I am indebted to Dr John Sainsbury of Brock University, St Catharines, Ontario, for this reference.

56. *Middlesex Journal*, 27/29 June 1771.

57. Cited by Richard Sennett, *The Fall of Public Man* (New York, 1977) p. 103.

58. *Public Advertiser*, 10 January 1784.

59. *Public Advertiser*, 15 February 1784.

60. Linda Colley, 'The Apotheosis of George III: Loyalty, Royalty and the British Nation 1760–1820', *Past and Present*, 102 (1984) p. 104.

61. Price, *A sermon ... at Hackney*, p. 25.

62. See John Money, *Experience and Indentity. Birmingham and the West Midlands 1760–1800* (Manchester, 1977) ch. 7.

63. Joseph Priestley, *Memoirs to 1795* (1809) p. 74.

7. THE MIDDLING SORT IN EIGHTEENTH-CENTURY COLCHESTER: INDEPENDENCE, SOCIAL RELATIONS AND THE COMMUNITY BROKER   *Shani D'Cruze*

1. This chapter is based on primary research undertaken for S. D'Cruze, 'The Middling Sort in Provincial England: Politics and Social Relations in Colchester, 1730–1800' (University of Essex Ph.D. thesis, 1990). It is not possible here to reproduce full references to the primary material cited in the thesis, though the kinds of primary sources used have been indicated and, by way of example, full references have been included in one or two cases (e.g. note 12).

2. P. Corfield, *The Impact of English Towns* (1982); C. Chalklin, *The Provincial Towns of Georgian England: A Study of the Building Process, 1740–1820* (1974); C. Chalklin and M. Havinden (eds), *Rural Change and Urban Growth 1500–1800* (1974); A. Everitt (ed.), *Perspectives in English Urban History* (1973); A. Everitt, 'The Banburys of England', *Urban History Yearbook* (1974) pp. 28–38; A. Everitt, *Landscape and Community in England* (1985); A. Everitt, 'Country, County and Town', *Transactions of the Royal Historical Society*, XXIX (1979) pp. 79–108; P. Clark (ed.), *Country Towns in Pre-Industrial England* (1981); P. Clark (ed.), *The Transformation of English Provincial Towns, 1600–1800* (1984); M. J. Daunton, 'Towns and Economic Growth in Eighteenth-Century England', in P. Abrams and E. Wrigley (eds), *Towns in Societies* (1978) pp. 9–33; P. Borsay, 'The English Urban Renaissance; the Development of Provincial Urban Culture c.1680–c.1760', *Social History*, V (1977) pp. 581–98; P. Borsay. 'Culture, Status and the English Urban Landscape', *History*, LXVIII, no. 219 (1982) pp. 1–12; P. Borsay, 'The Rise of the Promenade: The Social and Cultural Use of Space in English Provincial Towns c.1660–1800', *British Journal of Eighteenth-Century Studies*, IV (1986) pp. 125–40; P. Borsay 'Urban Development in the Age of Defoe', in C. Jones (ed.), *Britain in the First Age of Party, 1680–1750* (1987) pp. 195–220; P. Borsay, *The English Urban Renaissance: Culture and Society in the Provincial Town, 1660–1770* (Oxford, 1989). For a recent modification of the Borsay thesis see A. McInnes, 'The Emergence of a Leisure Town, Shrewsbury 1660–1760', *Past and Present*, no. 120 (1988) pp. 53–87; A. McInnes and P. Borsay, 'Debate: The Emergence of a Leisure Town: or an Urban Renaissance', *Past and Present*, no. 126 (1990) pp. 189–202. P. Langford, *A Polite and Commercial People, England 1727–1783* (Oxford, 1989) ch. 3, pp. 417–35; J. Black and J. Gregory (eds), *Culture, Politics and Society in Britain, 1660–1800* (Manchester, 1991).

3. A. F. J. Brown, *Colchester in the Eighteenth Century* (1969); A. F. J. Brown, *Essex at Work, 1700–1815* (1969); G. Martin, *The Story of Colchester from Roman Times to the Present Day* (1959) pp. 51, 71; P. Morant, *The History and Antiquities of the Most Ancient Town of Colchester* (1748) Book 2, p. 106; D. Stephenson, *The Book of Colchester: A Portrait of a Town* (1978) p. 91. The local newspaper, the *Ipswich Journal* (afterwards *IpsJ*) is a ready source for such genteel developments, for example: William Keymer's circulating library, *IpsJ*, 28 January 1786; Auricula Feasts, *IpsJ*, 15 April 1749; *IpsJ*, 21 April 1753; *IpsJ*, 4 May 1754.

4. J. Patten, 'Urban Occupations in Pre-Industrial England', *Transactions of the Institute of British Geographers*, n.s., II (1977) pp. 269–313; P. Corfield, 'Class by Name and Number in Eighteenth-Century Britain', *History*, 72 (1987) pp. 38–61; for the 'pseudo-gentry', see A. Everitt, 'Social Mobility in Early Modern England', *Past and Present*, no. 33 (1966) pp. 56–73; McInnes, 'Emergence', p. 62. For an example of a leading Colchester clergyman, see the correspondence of Nathaniel Forster, B L Add. MSS 11277; Langford, *A Polite and Commercial People*, especially ch. 3.

5. P[ublic] R[ecord] O[ffice] PROB 11, Dodwell 393, 1793; *IpsJ*, 20 June 1788; E[ssex] R[ecord] O[ffice], St James's Land Tax Assessments, 1788.

6. D'Cruze, 'Middling Sort', pp. 12–14 and p. 19, n. 27. A comparison between land tax assessments for ten Colchester parishes for the 1780s and 1790s, and the population figures given in the 1801 census (*Victoria County History* for Essex, vol. II, p. 353) less 30 per cent to account for children, produced a figure of 13.8 per cent of the adult population paying rates on property valued at more than £2 per annum. The calculation has an inbuilt underestimate, since population was increasing over these decades.

7. The types of sources used to compile data on such middling individuals include local newspapers, wills, administration of estates, parish rates and land tax assessments, the corporation assembly book, borough quarter sessions and petty sessions, free burgess admissions, borough poll books, parish registers etc. All manuscript sources referred to are located in the Colchester Branch of the Essex Record Office unless otherwise stated.

8. Colchester Borough Petty Sessions, P/COR/1 4 March 1758.

9. L. Davidoff and C. Hall, *Family Fortunes: Men and Women of the English Middle Class, 1780–1850* (1987) pp. 60–9; L. Davidoff, 'Life is Duty, Praise and Prayer', *Fawcett Library Papers*, 4 (1981); J.Gilbert (ed), *The Autobiography and Other Memorials of Mrs Gilbert*, 2nd edn (1876).

10. Lexden and Winstree Petty Sessions, P/LWR/1, 11 July 1758; for the Shillito family see D'Cruze, 'Middling Sort', Appendix 5.

11. *IpsJ*, 8 May 1773; William Mayhew to Richard Savage Nassau, 2 October 1749, quoted in J. Bensusan Butt, *A Friend to His Country* (1972) p. 14; H. Perkin, *The Origins of Modern English Society* (1969) pp. 49–50; Davidoff and Hall, *Family Fortunes*, p. 199.

12. John Bartholomew: Will of Hannah Hopkins, ERO, Chelmsford, 313CR15 1749; will of Thomas Hopkins, ERO BW95 1747; deeds of the Fleece Inn, CPL638 (originally Colchester Public Library, now in Colchester Record Office); will of Hannah Bartholomew, wife of John, made 1736, proved 1739, ERO 233BR22; will of Elizabeth Freeman, ERO 246CR15, made 1746, proved 1747. Monday Court Book, 30 October 1738, for Bartholomew's prosecution for debt of Charles Walker; similarly, Monday Court Book, 13 October 1740, prosecution of Thomas Webb. Sale of the *Ceres* and later expansion of business activities: *Colchester Journal* (hereafter *ColJ*) 3 February 1739; *IpsJ*, 8 August 1747; *IpsJ*, 12 December 1747; *IpsJ*, 11 June 1748; *IpsJ*, 13 August 1748; *IpsJ*, 30 November 1754, sale of sloop *Friends Goodwill*. Role in prosecuting criminal cases at the Hythe: see Borough Sessions 1740, examination of John Till the younger; Lexden and

Winstree Petty Sessions P/LWR1 8 December 1758, P/LWR4 2 January 1760. Administrations of estates by Bartholomew: D/ACWb51, Joseph Gould, 1742; D/ABWb157, James Cork, 1746; D/ABWb158, Peter Creffield, 1748. For other estates settled, see: IpsJ, 27 April 1751, 3 March 1753.

13. D'Cruze, 'The Middling Sort', chs 3 and 6.

14. J. Boissevain, *Friends of Friends* (1974); J. C. Mitchell (ed.), *Social Networks in Urban Situations: Analyses of Personal Relationships in Central African Towns* (1969); E. Bott, *Family and Social Networks* (1957); R. J. Frankenberg, *The Village and the Border: A Social Study of Religion, Politics and Football in a North Wales Community* (1959). The formula for calculation of density is given in the notes to network maps.

15. D'Cruze, 'Middling Sort', pp. 172–5.

16. For Andrew Murrells, see: Assembly Book of 29 July 1734, 30 September 1735, 5 October 1736, 25 July 1737, 5 September 1737, 4 October 1737, 3 October 1738, 28 June 1738, 2 October 1739, 3 September 1739, 23 July 1739, 28 July 1740; Borough Sessions of Epiphany 1736, Midsummer 1739, Easter 1740; *IpsJ*, 15 April 1739.

17. J. Bensusan Butt, *When Gainsborough Painted a Colchester Attorney* (1972), and 'A Friend to his Country: William Mayhew and the Recovery of the Colchester Charter, 1763', *Essex Archaeology and History*, XVIII (1987) pp. 63–74.

18. See D'Cruze, 'Middling Sort', pp. 221–2, n. 39.

19. Gilbert (ed.), *Autobiography;* Davidoff, 'Life is Duty'; Davidoff and Hall, *Family Fortunes*, pp. 59–69, 478; J. Bensusan Butt, 'Jane and Ann Taylor as Engravers', *East Anglian Magazine*, XXI (1961–2) pp. 682–3.

20. Martin, *Colchester,* pp. 60–79; T. Wright, *The History and Topography of Essex* (1836) p. 333; Morant, *Colchester,* Book 2, p. 81; P. Morant, *The History and Anquities of Essex* (1768) Book 1, pp. 456–9; *Dictionary of National Biography*, vol. 21, pp. 1341–6, for the earls of Rochford, and vol. 16, p. 1188, for Rigby; L. Namier and J. Brooke, *The House of Commons, 1754–1790* (1964) vol. 1, pp. 276–8, vol. 2, p. 13, vol. 3, p. 310; G. O. Rickwood, 'The Members of Parliament for Colchester, 1747–1830', *Essex Review,* VIII (1890) p. 227.

21. J. M. Triffitt, 'Politics and the Urban Community: Parliamentary Boroughs in the South West of England, 1710–1730' (University of Oxford D.Phil. thesis, 1985).

22. J. Black, 'Eighteenth Century English Political History: The Local Dimension', *The Local Historian*, 23, 2 (1993) pp. 103–10; N. Rogers, 'Paul Langford's "Age of Improvement" ', *Past and Present*, 130 (1991) p. 205.

23. These statistics were obtained by correlating listings of members of the corporation in the borough assembly book for 1733–37 inclusive, and in the new charter of 1763, with a listing of names collated from all available Colchester nonconformist sources for the period: see D'Cruze, 'Middling Sort', p. 91, n. 35. For the situation elsewhere compare, for example, J. Barry, 'The Cultural Life of Bristol, 1640–1775' (University of Oxford D.Phil. thesis, 1985), where dissenters did sit on the corporation, and J. R. Smith, 'The Borough of Maldon 1688–1768; A Study in English Urban

History' (University of Leicester M.Phil. thesis, 1981), especially pp. 64, 96, 73, where they did not.

24. P. Langford, *The Excise Crisis* (1975); R. Sedgwick, *The House of Commons, 1715–1754* (1972) vol. 1, pp. 241–2, 409, 495, vol. 2, pp. 81–2; R. Porter, *English Society*, ch. 3; D'Cruze, 'The Middling Sort', ch. 6; Langford, *A Polite and Commercial People*, pp. 28–33, 53–7.

25. L. C. Sier, 'Charles Gray, MP of Colchester', *Essex Review*, LVII (1948) pp. 17–20; L. C. Sier, 'The Ancestry of Charles Gray', *Essex Review*, LXI (1952) pp. 94–6.

26. PRO SP 36/50/377, Charles Gray and Thomas Francis, 'Report to the Secretary of State of Defendants' Evidence to Support their Petition for a Pardon'. Other sources for the Gray case include: Borough Sessions, Epiphany 1739, Easter 1739; Assembly Book, 1739–1740; *ColJ*, 18 August 1739; *IpsJ*, 23 February 1740, 3 May 1740; PRO King's Bench pleas, KB 28 and index thereto, IND 6658; PRO C 111 Signet Office Ind. 16972 (his pardon of 3 May 1740).

27. Borough Poll Books, 1735 and 1741.

28. R. Trumbach, 'London's Sodomites: Homosexual Behaviour and Western Culture in the Eighteenth Century', *Journal of Social History*, XI (1977) pp. 1–34, especially p. 21.

29. PRO TS 11/854/2910; *IpsJ*, 19 January 1793, 13 March 1793, 20 July 1793; Colchester Borough Sessions, 1793; D'Cruze, 'Middling Sort', p. 442, n. 50.

30. Rebow papers, box 2.

31. D'Cruze, 'Middling Sort', pp. 386–8.

32. J. Innes, 'Jonathan Clark, Social History and England's *Ancien Régime*', *Past and Present* 115 (1987) p. 191; J. Brewer, *Party Ideology and Popular Politics at the Accession of George III* (1976); F. O'Gorman, *Voters, Patrons and Parties: the Unreformed Electorate of Hanoverian England, 1734–1832* (Oxford, 1989); J. G. A. Pocock, *Virtue, Commerce and History* (Cambridge, 1985); H. T. Dickinson, *Liberty and Property: Political Ideology in Eighteenth-Century Britain* (1977); J. A. W. Gunn, *Beyond Liberty and Property* (1983).

33. Butt, *A Friend*, p. 15; N. Rogers, *Whigs and Cities: Popular Politics in the Age of Walpole and Pitt*, (Oxford, 1989).

34. Handbill that forms the cover of Butt, *A Friend*. On popular Toryism, see L. Colley, *In Defiance of Oligarchy: The Tory Party 1714–60* (Cambridge, 1982) ch. 10; M. Peters, *Pitt and Popularity: The Patriot Minister and London Opinion during the Seven Years War* (Oxford, 1980); N. Rogers, 'Riot and Popular Jacobitism in Early Hanoverian England', in M. and J. Jacobs (eds), *The Origins of Anglo-American Radicalism* (1984) pp. 70–88. On popular participation in politics more generally, Brewer, *Party Ideology*, chs 9–12; N. Rogers, 'Aristocratic Clientage, Trade and Independency: Popular Politics in Pre-Radical Westminster', *Past and Present*, 61 (1973) pp. 70–106; M. Mullett, 'Popular Culture and Popular Politics: Some Regional Case Studies', in Jones (ed.), *Britain in the First Age of Party*, pp. 129–50.

35. Cover of Butt, *A Friend*.

36. P. J. R. King, 'Urban Crime Rates and Borough Courts in Eighteenth-Century Essex; the Impact of Local Court Availability', *Essex*

Journal, XXII, no. 2 (1987) pp. 39–42; an example of an affluent Tory was Thomas Boggis, baymaker: see J. Bensusan Butt, *The House that Boggis Built* (2nd edn, 1990); Morant, *Colchester,* Book 1, p. 71.

37. *IpsJ,* 14 October 1749; D/Y/2/2, pp. 355–8; D'Cruze, 'Middling Sort', p. 105.

38. *IpsJ,* 14 October 1749.

Notes on Contributors

JONATHAN BARRY is Lecturer in History in the Department of History and Archaeology, University of Exeter. He has published many articles on aspects of the social, cultural and religious history of south-western England in the early modern period, notably on Bristol. He is General Editor of *Studies in the Social History of Medicine* (Routledge). He is currently on a Leverhulme Fellowship to complete a study of cultural life in early modern Bristol (Clarendon Press, forthcoming) and chapters for the *Cambridge Urban History of Britain* (Cambridge University Press, forthcoming).

CHRISTOPHER BROOKS is Lecturer in History in the Department of History, University of Durham. He is author of *Pettyfoggers and Vipers of the Commonwealth: The 'Lower Branch' of the Legal Profession in Early Modern England* (Cambridge University Press, 1986) and is currently writing a book on *Law, Society and Politics in Early Modern England* (Cambridge University Press, forthcoming).

SHANI D'CRUZE is Subject Pattern Leader in History at Crewe and Alsager Faculty, Manchester Metropolitan University, and Honorary Lecturer at the Centre for Women's Studies, University of Lancaster. She has written articles on self-help, mutual aid, and the household in the nineteenth century, and is currently writing a book on the history of sexual assault in England c.1850–1900 (UCL Press, forthcoming).

PETER EARLE is Emeritus Reader in Economic History at the University of London. His writing divides between world maritime history and the social history of England in the early modern period. His main works in the latter genre are *The World of Defoe* (Weidenfeld and Nicolson, 1976), *The Making of the English Middle Class* (Methuen, 1989), and *A City Full of People: Men and Women in London, 1650–1750* (Methuen, 1994).

NICHOLAS ROGERS is the current Chair and Professor of History in the Department of History (Arts) at York University, Toronto. He is the author of *Whigs and Cities: Popular Politics in the Age of Walpole and Pitt* (Clarendon Press, 1989) and *Crowds, Culture and Politics in Hanoverian Britain* (Clarendon Press, forthcoming).

269

KEITH WRIGHTSON is Reader in English Social History at the University of Cambridge and a Fellow of Jesus College. He is the author of *English Society 1580–1680* (Hutchinson, 1982) and co-author, with David Levine, of *Poverty and Piety in an English Village, Terling 1525–1700* (Academic Press, 1979) and *The Making of an Industrial Society, Whickham 1560–1765* (Clarendon Press, 1991). In addition he has published many articles on English society in the early modern period.

Index

DATE DUE			
			Printed in USA